HIGH NOON

HIGH NOON

BOBBY ROBSON:
A YEAR AT BARCELONA

Jeff King

Virgin

First published in Great Britain in 1997 by
Virgin
an imprint of Virgin Publishing Ltd
332 Ladbroke Grove
London W10 5AH

Internal photographs courtesy of Editorral Don Balón S.A., Barcelona.

A catalogue record for this book is available from the British Library.

ISBN 1 852 27633 9

Typeset by TW Typesetting, Plymouth, Devon

Printed and bound by
Mackays of Chatham, Lordswood, Chatham, Kent

CONTENTS

Para Olga

ACKNOWLEDGEMENTS

Very special thanks to Bobby Robson – nice guys do win sometimes.

Thanks to José Miguel Teres at FC Barcelona; Javier Corbat at Videocomunicación; Juan Pedro Martínez at Don Balón; Enric Bañeres at La Vanguardia; José Antonio Albert, Carlos Mira and David Arquimba for the photos; Ben Dunn and Hannah MacDonald at Virgin Publishing.

Kindred spirits: Oliver King, Steve Ford, Tony Willis, Dave Cottrell and Michael Hodges at Goal; the bros Kelly; Honey for Luna (trash-talking Barça-funk).

Special thanks to Paul Hawksbee for the read and Antoni Closa for the research.

To Olga for the lost weekends. Hello Mum. Hello Dad.

PROLOGUE
Seven Days In May

WEDNESDAY, 22 MAY 1996

Out on the streets, it's an unusually muggy day for spring in the Mediterranean's most stylish city, but inside FC Barcelona's press suite it's cool and comfortable as Bobby Robson takes the stage for his ritual investiture. Opening salvos from journalists question his ability to handle the demands of such a football-obsessed city, but the man in the spotlight beams his way through an hour-long grilling like a kid with new football boots. Pressure, what pressure? At 63, Robson boasts a formidable pedigree: England's best World Cup result on foreign soil, league championships in Holland and Portugal, UEFA and FA Cup triumphs at Ipswich; quite simply, the kind of across-the-board success no other British manager has achieved. Ever. Now he's got the job he always wanted. No wonder he's chuffed to bits.

'I know Barcelona is a massive club, but I handled the pressure of eight years as England manager so I know all about great expectations,' he tells the packed gathering. 'If I've survived forty-five years in the game I must have a strong character and I still love a challenge. If not I wouldn't be sat here today, I'd be out playing golf with other ex-managers of my age.' He might have added, 'And I'm no stranger to a hostile press.'

No sooner had Robson taken over as England boss in 1982 than he was under the media cosh, at first simply for not being Brian Clough, the so-called 'people's choice'. Ninety minutes into his reign (a 2-2 draw in Denmark) and the *Sun* was dishing out 'Robson Out! Clough In!' badges while organising telephone polls to demand his resignation. Over the next eight years, things rarely got better. Whilst the quality press berated Robson for indecisiveness, the tabloids went for the jugular in what has become a depressingly familiar fashion: 'Plonker!' after a 2-0 Wembley defeat against the USSR in 1984; 'In the Name of God Go!' after three consecutive defeats at the European Championship in Germany; 'In the Name of Allah Go!' after a draw against Saudi Arabia in 1988. Eight years of headlines like that were enough to turn any man's hair grey. Only Robson's near-glorious farewell at the 1990 World Cup bucked the trend, but by then he was beyond caring.

So really, what could the Iberian press pull on him compared to England's finest? A couple of hundred journalists and enough cameras to film a Hollywood epic had turned up today demanding instant solutions to everything but Spain's trade deficit: 'What tactics will he employ?'; 'Which players will he get rid of?'; 'Who does he want to buy?'; 'How will he handle taking over from a legend?'; 'Does Jordi Cruyff have a future as a "spy" in the dressing room?' Kid's stuff, *chicos*. Perhaps. But did Robson realise that the very same multitude would hover outside his door after every match, every training session, and every tête-à-tête with his president? The England side plays some ten games a year. That's ten weeks of media-induced aggro; the rest of the time you're pretty much left alone, at least physically. And in the high-profile stakes, Ipswich, PSV Eindhoven and Porto are minor players on provincial stages compared to Barcelona. Robson would soon learn to live 24 hours a day with a tape recorder stuck up his nose.

At least the media here would give his private life a wide berth. Everybody knows that when Spain's sporting royalty (that's his royal highness, the King) goes skiing in the Pyrenees without the missus, he doesn't spend lonely nights in a log cabin fretting over issues of state. But you'd never, ever read about it in the papers. We're talking about the country that gave birth to *Hello!*, after all. Spanish celebrities can party to their hearts' delight and no one gives a damn, and what better place to do it than Barcelona? As Argentinian coach César Menotti put it to his successor, Terry Venables, back in 1984: 'Terry, if you like women, welcome to paradise!'

Menotti's liberal regime hardly encouraged professional standards, but you'll search fruitlessly for recrimination in the press archives. Of course, back in the mid-eighties, Spain was still in the teething stages of democracy after 50 years of General Franco's dictatorship, so censorship was hardly an alien concept when it came to the excesses of the powers that be, sporting or otherwise. Under the chain-smoking Menotti, training sessions took place at five o'clock in the afternoon, ostensibly because of 'bio-rhythms', in reality so that his Argentinian clan (come on down, Diego Maradona) could recover from their nocturnal frolics. Diego's uncredited role in the single-act drama that saw a famous actress dubbed the 'most expensive call-girl in Spain' speaks volumes about the media's live-and-let-live attitude.

Whilst a dirty stop-in compared to his predecessor, Venables was not one to mope about at home. A decade on, Barça's vice-president, Nicolau Casaus, recalls Dagenham's favourite son as a *'bon viveur'*. 'I've very fond memories of Terry. He used to sing on TV shows and he loved to wine and dine, but we never had a problem with that. On the contrary, the fact that he always had a smile on his face and lived life to the full was an advantage for him as a coach. That positive attitude was reflected in his approach to the game and his relationship with the players.'

Barcelona President Josep Lluís Núñez's first choice in 1984 was, in fact, Bobby Robson. 'I was actually offered the job twice,' says Robson, 'first, when I was manager at Ipswich. We'd played Barcelona a couple of times in Europe and impressed them, though both times we were knocked out. The first time it was 3-3 on aggregate and we lost on penalties at Camp Nou, the second time we won 2-1 at Portman Road but lost on the away goal over here. We got done by the referee both times, I'll tell you [*shaking his head at the memory*]. I couldn't take the job the first time because I was in the middle of a ten-year contract and Ipswich wouldn't let me go. They said they should get big money for me if I left, and Barcelona replied, "Well, sorry, we don't do that with coaches." They felt like guys should pay for the privilege of coming here! The next offer was when I was with England. I couldn't possibly walk out on my country the way Don Revie did, so I recommended Terry.'

Happily married, Robson's personal life is unlikely to attract the attention of the Spanish media. That's the good news. The bad news, make that the very bad news, is that every sports journalist in the country is on a mission to disparage misguided coaches. Spain has four daily sports papers. Barcelona alone has two: *El Mundo Deportivo* and *Sport*. Both dedicate some 25 pages a day to the life and times of FC Barcelona. That's half a newspaper every single day, come rain or shine or close season. Then there are two influential radio shows, *El Larguero* (The Crossbar) and *Super García*: that's $2 + 2 = 4$ hours of digging the sporting dirt every night of the week for three million listeners. And we still haven't mentioned what the

Spanish call *la caja tonta*, the silly box. Andy Gray and his state-of-the-art hardware? Pah! In Spain, such low-key TV harassment is beyond a coach's wildest dreams. The fact that a significant number of sports journalists are *señoritas* of deep voices and *décolletage* makes it even harder for besieged managers just to say no.

At least Spain's best-loved television pundit, Michael Robinson, is a fellow Brit, not that he underestimates Robson's task. 'It's a thankless job taking over from Johan Cruyff, he's the greatest football brain I've ever come across,' says the former Liverpool striker, now busy fronting Spanish League games for Canal Plus. 'Stepping into his shoes is the most difficult thing Bobby Robson has ever attempted. I remember feeling sorry for whoever had to come in at Liverpool when Kenny Dalglish left. It's hard to take over at a club that is used to success, especially when that success is so closely identified with one person.

'Historically, Barça have always had the reputation of being a rich club and a political standard-bearer for a region of Spain,' continues the man the Spanish call Robeen. 'But it's a club that has enjoyed very little success for the amount of money it spends. In the last twenty years or so, only Terry Venables had won the championship for them. Then Cruyff comes along and gives FC Barcelona everything it's always wanted and never had: he makes a habit of winning the league; he gets to four European finals; he wins the club's first ever European Cup. I wouldn't wanna ask a woman out on a date after Tom Cruise, would you? It's the same,' he laughs, 'unfavourable comparisons are inevitable.'

Robinson won't be pushed on whether Robson is the right man for the job, though. 'Ooh, bloody hell,' he exclaims. 'I don't know, he's a good manager and the club could have made a thousand worse decisions. I'm sure Núñez and the board think he's the right kind of man to pick up the pieces and pave the way for an easier long-term future without Cruyff: he's a father figure, open to dialogue, not authoritarian or too controversial.'

There is, it seems, one potential stumbling block. 'If Barcelona lose three games on the trot, the Catalan press will slaughter Robson; the players will begin to doubt him, and then you've got instability. Fabio Capello's situation at Real Madrid is different because he isn't following anybody. The singularly most difficult job Robson has is not winning the league, but taking over from Cruyff.

'The demonstrations against the board after they sacked him reflect an enormous rift at the club. He's taking a year's sabbatical and still lives in Barcelona, that means danger sat in the VIP box every other weekend. If things don't look promising early on, the opposition have got the focal point they need. But if the team doesn't do well, I don't think they'll have a go at Robson, it'll be primarily Núñez they attack. To be honest, Spanish fans think Núñez has got himself an old man who is a bit dozy, a bit of a dickhead. I think they are very much mistaken, but that's what they think. If Madrid get off to a good start, believe me, Bobby won't get much leeway.'

Not from the press, that's for sure. On presentation day it may be 'Welcome, Meeester Rrrobson', but the knives will be out long before September if pre-season displays are slightly less than majestic. For the moment, the new boy in town seems happy to be dealing with a media obsessed with footie rather than bootie or hootie. 'Handling the press is part of your work, you should never worry or get over-emotional about criticism. What I've liked over the last six years in Holland and Portugal – and it's the same here, I guess – is that they're just interested in the sport. I think that's maybe a better situation than back home with the tabloids delving into people's private lives.'

THURSDAY, 23 MAY

Whatever Happened To The Likely Lads? Bobby Robson may have departed his native North-East in the days when its shipyards served the world, but half a century down the line a Geordie lilt still bubbles permanently below the surface. When he gets melancholy he sounds uncannily like James Bolam admonishing Rodney Bewes. Even as a schoolboy in Langley Park, Robson knew he wanted to be a footballer, but it's a long way from County Durham to Camp Nou. Surely even boyish dreams can only go so far?

'I don't think your imagination can ever stretch this far,' he says, smiling at the memory. 'As a kid I was immersed in the game and my only desire was to play football; where that would take me was beyond my dreams. When I signed as a pro at Fulham, I was desperate to make it 'cos I was so afraid not to. What would happen to me if I didn't, I kept asking myself? But in terms of having such a long career, going into coaching and management, where I've been the last few years, that's beyond the imagination, really.

'You never forget where you come from, though. I've just read

Michael Caine's autobiography. He struggled and had a hard time of it, too. He was down to his last penny, then he gets a little bit of luck, he builds on it, and all of a sudden he's a star. He talks about making it from a working-class background and I can identify with that. You still have to pinch yourself sometimes to make sure you've really made it. I left school at fifteen and worked for two years as an apprentice electrical engineer, but that wasn't for me, I knew that. All I could wait for was to get to seventeen, 'cos I felt I could be good enough then to sign as a pro. All I ever wanted to do was play football professionally.'

Robson is one of a score of legendary managers who are either Scots or hail from the North-East. What did they put in the porridge up there? 'I think it's because they're hotbeds of football, it's where the game is played with the most passion and feeling, it's a very large part of people's lives. If you grow up in that environment, in that frenzy of football, it has a great impact on you, and out of those areas, especially the coal-mining areas before, it's a way into a better life. And it produces good characters, people who are honest and loyal and want to work.'

Of course, you can hardly find a seam of coal in England any more, let alone shout down a pit-shaft for a ball-playing wizard. Robson admits that current players find it more difficult to buckle down. 'It's not across the board, but there are players who have the talent but don't make it because life is too easy for them. They don't come into the game with the best attitude and motivation, so they fail. In the past, a lot of people from those tougher backgrounds simply didn't want to go back, not because of the people, but because of the areas.'

Robson's second day on the Med isn't spent in the Barça boot room discussing plans for the future or watching videos of his future charges. The more mundane business of looking for somewhere to live has to wait a while, too. Day two in Barcelona is spent paying homage to the city's Fourth Estate. In tow as translator is 33-year-old José Mourinho, Robson's assistant at Porto. The coach's high opinion of Mourinho is reflected in his habit of using the royal we; 'We intend to do this, our plans are . . .', etc. First port of call is *Sport*, a sporting tabloid that could have been spawned by the *Sun*. Robson is late, though for once he's got a genuine excuse: his car broke down.

Given a reputation for tardiness and a Big Jackish ability to confuse names (apocryphal or not, those tales of an England captain called Bobby just won't go away), Robson has made a wise choice in coming to Barcelona. If, as often suggested, punctuality is the virtue of the bored, the Spanish must be the most exciting people in Europe, and the new coach can always blame his problems with names on the language. Hemmed in by the paper's top brass, and unfazed by the incongruousness of the surroundings (the Spanish executive class is obsessed by cod Britannica), Robson maintains his optimistic line vis-à-vis *la presión*, one Spanish word he is already familiar with. 'Everybody's talking about the same thing; the pressure. Even before we start training or playing games, I can sense the weight of expectation all around me. But my aim is to kill off that pressure before it gets to me. I want to enjoy my work here.

'It's a case of when in Rome, isn't it? Barcelona is a high-profile club, so I have to adapt to the circumstances. What I can't do is try and change the reality of a club with a hundred years of history behind it. When I was in Portugal, I adapted to their way of life and expectations, and I'll do the same here. That doesn't mean I'm going to abandon my own ideas and personality, a coach can never do that. I'm perfectly aware that I've arrived at a delicate moment. For a club as big as Barcelona, two years without winning anything is too long and the whole city demands instant success. But football managers never get offered jobs at the best possible time, do they? If Barcelona had spent the last two years winning things they wouldn't have changed their coach in the first place. But if I was scared of the challenge I wouldn't be here, would I? The fact that I've left a fantastic club in a great city, with marvellous supporters and after winning the last two leagues, the fact I've left all that to come here is proof that nothing frightens me.'

In two and a half years at Porto, Robson transformed an incorrigibly conservative side into one committed to winning things in style. Strange, then, that the Spanish have welcomed him with sombre hints about defensive obsessions and a British school of football (not a compliment over here) that threatens Cruyff's attacking legacy.

Scurrilous reporting aside, Robson is clear about his priorities now that he's finally made it to Barcelona. 'The most important thing when you arrive at a new club is to know exactly what you want and what needs to be changed. The basis of the squad here is excellent, but I'm going to make changes, because the situation has changed. I know exactly which players I want and the club has already got my list of reinforcements.'

FRIDAY, 24 MAY

'He's an authentic English gentleman,' says Antoni Closa, author of the acclaimed history *Cròniques del Barça*. 'Well-mannered, courteous, a nice person and a good coach.' And that's just the other ex-Fulham manager.

Craven Cottage is not an obvious breeding ground for great managers, yet sleepy Fulham has produced two for one of Europe's biggest clubs. The aforementioned gentleman is Vic Buckingham, in his playing days a stylish full-back at Tottenham, and later manager at West Brom, Fulham and Sheffield Wednesday. In his one full season at Camp Nou, in 1970/71, Buckingham led Barcelona to second place in the League and victory in the Spanish Cup. 'It's a strange coincidence,' muses Robson. 'I played for Victor, as well – at the Hawthorns and Craven Cottage. I admired and respected him a lot, I was very sad when he died last year. He was definitely one of the good guys, very extroverted, and he was very successful here, Barcelona didn't want to get rid of him, you know? He only left because of bad health [*severe back problems*]. I hope I can repeat his success.'

It was, in fact, Buckingham's sacking in January 1968 that gave Robson his first managerial opportunity at Fulham. Buckingham had previously been dismissed by WBA after being cited in a divorce action. Albion's then chairman, Bert Millichip, obviously grew more permissive with old age. As the tabloids delved into Robson's private life with twaddle about extramarital affairs in the build-up to the 1990 World Cup, the by then chairman of the FA, Sir Bert, would stand by his man. It was Robson himself who decided enough was enough and opted to join PSV Eindhoven once the World Cup was over. Naturally, the same tabloids that had spent eight years urging him to go attacked Robson for abandoning ship with Italy '90 looming. Strangely enough, Buckingham's road to Barcelona also passed through a Dutch championship, at Ajax in 1960, where (and this is getting really spooky) he discovered a prodigious junior called . . . Johan Cruyff!

Robson won consecutive championships at PSV and thinly veiled criticism of his coaching methods. When *World Soccer* asked defender Berry Van Aerle what he'd learnt from Robson, he

10

responded, 'The only thing he taught me in two years was English.' After the 1992 title triumph, PSV didn't renew the coach's contract.

The initial move to Holland represented a footballing culture shock, but Robson is convinced that the role of the Continental coach has increased his longevity. 'What I like is that you're not involved in the complete running of the club. In England you do everything; at Ipswich I was responsible for buying and selling, negotiating contracts, developing youth policies, meeting parents, going to board meetings, dealing with the press, helping with the commercial side of it . . . the whole works. When I went abroad to Holland, I found I actually had time to plan my training sessions. It's the same at Barcelona – I'm responsible for coaching and getting results at first team level, that's the job. That's not to say that the football side of it is easier. You're playing against sides you don't know much about – at best, you've watched them a couple of times or read a couple of reports – and you're expected to produce a winning team overnight. The tactical equation is more sophisticated, too. How are you going to play at home and away, what system do your opponents use, how you need to adapt? It's a difficult science.'

Not that he envies managers back home in Britain. 'How much spare time do you think Alex Ferguson gets? Manchester United are such a massive club he must get dragged away from his coaching a lot. I'm sure Brian Kidd spends more time with the players. I couldn't do that here; if I did I'd lose my job.'

He may not miss the dawn-to-dusk slog of English management but Robson admits he occasionally pines for England's green and pleasant. 'I did get homesick when I first went to Holland. I missed my children, I missed my friends. But when you're wrapped up in football, you lead such a full life it makes up for the little things you miss and the homesickness. A football lifestyle means everything else takes a back seat, wherever you are. You're so tied up with your job and you lead such a full life you haven't got time to brood.'

SATURDAY, 25 MAY

For several years now, *Força Barça* has been Catalonia's most popular television programme. A footballing cousin of *Spitting Image*, its team of grotesquely masked impersonators mercilessly lampoon the footballing powers that be: 'Stoichkov', the Bulgarian peasant with a hanky on his head; 'Romario', the fat little Lothario in a thong; 'Cruyff', the Scrooge with his eccentric Spanish; you're nobody in Barcelona until you've made it onto *Força Barça*.

11

It takes Bobby Robson just three days to join the select club. In his debut scene tonight, he's portrayed as a bungling English *coronel* being conned by the spivish 'President Núñez' in contract negotiations. Take one: 'Robson' happily accepts generous rations of *botifarra*, Catalonia's famous sausage, in lieu of cash bonuses, before dancing the flamenco as a smirking 'Cruyff' looks on from the wings. Then it's time for a song as a drag queen from Vegas croons her way through an ode to Robson with the following unforgettable lyrics:

> He's a gentleman with white hair who looks like a boy and
> works very hard,
> He loves Meryl Streep and his favourite group is the Beatles,
> He is Bobby Robson, Oh Mama, Oh Mama, he is Bobby Robson,
> Oh yeah, yeah, he is Bobby Robson.

And it loses nothing in translation!

SUNDAY, 26 MAY

You could be forgiven for thinking the Spanish have an inferiority complex, summed up by the sad cliché '*Lo de fuera es mejor*' – foreign things are better. Whether it's German *Vorsprung durch Technik*, Japanese hi-tech or the proliferation of blond kids in TV commercials, the Spanish have an exaggerated tendency to disparage what's on their own doorstep. The astonishing roll-call of nobodies that have managed Spanish football clubs (Colin Addison, anybody?) is arguably a result of the same hang-up.

Spain's manager, Javier Clemente, has long criticised what he describes as 'knee-jerk club presidents who contract foreign coaches just for the sake of playing to the gallery'. Ever the pragmatist, he's been a particularly vigorous opponent of Cruyff's 'suicidal footballing philosophy' and 'tactical naïvety'. Interestingly, Clemente makes an exception for the British. The outspoken coach from a decaying industrial overspill of Bilbao (a milieu often compared to northern England's industrial heartlands) is a self-confessed disciple of British football. However, few were aware that he had a mentor . . . until Bobby Robson arrived at Barcelona. 'Javier came over twice to have a look at English training methods when he was youth team coach at Bilbao,' recalls Robson. 'That was quite unusual at the time. Young Scandinavian coaches were starting to look to England, but he was the first from one of the major football countries. He was a nice lad and obviously lived and breathed football.'

'Bobby will always be one of my idols,' says Clemente, a man who sets enormous stall by loyalty. 'I went over to Ipswich in 1976 as a beginner without a clue about football, but he was never too busy to spend time with me. It was an unforgettable experience, and to this day I'm using coaching methods that he taught me. Bobby's an extraordinary coach. Just look at his track record; every club he's been at has won things, regardless of their pedigree. That's not luck. Nobody is that lucky.' Clemente is equally fond of Robson the man. 'He's a grand person, though perhaps not typically English like Terry Venables; Bobby's more laid-back but even funnier.'

MONDAY, 27 MAY

Johan Cruyff fires the opening shot in what promises to be a long-running battle. The word on the street is that Bobby Robson has spent more time talking shop with president Núñez in a week than Cruyff did in eight years. According to the dethroned Dutchman, a signed-up member of the directors-know-nothing-about-football school, 'At this rate, Robson will end up dancing to the board's tune.' The man in the dock is quick to disagree.

'It's one thing talking football with the board and another altogether letting them influence me. The president likes to know what my point of view is, and as I have to plan for next season, it's logical we meet to talk things over. But what I'll never do is accept outside influences on my coaching decisions. If I'm going to talk to the press every week, why shouldn't I do the same with the president? My relationship with Núñez and Joan Gaspart [*Barcelona's Machiavellian vice-president*] is excellent, but the responsibility for the playing side of things is all mine. Johan turned the dressing room into a bunker and that's the way I'm going to keep it.'

For the moment, Robson remains diplomatic about his predecessor. 'Johan Cruyff's achievements as a coach were incredible and nobody's expecting the fans to forget him overnight, but people have got to concentrate on the future. When the Presidency of the United States changes hands the country doesn't come to a standstill, so why should Barcelona be any different? I know the fans were divided about his sacking, but it's my job to regroup them around a new team. I haven't got a crystal ball, so I can't tell you what will happen in the future. But I've won four championships in five years at PSV and Porto, so it's obvious where my priorities lay. What's good football? It's football that people like to watch, but it's also football that wins games and titles. Everybody talks about what an attractive side Barcelona have been, but they haven't won anything in two years. What kind of entertainment is that?'

TUESDAY, 28 MAY

Barcelona's 49th coach in just short of a century's history has clearly done his homework. In an hour-long interview on *Gol A Gol*, a weekly football show on the local Catalan TV channel, Robson repeatedly comes back to the theme of Barcelona as 'A club that represents a whole nation'.

'I'm well aware what Fútbol Club Barcelona [*he always refers to the club's full and formal title*] means to the Catalans, and I know it's an enormous responsibility trying to provide them with the successful side they yearn for. I consider it a tremendous honour being given the chance to play a part in their future.' As Robson suggests, we're not talking just football here. 'They want the club to be their ambassador around the world,' he insists. Barcelona's legendary motto, *Más que un club* (More than a club), is indeed the reflection of a unique social and historical reality. Strictly speaking, Barcelona may be a club side; six million Catalans, however, will insist we're talking about their national side.

Franco's obdurate right-wing dictatorship (1939-75) saw *el Barça* (pronounced Barsa) become the flagship of Catalonia, a fiercely independent region (or country, as its natives would insist) in the north-east of the Iberian peninsula. With free political speech banned, the Catalans embraced football as a means of expressing their identity and FC Barcelona's sporting arena was transformed into the high church of Catalan nationalism. It provided a haven where the locals could congregate *en masse*, speak their outlawed language (that's what you get for taking the wrong side in the Spanish Civil War) and vent their anti-Franco spleen, especially when Real Madrid, 'the Regime's team', came to town. James Joyce once said that the soul of a culture is to be discovered in its music halls. He'd obviously never been to Camp Nou.

The club's structure reflects the grass-roots nature of its support. There is no wealthy magnate, patriarchal family or conventional board of directors; FC Barcelona is a sports club owned and controlled by its 100,000-plus *socis* (members). Every five years, each *soci*, from Josep Lluís Núñez down to the Juan-come-latelys with the ink still wet on their membership cards, casts a single vote in the presidential elections. Neither the victorious candidate nor his chosen board have any direct financial interest in the club; their only interest is to serve club and country, i.e. Catalonia. And this is not about a token nod to democracy with the real action going on behind closed doors, either. At a financial level, the club's finances are transparent; accounts and budgets have to be passed by an annual assembly comprised of 10 per cent of *socis*, selected by a legally rubber-stamped draw. Surplus money (the club is run so impeccably there is always a profit) either stays in the bank or is reinvested in the team and the club's ever-increasing patrimony: a small city of stadiums and installations, a museum with priceless works of art (Picasso, Miro *et al*), a listed building that houses a football academy, etc.

That's the democratic theory; cynics would claim that Núñez, president since the club's first democratic elections in 1978, and his sidekick, Joan Gaspart, have done very nicely *gracias* by their association with Barça (it's safe to say that neither Núñez's construction empire or Gaspart's chain of hotels has suffered from the fawning attitude to Catalonia's most important civil institution). At the beginning of the 1996/97 season, the club boasted 103,850 *socis* and 80,000 season ticket holders. Every season ticket holder is a *soci* but not vice versa, an anomaly explained by either a sentimental commitment to the club/Catalonia, or the quasi-VIP status being a *soci* confers. It's not unusual to get talking to a stranger in a Barcelona bar who within five minutes will have whipped out his wallet, not to buy you a drink (getting your round in is an alien concept here), but to flash his *soci* card. It's no more unusual to then learn that he hasn't been to a game in years! Businessmen, journalists and politicians who privately detest FC Barcelona are forced to go along with the charade in public. Anything else would mean bankruptcy, unemployment or political suicide.

Even in the purely sporting sense, Barça is 'more than a football club'. Its professional ranks also boast one of Europe's most celebrated basketball sides (Spain's second sport) and both the ice hockey and handball teams have been European champions. But economically, all other sections, professional and amateur alike, survive off the largesse of the football team. That leaves the coach with little margin for error.

If he's unsuccessful, Robson's brief reign (the chances of failing and hanging around to tell the tale are non-existent) will mark the end of a much longer one. President Núñez has been re-elected four times since first taking the reins in 1978, but after sacking the club's most celebrated coach in despotic fashion, his popularity is at an all-time low. With presidential elections due in 1997, he would do well to ask the club's most illustrious *soci* (c/o the Vatican) to say a prayer on his behalf before the new season kicks off. If not, Johan Cruyff won't be the only *soci* voting for a change in '97.

HIGH NOON
The 1996/97 Season

SATURDAY, 31 AUGUST

If you belong to the ever-growing band of cynics who are convinced that a career in football involves selling your soul to the highest bidder, you clearly need a dose of Bobby Robson. If there's a footballing love potion, he's definitely got the recipe.

'Money is important,' admits Robson, 'but it's not top of the list when I'm making decisions about my career, certainly not any more. My ambitions now are sporting ones. Right now, that means winning the league with Barcelona.' John Smith, founder of the sports marketing company First Artist, has known Robson for fifteen years. 'As befits a man of humble origins, Bobby's never been a man to sell himself short at the negotiating table, but he's never lost that sense of how lucky he is. When he was England boss, I turned up at training one day in a Bentley, and he was, like, "John, that car's a work of art. Go on, give us the keys for a spin." He's always maintained a measure of awe about the things money can buy.'

Even the hardened cynics of the Spanish press corps have been taken aback by Robson's unadulterated enthusiasm. Witnesses to his Geronimo-like whoops of joy as he biked at pre-season training camp in Holland would have to agree, the expression 'You're as young as you feel' could have been invented for Robert William Robson, born Sacriston, County Durham, 18 February 1933. Twenty-four hours before the season proper begins and Robson is in expansive mood. At a time of life when most of his contemporaries are planning nothing more strenuous than a round of golf (Valencia's Luis Aragonés is the next oldest coach in Spain at 58; Alex Ferguson is the Premiership's senior citizen at 54), Robson is raring to go. Punching the air, his fist and the table when words alone won't do, he's barely able to contain his enthusiasm for the coming season. 'I just relish a challenge. I'm still immersed in football, I'm very much

19

in love with the game and you never cease to learn. I'm always motivated by it. And if I didn't work I wouldn't know what to do ... yes, I play a game of golf, yes, I like watching a bit of TV and reading a good book, and yes, in the winter I like to go skiing; but nothing compares to being in charge of a football club. Football is still my passion; I need that adrenalin rush every Saturday. I'm not ready to retire and until this gut reaction of mine tells me it's time to do so, I won't.'

If you take the Spanish press at their word, taking over at Barcelona is the biggest challenge of Robson's career. He begs to differ. 'You can't compare it with the enormous responsibility of the England job, can you? [*His habit of ending a sentence by seeking approval is an endearing one.*] As a coach, managing your country is the pinnacle. The problem is when you hit the apex, where else do you go? Most people retire from that position. I was too young and didn't want to anyway, or I thought I was too young. Personally, I wanted to further my education and that meant going abroad, that's what stimulated me. Going back to English club football would have been a step backwards. Now I'm back in club football at the very top. And I really think Barcelona are the biggest club in Europe: AC Milan, Real Madrid, Bayern Munich or Manchester United are there and thereabouts, but we're arguably the biggest; simply because more people come here to watch Barcelona play than any other club in any other city in the world.' The same reasoning that sent him abroad after the England job could send him into retirement after his spell at Camp Nou. 'Where do you go after Barcelona?' he muses. 'My feeling is that this could be my last club, but you never know.'

The club has certainly spent on a record-breaking scale to give Robson the raw material to win the league; a cool £27 million on Ronaldo (£12.8 million from PSV Eindhoven), Giovanni (£5 million from Santos), Vítor Baía (£5 million from Porto), Stoichkov and Couto (£2 million each from Parma), not to mention the investment in Pizzi, Blanc and Luis Enrique (last season Europe's top scorer, a 1996 French Double winner and an automatic choice for Spain), who don't work for peanuts, especially when there were no transfer fees involved. Rather than dwell on the attendant pressures, Robson considers the ability to spend a bonus. 'I've never had the luxury of really big money before, not at PSV or Porto, so I've enjoyed spending big. People ask me if it's more fun developing players and taking money off the big boys, or splashing out money.' Robson laughs. 'Ask me again at the end of the season! At Ipswich the backbone of the club was the youth policy and that was a long-term affair, but Barcelona can't wait. So to some degree you have to try and buy your way to honours.'

As some of the initial names on Robson's shopping list (Emmanuel Amunike, Secretario, Rui Costa, Alan Shearer) fell by the wayside, the Barça board seemed intent on negotiating with every agent on the globe of their own accord. Strike One: Giovanni, a seven-million-dollar video signing from Santos. Robson, in common with the rest of Europe, had never heard of him. Whilst the wheeling and dealing went on at a furious pace, Robson was back home in England following Euro 96. Not surprisingly, the Spanish press decided Barça's new coach was a decorative figure when it came to transfer decisions. A poll in *Sport* suggests that a majority of the fans also believe that Núñez controls the hiring and firing. 'This will only lead to trouble,' suggests the accompanying editorial. 'For Robson, because he gives the impression he's a soft touch, and for Núñez, because he won't be able to use the Englishman as an alibi if early results are disappointing. As for the club's press release claiming that it was Robson's decision to get rid of Jordi Cruyff, nobody seriously believes that.'

Robson rubbishes the notion that he isn't in control. 'The decision to sell Jordi was mine and it was purely a footballing one. With the exception of Pizzi, Luis Enrique and Blanc – players who were tied up before I arrived – the club has bought nobody without my consent. I gave the board a list of players for the positions I felt needed strengthening. I said, Look, there's seven players – I'm talking about one position here, mind you – buy me one of those. Some of them got complicated because of wheeling and dealing, and that would open the path for other options. I made enquiries about Ginola, but in the board's opinion, Newcastle wanted too much for him given his age. Stoichkov was on the same list in his position and the conditions were more favourable, so we went for him instead. Admittedly, I didn't know much about Giovanni when I arrived, but the president threw videos at me for two days and he looked like a player who could conjure something up out of nothing. He's a bit timid and shy, but having Ronaldo alongside him helps, and he's coming on nicely.'

Ah yes, Ronaldo, that's what the Spanish call *una palabra mayor*, a big word. The Brazilian's performance in his first game, last week's

5-2 victory against Atlético Madrid in the Super Copa (Barça won Spain's equivalent of the Charity Shield 6-5 on aggregate), has got his new boss just slightly excited. 'He's going to be sensational,' drools Robson, whose constant high enthusiasm count goes off the chart at the mention of his teenage Brazilian. 'He's fabulous working in small spaces in the box, he can take defenders clean out of the game with a feint or a turn, and then he knows instinctively the right ball to play, whether to shoot or pass. He can also drop back forty yards, pick the ball up and go off on runs taking on whole defences on his own. I think he'll be the key player in the Spanish League this year. He must be one of the greatest players in the world. And he's only nineteen!'

He's not a Geordie, though. 'I spoke to Ray Harford on three occasions and he told me Shearer was not for sale at any price. I think he would have come to Barcelona, so I suppose it was all about timing. If Ray had given me some leeway and let me talk to the player, who knows? But as he insisted Blackburn didn't want to sell I decided not to rock the boat. I'd originally had my mind on Ronaldo anyway; at that stage PSV were holding out for more than the fourteen million dollars we were offering and I thought we could get Shearer for roughly the same amount; that was before his price shot up and up. But at the end of the day, I'm very happy with what I've got. Shearer is a traditional centre forward who holds the ball up for you and he's a great finisher, but he can't do the things Ronaldo can.'

As Robson admits, it's not just about his all-star forwards. 'You can't just overload on attacking if you want to win things; you need a solid foundation to strike from, as well. Nadal, Abelardo, Sergi and Ferrer already made for a good defence; now we've got Blanc and I've bought Fernando Couto who was with me at Porto before he went to Parma. He's a big strong defender and he can cause problems when he goes forward for dead-ball situations. I've worked with Vítor Baía every day for the last two and a half years so I know his qualities and character, too. I bought him because I felt we needed a class goalkeeper. He's one of the best in the world and he'll win us an awful lot of points over the season. Add that to the variety up front, and I've got to be positive about our prospects.'

Atlético Madrid coach Radomir Antic, for one, claims that Barça have been signing players willy-nilly. He insists that Ronaldo and Pizzi, the league's top scorer last season at Tenerife, won't fit together in the same side. 'Obviously I don't agree,' smiles Robson. 'I remember Raddy from his Luton days with David Pleat and he had a fabulous season at Atlético last year. I suppose he thinks he has to outpsych us and that's his opening shot! But one of the reasons we bought Ronaldo is because he gives us completely different options to Pizzi. Other people have claimed we've got too many playmakers with Giovanni, De la Peña and Guardiola; but we've got sixty-odd games, so competition is very important. I won't just have a first-choice eleven, I'll need to rotate: Stoichkov, for example, is thirty, he won't play sixty games, maybe he'll play thirty-five; that means somebody else has to play twenty-five. It's always nice to play your best team, but nobody can possibly play sixty games in a season, you'd have no legs by March, especially here. The Spanish League made a big mistake expanding to twenty-two teams.'

Robson has never denied that he's taking over from a legend. With the serious business about to get under way, was that still in the back of his mind? 'Well, I respect who I'm taking over from and what he's achieved,' he says, in the cautious tone he reserves for talking about his predecessor. 'Johan Cruyff was one of the greatest players the world has ever seen; he's in that league with Pelé, Beckenbauer, Di Stéfano, Maradona and George Best, if you like. And I'd never deny that he had marvellous success here as a coach. I know about the reverence towards him in this city, but, um . . .' He pauses and grins. 'What was the question? No, seriously, if we start the season well and winning games, whoosh, his name will disappear into fresh air! I don't mean that disrespectfully, nobody will ever forget what he's done for Barcelona, I just mean the fans won't be looking backwards. However, I'm a realist; if we start badly and lose two or three games in a row, I know the fans will be chanting his name. But if that bothered me I wouldn't be here, I'd be going' – he feigns incredulity – 'Wow! Johan Cruyff, I can't follow him. Wow! He's won everything. Anyway, I've got my own CV, I'm experienced, I know how to build a team and how to make them play. If you can manage England you can manage any club, can't you? You're picking the best players in the country and you've got to handle the Bryan Robsons and the Ray Wilkins, and Peter Shilton and Ray Clemence, those are big guys. If you can't handle the big guys you're no good as England manager, the job will kill you. I had it for eight years, Graham had it for three, Terry for two. I had it for eight.'

The extensive televised pre-season calendar for Spanish clubs means that Robson has already had a good look at his rivals. It is early days, but where does he see the main challenge coming from? 'Real Madrid are a very big danger. They had a poor time of it last season, but they'll be a far better team this year. They've bought some extraordinary players: Mijatovic and Suker obviously, Seedorf is a good all-round player, Roberto Carlos has got a fantastic left foot, Secretario from Porto is a very good defender. Fabio Capello's situation is similar to mine, he's only had a month with his players and he's trying to get everything together quickly. Everybody's expecting immediate results, but you can't build a team in such a short space of time. If he does have an advantage, it's that he knew he was joining Madrid several months ago, that gave him more time to plan his signings; to look around and see what's available. I suddenly got offered the Barcelona job in May and had to start from scratch, and Mijatovic is already gone, Suker is gone, Seedorf is gone, we've missed out on some good players. But we've tried to make up for that and we've signed quality.'

A combination of Euro 96 and stop-press signings means that Robson has barely exchanged how-do-you-dos? with half of his players. 'You really can't expect to get everything together in one month,' he insists, 'and Jesus, look at the injuries I've had: Nadal, Stoichkov, Oscar . . . and then Ronaldo arrived late because of the Olympics.'

Unlike pundits who see the title race in terms of Real Madrid v. Barça, Robson refuses to underestimate double winners Atlético. 'I like Atlético, very much,' he says emphatically. 'The other night we ended up winning 5-2 so the press are going overboard, but at 2-2 it could have gone either way. They're a solid, well-organised side and I rate Antic very highly. He's an extremely meticulous coach, sticks to the basics, doesn't try to invent anything. Valencia could have another good season, too. I'm convinced Romario will score a lot of goals for them. But the Spanish League is full of tough games. Teams like Athletic Bilbao and Betis may not challenge for the title, but when Barcelona go to play there, you're going to get a bloody tough game!'

Closer to home, Robson is clear about what is required of him and when. 'There are no tomorrows at a club like Barcelona, it's all about instant success, especially now we've spent so much money. I know I'm expected to win the league straight away. Anything we do in Europe will be a bonus, but we have to get back into the Champions League.'

SUNDAY, 1 SEPTEMBER
Oviedo 2, Barcelona 4 (Stoichkov 47, 50, Luis Enrique 76, 89)
Carlos Tartiére, 20,000
Baía, Ferrer, Nadal, Popescu, Sergi, Amor, Guardiola, Luis Enrique, De la Peña (Abelardo 71), Ronaldo (Pizzi 65), Stoichkov (Cuéllar 65).

The Spain of 'Sun, Sea, Sex and Sangría' is a cliché designed to attract the throngs of northern Europe. It's also a fallacy guaranteed to exasperate 95 per cent of Spaniards. The country's tourist board has long had its own slogan: 'Spain is Different'. In truth, 'Every part of Spain is different' would be more appropriate. Barcelona are one of 22 sides in the country's top flight. During the season that kicks off today, Robson's travels will demonstrate that attempts to squeeze Spain into a convenient soundbite are fruitless. Any notion he had of his new country's homogeneous nature is dashed by an opening day trip to Oviedo, capital of the northern province of Asturias, a region of undulating hills with a radical mining stock that puts South Wales to shame (and where the natives' tipple is not *sangría* but a wicked cider). *Y Viva España?* Matadors? Flamenco? Hardly.

From the rugged coastline and blue seas of the Mediterranean (Barcelona and Espanyol) through a Basque country of industrial cities surrounded by lush countryside (Athletic Bilbao and San Sebastián's Real Sociedad) to rain-swept Galicia (La Coruña's Deportivo, Vigo's Celta, Santiago's Compostela); from the tropics of the Canary Islands (Tenerife) through the country's stiflingly hot flatlands (Real Madrid, Atlético Madrid, Rayo Vallecano and Valladolid) to Andalusia, the land of olive groves and the *siesta* (Sevilla and Betis); Spain's footballing geography is about as diverse as it gets. Lest we forget, Barcelona is closer to Paris than it is to Seville. As for the Spain beloved of the lager-swigging masses, Torremolinos, Benidorm, Magalluf and their like, dispersed across and beyond Spain's mainland, they have more in common with kiss-me-quick English resorts of fading postcards than anywhere else.

Robson certainly couldn't have asked for a more comfortable debut than a visit to Real Oviedo. This part of Asturias is Barça-friendly (the annual congress of Barcelona's supporters' clubs was held here last Monday) and the opposition even more so. At just 30, Oviedo's diminutive coach, Juan Manuel Lillo, is younger than many of his players and boasts a voice so squeaky it makes you wonder where Alan Ball went celebrating World Cup glory in '66. Lillo, a man with no professional experience as a player, was kicked out of relegation-bound Salamanca halfway through last season. Given that unenviable pedigree and Oviedo's failure to reinforce, their fans would happily settle for a repeat of last year's fourteenth position; beating the likes of Barça is definitely not on their agenda.

As for the level of expectation at Camp Nou, Bobby Robson would do well to come to grips with one fundamental truth: FC Barcelona are not in competition with 21 other sides, they are in competition with Real Madrid. Put another way, a Madrid or Barcelona coach never comes first or second, he comes first and last. And even if Robson produces a winning team he's not guaranteed to keep his job; sometimes, it's not enough to succeed; your rival must fail, too. In January 1992, Raddy Antic was sacked by Real Madrid halfway through the season with his side top of the league! 'Barcelona [*three points behind at the time*] are playing more spectacular football,' argued the Real president. It's against this kind of standard that Robson's achievements will be measured.

A week ago, Robson was resigned to opening the season with a depleted cast. Extended pleading with the Portuguese and Brazilian FAs means that Baía, Figo, Ronaldo and Giovanni are all present and correct in Oviedo, even if leaden of foot after early morning flights back to Spain. With the benefit of hindsight, the £70,000 Barcelona invested hiring two private planes would have been better spent elsewhere: Figo sits out both Portugal's game against Armenia and Barça's debut with a twisted ankle, Giovanni remains on the bench after yesterday's goalscoring double against Holland, and neither Ronaldo nor Baía play decisive roles in the proceedings.

Robson has consistently reminded everybody that his team are at the rehearsal stage. His players spend the first 45 minutes of the season endorsing the managerial line. Luckily, Oviedo are unable to capitalise on their better-looking approach work and two magical assists after the break from Ivan de la Peña, the shaven-headed prodigy they call 'Little Buddah', confirm that individual genius can compensate for the most shoddy collective performance. Ronaldo may be football's Michael Jordan (he wears the Nike, he's got the same barber; damn it, they're both forces of nature), but he hasn't got Jordan's legendary shirt. Number 23 at Barcelona is reserved for a more cerebral prodigy. When Ronaldo enters the fray there's a buzz; every time De la Peña gets the ball there's a hush. It's as if the fans fear that an outrush of breath would knock the little genius off his stride.

Twice Hristo Stoichkov adds the finishing touch to De la Peña's assists. The Bulgarian celebrates his back-on-the-block goals with effusive kissing of the colours. For once, it's not just about a mercenary playing to the gallery. After a year of Cruyff-imposed exile in Italy, Stoichkov is back at the club he never wanted to leave in the first place. And after turning down a more lucrative offer from Galatasaray to 'come home', he's entitled to his display of affection. The last 25 minutes produce sloppy defending all round and the game finishes 2-4, the first time Barça have opened a league campaign with four goals away from Camp Nou. 'We played very badly in the first half and were lucky not to go behind,' says a candid Robson, 'but even with Giovanni and Figo missing and Ronaldo really tired, we've obviously got players who can turn a game in a moment.'

Robson's introduction to Spanish football confirms the if-it-moves-book-it philosophy of the country's referees; nine yellow cards in a game that could hardly be described as bad-tempered. Luis Enrique, another Barça debutant, gets booked for celebrating the first of his two goals with a quick striptease, clearly a more punishable offence than the eight fouls he'd previously logged up. Elsewhere, Valladolid's club doctor was sent off at Rayo Vallecano whilst attending an injured player. In the words of the referee, 'I didn't like the way he looked at me.'

MONDAY, 2 SEPTEMBER

For the first time since he arrived at Barcelona, Robson gets to take training with his entire foreign legion. Laurent Blanc, or Blank as the Spanish insist on calling him, has recovered from a pre-season ankle injury, while deadline signing Fernando Couto is reunited with his mentor from Porto. Ronaldo, Giovanni, Figo, Stoichkov, Prosinecki and Baía complete a foreign line-up to die for. Unfortunately, most of the locals have done a runner. Javier Clemente has called up seven Barcelona players for Spain's World Cup qualifier against the Faeroe Islands. Nadal, Abelardo, Luis Enrique, Sergi, Amor and Pizzi all featured in Euro 96, and there's a recall for midfield stylist Pep Guardiola, out of favour since the 1994 World Cup.

Depending on the prevailing balance of power, the Spanish national side is generally dominated by either Barcelona or Real

Madrid players. Clemente's latest squad includes only two Madrid players (matching the two from reigning champs Atlético). The coach may be a prickly character, but even if he was diplomacy itself he'd be on a hiding every time he names his squad. If players from Barça dominate, the Catalan press will complain that Clemente is undermining their side's league campaign; if players from Real Madrid dominate, they will suggest he's anti-Barcelona. Needless to say, whichever argument dominates in Barcelona, the opposite applies in Madrid.

TUESDAY, 3 SEPTEMBER

Post-Bosman, the Spanish League is something of a misnomer. The Spot-the-Spaniard League would be more appropriate. (Saturday's opener between Deportivo La Coruña and Real Madrid). John Toshack's line-up boasted three Frenchmen, two Brazilians, a Moroccan, a Cameroonese, a Serb and just three Spaniards. A combination of Bodo Illgner's eleventh-hour arrival from Cologne, injuries and international duty dictated that Fabio Capello fielded just three foreigners (Mijatovic, Suker and Roberto Carlos), but that's as home-grown as Madrid are going to get.

Spanish clubs, big and small alike, have spent the summer scouring international markets with unparalleled relish. As the action commences, 150 foreigners are on board in the top flight alone. A TV-financed spending spree has seen Spain's footballing barons invest £130 million in the transfer market, almost as much as the Premiership and the *calcio* put together. In the wake of the Bosman ruling, EU citizens are obviously in demand, and some 33 EU players are on duty compared to five this time last year. But changes in the league's regulations mean that foreigners are now welcome irrespective of their passport. Spanish clubs can now sign up to six non-EC players, four of whom they can field simultaneously. The fledgling states of the former Yugoslavia maintain their status as market leaders with a combined total of 37 players, followed by the traditional Hispanic-friendly territories of Argentina (21) and Brazil (13). Players from 59 countries make the Spanish top flight the most cosmopolitan on the planet.

Of the 500,000 foreigners legally resident in Spain, 65,000 are Brits (only Morocco boasts more). Unlike Australia, Costa Rica, Bolivia, Ghana and Israel, however, the home countries can't muster a footballer between them. The young untouchables aside – that's

Giggs, McManaman, Fowler and stop counting – Spanish clubs are simply not interested in buying British. A combination of silly prices (why buy 31-year-old Gary McAllister for £3 million when you can get 20-year-old Clarence Seedorf for the same price?), and the feeling that British players are like fish out of water away from the hurly-burly of the Premier League, are the main reasons. And while the English enthuse about their influx of foreigners, the Spanish view the Premiership as essentially a retirement pasture for old crocks (Vialli, Gullit, Futre) or a step down the ladder for rejects. Familiar names like Dumitrescu, Raducioiu, Jerkan and, of course, Jordi Cruyff were all discarded by their Spanish clubs. Harsher Italian critics might say the same of Ravanelli, Carbone, Silenzi, Asprilla and Bergkamp.

As a man in a privileged position when it comes to spreading goodwill and money around, does Robson think English clubs were out of synch when it came to transfer fees? 'Well, yes, seven million pounds for Ravanelli, for example, is an awful lot of money. But how do you change the market? I think twenty million dollars for Ronaldo is excessive but unless we pay that money we don't get him. You cough up and get the player you want or you settle for somebody else who perhaps won't win you things.'

At least Robson is working for one of the winners in the new world order. 'The Bosman ruling makes a difference to most clubs, but sadly it will favour the big guns who can now choose from even more players,' he admits with commendable frankness. 'Before, you could get a player on a long contract at a smaller club, now you'll be lucky to get them on a one- or two-year deal. I was guilty at Ipswich of developing this loyalty thing with long-term contracts and players would actually stay with you. I don't think you'll see that any more – unless you're a big club and you explain the situation to players, like we did with Ronaldo. You have to say, "Listen, I can't pay twenty million dollars for you and give you a two-year contract, you have to understand that, and if you can't, don't sign." Ronaldo wanted to sign so he tied himself to the club for the rest of his career, but he gets a lot of money in return so he can't complain. There's no question about it, the Bosman ruling will help the big clubs; now they can commandeer all the best players. They could in a way before, but perhaps it took them longer to get what they wanted.'

At nineteen, Ronaldo is guaranteed well over a million pounds per annum for the next eight years. Will that affect his motivation and desire? 'That's a question you'd have to ask Ronaldo,' says Robson. 'I think he'll handle it from what I know of him. I don't think he'll go, "Christ, I'm a twenty-million-dollar player so I've got to play like one, it's going to worry me." I don't think he'll be concerned about the money, to be honest. Personally, I think it's a great investment because we've got a superstar for the next ten years.'

THURSDAY, 5 SEPTEMBER

In his three and a bit seasons at Camp Nou, Terry Venables surrounded himself with fellow Brits (coach Alan Harris, Steve Archibald, Gary Lineker and Mark Hughes). Bobby Robson denies plans to establish a Portuguese clan – 'It's just a case of being comfortable working with people I know' – but if he'd succeeded in buying Amunike and Secretario we're talking near as damn it. Porto old boys Mourinho, Baía and Couto, plus Luis Figo (who played for Robson at Sporting Lisbon), and the Portuguese-speaking Brazilians, will ensure that Spanish has a serious competitor in the Barça dressing room this season.

Linguistic hegemony aside, Michael Robinson reckons there could be psychological reasons behind Robson's accumulation of *amigos*. 'I'm sure one of the motives for buying so many new players is to establish his authority in the dressing room. Robson needs the players to accept his authority as the new man in charge, and not have sixty or seventy per cent thinking, "Well, with Johan we did this, that and the other." I think that's why he has gone back to Portugal and signed people who know and respect him. The other players will use that as a reference; the sceptics in the dressing room who were thinking, "What's he like, ain't he a bit old, is he any good?" But if he's got the dressing room backing of players who'll say, "Hey, he's all right, he knows his business, he knows his job," that will help win over the doubters and give him a sort of credibility.'

SATURDAY, 7 SEPTEMBER

Barcelona 2, Espanyol 1 (Giovanni 84, Pizzi 92)
Camp Nou, 100,000
Baía, Luis Enrique, Couto, Nadal, Sergi, Popescu, Guardiola (De la Peña 71), Figo (Pizzi 71), Giovanni, Ronaldo, Stoichkov

In Spain, *un derby* is any game between major rivals, regardless of geography. Hence *el gran derby* is Barcelona against Real Madrid;

not Real v. Atlético Madrid, and certainly not Barça v. Espanyol. Camp Nou and Espanyol's Sarrià stadium lie barely a mile apart on either side of Barcelona's main thoroughfare, *la Diagonal*. Driving in from the north, it's an impressive gateway to the city: Space Age office blocks, wide tree-lined sidewalks, and signposts that evoke great football. 'Turn Right' for Camp Nou or 'Turn Left' for Sarrià, the venue for that classic Italy v. Brazil game at the 1982 World Cup (and still the scene of summer homage by nostalgic *tifosi*). Sarrià sits at the heart of Barcelona's most exclusive residential neighbourhood. Sadly for Espanyol, the north side of *la Diagonal* is upmarket in property terms, but in every other sense the club is a distinctly poor relation. Bobby Robson's home debut is against a local rival that has lost all but four of its 37 visits to Camp Nou, and it's fifteen years since their only win at Fortress Barça. A case of 'Budgies' (Espanyol's self-deprecatingly cute nickname) to the slaughter?

It may be a new season, but a turbulent past filters through the stadium's every pore. Twenty minutes before the 8.30 p.m. kick-off, a blackboard in the press suite still cites the players who took part in the final fixture of the 1995/96 season. Well, most of them, anyway. One hundred and ten days and a footballing revolution later, Celta's line-up remains intact. However, an eager-to-please Camp Nou volunteer has taken it upon himself to erase the names of the Barça disciples who were expelled with the Dutch Antichrist. In the club shop, you can still purchase postcards of the long-gone Eusebio, Korneiev and Nando, but there's not a Johan or Jordi in sight.

Awesome is the only word that does justice to the five-tiered Camp Nou skyscraper. The world's most impressive football stadium with the world's silliest name. FC Barcelona upped sticks in 1957 before deciding on a name for their new residence, so the fans started referring to it as *el camp nou*, the new ground. The dithering board never made up its mind and four decades on the not-so-new arena retains its temporary moniker. Inside a stadium that makes Old Trafford's 'Theatre of Dreams' look like an off-Broadway fleapit, the Gol Nord is awash with flags: the red and yellow stripes of Catalonia's *senyera*, the green and yellow of Brazil, and the cross of St George. For the moment, Bobby Robson is up there with his Brazilians in the popularity stakes, though it'll be a miracle if he ever competes with the Bulgarian Messiah.

As the fans manoeuvre their way through the building site that poses as the Camp Nou environs (permanent according to the grumbling *socis*, though in this case a new underground carpark is to blame), it's clear from the number of youngsters in undersized shirts that '8-Stoichkov' is back on friendly territory. Unlike in England, replica shirts are not *de rigueur* gear at the footie (the only punters you'll find wearing the colours in Barcelona are tourists), but does the unwillingness to invest in new gear reflect scepticism about Hristo's staying power the second time around? Few players in Barça's history have been as revered as the former European Footballer of the Year, but even the original Hristo (Christ in Bulgarian) had his card marked by his early thirties.

They Used to Play on Grass was a Terry Venables novel translated into Catalan in his days as El Tel. A decade and more on, it threatens to provide the subtitle for Bobby Robson's season. From the press box at the top of Camp Nou, the pitch looked green and true. Yet something is clearly amiss as Robson spends his pre-match walkabout treading down the pitch, oh so gingerly . . . again and again. Barely ten minutes into the season's proceedings and it's clear why. The club may have reseeded its pitch for the umpteenth time this summer, but before Ronaldo & Co. have worked out which way they're kicking, the grass has cut up so dramatically you fear for their safety.

On a surface unfit for football, the game was memorable only for a delirious finale. Espanyol's hopes of a surprise victory are still intact when, with just six minutes to go, Giovanni equalises. Then, in the 92nd, minute, Ronaldo picks up the ball 30 yards from goal and demonstrates just why he cost 20 million dollars. Forcing his way around and through defenders, he unleashes a divot-assisted rocket that the 'keeper can only parry; Pizzi strokes home the rebound before leading a mad dash to the corner flag. Vítor Baía, clearly a graduate of the Tony Adams School of Celebrations, almost laid waste to Barça's prize investment after a hop, skip and jump onto the celebrating pack that left Ronaldo nursing a bruised head. Bobby Robson was somewhat more controlled on the bench. When Giovanni equalises he limits himself to hoisting up his socks. Amidst the mayhem that greeted the overtime winner, he simply patted the team delegate on the back. After the game, he dedicated the victory to Barça's president on his 65th birthday. Johan Cruyff, now a season ticket holder, leaves early and misses the injury-time winner. It's safe to assume he isn't off to celebrate happy birthdays with Josep Lluis Núñez.

'The pitch clearly helped the Brazilians,' moans Espanyol captain Jordi Lardín afterwards. 'It was like playing on a beach.' At least there weren't many Espanyol fans on hand to witness their latest capitulation to Goliath. It may have been a derby, but you could have squeezed the visiting contingent into a matchbox. Spanish football fans don't travel in any great numbers for many reasons. There's the country's size (fractionally smaller than France, Spain is the second biggest country in Europe besides Russia), the unwillingness to 'put money in the enemy's pocket', and, frankly, the sheer danger. Despite much pontificating to the contrary, one of the reasons hooliganism has never taken root in Spain is precisely because of the ugly nature of football rivalry. There are clubs that are friendly for political reasons (Barcelona are particularly welcome in the Basque country, Espanyol and Real Madrid fans are practically blood brothers), but in cases where there is no love lost, you travel at your peril. And unlike in England, where even in the bad old days there existed a twisted hooligan code (i.e. little kudos attached to attacking 'civilians'), Spanish hostilities are indiscriminate. Women, children and bespectacled parents – if you're wearing the wrong colours you'd better stay out of town. Or even the other side of town.

Despite the board's recent attempts to Catalanise the club, Espanyol have never shaken off the stigma of being, as their name suggests, a Spanish team in enemy territory, and the continuing stigma of a nasty group of right-wing *ultras* is a reminder of a traditional source of support. For decades, FC Barcelona acted as an integrating force for Catalonia's new arrivals, while Espanyol drew their support from sectors hostile to notions of the region's independence (soldiers, policemen, civil servants, fascists). They might boast more Catalan players (today, Toni, Herrera, Lardin and Javi to Barça's Sergi and Guardiola), but Espanyol are still very much the neighbours from outer space.

The fans may be used to it, but Robson will take a while to get blasé about crowds of 100,000. 'Do you realise you could squeeze every last man, woman and child from Ipswich into Camp Nou? Football's sway in this city is overpowering. In Ipswich it's far more laid back; if they win they don't get too excited and if they lose they don't throw stones. If you lose here, well . . .' He pauses and decides to change the subject before it follows its natural course, but his look says it all. 'At Ipswich, I had the most civilised way of life any football manager could hope for. The Cobbold family were beautiful people to work for, they treated winning and losing exactly the same. If we lost John Cobbold would say to me' – he adopts a placatory tone – ' "Bobby, Bobby, it wasn't our turn to win today." I used to say, "But, ah, Mr John . . ." and he'd interrupt me, "Bobby, Bobby . . . if we hadn't lost today the other team wouldn't have had the pleasure of winning." ' Somehow it's difficult to imagine *la familia* Núñez being so charitable.

SUNDAY, 8 SEPTEMBER

Today's headlines are dominated not by the Camp Nou debut of Robson's new-model Barça, but the excuse for a pitch. 'Scandalous,' grumbled Gica Popescu as he trooped wearily off, and that's about as mild as it gets. 'It's difficult to play decent football on that pitch,' admitted Robson, a bit like saying you can't play snooker in a swimming pool. Ronaldo was more forthright. 'In the run that led to the winner, I don't know which was more difficult, getting past the Espanyol defence or over the pitch.' The Olympic stadium at Montjuïc was the setting for Barça's pre-season games and there is plenty of support for taking Thursday's Cup Winners' Cup debut there. 'I'm sure there are season ticket holders that wouldn't mind making the sacrifice,' insists Ronaldo. 'They must realise that the result and avoiding injuries are more important. The pitch is in a dreadful state and the players are frightened of getting injured.'

With Spanish football's highest 1996/97 budget (£50 million) and a lunar crater of a pitch, Barcelona may take top prize in the ineptitude stakes, but their situation is not unique. Champions Atlético Madrid were forced to take their home debut across the city to Real's Bernabéu stadium after it was discovered that their freshly laid pitch was infected by caterpillars. Like Núñez (and every other president in Spain), Atlético's Jesús Gil made his fortune in the construction business.

WEDNESDAY, 11 SEPTEMBER

Romario, Barcelona's last great Brazilian, is at loggerheads with another coach. Back in Spain at Valencia, he reacts angrily to being dropped by Luis Aragonés for tonight's UEFA Cup game against Bayern Munich. His message to the board, 'Make your minds up, it's me or Luis!' No doubt keen to avoid similar revolutions, Bobby Robson calls time-out in training to warn his players not to wash their dirty linen in public. He's particularly annoyed that a row between Stoichkov and Guardiola after the Espanyol game has been leaked to the press. Barça fans may worship the Bulgarian, but the dressing room was never teeming with his bosom pals. As Guardiola puts it, 'It's not the first time this has happened, and it won't be the last.'

Given that Núñez has spent the last few days claiming it was 'impossible' to take tomorrow's game to Montjuïc, Robson admits he was 'surprised' to receive a midnight call informing him that Barça will play at the Olympic Stadium after all. A stormy weather forecast and the 'Miracle of Vicente Calderón' provoked a change of heart. At midday, half of Atlético Madrid's playing area resembled a beach; at half past eight, they kicked off their Champions League game against Steaua Bucharest on a freshly laid pitch as true as a bowling green. Ninety minutes and a resounding four-goal victory later, Núñez was on the blower.

THURSDAY, 12 SEPTEMBER
Barcelona 2, AEK Larnaca 0 (Ronaldo 19, 77)
Olympic Stadium, 29,199

Thirty thousand fans brave the pouring rain to trek up the 'Magic Mountain' of Montjuïc. 'Now we'll have to take a full-strength side to Cyprus,' laments Robson of what was definitely an excuse to stay at home. Three games into the season, the press leap on the performance to criticise the team's 'continuing lack of chemistry' (!), but as centre forward Pizzi observes, 'It's pointless trying to read anything into our performance, it was just one of those nights when the ball didn't want to go in the net, it's as simple as that.'

The Cypriot's line-up included a carpenter, an insurance salesman and a soldier; a slightly different pedigree to Barcelona's last Cup Winners' Cup opponents, Manchester United in the 1991 final. Robson is convinced that the men from Old Trafford are set for another successful Euro-campaign. 'I think Manchester United will do well because they've learned. English sides forgot how to play in Europe. No top side in England plays defensively away from home and they don't know how to kill a game. I remember a game between Newcastle and Bilbao a couple of years ago. Newcastle were winning 3-0 at home but they wouldn't sit on it, they kept going for the fourth goal, they left a door open at the back, and suddenly it's 3-2. You lose 1-0 away from home and you're out! We were out of

Europe so long we forgot how to play two-legged football. We'd play one-game knockout like FA Cup ties, and we've had to learn again.'

SATURDAY, 14 SEPTEMBER

In a country where snap judgements are the norm, the press have already reached a unanimous verdict: Robson's Barcelona may be winning but the sum of the parts doesn't add up and the team remains dependent on flashes of genius from one or other of its superstars. Before setting off for tomorrow's game at Racing Santander, Robson takes this argument on board. 'It's important to have players in a collective who can tip the balance, the way Maradona did at the 1986 World Cup. Without him Argentina would never have won the World Cup. So if you've got a Maradona, a Cruyff, a Di Stéfano or a Romario in your team, of course they are going to make the difference. Every player in the team has his part to play, but if you've got a twenty-million-dollar footballer like Ronaldo, it's logical that he makes the difference. That's his obligation.'

SUNDAY, 15 SEPTEMBER
Racing Santander 1, Barcelona 1 (Ronaldo 31)
Nuevo Sardinero, 21,000

Despite their being the kind of opposition they regard as cannon-fodder, Barcelona can't seem to get the hang of Racing. It's now fourteen years since Barça last managed a victory at the tiny Nuevo Sardinero (the New Sardine Beach) stadium on the Cantabrian coast. Before the game, Robson had insisted, 'This is the kind of away game we must win if we're serious about winning the title.' Well, if it's any consolation, Barça have done far worse here in recent years and gone on to win the league.

It all started so promisingly, too. Ronaldo's first league goal was the kind of opening strike legends are made of. Killing a long ball from Guardiola on his chest and sweeping past his marker in one simultaneous movement, he then sent the 'keeper on reconnaissance in one direction before rounding him in the other. Sadly, that was the last time Barça got the ball to their boy wonder in decent conditions. Almost despite themselves, Racing equalised with fifteen minutes to go. Robson seemed genuinely ruffled by his side's inability to mesh. He spent most of the second half gesticulating from the touchline and after the game his reprimands echoed beyond the dressing room: 'No, no, no, that's not the way to play football.' Once the man the players have dubbed *l'Avi* (Catalan for granddad) regained his more familiar composure, he told assembled journalists, 'In the second half, we've not done anything right at all. We keep giving the ball away and we've not had a single shot on goal until the last five minutes. There's no way we can continue to let other sides dominate us.

'Ronaldo's goal was a marvellous example of how you make goals out of nothing, but we've really got to work on getting him more involved, even if he was a bit static today. Our playmakers, the technical players like Guardiola, have wasted lots of possession today [*at this point he pauses, as if shocked by his own severity*] but that's not a criticism.' It certainly sounded like one.

'There have been games when I've lost the ball less,' admitted the contrite midfielder, though as the only survivor from a side that was thrashed 5-0 at Santander two years ago, he might have added, 'Thank God for small mercies.' On the opposing bench was Marcos Alonso, a member of the last Barça side to win at Santander, in 1982. 'Barcelona have changed overnight,' he observed. 'Personally, I preferred Cruyff's more courageous tactics. There's plenty of quality in Robson's side but they only play in short bursts.'

MONDAY, 16 SEPTEMBER

Ronaldo denies the existence of what the press has described as '*Ronaldodependencía*'. 'I've got plenty of teammates who can score goals, it's just that I'm receiving all the good passes. Our success depends on the whole team, not just one player.' Nonetheless, assistant coach José Mourinho echoes Robson's comments of the previous day. 'We've told him it's no good scoring a wonder goal and spending the other eighty-nine minutes sleeping. I'm sure he's got the message.' Ronaldo's scoring record currently stands at 118 goals in 121 games for Cruzeiro, PSV and Barcelona. God knows what'll happen if he decides to stay awake for a whole game.

The world's last great solo act, Diego Maradona, could take some advice from Ronaldo on getting enough shut-eye. Visiting Spain to rustle up sympathy for his 'medical problems', he trashes the lobby of an Alicante hotel at six o'clock in the morning. That's six o'clock in the morning before going to bed.

TUESDAY, 17 SEPTEMBER

Ronaldo responds to Mourinho's Santander jibes. 'It would have been better if he'd told me face to face, rather than going to the press with it, that would have been more professional. I played badly at Racing, but so did everybody else. I'm in the team to carry out the coaches' orders, but if I don't get the ball there's not much I can do.'

A furious Martin Edwards flies back to England after Barcelona refuse to discuss Manchester United's offer for Miquel Angel Nadal. 'I don't understand Barcelona's attitude. We've agreed terms, and now they turn around and say he's not for sale. Still, the player definitely wants to join us, so I'm not giving up hope.' Bobby Robson denies rumours that his international defender is about to join United. 'Nadal is not for sale, it's as simple as that. I've got twenty-four players in my squad and I need every last one of them.' According to the Spanish press, Barcelona will sell Nadal, but only if United double their current £2.5 million offer.

FRIDAY, 20 SEPTEMBER

One week's intensive sodding about later, Bobby Robson gives his newly laid green the thumbs up. 'I'm very happy, in a month it should be perfect. Today we've done all the things we'd normally do in training and the pitch has held up perfectly. The players will be able to take the field now without worrying about the surface.' In the end, Barcelona decided to ape Atlético Madrid and replaced their turf chunk by chunk using a revolutionary new method called . . . sodding.

Michael Robinson, in town for Sunday's game against Real Sociedad, assesses Barcelona's start. 'Even though they've not played well so far, Barça are clearly a side that will score a lot of goals. I'm sure there won't be half a dozen games all season when they don't score two or more. You'll get the nit-pickers who'll say, "Yeah, but what about the style?" but in the two games I've seen, I was amazed by their potential in fifteen-minute bursts, and that'll do me at this stage of the season. The Espanyol game reminded me of when we used to play football in the school playground, and the good players – the goodies – would give the bad players a ten-goal start. Then, after a while, the teacher comes out into the playground and says, "In five minutes, you've got to be back in." All of a sudden, you realise you've only got six or seven goals so it's like the seventh cavalry. It's the same with Barcelona, they give me that unbelievable sense of "This is a powerful football team when they put their minds to it". In the second half against Oviedo, it was as if the players were thinking, "Well, we played crap in the first half, we've got to do something now," so they've scored two goals straight away. I think they've got an artillery of enormous magnitude ... they're my favourites to win the League.'

SATURDAY, 21 SEPTEMBER

At his routine weekly press conference, a visibly irked Robson attempts to lay to rest the week's sideshows. On José Mourinho's 'sleepy Ronaldo' dig, he insists, 'That was just a throwaway comment intended as an example and it's been taken out of context. From now on we'll have to be careful not to give examples, or just say, "No comment." I've spoken to Ronaldo and he knows he enjoys our total confidence and that everything we do is for his own good. You have to put yourself in his shoes; he's only nineteen and every single day he's in the papers and people are looking for a story for him. Our job is to guide him, to help him keep on track. I remember what happened to George Best. On the pitch he was unstoppable, but by the time he was twenty-five he was practically finished because nobody put the brakes on off the pitch either: discos, parties, booze . . .

'We want a good relationship with the press, and we know you're only doing your job, but I'd like you [*journalists*] to come and sit up here for just ten minutes. So let's try and not misinterpret what's being said.'

Robson fails to play the tough guy for very long, though. A nice man who loves to talk football is a nice man who loves to talk football, try as he might to get angry. Twenty minutes after a prickly and hour-long press conference, he's still chatting affably to journalists who have stayed behind to chew the fat. The attempts of Barcelona's press officer to drag him away for dinner on time are as fruitless as ever.

Back at the team's hotel, conversation turns to England and Glenn Hoddle's forthcoming Wembley debut. Almost fourteen years to the day since he walked out at Wembley for his own home debut, Robson will be back in London next month to see Hoddle follow in his footsteps. And cometh the hour, he'll know exactly how his former charge will be feeling. 'You can be the calmest, most confident person in the world, but before your first match at

39

Wembley, there's definitely a feeling of nervous tension within you, a feeling of "Gee, I hope everything goes all right". You're not afraid, otherwise you wouldn't have taken the job, but there's so much riding on that match for you personally, you pray the team are going to play well. But you're excited and very proud, as well. Winning a game at Wembley as England manager is one of the greatest feelings in the world.

'You know you've got to build a team, so one of your priorities is to look at different people early on, but the Poland game is a World Cup qualifier so Glenn can't afford to experiment. He certainly can't expect the benefit of the doubt from the press when he loses, whatever the nature of the fixture. People say, "Experiment in a friendly game, it doesn't matter if you lose" . . . It doesn't matter if you lose! I hope nobody's told Glenn it doesn't matter if he loses. I once tried out some new players in a friendly in Saudi Arabia, and though we didn't lose, it actually finished 1-1; I got hung, drawn and quartered. I had a look at Pallister, Gascoigne and Seaman alongside your Robsons, Linekers and Beardsleys, so don't tell me I picked bad players. Last week, Gica Popescu came back from losing against Saudi Arabia in Romania, and I asked him what happened. He said, "Too many debutants, mister." I had to laugh!'

Seven players – Peter Shilton, Bryan Robson, Chris Waddle, John Barnes, Gary Lineker, Kenny Sansom and Terry Butcher – played more than 50 times for Robson's England, and he's quick to add Peter Beardsley (45 games) to his list of stalwarts. Does he think Hoddle, who he capped 40 times (and who doesn't make his list of goodfellas), has a similar hard core of quality at his disposal? 'You'd have to say Shearer straight away and I know Glenn rates Barmby. I think Anderton and McManaman are young enough and good enough to be part of the England scene for a long time. Then, of course, there's Beckham. Glenn needs to nurse him and he won't play every game, but once he matures and gets his strength, at maybe twenty-four or twenty-five, he's going to be very, very good. He's certainly spoilt for choice up front. I had the Lineker and Beardsley partnership later on, but there were players I capped – Kerry Dixon, Luther Blissett and Peter Davenport spring to mind – who are not comparable to some of the players who are struggling to get a game at the moment, the likes of Fowler, Ferdinand and Collymore.'

Of course, an embarrassment of riches brings its problems, too. Robson once joked that he'd have to field 20 players a game if he played everyone the press was pushing for. And then there is pressure from partisan fans. After ending Kevin Keegan's international career, Robson was barracked and spat at when he first went back to Newcastle. As he admits, that kind of dual-edged pressure can make the England job unbearable. 'Glenn will find that difficult at first, but you have to try and ignore it. You've got to be your own man and make your own decisions. The problem is when it gets personal and starts to affect the people around you. Graham Taylor's wife nearly had a nervous breakdown because of the pressure he was under. She was delighted when he resigned. People used to say to me, "Have you read the *Sun* today?" I'd say, "Listen, don't tell me, I don't want to know." You're better off without it, aren't you? They're never going to reflect what you think, they write to sell papers, that's their job. Being bad is their job and they're brilliant at it!'

As Robson points out, even when you get things right, you rarely get credit for it. 'When I switched to the sweeper system at the 1990 World Cup, I was crucified for using tactics I'd supposedly ignored for eight years. Then when it worked, the press suggested it was the players' idea, anyway!' As he attempts to win the championship in a third country, Robson admits his England days are becoming distant, albeit fond memories. 'There are still several players involved that made their debuts for me, and I'm proud they've lasted the course, but I don't really see England as my team any more. Now I'm just another fan.'

SUNDAY, 22 SEPTEMBER
Barcelona 3, Real Sociedad 2 (Ronaldo 1, 89, Pizzi 74)
Camp Nou, 90,000

It may have been the day rain stopped play (hardly circumstances Río de Janeiro prepares you for) but it was still 'Happy Birthday, Ronaldo'. Barely a minute into the game and the Brazilian crashed the ball home with a virulence that suggested dismay at abandoning his teens. Any notions of a similarly rapid start to the second half were dispelled when a rainstorm-induced power cut left Camp Nou shrouded in darkness for 20 minutes. 'After the break we found it difficult to adapt,' grumbles Bobby Robson, 'though I was delighted at how the pitch held up in such hellish conditions.' Real Sociedad from rain-seduced San Sebastián had no such problems, though in fairness their equaliser was the result of a fluke deflection. Once again, the introduction of Pizzi and De la Peña prompted a grandstand finish. The Hispano-Argentinian needed his customary five minutes before restoring Barça's lead, and 'Little Buddah' invited Ronaldo to round things off and send his mum (who was still powdering her nose when Junior opened the scoring) into tears. The Basques did pull a goal back with a last-minute penalty, but by then it was all over bar the raining.

MONDAY, 23 SEPTEMBER

Robson spends the afternoon at Barçamania. Covering four blocks in the city centre, the annual fair boasts 140 stands and more than 2,000 FC Barcelona-licensed products. 'Barcelona's capacity to surprise me never wears off,' says Robson between signing autographs and generally spreading goodwill. 'I've travelled all over the world and I'm familiar with how lots of big clubs work, but I've never seen anything remotely like this fair. You have to see it for yourself to believe it. Barcelona really are a unique club.'

Over four days, nearly 600,000 punters share his enthusiasm.

WEDNESDAY, 25 SEPTEMBER

FC Barcelona celebrate 39 years at Camp Nou with Mass in the club carpark. Like most Spanish clubs, Barça like to shroud their activities in a religious aura. Lots of Hail Marys and making the sign of the Cross aside, no championship celebration is complete without a visit to the holy shrine of Montserrat to pay homage to *la Moreneta*, Catalonia's black madonna. Not that all the holy guys are on their side. 'Where there used to be paintings of the Last Supper, now there are posters of Ronaldo,' grumbles one Catalan bishop as he bemoans an increasingly secular society.

Meanwhile, in Cyprus, Robson expresses his own indignation at the non-believers. 'I really don't understand the stick we've been getting when we've still not lost a game,' he tells journalists at Barça's temporary HQ in Limassol. 'If it's like this now, what will it be like when we lose a game? I know we're only at seventy to seventy-five per cent, but we've got eight new players. That's a lot of new faces, and they're all used to playing in different styles, so I'm happy with the way things are developing. I'm sure we'll be successful and entertaining. Just be patient.'

Rumour has it that Nadal won't play against AEK because a pact dictates he shouldn't be cup-tied. Robson firmly denies any such agreement. 'There is no pressure on me to leave him out, whatever happens will be my decision. It's a long season and we've already seen with all the injuries that we need a big squad.'

THURSDAY, 26 SEPTEMBER
AEK Larnaca 0, Barcelona 0
Zenon Stadium, Larnaca, 7,000

Robson's men ease their way into the next round of the Cup Winners' Cup, but top billing in *Sport* is reserved for Manchester's most wanted looking forlorn on the bench. 'Nadal Is Going,' guarantees the headline. Clearly the press are not convinced that Robson is pulling the transfer strings.

Ronaldo sits out the game as a precaution after pulling up in training with a sore pubis, and with Pizzi and Stoichkov (out for a month) also missing, Barça cruise through the game with little enthusiasm (admittedly proceedings are tedious, but does Ronaldo need to spend the whole game gabbling on his mobile phone in the stand?). 'It was like a training session,' is Robson's summing up of a dull game. In reality, it must have been difficult to take things seriously at a ground with tree-lined open spaces on three sides. A tiny pitch and swamp-length grass were hardly conducive to party tricks, either. 'I'm just glad we didn't pick up any injuries,' adds Robson. He also warns against reading anything into Nadal's non-appearance. 'I preferred to let Abelardo and Blanc get a game under their belts.' Reflecting a rather different agenda, the still-not-cup-tied player admits, 'I breathed a sigh of relief when Robson made the third substitution.'

FRIDAY, 27 SEPTEMBER
Josep Lluís Núñez's attempts to exorcise the Cruyff legacy are continued when Valencia keeper Andoni Zubizarreta is offered the chance to return to Camp Nou when he hangs up his boots with Valencia. Spain's most capped player was told he'd played his last game for Barça after the 4-0 defeat against Milan in the 1994 European Cup Final . . . on the bus to Athens airport! Such a callous *adiós* was no reward for eight years of sterling service, and the fact that one of the men who benefited from his departure was Cruyff's son-in-law suggests the coach's motives weren't entirely honourable. At the time, Jesús Angoy was 28 and still in Barça's nursery team

(average age 19.3). Now 30, he is out of the game and reduced to casting sessions as a kicker for Barcelona Dragons American football team. In his defence, Cruyff could argue he is merely abiding by local custom. Josep Lluís Núñez and Atlético's Jesús Gil have sons on the board and poised to take over the reins, while Real Madrid President Lorenzo Sanz has both his boys on the playing staff! And one of the young Sanzes is engaged to the daughter of the president of the media mogul who is underwriting Madrid's huge debt, and . . . well, we could go on all day.

SATURDAY, 28 SEPTEMBER

Tonight sees the premiere of *El Culé Kulé*, a play about a *culé* (a Barcelona fan) called Kulé whose marriage hits the rocks because of his footballing obsession. Barça fans have been known as *culés* since their pre-First World War days at the Carrer Industria stadium. Legend has it that on walking past the ground on match days you could see lines of bottoms (*cul* in Catalan) hanging over the top tier. Hence the name. Barcelona must be the only city in the world where total strangers greet you with a smile and 'Hi, I'm a bum-boy'! As for *El Culé Kulé*, well, there are no bums on seats when Barça are in town; naturally the play is cancelled on match days.

SUNDAY, 29 SEPTEMBER

Zaragoza 3, Barcelona 5 (Ronaldo 56, 85, Figo 21, Popescu 73 pen, Luis Enrique 82)
La Romareda, 33,000

Five days after La Romareda play host to the sole European leg of Michael Jackson's world tour, Barcelona and Arsenal's favourite Spaniards produce their own thriller. With an hour on the clock, Barcelona are 3-1 down and grateful that one-sided football matches can't be stopped. While Nadal, Couto and Sergi take it in turns to be tormented by Gustavo López, his fellow Argentinian, Kily González, all but declares war on 'No, *you* go first' Ronaldo and Giovanni (what is it about Argies and Brazilians?).

However badly they play for the first hour, writing off Robson's side is rapidly becoming a mug's game. Ronaldo has already broken the offside trap and another grounded 'keeper's heart to make it 3-2 when the game turns on a 73rd minute flashpoint. Zaragoza's Solana decks Couto in a penalty-box mêlée and at the instigation of his linesman the referee awards a penalty and flashes the red card.

Unfortunately, Mejuto González's eagle-eyed accomplice (a school janitor by day) prompts him to send off the wrong man. The antics of the Zaragoza players, who, led by the typically insubordinate Gustavo Poyet, threaten to walk off in protest, see the game delayed ten minutes before Popescu slots home the penalty.

With their opponents in a state of barely controlled frenzy, Barcelona only have to keep their nerve to win. With eight minutes to go, Luis Enrique unleashes a furious shot from the edge of the box to put them ahead. Three minutes later Ronaldo charges past three defenders and the 'keeper as if they are Chinese whispers to seal an epic comeback at 3-5. It's official: the art of dribbling around goalkeepers is no longer confined to Pathé newsreels; four of Ronaldo's five league goals have been scored after leaving a 'keeper sprawling on the deck. Most of the home crowd miss his latest extravagance, having followed the belligerent example of their board of directors and abandoned the stadium *en masse* after Barça's fourth goal.

The fever-pitch atmosphere is obviously catching. Bobby Robson barely moves from his corner of the bench in 90 minutes and opts out of the post-match niceties with what is later diagnosed as a raging temperature. After the game, thousands of Zaragoza fans loitering with intent force the Barcelona party to cross the pitch in darkness before sneaking out through a back door. Still, the 296-kilometre journey home (Espanyol apart, Barça's shortest road trip) must have been a satisfying one. Barcelona are top of the league!

MONDAY, 30 SEPTEMBER

Robson misses training with the flu and avoids the on-going controversy about yesterday's sending off. In reality, a candid camera proves that the referee was reluctant to send anybody off. Mejuto's initial response to his linesman's observations was, 'Don't fuck with me, Rafa, for fuck's sake!' before asking poor Rafa if he was sure a good dozen times. Maybe he did send the wrong man off, but did Solana do the decent thing when the crowd was raging for blood? No, *señor*. Spanish referees may be bad, but cheating players, haranguing directors and hot-blooded fans don't help, do they?

Meanwhile, the Spanish press are busy comparing Ronaldo to Pelé, Maradona, Superman, *et al.* The Brazilian certainly loves his football. Commenting on having to play again on Wednesday against Tenerife, he flashes a boyish smile and insists, 'I wish I could always play twice a week. I wish I could play football every day.'

TUESDAY, 1 OCTOBER

Who says money doesn't talk? Five games into the season and the summer's big spenders (Barcelona, Deportivo, Real Madrid and Betis) occupy the top four places. At the other end of the table, the newly promoted and dirt-poor pair, Hércules and Extremadura, have reserved lightning-fast returns to anonymity with three points between them; courtesy of . . . Hércules 2, Extremadura 1.

At the top of the scoring charts, it's a case of where's-the-R-in-samba? Ronaldo heads the pack with five goals followed by fellow Brazilians Romario and Rivaldo (Deportivo) with four apiece. Today, Deportivo announce the signing of Atlético Mineiro striker Renaldo; it'll be a commentator's nightmare if that lot ever get into the same Brazilian team.

Having made the peace with his coach and scored twice yesterday, Romario is in confident mood. 'I need a few games under my belt to get back to one hundred per cent, so if I was the coach I'd pick Ronaldo at the moment, too. But once I'm in form, I'm sure I'll get back in the Brazil side.' In his one full season at Barcelona (1993/94), Romario scored 30 league goals. No big deal according to the dewy-eyed striker. 'There's still almost forty games to go; scoring thirty goals is not particularly difficult!'

A well-again Robson muses on the Zaragoza fracas. 'I wouldn't deny the sending off changed the game. Did Couto make a meal of the thing? I don't know. But Solana wasn't very smart hitting him, was he? I'd kill one of my players if he did that [*the smile suggests he's joking*].'

WEDNESDAY, 2 OCTOBER

Barcelona 1, Tenerife 1 (Popescu 78)
Camp Nou, 80,000

Robson's side may have gone into the game as unbeaten leaders, but there are still question marks against their overall performances. Great players, not so great team is the general feeling. Tonight, the benefit of the doubt lasts 30 minutes before Robson catches the first timid whistles of the season. Ironically, the discontents resurrect a major factor in Johan Cruyff's downfall; chants of 'Iván, Iván, Iván De la Peña . . .' *ad infinitum*. Cruyff, normally so willing to give youth a fling, was strangely unwilling to hand the creative reins to a player destined for greatness. His detractors claimed he was frightened that the little guy would outshine the hapless son Jordi.

Strangely, Robson seems to have inherited the Dutchman's misgivings, despite an under-achieving midfield. With Giovanni a lackadaisical presence and Popescu blustering to unpredictable effect, Guardiola is rapidly becoming a one-man supply line. And the talented but infuriating Luis Figo continues to run up blind alleys. 'For every hundred passes Figo receives from Guardiola he wastes one hundred and one,' jokes Enric Bañeres, sports editor of the Barcelona broadsheet *La Vanguardia*. Robson, insists it's all a matter of time. 'Any problems are down to the players' form, not the system.'

Barça went ahead with a Popescu goal after their sixteenth corner; De la Peña came on halfway through the second half and promptly missed the chance to make it two. Tenerife equalised from their first corner in their only serious goal attempt in 90 minutes. For once, Ronaldo didn't ride to the rescue. César Gómez spent the game so tight up the Brazilian's arse he was in danger of being arrested for lewd behaviour. Asked before the game how he would approach marking Ronaldo, the Tenerife centre half replied, 'Pray a lot.' After the game, he admits, 'That was the most difficult marking job I've done in my life. I feel like I've just played five games.' We don't know if he enjoyed a post-coital fag.

'Maybe we expect Ronaldo to score two goals a game,' is Robson's wise summation. 'But you can't expect a twenty-year-old to win you every game, however special he is.' As for the barracking: 'The public are impatient, but they pay their money so that's their prerogative. But nobody wins the league in October. Come and talk to me after forty-two games.' Real Madrid's victory against Espanyol leaves Capello's side, also barracked by their own supporters, top on goal difference.

'It's tough enough without being booed off the park when you're top,' says Robson later. 'It's not as if there's ever an easy game here. In Portugal, there were one or two games, especially at home, that you knew were a foregone conclusion. Here it's different. There's a very similar level now to England. All of the top-flight clubs have a bit of money to spend, so if there's a weakness they can go out and add another piece to the jigsaw. If you're slightly off your game you'll drop points whoever you're playing. OK, there are teams like Extremadura who have come up and are finding the transition difficult, but look at Sevilla and Zaragoza; you wouldn't expect them to be down the bottom, would you? And next year we'll be down to twenty teams, so those weak two will be gone. You won't be able to pick up six points off Extremadura next year.'

THURSDAY, 3 OCTOBER

UEFA rubber-stamp their new Champions League format. As of next season, the runners-up of the eight countries with the highest coefficient will also qualify for Europe's premiere competition. 'This is a decision that not only benefits FC Barcelona as one of the prime movers for this change, but the whole of Europe's footballing élite,' announces a satisfied club spokesman without a hint of sarcasm. Why's that, you might ask? Well, how about a Barça curriculum that boasts eighteen runner-up spots compared to fourteen league titles for starters? Some of the countries that benefit from the two-contestants ruling – Italy, Germany, England – boast several potential champions; elsewhere, a perpetual monopoly on the top spots will lead to quasi-franchise status for the lucky likes of Porto, Benfica, PSV, Paris Saint-Germain, and, of course, Real Madrid and Barcelona.

SUNDAY, 6 OCTOBER

Javier Clemente takes time off from preparing for Spain v. Czech Republic to rubbish the notion that Bobby Robson is keeping the Camp Nou bench warm for him. 'I know that's what people are saying, but there's absolutely nothing to it. People say I'm in cahoots with Núñez, but we've had a good relationship for years and I've not got the job yet, have I?'

For the moment, if he's genuinely on Robson's side, perhaps he should ease up on the eulogising. 'Barça are the strongest team I've seen in my life,' he says. 'I think they've got twenty-two full internationals; even Di Stéfano's Real Madrid didn't have as many. Admittedly, Sacchi's Milan was a team made in heaven – Van Basten, Gullit, Baresi, Rijkaard and Maldini were great players at their peak, while Ronaldo, for example, is only twenty – but even that squad wasn't better than Robson's.'

At least he rejects the theory that Núñez is usurping the coach's responsibilities. 'Núñez is incapable of interfering with playing matters. Bobby is a seasoned coach with a strong personality. If the board did try to impose things on him, there is no way he'd swallow it. Believe me, he picks the team.'

MONDAY, 7 OCTOBER

Robson heads back to England, leaving José Mourinho and six players to improvise a training session. 'Basically, I'm losing a week's work. The background to all this lies in the war between UEFA and FIFA. It's ridiculous. We've paid twenty million dollars for Ronaldo and we can't even count on him for all our important games. I don't understand why UEFA can't control this situation. At the very least, all the international sides should play their games on the same date.'

WEDNESDAY, 9 OCTOBER

Barcelona may be leaking goals at an unhealthy rate in the league, but the Czech Republic are incapable of breaching the Barça wall in Prague. The heroics of Luis Enrique, Nadal, Abelardo and Sergi aside, Spain's goalless draw was most newsworthy for the debut of Real Madrid's own wonderkid, Raúl. 'I'm convinced he's a player who will do great things for Spain,' says Clemente of his nineteen-year-old striker. For the moment, Raúl has got a head start on Iván de la Peña, his room-mate in the under-21 and Olympic sides. Barcelona's prodigy barely managed an hour in yesterday's under-21 fixture, a year to the day after Barcelona won 5-1 at Betis in a game that was heralded as the birth of the 'Little Buddah Brigade'. Eight home-grown players made the starting line-up that day and three more came on as substitutes. They may be youngsters, but for the likes of De la Peña, Roger, Celades, Toni and Moreno, a year in football must seem like an awfully long time.

While Bobby Robson is watching England beat Poland, Ronaldo shares the stage back home with Cilla Black's Spanish wannabe on *Sorpresa, Sorpresa*. The blushing Brazilian makes one twelve-year-old's night with an on-stage kickabout and then feigns injury so a masseuse can come on down and rub his priceless thighs. He rounds off his man-of-the-people act by donating £7,500 to charity (about what it must have cost Antena 3 Televisión to invite his clan to Madrid for the night). The insurance guys must have been sweating when Ronaldo faked his injury. 'Aside from the club's insurance I've got a private policy with an Italian company,' says Barça's most-prized asset. 'I pay twenty thousand dollars a year and I'd get three million if an injury ended my career.'

FRIDAY, 11 OCTOBER

Robson confirms that Stoichkov will make his comeback in tomorrow's game at Compostela. 'We want him to get a game under his belt so that he feels confident about his fitness for a tough game against Red Star.' The Bulgarian is back in typically belligerent mood. 'There are lots of clueless people sermonising about things they don't understand,' he claims in an interview with *Televisión Española* (the only people he deigns to talk to at the moment). 'It's impossible to build a new team overnight; there's absolutely no need to get worried or start criticising prematurely.' It's not just journalists Hristo has got it in for. The presence of more than a thousand fans at Santiago de Compostela airport means the police have to usher the players to their coach through a restricted area. Typically, Stoichkov decides to go his own way. One run-in with *la policía* later, he can thank God that Bobby Robson is one of life's diplomats.

One or two newspapers have suggested that Robson was neglecting his responsibilities by spending five days in England. 'It's been suggested that I was at Wembley working for TV as a commentator,' he says. 'Well, that's not true. I was doing my job, that's why I went to see England against Poland. I wanted to have a look at some Polish players.' As if unconvinced by his own motives for the extended trip, he adds, 'Anyway, I had permission from the president. I had important personal reasons for going to England.

'These stories about me doing television are absolute bloody lies,' he complains in private, 'apart from watching the games, I go back to see the doctor. I'm in excellent health now, but I have a personal check-up every three months as a precaution.' As he admits, you can never be too careful. 'My operation (to remove a cancerous growth on his nose) was a real lifesaver, but ironically, the doctors discovered it by chance. Mind you, I was unlucky in the first place. I don't smoke or drink and doctors told me there was a less than 2% chance of getting something like that.'

SATURDAY, 12 OCTOBER
Compostela 1, Barcelona 5 (Ronaldo 35, 46, William o.g. 1, Giovanni 16, Figo 65)
San Lázaro, 12,000

Rich man, poor man. While Robson and his players were scattered around the globe this week, Compostela were one of three top-flight sides without a single player deemed worthy of international duty. Maybe Compos coach Fernando Vázquez should have taken the week off as well. Michael Robinson, for one, reckons coaches have problems when they get 'too much time to think'. The ten days Vázquez had to plot tonight's game (that's the ten days in which he decided not to mark Ronaldo) suggest the former Liverpool man is right. As for thinking a suicidally advanced back four would deter the lightning-fast Brazilian, well, that was tantamount to putting a paper bag over your head to fend off Mike Tyson.

Like Iron Mike in the good old days, Ronaldo dithered not. After 30 seconds he strolled through the right flank of Compostela's defence to send an invitation the Brazilian William just couldn't refuse (unfortunately for Compos, Ronaldo's fellow countryman was making his home debut). Fifteen minutes later, he ambled down the opposite flank to create a chance even Giovanni couldn't miss. After 30 minutes, the youngster decided to make things a bit harder for himself. Picking the ball up in his own half, his dribble past anybody who got in his way was reminiscent of Maradona's classic against England.

A decade on, Robson's reaction is understandably more appreciative. After placing hands on head in amazement, he turns to the crowd, arms wide apart in 'What can I say?' mode. Equally nonplussed, they just applaud. 'You can go anywhere you want in the world, and you won't find a player who can score goals like that,' he enthuses after the game. 'Can anybody, anywhere, show me a better player?' And not a 'Hand of the Rascal', as Robson describes Diego's other effort, in sight.

Admittedly, Compos were about as solid as their name suggests, but the Ronaldo show aside, it was an encouraging performance. On the flight back to Barcelona, Ronaldo hijacked the captain's microphone to run through a litany of Robsonisms (Rory Bremner can sleep safely, though, for the moment; the Englishman's stock training phrases don't offer much material). This on a day when Robson appeared for the first time in public speaking Spanish, or make that Spanglish. His pitchside interview for TV3 before the game won't win him awards as International Linguist of the Year, but it'll win him plenty of friends for effort.

Not such good times for another Brazilian superstar. After turning up late for training on Thursday, Romario was dropped for Valencia's game against Sevilla. 'My alarm didn't go off,' was his less than convincing excuse. What was that about 'Genius is one per cent inspiration, ninety-nine per cent perspiration'?

SUNDAY, 13 OCTOBER

The adjective most applicable to Spanish football is 'exaggerated'. Whichever paper you buy today, you'll find a cover worshipping at the altar of Ronaldo 'Pelé and Di Stéfano rolled into one', anyone? He seems determined to rewrite the TV scripts, as well. The late night highlights programme *El Tercer Tiempo* (The Third Half) used to open by selecting the weekend's MVP. 'It's a bit of a redundant exercise now Ronaldo is in town,' says presenter Paco González, only half in jest. 'From now on, we're going to take it for granted that Ronaldo is the star turn and start the programme by choosing the second-best player of the week. Otherwise, nobody else will get a look in!'

It's not simply about journalists trying to sell papers, either. 'I don't know about Brazilian, he's more like a Martian,' says former Real Madrid boss Jorge Valdano. Canal Plus sent a team to Manchester to follow the fortunes of Jordi Cruyff in yesterday's game against Liverpool. Back at 'Chez Jordi', the ex-Barça player sank into his sofa after Ronaldo's televised wonder goal and exclaimed repeatedly, 'Did you see that? Did you see that? Just incredible. It's amazing what he can do.'

Given Jordi's unenthusiastic opinion of English defences, it's a shame for 'Super Sky' that Ronaldo doesn't ply his trade in the Premiership. 'It's unbelievable the amount of space you get here,' he argues. 'Sometimes a big hole opens up for you at the back and you think to yourself, "How can they possibly leave you so much space?" English players think with their hearts and not with their heads.'

MONDAY, 14 OCTOBER

Robson's assistant, José Mourinho, has had to deal with plenty of sniping about his coaching pedigree in the last couple of months. Now it's his sexual preferences under the microscope. Ever since Barça's new coaching tandem arrived in town there have been whispers that their relationship goes beyond the professional (nobody seems to know where it started, unless being a clueless, Calvin Klein-clad pretty-boy suddenly makes you gay). 'I'm anything but homosexual,' says Mourinho, who abandons his usual line in smarm for a clear-the-air interview with *Sport*. 'It's sad that people should think that, but it really doesn't make any difference to me. It's ridiculous. Bobby Robson is married with three kids, I'm happily married and my wife is expecting our first baby. Anyone who knows me will tell you how much I like women. I'm here because of my professional relationship with Bobby. When he asked me if I wanted to come to Barcelona, I said, "Here, or the end of the world." I couldn't have a better teacher than him.'

When the Englishman arrived at Sporting Lisbon in 1992, Mourinho was a pedigreeless 28-year-old coaching kids. Four years later he's assistant coach at one of the world's biggest clubs; no wonder he's happy to follow his mentor. For his part, Robson just smiles when asked about Mourinho's denials. 'Don't get me involved. I don't know what you're talking about, either.'

WEDNESDAY, 16 OCTOBER

Robson berates journalists for not focusing on the Red Star game. 'Today's papers are full of Nadal transfer rumours, De la Peña talking to Roma stories, Figo and Juventus gossip and, of course, Ronaldo, Ronaldo, Ronaldo,' complains the put-upon coach, waving his arms around to stress his annoyance. 'Hey, what's going on here? In the last two days, I've seen barely a word in the papers about Red Star and what is probably our most difficult game so far. In two weeks, we've got to go to Belgrade and I can tell you from experience, that's going to be very difficult. I went there in 1987 with England and the atmosphere was very hostile.

'Ronaldo's important but so are the other players,' he says of his absentee striker. 'Their pride is wounded and they're determined to prove we're not a one-man team.' On the other side of the world, another coach who's seen a thousand battles, Brazil's Mario Zagalo, is doing his best to get Ronaldo's feet back on the ground. 'I had a long chat with him on Tuesday and told him not to get carried away with all the praise,' he says. 'Personally, I don't like all the hype; it's ridiculous that all the responsibility at a club like Barcelona falls on the shoulders of a twenty-year-old.' Especially, it seems, when he's still got a lot to learn. 'Ronaldo's not very good in the air and he still doesn't understand the meaning of teamwork. He's going to be an all-time great but Pelé was a more complete all-rounder at twenty.' Reminiscent of one studio's assessment of a young Fred Astaire? 'Can't act. Slightly bald. Can dance [score] a little.'

Tomorrow's game against Red Star Belgrade will see Robson come face to face with Vladimir Petrovic, a man whose 22 games for Arsenal in the 1982/83 season did scant justice to his talents as one of Yugoslavia's all-time greats. As a footballer, Petrovic was elegance personified; as a coach he is a stony-faced realist. 'Football has changed considerably since I played against Barcelona in the early eighties,' he argues. 'Maradona played in that side. Now they could field eleven top foreigners if they wanted to. Football is just a business now. It's sad, but that's the way it is. If we can beat Barcelona, our fans will be delighted because it would mean a victory for the poor guys.'

THURSDAY, 17 OCTOBER
Barcelona 3, Red Star Belgrade 1 (Giovanni 33, 35, Figo 54)
Camp Nou, 74,000

Despite the presence of a referee called Serge Leon, tonight's game was more pot-boiler than spaghetti western. Two goals from Giovanni cancelled out Red Star's disquieting opener and premature whining from an impatient crowd. Figo notched a third and if Popescu hadn't missed a penalty the return would have been a formality. 'It needed another goal to settle things,' admits Robson. 'But with Ronaldo back for Belgrade, we've got to fancy our chances of an away goal or two.'

Not for the first time this season, he's forced to defend a player who is rapidly becoming the Camp Nou whipping boy. 'It's a shame Gica missed the penalty, he was our best player tonight and really deserved a goal. He was up and down the pitch non-stop and getting in the box; you need to be incredibly fit and strong to do what he does.' His critics suggest a little less hustle wouldn't go amiss. 'The midfield is a battlefield of influences, even against your teammates,' says Enric Bañeres. 'Popescu is crowding Guardiola's space, and Pep can't or won't impose himself.'

Once again, Nadal missed the cut for a European game. Word has it that he refused to play. Robson fends off the claims with a bemused look and a slow-motion denial. 'Nadal ... did ... not ... ask ... not ... to ... play. He played three times last week, and I'm just trying to give everybody a game. It's an old story, and my position is exactly the same.' Asked if he had any advice for a player who claims he is 'sick of the situation' and suffering sleepless nights, Robson is unmoving. 'I don't sleep, either. He should forget Manchester United. It's over, finished.'

SATURDAY, 19 OCTOBER
Reports from Brazil claim that Milan are willing to pay Ronaldo's 4,000 million pesetas buy-out clause (all players in Spain have one,

and if they pay it they can walk). 'I'd obviously look at any offer, but why would I leave Barcelona? I've only just arrived.' While the press grills the player on the veracity of the story, his coach waits patiently before taking the stage for his weekly press conference. Bobby Robson refuses to be drawn on what he describes as 'just rumours', adding with a smile, 'It snows in Milan in January and I know Ronaldo doesn't like the snow.' After the usual round of questions on comings and goings, he applauds ironically when a journalist finally asks him a question about tomorrow's game against Logroñes.

Davor Suker and Pedja Mijatovic share five goals as Real Madrid thrash Real Sociedad 6-1, on what was a fitting occasion on which to share their first glory night at the Bernabéu. Before the game, Ferenc Puskas (512 goals in 528 league games for Kispest and Real Madrid; beat that, Ronaldo!) did the kick-off honours with football's most famous left foot. Puskas fled Hungary after the Soviet invasion of 1956 and went on to win five championships and three European Cups, most memorably in 1960. Who can forget his four goals in Real Madrid's 7-3 thrashing of Eintracht Frankfurt as the Swinging Sixties kicked off early in Scotland? What the Sex Pistols' legendary 100 Club debut was to punk, Real's crowning glory is to football.

SUNDAY, 20 OCTOBER
Barcelona 8, Logroñes 0 (Stoichkov 21, 55 pen, Giovanni 29, 42, Ronaldo 40, 87 pen, Pizzi 82, Clotet o.g. 77)
Camp Nou, 95,000

Bobby Robson enters the press suite after the game sporting a big grin and doing the Winston Churchill – that's two fingers that rapidly converge to signal a zero. Not only had Barcelona scored eight goals, but for the first time this season they'd registered a clean sheet. It was also, perhaps not coincidentally, the first time Robson had been able to field what he privately admits is his first-choice eleven: Baía in goal; a back four of Luis Enrique, Blanc, Couto and Sergi; Guardiola and Popescu as midfield pivots; Figo, Giovanni and Stoichkov as a right-to-left first line of attack; and Ronaldo as centre forward.

It says everything about a puny Logroñes that, eight goals to the bad for the first time in his career, goalkeeper Andoni Cedrún was their best player. A standing ovation for the veteran 'keeper as he left the field was just reward for one of football's good guys. With

Barcelona 4-0 up, Hristo Stoichkov (nobody calls him a good guy and lives to tell the tale) was on the receiving end of harsh words from his teammates when he stamped on Popescu's prerogative to take a penalty. After the game, Robson throws some light on an unseemly incident. 'We'd agreed that Stoichkov would take the penalty if the scores were tight, but if we were two or three goals up Gica was supposed to take it. But as the foul was committed on Stoichkov, he obviously thought it was his call.

'What can you do?' He shrugs. 'That's Stoichkov for you.' Excuse me – ignoring your coach's instructions and riding roughshod over your captain? After sprinting back to the centre circle, the unrepentant Hristo gave the bullfighter's four-sided. Predictably, given their sympathies, the fans reacted with an ovation. After the game, Robson offers Stoichkov a lesson in humility when he sympathises with Logroñes coach Miguel Angel Lotina. 'I felt really sorry for him when we went off 4-0 up at half-time.' Not that his condolences extended to telling his men to ease up. 'In the break, I said to the players, "Look, the game is over, but are you going to be ambitious or not?" I was delighted at their response; we could easily have scored a dozen.' Not surprisingly, Robson reacts with untypical churlishness when asked if the players are getting used to his system. 'We've scored sixteen goals in a week and you're still talking about systems?' he barks. 'That's simply not a question any more.'

On the pitch for a pre-match warm-up, Logroñes centre forward Manel made a beeline for Ronaldo with his camera and a photo request. The Brazilian happily complied, but hey, nothing comes free in life. A couple of hours later, the star-struck Manel was sent off for insulting the referee after Ronaldo scored from a disputed penalty. Still, in years to come he can show his kids the photo of the day he played against the world's best player. Let's just hope they don't ask him the score!

Manchester United lose 5-0 at Newcastle, their biggest defeat since a 6-0 thrashing at Ipswich in 1980. 'I remember that game very well,' smiles Robson. 'Not only did we score six but we missed three penalties. And I can tell you who missed them: Thissjen, Beattie and Mick Mills.' A 6-0 thrashing of Man Utd is always going to stick in the mind, but Robson reveals that he carries an extensive personal archive around in his head. 'I remember games quite well, things tend to stick. I can still remember things Johnny Haynes did in games. You don't remember everything, but in principal, things stick.' It's certainly a good job he's got a good memory. 'I do wish I'd kept more books or press cuttings,' he admits. 'I've got a couple of videos of Ipswich in cup finals but that's about it. I've moved around a lot so I've never kept things. I've still got my house in Ipswich where I keep things, but I'd need a bigger house if I'd kept everything!'

MONDAY, 21 OCTOBER

'*Uno . . . dos . . . tres . . . cuatro . . . cinco . . . seis . . . siete . . . ocho* Mambo!' Forget the Dream Team or the Samba team; 'The Mambo Team Is Born,' boasts the front cover of the Madrid-based sports daily *AS*. Fittingly, 'Mambo No. 8' was the theme tune of one of Barcelona's favourite sons, Xavier Cugat. Hollywood's King of Rumba was a man who did things in style; after decades of lending his irrepressible swing to MGM musicals, he retired to his native city and held court at the Ritz (owned by the family Gaspart) until his death in 1990.

Stoichkov's penalty tantrums threaten to lose him one of his few allies in the dressing room. Compared to most of the players' off-the-record observations about the Bulgarian, Popescu is diplomacy itself: 'We'd agreed I would take the penalty but Stoichkov must have forgotten. What was I supposed to do? Kick up a fuss in the middle of the park? Have a fight with him?' Nonetheless, for the first time this season, Gica decides to give post-match dinner with Hristo a miss.

The so-called football wars threaten to spill over into the political arena. According to press reports, Jordi Pujol, president of Catalonia's autonomous regional government, has thrown his weight behind the Antena 3 Televisión bid to wrest football rights away from Canal Plus. If Antena 3 do secure exclusive rights, they have promised to cede a weekly game to their allies at Televisió de Catalunya. But why should Pujol be interested in the amount of football on television? Simple: because football tops the Televisió de Catalunya rankings and that's football broadcast in Catalan. Attempts to redress the balance of 50 years of linguistic censorship, televised football equals millions of punters listening to and so the story goes, learning Catalan. What's more, no politico can harbour serious aspirations in Catalonia without courting FC Barcelona. You'd never catch Pujol at Camp Nou for an untelevised fixture against no-mark opposition, but if it's Real Madrid or Manchester United live, you can guarantee he'll be hobnobbing it in the presidential box.

HIGH NOON

The fanfare that greeted the 20th anniversary of radio's *Futbol en català* reflects Barça's importance to the linguistic crusade. After four decades of suffering the pseudo-fascist rhetoric of the Spanish school (characterised by the baroque Matías Prats – imagine the BBC World Service on acid), the birth of Joaquim Puyal's radio show in 1976 came as a liberating force in Catalonia. 'My generation has learnt more Catalan listening to Puyal commentating on Barça games than reading classic literature or studying prose,' says *El País* columnist Sergi Pàmies.

TUESDAY, 22 OCTOBER
Stoichkov reacts to the controversy over his penalty antics in typically diplomatic fashion. 'Maybe I have got enemies in the dressing room, but when I take the field that's all forgotten. I give everything for ninety minutes and when the game has finished I go my own way. If other players are pissed off or don't like me that's their problem. All I'm interested in is playing football and scoring goals.' He also denies rumours that he is only back at Barcelona because he's the light of Núñez's eye (stories about the Bulgarian's wife crying down the president's phone from Italy are legendary). 'I'm here because Robson wanted me here. Anybody who thinks my return was down to Núñez is stupid.' Whatever he really thinks of Stoichkov, Robson is trying to end the continuing penalty controversy. 'We've talked about it, but it really is a side issue, it's not important,' he insists, adding amiably, 'I'll have to take the next one myself.'

WEDNESDAY, 23 OCTOBER
Sevilla 0, Barcelona 1 (Luis Enrique 77)
Sánchez Pizjuán, 55,000

If the secret of winning championships is to bag the points on your off-days, tonight's game augurs well for Barcelona. Against a chronically goal-shy Sevilla (four goals in eight games so far, one shot on target tonight), Barça were undeniably poor but secured three more valuable points. Juan Antonio Pizzi, for one, was not doing cartwheels after the game.

With thirteen minutes to go, Luis Enrique did what Roger Hunt, bless him, should have done, by nodding the ball home after a teammate's shot ricocheted between crossbar and goal line. Unlike

Geoff Hurst's effort in June 1966, Figo's shot definitely crossed the line. As the ref gave the goal to Luis Enrique anyway, it was also a case of better safe than sorry. Bobby Robson's instant response to the goal was to replace Pizzi with Nadal. Now he isn't the first manager to shut up shop with an extra defender, but he's surely the first to drag off the current European 'Golden Boot' for tactical reasons 20 minutes after bringing him on. Pizzi reacted first with understandable astonishment, and then with anger. Attempts to placate him as he took his still-warm place on the bench were greeted with a torrent of abuse and a flying tracksuit that missed Robson's head by a whisker. Michael Robinson, commentating on the game for Canal Plus, accused Robson of 'displaying all the tact of Henry VIII'.

'I know it must be difficult for Pizzi,' admits Robson afterwards. 'But it was a difficult decision for me, as well. When I felt we'd won the game, my decision was to secure the result; that meant taking a forward off. The choice was Pizzi or Ronaldo; my choice was Pizzi.'

On the day when Pelé celebrated his 56th birthday, a lacklustre Ronaldo landed back in the land of the mere mortals. O Rei may have a pretender but a dose of early caution wouldn't go amiss. 'Ronaldinho is just starting out so people really shouldn't compare us,' says football's best ever. 'It may be unintentional, but it can only harm him.'

THURSDAY, 24 OCTOBER

Depending on whose testimony you choose to believe, Pizzi turned up for training this morning determined to put last night's incident behind him, or he refused to apologise to Robson for his bout of tossing the tracksuit. Whatever. Not for the first time this season, what should have been a storm in a teacup threatens to run and run. After the game, a placatory Mourinho had claimed, 'We've got to help Pizzi on this one.' Robson's idea of a gee-up is to drop the Argentinian from Saturday's squad to face Valencia.

The player responds with a lengthy press conference accusing Robson of a 'lack of respect' and 'personal vindictiveness'. Though more sparing in his explanations, Robson dismisses notions of a vendetta. 'It's not personal, it's a question of discipline.' Naturally, the press have taken Pizzi's side. The front page of Marca (not only Spain's best-selling sports paper, but the country's best-selling newspaper full-stop) boasts a photo of Robson strapped into a doctor's chair and the headline 'Robson in the Electric Chair'. Pichi

Alonso, a striker in Venables's Barça side and now a respected TV commentator, sheds his inveterate diplomacy to defend Pizzi, as well. 'What Robson did to Pizzi neither guaranteed success on the night or in the long run. His humiliation will leave scars that are hard to cure and his teammates have openly sided with him, too. They all feel affected by Robson's tactlessness. Would it have been so difficult to take Ronaldo off for the last ten minutes? It's not as if he was getting the ball.'

FRIDAY, 25 OCTOBER

Robson buries the hatchet and adds Pizzi's name to the squad for the Valencia game. 'We've had a chat and I've decided to forgive him. I'm a human being, too,' explains Robson, though the presence of troubleshooter Joan Gaspart at a clear-the-air meeting provokes suggestions that his change of heart was prompted. Robson does, however, point out that the Argentinian is not the innocent party the press would have us believe. 'My decision to exclude Pizzi from the squad had nothing to do with what happened in Seville. I can understand him getting annoyed when he was taken off, but I tried to meet with him three times on Thursday and each time he refused. That was clearly an act of indiscipline and that's why he was dropped. What do you think would happen if I refused to talk to the president, or if any of you [*gesturing to journalists*] did the same to your boss?

'Despite what's been reported in the press, there are absolutely no problems in the dressing room. We still haven't lost this season, we've won at Sevilla for the first time in six years, Pizzi is the one who doesn't want to talk to me, and to cap it all, I'm the one people want to put in the electric chair. Brilliant!'

SATURDAY, 26 OCTOBER
Barcelona 3, Valencia 2 (Ronaldo 15, 35, 74)
Camp Nou, 105,000

The King is dead. Long live the King! Romario's latest departure from Spain's playing fields (Valencia have sent their sleeping beauty back to Flamengo just four months after signing him) makes it unlikely that Brazil's finest will ever come face to face. Oh well – Ronaldo seems intent on satisfying the purists on his own. At his current scoring rate, he has every chance of emulating Romario's 30 goals in his one full season at Camp Nou. And having already followed the Brazil-to-Barcelona-via-Eindhoven path, it won't be his first case of career déjà vu.

Bobby Robson, once Romario's coach at PSV, is another thing the strikers have in common. 'Ronaldo will be better than Romario,' he argues. 'They've got a similar technical level, they're both very quick over shorter distances and great dribblers. But Ronaldo is bigger, stronger and far more dangerous over longer distances.'

The Spanish are fond of saying comparisons are odious. Luckily for Romario. Even at his peak, the little guy would have struggled to live with Ronaldo on tonight's form. His two first-half goals were merely splendid, the second-half winner was breathtaking. After the game Robson concedes that he's never seen a player start a season so impressively. When asked if Ronaldo could get any better, his expression suggests, well, the inconceivable. 'A player is obviously not at his peak at twenty, so he should get better,' he muses, adding with a smile, 'it's hard to imagine him getting any quicker.' The way the youngster hurdled through Valencia's defence for the winner was pure Ed Moses. His late winner provoked the ultimate Spanish tribute, the mass hankie wave. Perhaps unaware of the ritual and how to pay homage to matadors, Robson simply turned to the crowd and gestured towards the heavens with a finger.

In a roll-call of football managers who are accommodating with the press, Bobby Robson would appear very near the top. But as a correspondent from the local paper *Avui* discovers, the manager/journalist relationship is always an unequal one. Even with the good guys, it's the friendly-questions-only syndrome. 'Does the Pizzi affair prove that you don't control the dressing room?' Robson's reaction is to guffaw. He isn't laughing. After eyeballing the squirming journalist for what seems an eternity, he answers, '*I* think I'm in control.' Another extended pause. 'Don't you?'

The man from *Avui* was clearly a sucker for punishment. 'How does the team need to improve?' he insists. The response to a probing if hardly incendiary question borders on the churlish. 'Such as?' Another long and awkward silence. 'We've won and we're top of the league. Why is everybody trying to punch holes in us?' With the press conference wrapped up, Robson is still fuming. 'Who is that guy?' he demands of Barça's press secretary while he paces up and down the press stage. 'I'd like to meet that fella in the street, just me and him,' then, perhaps remembering that he is 63, he adds, 'especially if he was walking and I was in my car! It's people like that who give journalists a bad name.'

Paul Hawksbee is not in Robson's bad books, at least not yet. Arriving at a desolate Camp Nou fifteen minutes before the game, the *Goal* editor rubbished predictions that the game would attract a packed house. Fifteen minutes later, 105,000 fans brought the house down as referee Japón Sevilla blew his whistle to get proceedings under way. The Spaniards' incorrigible unpunctuality wins the day over soaking up the big match atmosphere every time.

SUNDAY, 27 OCTOBER

Barcelona's eight wins, two draws and 33 goals represent a best-ever return in their first ten league games. No wonder Robson gets ruffled by the carping. As for the one-man-team argument, the 21 goals scored by the rest of the team would make Barça Spain's highest scorers even without Ronaldo.

It's certainly a good job the youngster had football to fall back on. 'When I was a kid I always used to hoodwink my mum, I'd tell her I was going to school but I'd stay in the street playing football. I always had a ball at my feet. In Brazil, the street is the best university you can get.

'I don't like studying or reading,' he admits when asked why he's already given up his Spanish classes, adding, 'I am reading a biography of Garrincha, though.' He then messes it up by adding, 'I expect to finish it within six months.' Happily, Ronaldo's lifestyle *per se* is unlikely to give Robson any headaches. Apparently, the stinking-rich youngster spends most of his spare time at home playing with toys. 'The only problem,' says his sister, Ione, 'is that Ronaldo doesn't let my son touch the new ones until he's stopped playing with them.'

John Toshack may have plenty of Brazilians of his own, but that doesn't stop him waxing lyrical about Barça's prodigy. 'What I most like about Ronaldo is that he scores goals when it matters, not just when his team are two or three goals ahead and the result is a foregone conclusion. He proved that on Saturday. He scores the first two goals and says, "There you are, lads, that's the game won for you." Then, when Valencia equalise, he's gone, "Bloody hell, I've got to start all over again." So he picks the ball up on the halfway line and wins the game again.'

MONDAY, 28 OCTOBER

Spanish presidents are notoriously trigger-happy, but Miguel Angel Lotina, the season's first managerial casualty, has less cause to complain than most. A week after losing 8-0 at Barcelona, his Logroñes side lost 6-0 at Bilbao yesterday. Even in football there are times when you should get your coat and leave quietly. Or maybe his employers are just extremely puritanical. Lotina was one of the coaches asked to prescribe a Ronaldo antidote in last week's *AS* survey. His response? 'Everything I can think of is illegal!'

Ronaldomanía boldly goes, as well. In today's *USA Today* he shares front-page billing with New York Yankees catcher Joe Girardi, as the Bronx Bombers celebrate their first World Series triumph in eighteen years. Closer to home, *Sport* take the moral high ground to censure Sampdoria's midfielder Christian Karembeu, who has spent the last week posing in first Real Madrid and then Barça colours. 'Has he stopped for a moment to ask himself how Sampdoria fans feel about him parading around in other shirts? Maybe it's too much to expect Karembeu to identify with his team in the same way the fans do, but if he was honourable he'd show more respect towards the club that pays his salary.' Worthy enough sentiments. One slight problem, though. It was, you guessed it, *Sport* that sent a reporter to Italy to persuade the player to strike a pose in the first place. The fact that she is young and pretty gives Karembeu an excuse; the same cannot be said of the hypocrites in her editorial room.

TUESDAY, 29 OCTOBER

Manchester United's 6-3 defeat at Southampton rekindles the Nadal rumours. Asked if it was true that United would now meet the £5 million asking price, Robson jokes, 'I don't know if they are prepared to pay so much. All I know is that they've conceded eleven goals in two games and Alex Ferguson is bloody lucky he's not sat where I am!'

They may not have conceded eleven goals in a week, but Robson insists his side are still too generous in defence. 'With an all-international defence we really shouldn't be letting so many goals in,' he argues. 'It's clearly something we've got to work on.' The response from a less than contrite Sergi is immediate. 'Our defensive problems are tactical, it's not down to individuals at the back,' he moans. 'We attack as a team and defend as a team. Ronaldo might be scoring all the goals but he wouldn't do it without our support. And it works the other way round as well. He should be the first line of defence. If we don't close down opponents further up the field, they get to our area with men to spare and it's impossible to stop them scoring.'.

Asked if lazy-bones Ronaldo needed special protection from referees, Robson replies, 'The only way to protect him would be if the press didn't write so much about him. How about only four pages a day instead of ten?'

THURSDAY, 31 OCTOBER
Red Star Belgrade 1, Barcelona 1 (Giovanni 48)
Crena Zvezda, 80,000

A workmanlike draw in Belgrade means Robson can put Europe on the back-burner until March. When Red Star went ahead just after half-time it might have spelled trouble in a predictably volatile stadium. Luckily, Giovanni's volley within a minute silenced the crowd and effectively ended the contest.

Ronaldo, who struggled through the game with a thigh strain, is not the only follicly challenged attraction in Barcelona. Snowflake, the world's most famous albino gorilla, celebrates 30 years in town today with 40,000 birthday cards, a season ticket at the city's opera house, and autographed shirts from Barça and Espanyol (we're sure he appreciated the fruit basket more).

FRIDAY, 1 NOVEMBER
Ronaldo will not be fit to play against Sporting Gijón on Monday. 'It's easy to say I told you so once the horse has bolted,' insists Robson on his decision to keep Ronaldo on the park for all but thirteen minutes against Red Star. 'But if we'd lost 2-0 everybody would be asking why he didn't play. At half-time, we asked him if he wanted to carry on and he said yes. People should praise his attitude. Anyway, it's not an important injury, he'll be fit in a week. It's not a bad thing that people get used to us playing games without Ronaldo, there's no way he'll play all sixty games.'

SUNDAY, 3 NOVEMBER
Real Madrid President Lorenzo Sanz has spent the last few days insisting that Karembeu is his man. Categorically. Unfortunately, nobody has told Sampdoria who today confirm they have agreed

terms with Barcelona. Robson is delighted at the potential coup. 'Karembeu is the natural substitute for Bakero. He is versatile and he'll keep our squad level high. I saw him play three times at Euro 96 and was extremely impressed. We originally tried to sign him in June so I'm delighted we've finally got him. I don't understand why Madrid are so upset, it's a free market and we're all entitled to make the signings we consider convenient.'

MONDAY, 4 NOVEMBER
Sporting Gijón 0, Barcelona 0
El Molinón, 35,000

Tom Cruise may be the box-office king Hollywood way, but he can't compete with Ronaldo in Barça territory. October's top-ranked programmes on TV3 were 1) Barça v. Valencia, 2) Barça v. Red Star, and 3) *The Firm*. No wonder Spanish TV companies are at war over football. Thanks to a deal between the TV3-led FORTA (the association of regional channels) and Antena 3, Barcelona play their first-ever league game on a Monday. It's also their first league game without Ronaldo. For the first time this season, Robson's side fails to score in the league. At least two of the three factors are related.

Pizzi and Giovanni both missed sitters in the first ten minutes; the next 80 were a Sporting monologue. In the second half, Baía must have felt like one of those fairground rabbits as the Sporting players lined up to take pot-shots at him. Robson can consider himself fortunate that a run of lacklustre away performances (Seville, Belgrade and now Gijón) has come against such shot-shy opponents. Nadal was sent off after 40 minutes but with Julio Salinas and Eloy (attacking partners at the 1986 World Cup) struggling to turn back the years in Sporting's attack, he was hardly missed. As is customary, Robson is putting a brave face on things. 'After our efforts on Thursday, the last thing we needed tonight was to end up with ten men. At half-time I told the players it was very important to secure the point. I'm happy we've maintained our unbeaten record.'

The coach may be content with a point against markedly inferior opposition, but history dictates greater expectations. 'Robson reckons he is getting a bad press and asks why the fans moan about a team that's top of the league,' says Josep Maria Casanovas, the editor of *Sport*. 'But he's his own worst enemy when it comes to improving his image. Bringing on a defender [*Couto*] for his only forward [*Pizzi*] when the game is goalless and with thirty minutes left is not something Barça fans are used to. The best players in Spain should always play to win, even when down to ten men. It's embarrassing to see Barcelona struggling to hold on to a goalless draw as if they were the underdog.'

Few Barça fans will have missed the implicit message of the editorial; Johan Cruyff never settled for goalless draws, did he? The Dutchman once said, 'If the opposition score four goals, we'll score five.' It was no idle boast. His unflinchingly positive philosophy was best illustrated by a game at Rayo Vallecano in December 1992. Down to nine men and 3-1 behind, a flagging Barcelona looked down and out. With ten minutes to go they pulled a goal back, and then with five minutes left scored the equaliser. Any other coach would have been screaming at his men to hoof the ball out of the ground as the seconds ticked away on an against-the-odds comeback. Not Cruyff. No sooner had the game restarted than he was on his feet waving his men forward, anti-football simply not part of his vocabulary. That's a mighty hard act to follow.

TUESDAY, 5 NOVEMBER

Robson's 100th day in charge is a day for reflections. 'It's been exciting but difficult, especially having to overcome Cruyff's legacy. I know there were people who thought that I wouldn't survive this long, but I think we've got the club back on an even keel and expectations are high. The most difficult thing is dealing with the constant rumours, negative press and all the hangers-on. I've never experienced anything like it in my career. It's something I smell around me and it really gets to you. It hurts to think that people aren't giving me my dues.'

Being dubbed the board's puppet can't be pleasant either. 'Those rumours are just ridiculous. One of the things I like about Núñez and Gaspart is that they don't try to give me advice on my decisions. Let's be clear about this: the day Núñez or Gaspart tell me which players to pick, I'm out of the door and gone. It's not my problem if Cruyff had an unsatisfactory relationship with people at the club. Yes, we see each other occasionally, and they love to talk about football like coaches, but they don't ask me why I'm playing certain players, not that I'd allow it anyway.' Perversely, it was Robson's willingness to chew the fat that helped him get the job in the first place. 'The first time I met Núñez and Gaspart with a view to joining Barcelona –

years ago in a London restaurant – I talked tactics with them using salt and pepper pots and glasses. They've told me they never forgot that!'

As for the criticism in the wake of the draw at Gijón, 'The only verb that exists here is to win. It doesn't matter what the circumstances are. You've got to be in my skin to understand what the pressure at Barcelona is all about. Do you really think I could get away with four defeats in a row like Alex Ferguson, or with the kind of start Van Gaal has had at Ajax? I'd have been sacked long ago.'

WEDNESDAY, 6 NOVEMBER
You would have thought a club that boasts Montserrat Caballé as a season ticket holder would take nothing for granted until the fat lady sings. Joan Gaspart flew to Paris this morning, boasting that Karembeu was Barça's. He snuck back in the afternoon with his tail between his legs and the Frenchman's rebuff ringing in his ears. 'I'm sorry for Barcelona but I'll either join Real Madrid or stay at Sampdoria until my contract finishes in 1998. I gave my word to Fabio Capello and I intend to keep it.' A man of his word – how admirable. And absolutely nothing to do with the down payment Madrid have so generously rendered his agent.

THURSDAY, 7 NOVEMBER
Ronaldo admits he'll have to sit it out at the weekend. 'It still hurts,' he says of his troublesome thigh. 'I haven't trained properly for a week, so it would be stupid to take a risk against Atlético.' With Stoichkov injured again, Baía, Couto and Figo on World Cup duty, and Nadal suspended, that's half Robson's first-choice team suddenly unavailable. With Lopetegui, Cuéllar and Celades also on the injured list, and Prosinecki away with Croatia, replacements are at a premium, too.

Everybody knows that FC Barcelona is the flagship of Catalonia; now it seems a Catalan international side is back on the agenda, too. Convergència i Unió, the ruling majority in the region's autonomous parliament, is campaigning for access to international competition. Catalonia has never been a breeding ground of footballers to compare with the Basque country, Asturias or Andalusia, but the Spanish First Division boasts more than 30 Catalan professionals, and you could easily put a side together on a par with countries of a similar population (Sergi, Guardiola, Ferrer and half a dozen others would walk into the Scotland team). A quasi-official Catalan side made its debut against France as far back as 1912, and in the years before the Civil War played friendlies on a regular basis (including a 4-0 win against Bolton in 1929!). General Franco was having none of it, though, and two decades of democracy have produced nothing but a 1993 testimonial for Barça legend Ladislao Kubala.

'Nobody seems to think it's strange that Scotland and Wales have an international side,' says Jordi Pujol. 'The Catalan people would love to have their own team.' Until they do, and with Spain governed by the conservative Partido Popular, it'll be a while yet. Barça will continue to be Catalonia's surrogate representatives in the international arena.

FRIDAY, 8 NOVEMBER

Ronaldo or no Ronaldo, tomorrow's game against Atlético Madrid promises to be a cracker. Atlético's last three visits to Camp Nou have produced a series of epics (impossible comebacks, scores of red cards, refereeing scandals and goals galore: 5-3, 4-3 and last season's championship deciding 1-3) and Barça's 6-5 victory in the two-legged Super Copa suggests that Robson's arrival has done nothing to buck a spectacular trend. There's good news and bad news for the coach today. The good news is that Nadal's suspension has been lifted and he can play against Atlético. The bad news is that Baía's replacement, Carles Busquets, has gone and caught tonsillitis (this is the man who was sidelined last season after catching a red-hot iron in his living room). The even worse news is that Robson's third-choice 'keeper, Lopetegui, himself a Spanish international, is also injured. That leaves 21-year-old local boy Francesc Arnau on stand-by for an unscheduled debut in what Robson acknowledges is a dose of 'bad timing for a key game'.

Radomir Antic is unimpressed by Barcelona's attempts to cry wolf. 'They love to play the victim, it's always been the same. They've been whining that Ronaldo and the Portuguese are missing, but you can hardly complain when you've got Pizzi, Abelardo and Ferrer to replace them.' As for Robson's 'We're ten points ahead of Atlético' response to his suggestion that Barça were 'Ronaldo and eight defenders', Antic is not for turning. 'I try and respect older people, I don't know why he got upset by that. All I meant was that I was fed up with people harping on about Ronaldo.' And just in case we thought he was being disrespectful, he adds, 'Robson's side is still characterised by a confusion of ideas. His philosophy is completely different to Cruyff's, and the current Barcelona side is a mixture of the two.'

Ronaldo's absence on Saturday is not only a blow to Robson, but also to the club's balance sheet. For once, the Brazilian's spontaneity has done the club no favours. Several directors have acknowledged that Ronaldo's decision to declare himself unfit so early has had a negative effect at the box-office. Just in case it happens again, the ace has been asked to be more discreet in the future, i.e. keep the fans guessing till the last ticket is sold.

SATURDAY, 9 NOVEMBER
Barcelona 3, Atlético Madrid 3 (Pizzi 15, Luis Enrique 29, Giovanni 78)
Camp Nou, 90,000

Nineteen ninety-six has been the year of the big-screen anticlimax: *Twister*, classic trailer, rank bad movie; *Mission Impossible*, foot-tapping teaser, tone-deaf movie; *Independence Day*, mind-boggling previews, mind-numbing movie. If you want guaranteed drama, Barça v. Atlético is the only show in town. We give you Robson's cast of understudies against the reigning champions; and at number 28, Arnau.

The rookie 'keeper waits five minutes for his first touch, recovering Caminero's header from the back of the net – the kind of premature drama a debutant can definitely do without. His second intervention is a textbook header to frustrate an Atlético counter-attack. Unfortunately, in rushing off his line he clatters into the back-pedalling Sergi. When the stretcher appears, Camp Nou fears the worse; luckily for Arnau, the full-back is as tough as he is tiny. Up he jumps, the action shifts to the other end, and Barça are soon ahead through Pizzi and Luis Enrique.

The second half finds Robson's side playing their most flowing football of the season, yet suddenly they find themselves behind. With the Seventh Cavalry otherwise engaged, Robson sends on De la Peña to save the show. 'Little Buddah' wreaks havoc in the Atlético box and Giovanni taps home for 3-3. 'That was great entertainment,' says a beaming Robson afterwards, clearly not too put out by dropping a couple of points. Nor will he be pushed into complaining about another three goals conceded. 'Don't complain. Just be happy you've seen a great game.'

Unusually, Robson singles one man out for special attention. At Real

Madrid, Luis Enrique played his way into the Spanish side with his whirlwind performances, yet earned a reputation as a frustratingly imprecise footballer. Whatever Robson has done to him it warrants investigation. Whether at full-back, in midfield or up front, the league's finest athlete has rapidly become his country's in-form player, full stop. 'He got a knock in the first half and was only at eighty per cent, so we moved him up front after the break,' says Robson. Atlético's back four are still having nightmares about 80 per cent of Luis Enrique.

'It's impossible to see a game like tonight's in Italy, yet in Spain there are games like this every week,' says Laurent Blanc, who on tonight's form learned plenty about the defensive arts in the *calcio.* 'Italian sides are obsessed with keeping clean sheets, here sides play to score, that's the big difference.' It's not just the football he's sold on, though. 'Even the Nápoles fans weren't as fervent as the Catalans, but what's really struck me is the enormous amount of support we attract in the rest of Spain [*more than 600 of FC Barcelona's 1,000-plus supporters' club branches are based outside Catalonia*]. At places like Santiago de Compostela, Seville and Santander, the airports were at collapsing point because of all the fans.'

SUNDAY, 10 NOVEMBER

There are draws, there are goalless draws, and there are goalless draws that come dressed up as defeats. Twenty-four hours down the line, and Barça's point against Atlético is looking even better. Deportivo's goalless draw with Tenerife combined with the weekend's second sporting upset make sure of that: you'd have got 25-1 on Evander Holyfield demolishing the Tyson myth in Vegas; if there were bookmakers in Spain they'd have given you 140-1 on Logroñes keeping a clean sheet at Real Madrid. When 100,000 *Madridistas* packed Santiago Bernabéu for a glitzy presentation of 'Real Madrid All-Stars' in July, goalless draws against Logroñes (beaten 8-0 at Barcelona three weeks ago, remember) were not quite what the promoters had in mind. Fortunately, Europe's heaviest gamblers (the Spanish spend as much on lottery tickets as they do on insurance policies) prefer to flutter in other ways. How about 5,000 slot machines per million habitants compared to 1,000 per in the USA?

As Robson's stock rises in the wake of Barça's most impressive team showing so far, Fabio Capello is doing little to win friends and influence people at Madrid. His side may have been without Mijatovic and Suker today, but fans of a club that have invested £20 million in signings don't want to hear their coach making excuses for not beating eleven players who collectively earn less than 20-year-old Raúl. 'We need at least four more quality players,' moans Capello. 'When Robson wants to make changes he looks at his bench and sees internationals like Pizzi, Couto and Abelardo. When I look at mine I see Milla [*30-something midfielder*] and the president's son [*reserve centre half Fernando Sanz*]. Considering the players available, it was a good performance today and I'm happy with the result. And people better get used to it, 'cos that's as good as it gets.'

Admittedly, Madrid do lag behind Barcelona for strength in depth – despite his absentees, Robson's Saturday night bench seated Amor, Ferrer, Bakero (more than 80 caps between them) and De la Peña – but Logroñes? Come on, Fabio. For all the excuses about absent stars, no less than ten of Madrid's side today were internationals. 'We won't fool anybody playing that badly,' complains Madrid's President Lorenzo Sanz. Not surprisingly, Capello is unimpressed by the carping. 'It seems everybody in Spain gets off on criticising the teams at the top. Let's wait until the end of the season and see who they're criticising then.'

A weekend of World Cup action sees some 50 players miss their club games in Spain. Athletic Bilbao's 2-0 win against Valencia is a reflection of what might be if the Spanish League was indeed that. With Valencia's foreign legion missing on international duty, it was a rare case of a game between 22 Spaniards, though Athletic's Basques-only philosophy exists precisely because they don't consider themselves Spanish. If it was all about home-grown players, Bilbao might have a chance of rekindling former glories. As it is, unless the Basque country throws up a freak generation of footballing superheroes, the murmur of dissenting voices among their fans could eventually become a sacrilegious roar.

Jordi Cruyff is in town and back on Bobby's case. 'I've enjoyed the flashes of skill from individuals this year, but it's difficult to enjoy watching such a defensive side. It's pathetic settling for a draw against the likes of Sporting. What's the logic of spending so much on forwards and then being obsessed with defending? Barça have got a far better squad than Madrid, it's just a case of getting the best out of them.

'If we'd had Ronaldo in the team last season we'd have done a clean sweep. Look at the difference between the money they gave my dad and what they've spent this season. The board used Pantic [*Atlético Madrid's dead-ball king, a £300,000 capture from Greek club Panionios*] as an example of the kind of bargain he should be looking for, but as soon as he's gone, they go and spend five million pounds on a goalkeeper! Even if they'd all been drunk the board wouldn't have let Dad spend twenty million dollars on Ronaldo.' Ah yes, the Cruyff family's common enemy. 'Núñez needs the team to start winning things straight away so he can be re-elected as president, that's why he's spent so much money.'

WEDNESDAY, 13 NOVEMBER

A report by the Spanish Federation of Restaurateurs claims that television's football overkill will provoke the loss of 30,000 jobs in their sector this year alone. Meanwhile, a prostitute on a reality-bites chat show claims her business is suffering while an exasperated housewife implores her husband to get a lover instead of spending seven days a week plonked on the sofa watching football. Perhaps the two guests should swap phone numbers? Or maybe the disgruntled wife should get her own lover? A cartoon in today's *La Vanguardia* depicts a woman necking on the balcony while Hubby watches the big match inside. '*Viva el fútbol!*' she proclaims. 'A game a day, at least!'

The 4,000 budding waiters who queue halfway round Barcelona for 200 jobs at the Fashion Café demonstrate how desperate things really are in the catering game. The sheer volume of televised football aside (Pizzi, Amor and Luis Enrique notch a goal apiece as Spain beat Slovakia 4-1 in tonight's helping), there is also the problem of timing. Saturday's live game kicks off at half past eight. Even in stay-out-late Spain that cuts in to prime-time dining. Mind you, the sheer volume of bars in the country (twice as many as the rest of the EU put together) suggests a little shedding is overdue. At least FC Barcelona are doing their bit for the cause. As of tonight, you can feast on football and food at the same time at the brand-new Màgic Barça restaurant. Specialities include Wembley ice cream, Barça *canelones* and the RonaldoBurger (has Ronnie McDonald been told?).

THURSDAY, 14 NOVEMBER

Barcelona hold a farewell dinner at Camp Nou for José Mari Bakero, who is off to join Mexican club Veracruz. At 32 and on the fringe of the action, Barcelona's club captain could hardly turn down a three-year contract worth a million dollars a year. Ronaldo, who preferred to spend his evening at a concert by the Brazilian singer Caetano Veloso, was the only absentee at what was an official club function (ironic that the departure of such a down-to-earth character should coincide with the birth of a diva).

Josep Lluís Núñez would normally put a curse on the house of anybody who counts Johan Cruyff among his friends. For once he makes an exception. 'We're sorry to lose the player, but above all, we're sorry to lose Bakero the person.' Televisió de Catalunya say bye-bye with a video of the player's Barça highlights to the tune of Whitney Houston singing 'I Will Always Love You' (how do you translate taste bypass operation?).

FRIDAY, 15 NOVEMBER

The rain in Spain falls mainly on the plain. Try telling that to Bobby Robson. For the first time in a week, he's got more or less his whole squad to work with and torrential rain limits proceedings to a game of basketball in the gym. As for the rain falling on the plain, well, that's another myth about Spain. The flatlands of the central regions (*la meseta*) are about as dry as it gets. Meanwhile, it hasn't stopped raining in Barcelona valley for nearly a week. In fairness, it doesn't rain here that often, but when it does, boy, you'd better dive for cover (though not in a bus or the subway; they'll have immediately ground to a halt).

Whatever dubious weather forecasts one particular teacher concocts in the interests of challenging his charge's vocalising, their veracity is the least of his pupil's worries. 'I'm finding the Spanish very difficult,' confesses Robson with typical honesty. 'At my age it really isn't easy to absorb a new language. The other problem is time; apart from a twice-weekly class the only time I get to myself is late at night. But by the time I get home, I'm really too tired to sit down and study.'

Home is 'a beautiful apartment' in Sitges, a pretty coastal resort some 20 minutes from Barcelona by car. At least, Robson thinks it is. 'I try and keep my one day off a week totally free, but apart from that I hardly get to see Sitges,' he admits. 'Today is a typical day. Training in the morning, then I have my Spanish class, a couple of hours with journalists, and then off to do a radio show. By the time I get home, it's time to go to bed.' At the moment, it's home alone, too. 'My daughter-in-law had a baby last week so my wife's gone back to stay with her.' He adds whimsically, 'The hardest thing about working abroad is being away from your family.'

Robson has been married for more than 40 years now. Doesn't his wife, Elsie, ever grumble about getting dragged about so much? 'Well, no, she doesn't moan, but she's aware that she's packed and unpacked and made houses and we're still on the trail, still in the covered wagon.' And life on the road still has its surprises. 'I didn't know Sitges was Spain's gay capital until after I moved in,' smiles Robson, adding without a hint of malice, 'At least my wife will be safe!'

SATURDAY, 16 NOVEMBER

With Spain's December transfer window looming and with Robson admitting that he wants to sign 'at least a couple of players', the rumour mill grinds away incessantly. Emerson, Kanchelskis, Kinkladze and Ginola are just some of the more familiar names being bandied around. 'If you believed what you read in the press, I'd be signing players every day,' says Robson. 'Next thing you know I'll be signing Mickey Mouse or Father Christmas.'

Nadal is back in the English papers, too, this time as a possible swap for Boro's troubled Brazilian. 'Me and my wife are homesick,' grumbles Emerson as he arrives back from Brazil (last time we heard, Barcelona was in Spain). 'He's a silly boy,' says Robson. 'You can't just walk out on things like that. I'm surprised, 'cos he was a model professional at Porto. And there is no truth in the rumours we've spoken to him. I know how the English press work. First they publish the story, then they call to ask me about it.' He also denies rumours in the local press that unsettled defender Albert Ferrer could be on the move. 'I've told him not to even think about leaving. He's got to be patient and wait for his chance. I know he's not played for seven months, but I don't want to let him go.'

One somewhat happier Brazilian is Giovanni, though the two-goal star of his country's win against Cameroon admits having to curb his natural extravagance to keep the boss happy. 'I like to try something new to entertain the fans, whether it's a nutmeg, a chip, a back-heel or a dribble. I don't think Bobby Robson likes that too much, though. He always asks me to be more practical.'

MONDAY, 18 NOVEMBER

Barcelona 6, Valladolid 1 (Popescu 10, Ronaldo 30, Luis Enrique 35, Bakero 56, Figo 75, Roger 81)
Camp Nou, 85,000

Say what you like about Barcelona fans, but never let it be said they are dirty stop-ins. On a bitterly cold night by Mediterranean standards, 85,000 *culés* pay their respects to Bakero, the departing symbol of Cruyff's 'Dream Team'. That's 85,000 for a Monday night game that is live on television. A game against unattractive opposition. A game that doesn't kick off until half past nine in a city where public transport grinds to a halt at midnight. A Monday night game at a club where 30% of the *socis* live outside the city. It's nights like tonight which make FC Barcelona the clear winners in the world's highest average attendance stakes.

Fittingly, Bakero went out like a winner. From the moment the other 21 players lined up to applaud him onto the field until his departure after scoring Barcelona's fourth goal, the crowd barely paused for breath in between chanting his name (an especially stimulating experience for the fans sat next to celebrity *culé* Josep Carreras). Bakero celebrated his farewell goal with a now-characteristic gesture: flat on his back *à la* Charlie George, fists a-pumping. Robson immediately brought him off so he could milk the applause.

'It was a perfect night for Bakero, you couldn't have scripted it better,' says Robson. 'I was going to take him off with fifteen minutes to go, but when he scored that was obviously the right moment.' For probably the first and last time this season, Ronaldo was a bit player. After two weeks of electrotherapy and massages, he eased his way back into action gingerly. When he retired from the fray a minute after Bakero, it barely registered on the Camp Nou Richter scale.

The Spanish like to think their league is the best in the world, but if the season so far is anything to go by, it's beginning to resemble the top- and bottom-heavy Dutch or Portuguese models. The league leaders in Italy, England, Germany and France have lost either three games (Newcastle and Borussia Dortmund) or two (Inter Milan and Paris Saint-Germain). Meanwhile, three Spanish teams (Barça, Real Madrid and Deportivo) remain unbeaten after thirteen games.

WEDNESDAY, 20 NOVEMBER

Barcelona's football club, as opposed to its media conglomerates, finally go out and buy a player and Bobby Robson doesn't know who he is. 'The fact is we've never heard of Dragan Ciric,' says José Mourinho of the 22-year-old Partizan Belgrade midfielder, a £1.75 million signing who's scheduled to arrive at Camp Nou in July. 'I can assure you, we have never asked for him,' insists Robson's right-hand man. 'And I never lie.'

HIGH NOON

Despite his side's 3-1 victory against Besiktas in the UEFA Cup, Valencia coach Luis Aragonés, the man who briefly replaced Terry Venables at Barcelona, becomes the fourth managerial casualty of the season. Last season's runners-up are struggling in the league and Aragonés's role in the Romario fiasco made his *adiós* inevitable. His successor is former Real Madrid boss Jorge Valdano. Another president, in this case Sporting Gijón's José Fernández, responds to rumours that his coach will be the next to go with an allusion to England. 'The season has barely started and we're already playing the lottery with coaches. It's about time we learned from English football where a coach can last eight or ten years at the same club.' You don't say, José?

THURSDAY, 21 NOVEMBER

Bobby Robson's reputation as a 'company man' is bolstered today when he backs the club in an increasingly public row over bonuses. 'The board's offer is a good one. The players already earn a lot of money; if they want to earn more then they should do it by winning titles.' He also contradicts that fibbing beggar Mourinho's comments about Ciric. 'I know plenty about him. He's one of the best young players in Europe, some say the best Yugoslav in fifteen years; better than Mijatovic, Savicevic or Jugovic, even.'

FRIDAY, 22 NOVEMBER

It's only taken a couple of months for the Gallic bundle of energy they call Luis Fernández to make his mark at Athletic Bilbao. Only Barcelona have scored more than Bilbao's 26 goals, and asked to predict a score for tomorrow's game against Barça, he is typically cocksure. 'We'll win 5-4,' he boasts.

Sport jumps on that flippant prediction to attack you-know-who. 'Robson hasn't predicted a result yet, but given his philosophy, we're sure he'd rather win 1-0 than 5-4. He measures success by results, not spectacle.' Blimey, what has a man got to do to convince these guys? Fernández's Athletic are doing well enough, but it's Barcelona who have scored 42 goals in thirteen games. At an average of 3.23 a game that makes them Europe's most prolific scorers. No wonder Robson groans: 'The day we lose, I'd better take two weeks' holiday.'

As a player, the ungainly Fernández played Cyrano de Bergerac to Platini, Tigana and Giresse in France's most eloquent midfield; as a coach, his sides play with bravura and style. Despite being a self-declared fan of Johan Cruyff, he has long been tipped as a future Barça coach. 'I did have some talks with Barcelona last year,' he admits, 'but it never got as far as an offer.' The Dutchman may be gone, but Fernández remains a disciple. 'Robson is a good coach, but Cruyff is still my model. His attacking philosophy changed the face of Spanish football. Robson's Barcelona may be winning games 6-0, but with the same players Cruyff would be winning 12-0.'

Fernández has spent the past week exchanging pleasantries with José Mourinho. It started when the Frenchman accused Figo of 'diving so much he should be in a swimming pool'. 'Enough is enough,' replied Robson's number two. 'Week after week we have to put up with accusations from people trying to influence referees before our games.' Not surprisingly, Fernandez is not backing down. 'I was only joking about Figo. I've got no problem with him at all. But who the hell is this Mourinho nobody?' He adds with a sinister flourish, 'He'd better watch out, the benches at Athletic are really close. If I was him I'd sit tight on my own side and not move.' Unwisely, Mourinho rises to the bait. 'Maybe at some clubs the assistant manager carries the suitcases, puts out the cones, or gives out the bibs, but it's not like that at Barcelona. Bobby Robson treats me as an equal.'

If it's not stroppy opponents it's the peasants revolting. With Bakero on the sidelines until his departure, Robson had nominated Popescu as team skipper with little opposition. Now we're talking about club captain here, not important in practice, but significant symbolically. The players want Robson to put it to a vote. Either Guillermo Amor, born in Benidorm but at the club since he was eleven, or local boy Guardiola would be the players' (and the people's) choice. Robson steadfastly refuses. 'Popescu is second in line so he takes over.'

Grateful or not for his coach's support, Popescu goes about proving he isn't a yes man. 'I'm proud that Robson has given me this responsibility, but it's my job to defend my teammates, even if that means disagreeing with the coach.' Especially when it comes to money, it seems. 'We're not asking for what the Milan players get, just enough to put us on a par with other major European clubs.' The Romanian does, however, deny a wider rift between players and coach. 'We didn't like what Robson said about bonuses, but it's rubbish to say there's a split in the dressing room. You'll never get twenty-five friends in the dressing room, nobody has that many true friends; but there is mutual respect.'

Robson has his own grouses, too. He's particularly exasperated at dressing-room conversations filtering through to the press. Guardiola, for one, is taken to task for lamenting the absence of 'Dream Teamers' Amor and Ferrer from Bakero's farewell game. 'It was a particularly hard decision leaving out Amor,' admits Robson. 'Especially when only last week he played for Spain and scored, but somebody had to make way for Bakero.'

The out-of-favour Ferrer admits he's received a 'really good offer' to join Real Madrid and rejects Robson's request for patience. 'I've been sat on the sidelines injured for six months; if that's not being patient then I don't know what is,' says the Catalan defender. 'I'm not saying I've got to play, but if I've been fit for three weeks and I'm not even getting into the squad, it's difficult for me to accept Robson believes in me.'

Popescu claims that he too has received an offer from Madrid. 'Capello called my agent and made an offer, but I took no notice. I'm a hundred per cent Barça and that's the way it's going to stay. My ambition is to retire here.' Madrid President Lorenzo Sanz admits he's approached Ferrer, but denies interest in the Romanian. 'If anybody can prove Madrid have made Popescu an offer I'll pay them fifty thousand pounds.'

SATURDAY, 23 NOVEMBER
Athletic Bilbao 2, Barcelona 1 *(Abelardo 25)*
San Mamés, 46,000

If football was a logical game, an injury-stricken band of local boys wouldn't have a prayer against a team of expensively assembled stars from football's global village. Tonight, however, San Mamés, better known in Spain as the Cathedral, was a place where underdogs' prayers were answered. It was also a night when fortune favoured the brave.

Fernández was as good as his word and Athletic took the field with only two genuine defenders. Robson responded by deploying three centre-backs and depriving Ronaldo of company. The first 25 minutes were closely contested, but from the moment Abelardo headed them into the lead, Barça were always going backwards. Two second-half goals were the very least the hosts deserved. The otherwise invisible Ronaldo did hit the bar with a last-minute header, but an equaliser would have been grossly undeserved. 'A side that concedes so many goals is committing suicide by trying to sit on a one-goal lead,' observed *Sport*'s Antoni Closa after the game.

In stark contrast to the ants-in-his-pants Frenchman, who despite driving rain spent the entire game shirt-sleeved and touting for an Oscar on the touchline, Robson was in placid mood tonight, though Fernández's intimidating face-off with Mourinho after Robson's aide protested an assault on Figo perhaps urged caution. And only the swift intervention of the police prevented post-match shenanigans, as Guardiola and Figo squared up to the mocking Frenchman (who ushered the Barça players off the field with a censurable impersonation of Greg Laganis). 'A professional should never mock a beaten opponent,' complained Guardiola afterwards. 'I suppose he's not used to winning,' added Figo. Not surprisingly, the chastened Mourinho was most scathing. 'Fernández has done everything in his power to turn a game of football into a dogfight. I won't say any more, because I prefer to talk about men, not badly behaved kids.' Former Barça icon Bernd Schuster famously said that playing at Bilbao was like 'going over the hill in Korea'. Things obviously haven't changed much.

The defeat sees Robson fall two games short of Barça's best-ever opening run, Terry Venables' fifteen-game unbeaten start to the 1984/85 Championship-winning season. Coincidentally, El Tel also tasted defeat for the first time in Bilbao, then coached by Javier Clemente.

SUNDAY, 24 NOVEMBER
Robson chooses a bad day to take in his first Barça B game of the season, as the club's nursery side lose at home to Real Madrid B in the Second Division's version of the big one. 'I've seen the youngsters on TV but it's the first time I've seen them play live,' admits Robson, whose presence at the 25,000-capacity Mini Stadi (a ground that would put several top-flight stadiums to shame) was allegedly the result of a midweek 'suggestion' from the board.

Davor Suker makes it a miserable Sunday all round by scoring a hat trick for Madrid's grown-ups as they beat Valencia and leap-frog Barça to the top of the table.

Question. What do Suker and Nicolas Cage have in common? Answer. They're both allergic to metal. After Suker missed training for several days with mysterious aches and pains in his arms, Real Madrid's doctors have told him to ditch all his watches and jewellery. Little Junior, Cage's muscle-bound psychopath in *Kiss of Death*, worked out his frustrations with a similar infliction by dressing up in a waterproof cape and beating people to death with a baseball bat (wooden, naturally). Presumably, Suker will take less drastic action, though Madrid fans will hope his allergy doesn't extend to end-of-season silverware.

Robson continues to avoid the controversy over *les follies de Fernández*. 'I headed straight for the dressing room after the game and I didn't see what went on in the tunnel. I'm not interested in getting involved in that kind of thing; it's just not my style.' Diplomacy obviously doesn't extend to the Barcelona boardroom. As his name suggests, Fernández has Spanish parents. According to Barça director Antoni Pagès, that explains everything. 'I live close to France, and I know his kind of pseudo-Frenchmen are not looked upon kindly by the French. I'm familiar with the kind of mental problems these people have and Fernández is most definitely one of them.'

MONDAY, 25 NOVEMBER

Luis is clearly not a man to retire quietly to a neutral corner. 'I suppose I'd better apologise for beating Barcelona,' he says with more than a hint of malice. 'My players are so sorry they've spent the whole day in the dressing room crying.' He then shifts from irony to full-frontal attack. 'Barcelona always make excuses when they lose. When Paris Saint-Germain beat them, they weren't bothered about whether I was polite or not, what they did was try and sign me at the end of the season. Maybe they don't like it because I joined Athletic instead. They're harping on about me when they should be talking about their actors.' And just in case we don't get his drift: 'What's Figo ever won? Nothing. He should take a look at my CV.'

Barcelona finally reach an agreement with the players over bonuses. Not a single peseta for finishing runners-up (despite the fact it delivers Champions League status) shows exactly what second place to Real Madrid means around these parts.

TUESDAY, 26 NOVEMBER

Barcelona 'reserves' beat a full-strength Celtic 1-0. If it's any consolation to Tommy Burns, Robson's fringe side did include nine internationals. But why were Barça playing a midweek friendly in Glasgow instead of enjoying a rare break from just about the heaviest schedule in Europe? 'I asked myself the same question,' says Robson of the unwanted fixture. 'It's because of this impresario, Josep Minguella. He handles all of these transfers and as part of his payment Barça hand him the rights to friendly matches.' Robson wasn't the only one cursing agents tonight. The game was televised live (that's where Minguella makes his money, natch) and getting their tongues around the names of a team of unknown Scots proved beyond the Spanish commentators. Alan Stoobs was a particular thorn in their side.

Premiership matches are broadcast live in Spain at least three times a week. The regular commentators bow to no one in their knowledge of English football, but they do have problems with certain Anglo-Saxon inflections. Did you know, for example, that England boast a full-back called Graeme Le Socks and a midfielder called Nicky Boot? And who is the Highbury cult figure they call Steve Bulled? The man who marks Dianne Dublin or Yon Barneys (a slouch these days compared to Ryan Jigs)? And if Alan Stoobs is looking for a partner he need look no farther than Ibrox and Richard Goof. Cartoon characters abound – just ask Nicky Bambi. Luckily, the Spaniards don't have any problems getting their tongues around Bobby Robson (though malicious gremlins in the press occasionally dub him Booby Robson), and plain and simple Bobby Robson at that. For some reason, it was always Gary Winston Lineker and it's never less than John Benjamin Toshack.

FRIDAY, 29 NOVEMBER

FC Barcelona is 97 years old today. Ironically, the flagship of Catalan nationalism was actually formed by a Swiss businessman, Hans Gamper (not surprisingly the locals have appropriated him for themselves as Joan Gamper). Barcelona's distinctive strip reflects not some ancient Catalan folklore but the legacy of Gamper's former club in Switzerland.

Many of Spain's football clubs were formed by British industrialists at the turn of the century (why do you think they're called Racing, Sporting and Athletic?), and though Barcelona's footballing Brits were beaten to the punch by the 21-year-old Gamper, their early influence was considerable. 'Foot-ball Club' Barcelona's first game, in December 1899, was played against a group of the city's English residents, and the club's first two presidents, Walter Wild and Arthur Witty, were both English. Notwithstanding the legendary Mister Barrow, who was let go after a four-month trial because of his 'drink problem' (it apparently included not staying sober long enough to tell anybody his first name), the club's first coach was a former player called Jack Greenwall, appointed in 1917. Over the next couple of decades there was a steady stream of anonymous expats at the helm, a pattern only broken by Patrick O'Connell, a former Sheffield Wednesday and Hull City player who led Betis to the only league title in their history in 1935. He came close in his two seasons at Barcelona, too, but not as close as Bobby Robson's mentor, Vic Buckingham, whose side lost the 1970/71 title on goal difference to Valencia (who they then beat 4-3 in the Cup Final). When the unknown Terry Venables arrived at Barcelona in 1984, the German midfielder Bernd Schuster commented, 'He must be some bloke they picked up on the beach who fancies a few beers in the good weather.' Schuster's surprising awareness of the Barça Brits tradition aside, El Tel would finally seal a championship for the perfidious Albion.

Steve Archibald was top scorer in that Championship-winning side, but he wasn't the first British player to lead Barcelona's scoring charts; that honour belongs to one Charles Wallace in 1907/08. Neither was Archibald the club's most incongruous acquisition from Blighty. In 1910, a group of Barça players holidaying on the Costa Brava persuaded an English tourist to make up the numbers for a beach kickabout. The mysterious Mister Patullo impressed so much that he was recruited for the following season. After scoring 20 goals in 41 games he disappeared to England as mysteriously as he'd arrived. Even Gary Lineker got a move back to Tottenham.

SATURDAY, 30 NOVEMBER
Ronaldo insists that rumours of Italian and English suitors are more than paper talk. 'The offers are real and we're talking about incredible amounts of money. We've got to sort out this situation as soon as possible so I can settle down and concentrate on my game. Barcelona know my intention is to stay but I'm a professional and I've got to consider offers from other clubs. Alexandre Martins and Reinaldo Pitta [*two of his three representatives, the other is their Italian associate, Giovanni Branchini*] will be here next week and I'm sure the club will do everything in their power to find a happy solution.'

Reading between the lines, Ronaldo's dilemma (sic) can be summed up easily: Mo' money, *por favor*. The goofy youngster may look like butter wouldn't melt in his mouth, but as the Advocaat case demonstrated, he can work a room with the best of 'em. Barcelona's long-running negotiations with PSV Eindhoven looked to be going nowhere last summer as the Dutch club insisted Ronaldo was not for sale at any price ... until the player made his situation at PSV untenable by calling coach Dick Advocaat 'stupid'. Two days later he was Barcelona-bound.

SUNDAY, 1 DECEMBER

Reports from England claim that Manchester United are one of the clubs who are prepared to pay £20 million for Ronaldo. 'I've got no problem with English clubs,' is Robson's reaction to the latest rumours. 'The problem is the press making up these stories. Four months ago, Alan Shearer was supposed to be going to United, too. And what happened? They didn't have the money so he went to Newcastle, and they ended up signing Jordi Cruyff instead!'

More than a week before the Real Madrid v. Barcelona game, and four days before tickets go on sale, and the first diehards (geared up with sleeping bags, sofas, *et al*) take their place in the queue. Meanwhile, the more entrepreneurial touts are asking for cash deposits (non-returnable in case of over-booking)! Naturally, no self-respecting tout is going to freeze in a queue for a week, either. They get round that little problem by recruiting the homeless to 'save their places'.

MONDAY, 2 DECEMBER

Barcelona 3, Extremadura 0 (Giovanni 13, Popescu 40, Juanito o.g. 45)
Camp Nou, 70,000

Almendralejo is a dot on the map in the impoverished region of Extremadura, a land of ghost towns populated by ageing farmers whose only ally is a horse and cart, and where the neighbours speak Portuguese. It's also home to Club de Fútbol Extremadura, whose fifth-place finish in last season's Second Division was an unexpected blip on a history spent in the backwaters of Spain's regional leagues. Like Barcelona, Extremadura play in red-and-blue stripes (the club was formed by Barça fans in 1928); that's where the similarity ends. Only 70,000 fans make it to Camp Nou for tonight's game; that's still 42,000 more than the entire population of Almendralejo. Extremadura's annual budget is barely a million pounds and £20,000-a-year midfielder Antonio Ito is the lowest-paid player in the top flight (at only £980,000 less than Barça reserve Robert Prosinecki).

Not surprisingly, Extremadura's top-flight debut is proving to be one long tumble back towards the Second Division. A side that has exceeded expectations with six points in fourteen games was never likely to motivate Barça's all-stars, even without a trip to Real Madrid just around the corner. Robson's men sleepwalked their way to a 3-0 half-time lead and spent the second half avoiding physical contact and yellow cards. 'I'm very disappointed and I'd hope the players were, too,' says Robson. 'But don't expect me to lay into them with the Madrid game on the horizon; they're only human, after all. You'll always get lacklustre games against weaker sides; it happens here and it happens in England, Portugal or Germany. When it does, you've just got to make sure of the three points, that's the only thing that counts at the end of the season.'

TUESDAY, 3 DECEMBER
Forget the Old Firm derby, Liverpool v. Manchester United, Boca Juniors v. River Plate, or Milan v. Inter. If you're looking for trouble, Real Madrid v. Barcelona is the mother of all footballing rumbles. The sheer ferocity of the rivalry evokes antipathies that go way beyond the merely sporting. Madrid may no longer be 'the Regime's team' but the vestiges of regional (monolithic Spain v. independent Catalonia) and political (right-wing pro-Franco v. liberal anti-Franco) antagonism cast an indelible shadow over present-day rivalry. As the title of a recent book suggests, welcome to 'The Never Ending War'.

The sporting contention dates back to the turn of the century. In 1902, Real Madrid's first-ever game, and Barcelona's debut outside Catalonia, was a 3-1 win for the visitors in the capital. The first-ever Spanish Championship in 1928/29 was won by Barcelona with Madrid two points behind as runners-up. Subsequently, the rivals have rarely strayed apart at the top of the table. Atlético Madrid temporarily upstaged the big two in 1996, but as the dual stranglehold on the previous eleven championships (that's Madrid 6, Barça 5) suggests, the bipolar nature of the Spanish League is, if anything, becoming more entrenched. Not surprisingly, then, hostilities are as marked as ever.

The seeds of a more sinister animosity were sown during the so-called 'Dark Years' between the end of the Spanish Civil War in 1939 and the death of Franco in 1975. In the first months of the war, FC Barcelona got its first martyr when club president Josep Sunyol was shot down by fascists after accidentally straying behind enemy lines. Four decades of Franco's dictatorship would see Real Madrid converted into a symbol of a unified and powerful Spain. In the late fifties especially, the all-conquering Madrid were adopted as 'Franco's ambassadors' abroad (depending on which side of the barrier you stand, cause and effect take divergent paths; but lest we forget, republican Madrid withstood a two-year siege by the fascists during the Civil War, so clearly not everyone in the capital was a stormtrooper). Meanwhile, Barça became a symbol of resistance to the dictatorship far beyond Catalonia's own frontiers.

Times may have changed, Franco is long gone and Madrid's last Championship-winning coach was Jorge Valdano, a South American left-wing intellectual, but four consecutive Barça championships under Cruyff didn't kill off the lingering suspicion that Madrid maintain the sympathies of men in smoked-filled rooms (Real, that's 'Royal' Madrid, are one of scores of clubs blessed by the royal seal of approval, so please don't blame the King). Barcelona's *Boixos-nois* (Crazy Boys) still take great delight in burning the Spanish flag, while their even uglier counterparts on the hooligan fringe at Madrid, the *Ultras-Sur* (so-named after the South End of the Bernabéu where they congregate) love nothing better than to deck themselves out in Nazi regalia for the Barça game and entertain bystanders with nasty, right-wing chants.

Not that the men at the top set an example to be proud of. One 1995 exchange saw former Madrid president Ramón Mendoza call Josep Lluís Núñez 'a miserable dwarf'. Núñez, who once accused the late Madrid idol Juanito of 'leaving pregnant women on every street corner', responded by labelling Mendoza 'a senile old man'. Mind you, the latter-day directors have got a lot to live down to. The legendary Santiago Bernabéu, Madrid's president between 1943 and his death in 1978, actually took part in the fascist conquest of Catalonia during the Civil War, and later coined the infamous saying: 'Those who say I don't like Catalonia are wrong. I like and admire Catalonia; in spite of the Catalans.'

As for the biannual date itself, well, if you're attracted to displays of mass hysteria, you'll love it, though as Bobby Robson will find out on Saturday, it's strictly one-way traffic. Three seasons ago, a Catalan savings bank made the mistake of busing a coach-load of prize-winning schoolchildren to Madrid for the big game. The idea of a pleasant day's sightseeing was hastily abandoned given the barrage of abuse from the capital's gentlefolk and the party beat a hasty retreat to their hotel. Accompanied to the ground by a police escort worthy of a Middle Eastern head of state, the visitors were cordoned off in the most isolated heights of the Bernabéu, as far away from the *Ultras-Sur* as possible. But even a massive police presence couldn't protect the children from the catalogue of abuse hurled at them from the surrounding 'ordinary' fans. Amidst jolly asides about Franco and his gas chambers, many of the bewildered children were reduced to tears. It's safe to say *la Halifax* will not be arranging a repeat visit.

The atmosphere at Camp Nou when Real come to town is not as sinister, but it's barely less charged. After Madrid beat Barça in the 1993 Super Copa their (silly) lap of honour was met by such an avalanche of UFOs that the players were forced to retire to the centre circle and await a police escort off the pitch. On arriving back in the capital later the same night, the victorious Madrid team were greeted at Barajas airport by an unholy alliance of President Mendoza and the *Ultras-Sur,* doing the Iberian pogo and chanting anti-Catalan ditties. All for the benefit of a live TV audience!

It gets little better when proceedings take place on neutral territory. The 1990 Cup Final saw Valencia turned into a battlefield, on and off the pitch. Barça fans were met at the train station by the *Ultras-Sur*, kitted out in motorbike helmets and armed with bricks and mortar from an adjoining (and suspiciously unmanned) building site. Despite the awful predictability of the welcome, it took the police 25 minutes to respond, leading to conspiracy theories and accusations of an anti-Catalan plot. The game reflected its ugly surroundings and it was a miracle, combined with the tact of a referee afraid he might have a riot on his hands, that only one player was sent off (Madrid's Hierro) and another stretchered off (Barça's Aloisio after a savage off-the-ball assault by Hugo Sánchez). The fun and games continued on Barça's lap of honour (they won 2-0, a result that kept the under-pressure Johan Cruyff in a job) when Zubizarreta was felled by a bottle and left with a gaping head wound. Afterwards, Madrid captain Chendo was still doing his worst to make the peace. 'What hurts most of all is that the King's Cup has been won by a team that's not Spanish,' he insisted.

It was in 1953 that full-blown hostilities broke out. Four decades on, the Di Stéfano case still rankles in Catalonia. In that year, a titanic struggle took place for the signature of the world's best player, the Argentinian Alfredo Di Stéfano. No sooner had Barça announced his signing from River Plate (with FIFA's blessing) than Real Madrid countered with claims that he was joining them from the outlawed Millonarios of Colombia, the club he'd joined after walking out on the Argentinians. The Spanish military authorities decided on a Solomon-like resolution and dictated that the player alternate between the rivals, season by season. The outraged Catalans refused to accept the compromise, and after a token indemnification Di Stéfano was handed on a plate to Madrid. That victory in a transfer tug-of-war was the most important 'result' in the history of the two clubs. In the Silver Spear's first season in Spain, Real Madrid won their first Spanish title in 21 years (why Madrid hadn't won the title in the first two decades of Franco's Real-worshipping dictatorship is a question the conspiracy school conveniently ignore). In the ensuing decade, he went on to score more than 300 goals, including an unparalleled 49 in 58 European Cup ties as he led Madrid to five European titles in a row. The Catalans, meanwhile, had to wait until 1992 to register their sole European Cup triumph. Or, as Madrid fans like to put it: How many European Cups have Barça won? Two. The first and the last.

Not surprisingly, only a handful of players have played for both clubs. Bernd Schuster's crossing of the lines in 1988 was the first case in a couple of decades; and then came Michael Laudrup. If pushed, Barça fans could rationalise the flight of the more visceral Schuster, but how, they asked, could a character as dispassionate as the Dane stab them in the back so cruelly? And after a four-year spell of Laudrup-inspired hegemony, how they suffered as 'Judas' led Madrid to the 1995 Championship. The savageness of the reception he received on his Camp Nou return was simply frightening.

Press-box decorum was abandoned for the night as neutrals in the front row found themselves wiping phlegm from the back of their necks every time Laudrup went near the ball. And that was as civilised as it got. The only thing missing from a Camp Nou awash with 'Laudrup Die' and 'Traitor' banners was the guillotine itself.

As the sad Dane trudged off the pitch after a mercy substitution, the cacophony of abuse must have echoed beyond the Pyrenees. They may beg to differ in East Anglia, but you get the feeling that Ipswich v. Norwich is not quite the same thing.

Bobby Robson would certainly settle for a repeat of Terry Venables' first away day in the Spanish capital. When he perused the fixture list for the 1984/85 season, Venables must have wondered if the Spanish gods had it in for chirpy cockneys. Barça's opening fixture? Real Madrid, away. Fortunately for El Tel, his baptism of fire turned into a stroll as Barça won 3-0 with a goal from fellow debutant Archibald thrown in for good measure.

Robson's personal memories of the Bernabéu are similarly happy. In October 1973 his Ipswich side knocked Madrid out of the UEFA Cup with a goalless draw in Spain after a 1-0 win at Portman Road. Even better was a 4-2 win with England in February 1987. 'That was one of my happiest moments as England manager,' he recalls. 'It was on my fifty-fourth birthday, and Gary Lineker scored all four goals on home turf, so to speak.' Lineker was not slow to register the wider significance of FC Barcelona. It was his comments after those goals in Madrid that guaranteed him hero status among the Catalans. Asked what it felt like to put one over on his host nation he replied, 'I don't play for a Spanish team, I play for a Catalan one!'

Both Robson and Fabio Capello have been around long enough to avoid unnecessary hyperbole. 'Any fan who has lived here all their life can tell you more about the rivalry than me,' says Robson. 'But I must admit I've never witnessed anything like the expectation for this game. Not in England, Holland or Portugal. It's got to be the biggest club game in the world.' Capello, a man prone to understatement, agrees. 'Everybody says that the Italians are more intense about their football than the Spanish, but not even a Juve v. Milan provokes this kind of passion. Football's place in Spanish culture is twice as far-reaching as in Italy. I've certainly never heard of Italian fans sleeping three days in the street just to get a ticket. The level of expectation is incredible.'

Wisely, Robson refuses to be drawn on the game's political connotations. 'As far as I'm concerned it should never be more than sport. That's my life, it's what I understand and the only thing I'm interested in. Barcelona and Real Madrid are the two biggest football clubs in Spain, that's what Saturday's game should be about, nothing more. And though I'd love to win, it's only worth three points, the same as any other game. With seventy-eight points to play for after Saturday, it's hardly a championship decider, is it?'

Paris may be on red alert after a bombing at the Port-Royal station, but Spanish tourists interviewed on TV3 have other things on their mind. 'There are so many gendarmes down here it must be the safest subway in the world,' says one singularly unconcerned backpacker, adding, 'Do you know where we can watch Madrid v. Barça on the telly?' He'll be happy to learn that France is one of 40 countries taking a live feed of Saturday's match.

THURSDAY, 5 DECEMBER

Despite two decades of democracy, Spanish society still runs on *noblesse oblige*, and nowhere more so than in the capital. The capacity at Santiago Bernabéu is a whopping 106,000, but once season ticket holders, supporters' clubs and assorted hangers-on have been accounted for, a mere 7,000 tickets are available to the general public. Less than two hours after the box-office shutters go up, the *No Hay Billetes* sign announces the bad news for the know-nobodies.

All the tickets may have been snapped up, but the players are still selling the game as if their lives depended on it. 'It's the most important occasion of my life,' says Ronaldo. 'Even in Brazil the build-up to a big game doesn't last two weeks!' Six hundred and twenty-one miles away in Madrid, Roberto Carlos gets even more carried away. 'I'd give my life to win this game,' he claims. Most players make the right noises about the fans, but the Brazilian with a heart as big as his thighs has been offering moral support and spare tickets to fans who queued to no avail. Bodo Illgner, meanwhile, hands his entire allocation straight back to the club. Blimey, he may be German, but has the man got no friends? Perhaps he fears egg on the face and wants to discourage witnesses. The giant 'keeper has been suffering from gastro-enteritis this week; rumour-mongers suggest it's a bad case of Ronalditis. 'It's not the first time I've had a bad stomach or faced a star forward, and it won't be the last,' he says. 'I wasn't scared of Maradona at the 1990 World Cup, so I'm certainly not going to be intimidated by Ronaldo.'

Continuing in Good Samaritan mode, Roberto Carlos does his best to cheer up his 'keeper. 'You don't have to kick Ronaldo to stop him,' he says of his home-boy. 'You've just got to make sure he doesn't get the ball. Then he gets really frustrated. When Ronaldo arrived at Barça he was doing things people in Spain had never seen before and everybody put him on a pedestal, but nobody asks why he didn't get a single game at the 1994 World Cup. He's still a beginner, that's why. When he gets the ball he forgets there are other people playing. He's just obsessed with scoring great goals.

'He could be better than Pelé or Maradona, but it's not just about what he does on the field. Pelé was the best ever because he knew how to use his head, as well. It's like Julia Roberts – you might be crazy about her as an actress, but when you read about the scandals in her private life, you realise there's something wrong. I'm worried about Ronaldo; he's made such a good start that people demand too much. And wherever he goes, he gets stared at like he was a freak.'

Freaky-deaky or not, Ronaldo agrees it's difficult to get out and mingle. 'Spanish fans are even more fanatical than in Brazil. The harassment is much more relentless here. Everywhere I go, I've got thirty people following me to the car wanting something from me and trying to touch me.' He should worry. The king of American sports, Michael Jordan, once had a woman beg him to run her over in his car just so she could tell her friends.

Stoichkov admits defeat in his bid to be fit for Saturday. His troublesome thigh is very good news for Capello and his boys. One of the reasons the Camp Nou congregation worship at the feet of Hristo is because he detests Real Madrid. 'There's just something about them that gets up my back,' he insists. In his original five-year spell at Barcelona, Stoichkov's record against Madrid swung from the sublime (spectacular winning goals, last-minute winners) to the ridiculous (a brace of sendings-off and a notorious spot of bother after stamping on the referee's foot in the 1990 Super Copa).

FRIDAY, 6 DECEMBER

A single Bank Holiday Friday in Madrid proves that Ronaldomanía gets to the parts other footballing crazes can't reach. Two thousand screaming fans packed into the capital's airport recall a legendary reception for *los Beatles* in 1966. Given the 'libidinous lifestyles' the Fab Four represented, that reception was seen as a death blow to Franco's morally repressive regime. The majority of today's welcoming committee are decidedly liberated kids; most have but one name on their lips, the Fab One from Brazil. 'I've never seen anything like it,' admits Nicolau Casaus, a two-decade veteran as unofficial club ambassador. 'Two thousand people at Barajas cheering Barcelona; it's more like Paseo de Gràcia [*Barcelona's elegant central avenue*] than Madrid.'

Even Bobby Robson is forced to jettison his just-another-game routine. 'Tomorrow's match is clearly special,' he admits. 'It's much more than one football team against another: it's a city against a city, a nation against a nation.' It's not Ol' Blue Eyes, though. 'If something was really important to me, I'd queue all day, too,' he insists. 'I'd do it for Sinatra!'

Robson has been around football a long time, but he's never experienced anything like Barça fever. 'I still can't quite believe it,' he says, shaking his head, sat in his room at the team's hotel. 'We were in Menorca for a pre-season tournament, and we couldn't get near the training ground because there were five thousand people blocking the road. I don't even know how they all found out we were training at this particular place; it was supposed to be a secret! Even when we got inside, we couldn't get on the pitches. I thought that was unique, but then we went to places like Bilbao, Santander and Oviedo and it was the same. I've never seen anything like the reception we get here, not at PSV, not in England. I had four years in Portugal, and I never saw anything remotely like the hero worship here. We'd leave the hotel in Lisbon or Porto for a big match and there might be a dozen people, all very calm with their "Good luck, misters", but nothing excitable, no screaming and yelling like they do here.

'I'm amazed by the patience the players show with the public. They're very considerate; even when they get knocked over in hotels and airports. In Bilbao our hotel was ridiculously crowded, but they still stood there and posed for photos. And the fans here are quite rude sometimes, they just grab your coat or your arm and go, "Sign there, mister"; they're very physical. I think it's hard for the players to be so giving every minute of the day. You can't go anywhere without being recognised.'

Over-burdened they may be, but Robson is arguably guilty of seeing his charges through rose-tinted glasses. Some of the players are indeed courteous (Amor, Barça's longest-serving player in the wake of Bakero's departure, is a prince among men), but others are either calculating (Guardiola is fine when a camera is around, less so otherwise) or friendly/stroppy according to their mood (Stoichkov). It is hard, though. Even Gary Lineker, born a man of the people, was known to slip out of the back door at Camp Nou to avoid the waiting hordes.

HIGH NOON

SATURDAY, 7 DECEMBER
Real Madrid 2, Barcelona 0
Santiago Bernabéu, 106,000
Barça: Baía, Luis Enrique, Blanc, Nadal, Sergi, Popescu, Amor (Ferrer 54), Guardiola, Figo (De la Peña 82), Giovanni (Pizzi 64), Ronaldo
Madrid: Illgner, Secretario, Hierro (García Calvo 87), Alkorta, Roberto Carlos, Víctor, Seedorf, Redondo, Raúl, Mijatovic (Sanchis 84), Suker (Amavisca 65)

The season's first 'Game of the Century' throws up a kaleidoscope of staggering facts and figures: 106,000 fans at the Santiago Bernabéu, a million pounds at the gate, £75 tickets fetching £500, a twelve-hour preview on TeleMadrid, 500 accredited journalists, more than a thousand police ... and an all-star cast of footballers from nine countries, including eleven debutants in Spain's big one. Unfortunately for Bobby Robson, it only delivers two goals, neither of them scored by Barcelona. Suker and Mijatovic get a strike apiece and both convert, Ronaldo has three (by his standards routine) chances, and misses the lot. 'We lost because I missed three open goals,' he admits afterwards.

Despite the youngster's willingness to shoulder the blame, the press would soon be shopping for more convenient scapegoats; *El Periódico*'s 'Capello 2 Robson 0' anyone? Stats in hand, Robson's claims that his side had 'played better than Madrid' were defensible. Barça did indeed hit the bar twice and have two shots cleared off the line. 'We're not likely to miss as many chances or be so unlucky again,' he insists. However, the physiognomy of the game told a rather different story. 'You can draw one incontestable conclusion from today's game,' argues *Sport*'s Josep Maria Casanovas. 'Madrid have got themselves a team, Barcelona a bunch of individuals.'

'There's no reason to panic,' advises Robson. 'If a team loses faith because it loses one big game then it doesn't deserve to be challenging for titles.' A third of a way through the season, his inability to impose a style of play on his side is beginning to inspire doubts, though. On a night when plan B (the three centre-halves) was expected, Robson experimented with Amor as an extra midfielder instead. Even if the strategy had worked (it didn't; Seedorf and Redondo were a more consistent presence at the game's heart), a game at the Bernabéu is hardly the occasion to experiment, claim the snipers. In contrast to Robson's chopping and changing, Madrid fans can cite team and system on autopilot. Tonight's result was not

92

decisive; the seeds of doubt planted in the minds of the vanquished could be. As Capello argues, 'Our victory is most important for what it means psychologically.'

Predictably, the atmosphere was charged. 'A hostile reception doesn't usually bother me in the slightest,' admits Robson later. 'I love the edge at the big games, that's what football's all about, but Madrid was especially volatile. I'd heard about it, but I was still surprised by the intensity. The stadium's built for it, too. Camp Nou curves upwards and outwards, whereas the Bernabéu is like four vertical walls, so it feels like the public are right above you, breathing down your neck. You'd get hostile days like that in England on a much smaller dimension, at places like the Den and West Ham, but at Real Madrid it was colossal. It's a hundred thousand people bearing down on you. As a club match, it really is an extra degree in terms of hostility.'

The first live broadcast of Real Madrid v. Barcelona, in February 1959, led to such a rush for televisions that a week before the game there wasn't a set left for sale in the whole of Barcelona. Thirty-seven years on, everybody's got a telly, but a power cut in Catalonia's La Cerdanya region meant that half a million homes were left powerless for the hours that encompassed the big game. That's what you call bad timing. It's also the kind of coincidence that can leave a government monopoly with a rebellion on its hands. You can shut down the ski resorts of La Molina without a revolution, but not Madrid v. Barça. Within a week, the local authorities were suing their Spanish suppliers for damages and negotiating with 'cheaper and more reliable' French electricity companies across the Pyrenees.

SUNDAY, 8 DECEMBER

	P	W	D	L	F	A	PTS
Real Madrid	16	11	5	0	33	12	38
Barcelona	16	10	4	2	46	21	34

The post-mortem begins here. Most commentators agree that, yes, Barcelona were unfortunate in Madrid, but insist that Lady Luck's whims on the night shouldn't mask a worryingly negative trend. As Barcelona's daily *La Vanguardia* (arch-enemies of Cruyff, and thus desperate to acclaim Robson) headlines, 'Barça Are Going Backwards'. In six games, a four-point lead over Real Madrid has been transformed into a four-point deficit. The good news for the beleaguered Robson is that a combination of World Cup fixtures and Spain's Christmas shut-down means that his side have only one (in theory comfortable) game at home to Celta before potentially unhappy New Year trips to Deportivo and Betis, second and third respectively. That gives him plenty of time to sit back and take stock. The bad news is that the lull in proceedings means the big-game autopsy will run and run. Joan Pi, 20 years a reporter on the Barça beat, sums up the consensus on the alleged Barça malaise.

'You name it, Robson's been accused of it,' he smiles (these guys hate a successful coach). 'Continual tactical shifts betray the lack of a clear system and several players are not being used in their best positions. We've got the best striker in the world and the team is incapable of getting him involved more than sporadically. Basically, because there's a serious lack of creativity in midfield. But we're not talking just tactical problems; there's a palpable division between automatic choices and the rest, as well. That leaves half the squad demoralised. And the untapped potential of De la Peña and Pizzi is a crime.'

It gets personal, too. 'Robson's lack of personality is a major problem. Can you imagine Fabio Capello travelling to Barcelona for a photo opportunity on the eve of a crucial game? Robson caved in to the players on tactics for the Madrid match, too. He'd planned to use three centre-backs but was persuaded to reinforce his midfield instead. Nobody is convinced by his signings, either. Baía doesn't look like a five-million-pound 'keeper and he buys Couto for two million then drops him for the first big game of the season. Barcelona have spent nearly thirty million pounds in signings and the best player so far has been Luis Enrique, who cost nothing!'

Naturally, Robson isn't about to get into a blow-by-blow debate with the press about the wisdom of his decisions. But even off the record, his reaction to the critics is measured. 'People complain about tactical changes, but if we've made changes, we've done so with a great deal of thought and planning. I've got a basic idea in my head of how we should play, but you have to be flexible and adjust the team according to the circumstances. We rejigged things against Valencia, it worked very well and we won. We made similar changes in Bilbao, with the three centre-halves, and we lost on two free kicks. We changed the system for the Bernabéu with just one out-and-out attacker because we wanted to reinforce the midfield. But let's be clear about what's happening here. The reason Ronaldo, Giovanni and the rest are moaning about the system is because we've lost at Bilbao and Real Madrid. What about when we were winning games by half a dozen goals with the same tactics; they weren't complaining then, were they?

'If you're going to reinforce the midfield or defence, you can only do that by taking an attacking player out. Against Madrid, we may have fielded one less striker, but we were still getting people forward to support Ronaldo. Sadly, during this last month his form and work-rate have dipped; that's got nothing to do with the system.

'People say something must be wrong when our best player is Luis Enrique who came on a free. But that's not really true, is it? He came as a result of being out of contract, but he wasn't exactly a giveaway. As for this first choice v. subs thing, he proves anybody can get in the team if they deserve to. When I arrived he didn't feature in my thinking as a first choice, but he's made it impossible to leave him out. It's a case of show me what you can do and you'll be in the team.' `

Of course, in terms of transfers, the most controversial was the money spent on Baía. 'You ask me if it's justified paying five million pounds on a 'keeper with one year left on his contract. Well, it's a good point, but that's not to say that after one year he would have come here anyway. As a free agent there was the risk that we'd have been competing for him with three or four clubs. And the club decided we needed a goalkeeper now. By paying that money and giving him a long-term contract, we've secured the goalkeeping position for eight years. So that amount of money over a decade is not a bad financial investment.'

It doesn't get you the best in Europe, though. 'Baía is probably in the top three, but David Seaman is definitely number one.'

MONDAY, 9 DECEMBER

Robson's most wanted finally arrives at Barcelona to stay. Sporting Lisbon's Emmanuel Amunike was the coach's first transfer target on arriving at Camp Nou, but despite parading the Nigerian before the press in June, Barça pulled out of the deal when a medical revealed a troublesome knee. Both the player and Sporting cried foul, and it's since been rumoured that the injury was a Núñez-inspired smokescreen to dissuade Robson. The coach insists it was anything but. 'We told Amunike that if he played regularly until Christmas and didn't break down, we'd go ahead with the deal. That's what has happened.'

The arrival of Nigeria's Olympic match-winner coincides with an exodus of his new teammates. No less than seventeen Barça players head off for international duty today while Robson takes advantage of the enforced lull to fly to England. Before catching his plane, he enthuses about his new signing. 'If you like Figo, you'll love Amunike,' he tells journalists at Barcelona airport (like lookouts in the westerns, these men are permanently on duty, just in case). 'He gives us a whole range of options on the left flank. He's a great crosser of the ball, he scores goals with both feet and he's good in the air.' And he adds rather bewilderingly, 'He's got the strength of an African player and the technique of a European. He always gave me problems at Porto.'

Meanwhile, the Rio-bound Ronaldo continues to reflect on Saturday's disappointment. 'I'm not Superman and I can't win games on my own, I'm just a twenty-year-old footballer who hates losing. I'm sorry, but I do miss chances sometimes.' As the player heads home for a few days off and Brazil's game against Bosnia, his management team arrive in town to negotiate a headhunters-busting deal with Barcelona. Talk is of a double-your-money £50 million get-out clause and a two-year contract extension that would keep him at Barcelona until 2006 ... in return for £2.5 million a year. Sorry, Ronaldo, for that kind of money anything less than Kryptonite-fuelled performances will be considered a fraud. According to one of Ronaldo's managers, Alexandre Martins, even the man of steel needs a coach who can get the best out of him. 'He spent too much time against Madrid dropping deep because he wasn't getting any decent service,' says the budding coach. 'If he has to drop into midfield to pick up the ball then his goalscoring ratio is going to fall. I suppose Robson has got his system, but maybe the players still haven't caught on.'

Today *Sport* publish their annual calendar, aka as the footballer's kiss of death. Of the 1996 pin-ups only Popescu (*Señor* March), Figo (May) and Guardiola (October) are regularly getting a game this season. The rest are either long gone (Kodro, Jordi Cruyff, Bakero) or forgotten (Celades, Prosinecki, Busquets). January's boy, Ronaldo, seems a safe bet to keep getting a game if he wants one, but as for the rest? Well, the arrival of Amunike doesn't bode well for one man. 'We signed Stoichkov in the summer because Emmanuel failed his fitness test,' admits Robson privately. Barcelona have certainly spent generously in the search for a left-flank companion for Sergi: Cuéllar,

Stoichkov and Amunike make for an £8 million investment and an abundance of sweet left feet.

TUESDAY, 10 DECEMBER

At the beginning of the season, Bobby Robson suggested that Ronaldo's price tag and superstar salary wouldn't be a burden. On the contrary, he argued, it would 'keep his mind on the football'. He could hardly have imagined that four months down the line, his star striker would be angling for more money. 'There is a definite connection between his declining form and the recent pay talks,' he says, reacting to news that Barça have signed a draft agreement to double the Brazilian's money. It's an admission that is accompanied by a sigh and a shake of the head. 'It's unethical that a player is renegotiating a contract just four months after joining the club. The kid started the season playing very well, and his people are very clever so they start talking about Manchester United and Arsenal and Milan. I told Joan Gaspart, "Don't panic about that, they're not coming in, they haven't got the money for him." Man Utd won't pay four million pounds for Nadal, so they ain't going to pay twenty million for Ronaldo, so forget about it. But they want to bind the player to the club by raising his get-out clause, so they have to renegotiate his contract. I don't think it's right, but I suppose it's inevitable. There's too much talk about money at this club, and everything gets leaked to the press. I fail to understand how club business becomes public; that's no way to run a club. It's very sad and you risk alienating the fans. The less you let on about money and what people are earning the better.' Especially in a country where a third of the working population survive on £600 a month and short-term contracts (to say nothing of the 20 per cent unemployed).

'The negotiations are handled by the board,' Robson continues, 'so there are transfer stories in the press every day. Draw your own conclusions. If the Nadal thing had been between me and Alex Ferguson, or Bryan Robson, it would have never got into the press; whatever we said would have stayed private. But they don't like it that way here. In England you tend to negotiate club to club and the impresarios play a less important role, though it's starting to change now with all the foreigners. In thirteen years at Ipswich, I never once did a deal with an agent. It was always club to club. Here, because of presidents and agents speaking all the time, there are leaks. It's never one to one, there are always three or four people on each side talking about the deal, and then boom boom!, it's out in the open. One person will always open their mouth.'

WEDNESDAY, 11 DECEMBER

Word has it that Barça's Brazilian duo may be on their way to Coventry. Enric Bañeres, the decidedly sober sports editor of *La Vanguardia*, claims that Ronaldo and Giovanni are the victims not of a daring bid from the Sky Blues, but of a boycott by several of their teammates. 'Irrespective of the system Robson uses, Ronaldo and Giovanni are not getting decent service; it's simply a question of their teammates not wanting to pass to them. In the game against Madrid, there were times when Ronaldo would be screaming for the ball in great positions, yet the player in possession utterly disregarded him. As for Giovanni, half the team ignored him totally. It's no coincidence that Ronaldo's best two goals this season – against Compostela and Valencia – were a result of him dropping deep to win the ball himself. On Saturday, Ronaldo received half the passes Figo did and a third that Sergi did. Where's the logic in that? Even more staggering are Giovanni's stats – he's supposed to be the link between midfield and attack and yet he received one pass from Guardiola in the whole game!' In private, Robson would later confirm the latter, adding with a grimace, 'And Pep gave the ball to Sergi thirteen times.'

Meanwhile on his flight to Brazil, Ronaldo wandered up and down the aisle asking journalists why they thought Pep wouldn't pass to him. According to Bañeres, it could be a simmering case of jealousy. 'It's understandable that the home-grown players are fed up with the arrival of so many foreigners. Good old xenophobia aside, there are sentimental reasons for being upset at the way local players have been pushed aside. And all the hype about Ronaldo makes the other players feel undervalued. But they should ask themselves one question: what did we win in the last two years without a genuine superstar?' Bañeres is not suggesting that Robson is to blame for the in-fighting, but he insists it is his job to find a remedy. 'It's up to the coach to do something about it. How long do you think a player would last at the Chicago Bulls if he refused to give the ball to Michael Jordan?'

Not surprisingly, the Spanish players plead an energetic not guilty. 'The idea is ridiculous,' says Sergi. 'There's no racism in the dressing room, no split and no boycott. It's stupid thinking that just because the foreigners are more famous and get paid more money that they are isolated from the rest of us.' Of course it is.

THURSDAY, 12 DECEMBER

Unlike his incessantly verbose counterparts in Madrid, Josep Lluís Núñez combines periods of verbal hibernation with short bursts of conference-length vitriol. Today he breaks one of his more enigmatic periods to set the record straight on his under-fire coach. It's taken less than four months of the season for 'Robson Under Pressure' stories to hit the front pages and the Real Madrid defeat has sparked a succession of predictable 'Who's next for Camp Nou?' headlines (take your pick from Van Gaal, Clemente, Antic and Heynckes). According to Núñez, the speculation is a media-induced nonsense.

'There is no way we have considered sacking Bobby Robson,' insists the Barça president. 'We've had absolutely no contact with any of the coaches mentioned in the press; it must be their representatives filtering names to try and provoke our interest. And the arrival of Amunike is a declaration of intent; if we were thinking of replacing Robson, do you seriously think we'd have signed his prime target?'

Núñez also suggests that if Sevilla come up with the money for Prosinecki (a cheque for £750,000 bounced yesterday!) there could be more reinforcements. 'We're prepared to buy more players if Robson asks for them.'

Guardiola, the local boy who best embodies Catalan sentiments, also lends his support to Robson. 'I'm not too worried about losing to Real Madrid. What worries me is the hangover, all the soul-searching and a lack of confidence in the team. We're breathing down the neck of the leaders in the league, yet one slight setback and it's a catastrophe. After so long with Cruyff, we've had to change habits, and we were never going to assimilate everything overnight. But what we can't do is change philosophy every five months. That's what really frightens me.'

Not that Robson seems too concerned by the rumours. Even if it meant cutting short a get-to-know-you session in England with granddaughter Isabel, he admits he 'couldn't wait to get back to work', albeit for a training session with five fringe players. 'I've got more important things to think about than newspaper stories,' he smiles.

Robson may be delighted at finally getting his man, but Amunike's arrival gives the press an excuse to make up some fresh nonsense. Take your pick from a) Núñez is preparing his alibi – i.e. when he sacks Robson he can say, 'It's not my fault; I gave him all the players he wanted, even Amunike!', or b) Robson must be getting commission from Portuguese agent Jose Veiga, that's why he's signed Amunike, Baía, Couto, etc.

FRIDAY, 13 DECEMBER
If you're a *sofaball* player, as the natives call their couch potatoes, you could do worse than move to Spain. In the last year, the country's television channels have broadcast 944 football matches (domestic games, internationals, the Premiership, Italian and Dutch Leagues, etc.) at a mind-boggling 2.6 games per day. Of the top ten ranked programmes of '96, six have been football matches. Last week's Real Madrid v. Barça heads the overall rankings ahead of the Atlético v. Barça Cup Final and England v. Spain.

A bank transfer arrives ten minutes before Barcelona's final deadline and Robert Prosinecki (a man who enjoys a lie-down and a packet of fags or two) is finally a *sofaball* – sorry, Sevilla – player. 'Robson was clear about what kind of team he wanted and which players fitted into his scheme, and I obviously wasn't one of them,' says the departing midfielder.

SATURDAY, 14 DECEMBER
Whatever happened to hard news? Spain meet Yugoslavia tonight in a decisive World Cup game and the best Barcelona's café-dwellers can read with their morning *café* and cakes (if you've got a sweet tooth, move here now!) is the Catalan sports press doing their best to imitate *Hello!*.

'Ronaldo In Love,' headlines *Sport* with a photo of our hero in the arms of Susana Werner, Fluminense model, actress and Romario's ex. 'He's An Angel,' boasts *El Mundo Deportivo* with another cover spread of the doting couple. Inside, nineteen-year-old Susana reveals she'd only in fact met Ronaldo once before his present visit to Río, and that was six months ago at a party. The lightning chain of events poses one question (how can you fall in love on the phone?) and answers another (who was Ronaldo wooing by mobile on those away trips?). Mind you, his latest cover belle (we've already had several strip-kiss-and-tell stories) should take Ronaldo's declarations of undying love with a pinch of salt. 'He's got so many girlfriends nothing surprises us now,' says sister Ione of her handsome bro' (we don't think!). 'The only real surprise would be if he stuck to one girl.'

Just in case any of *Sport*'s readers prefer something more demanding with their breakfast, today's paper comes with a free gift ... the latest Barça-garbed Warner Bros doll. We give you Claudio the Cock. No wonder Bobby Robson takes criticism from these guys with a pinch of salt. The publishing industry in Catalonia seems to abide by the motto 'Keep 'em sweet with a Barça treat'. Offers so far this season include the footy-playing Looney Tuners, *La Vanguardia*'s 'Big Barça Album'; three months of glossy photos and a swish presentation box – *El Mundo Deportivo*'s collections of Barça coins (a solid silver variation on Esso's 1970 World Cup vintage) and holographic cards (see Koeman win the European Cup in sparkling 2-D!). Also on the way are *Sport*'s collection of Barça cutlery (naturally, the knives came first) and a Barça CD-ROM.

Spain ignore the snub from the Catalan press to beat the highly fancied Yugoslavs 2-0. Pep Guardiola's performance as creative spring lends support to the view that Robson has got his midfield pivots playing back to front. The Barça coach insists that Gica Popescu is more effective carrying the ball forward. The problem according to everybody else is that the Romanian lacks the finesse of a playmaker and Guardiola's more incisive eye is wasted in a holding role.

The player himself is not getting into that debate, but he does use Spain's performance against Yugoslavia to strike a plea for the country's home-grown talent *per se*. 'It's ridiculous how everybody harps on about the foreign stars and ignores the Spanish players, especially when we've got a national side that are unbeaten in 25 games. We've got this big inferiority complex here, don't ask me why. Today we've played against one of the best sides in Europe, full of the so-called stars of our league [*Mijatovic led seven Spanish-based Yugoslavs into action*], and we've beaten them comfortably. Sergi and Ferrer are the best two full-backs in Europe, Hierro is one of Europe's top players full stop, Luis Enrique is a phenomenon, half of England wants to buy Nadal ... any club in Europe would pay a fortune for Raúl, Alfonso and Kiko. And Mijatovic was marked out of the game by Abelardo, who can't get into the Barça side.'

SUNDAY, 15 DECEMBER

An interview with Robson, recorded for *Transworld Sport* in the build-up to the Real Madrid game, but shown on Canal Plus for the first time yesterday, has done little to improve his deteriorating relationship with the local press. 'It's their team but they want to hurt it,' he barks when asked about the Catalan media. 'I really don't understand it. Barça is a great club and they've got a very, very good team, but the press just want to hurt it.'

The Fourth Estate react with a resounding chorus of 'We call it as we see it'. In fairness, few journalists want to criticise Robson personally, and almost every diatribe is prefaced by 'He is a very nice man, but . . .', yet it's widely held that he should be getting more out of Barça's 'strongest ever squad'. 'Robson had a credibility problem even before the season began,' argues *La Vanguardia*'s José Martí Gómez. 'Off the record, there are members of the board who have insisted that he wasn't up to the job from the very beginning. And everybody thinks that Mourinho is a joke.'

'The carping is just a knee-jerk response to a couple of defeats,' insists Robson. 'After losing an important game, people always start crying. You can't stop it, the only thing you can do is open the umbrella and protect yourself until the weather changes. Everything gets exaggerated in football. I was aware of the magnitude of the club and the repercussions of its victories and the way defeats are magnified, but it is a special environment here. Look at Tottenham; they've just lost three games in a week and Gerry Francis doesn't have to put up with one-tenth of the pressure I do. And Tottenham are a big club, too. A young coach would never have survived this situation; you need to be mentally strong and be clear about your ideas. If I was afraid, things would get worse, but panic is a symptom of stupidity and inexperience. There is absolutely no motive for panic. I honestly believe we're still favourites for the league.'

In private, Robson denies attacking the Catalan press *en masse*. 'I said that I was annoyed by some of the press, I'd be stupid if I said I was at loggerheads with all of them. Journalists have got their responsibilities and I accept that, but they should learn to exercise that responsibility. We're all supposed to be in the same boat, you know – FC Barcelona is the most important thing. But there are so many personal interests and pressure groups floating around, you can't possibly keep everybody happy. I'm constantly being misinterpreted, too. It got so bad I even considered giving up interviews. Only after a lot of thought did I decide it would create more problems than it would solve. There was lots of pressure managing England, but the pressure was more spread out; we only played maybe once a month. If you're playing every three or four days, you're wide open to attack.'

Not least from the *vox populi*. Today, Barcelona's best-selling tabloid, *El Periódico*, boasts a cover featuring Catalan celebrities giving Robson the thumbs-down under the headline 'Nobody Likes This Barcelona Team'. It's not just the famous (tennis ace Sergi Bruguera and writer Manuel Vázquez Montalbán among them) who are unconvinced, though. Twenty-three messages on the readers' page urge the club to get rid of Robson. Worse, there is not one single punter in his corner! 'Robson Go Home For Christmas' is about as polite as it gets.

In between sessions of beach volley for the paparazzi (with his new babe), Ronaldo is keeping in shape with the Flamengo physiotherapist, Milton Petrone. The man who nursed the youngster back to fitness after a knee injury earlier this year is not impressed by Ronaldo's physical condition. 'After his injury and before the Olympic Games, I sent PSV a video and a summary of what kind of exercises Ronaldo should be doing. I don't know if it was passed on to Barcelona, but looking at him, I'd say his training leaves a lot to be desired. A player who is valued at fifty million dollars should have a personalised work programme to keep him in tiptop shape. At Barcelona, he does plenty of work on his speed but not nearly enough on other aspects. And it's no good training just once a day. Ronaldo should be doing an hour and a half of special exercises on his own, as well.'

MONDAY, 16 DECEMBER

Robson rubbishes Petrone's accusations of sub-standard fitness. 'That guy's just out for publicity. Do you know what Mario Zagalo said to him? "Keep your mouth shut! If you want to get in the papers go and hang yourself from a tree." I know we've conceded too many late goals, but it's definitely not because of fitness; a lot of those goals have been down to individual mistakes or a lack of concentration, it hasn't been because we've been tired in the last five or ten minutes. The two goals that lost us the Bilbao game came from free kicks; that's not a question of tiredness, is it? I'm quite happy with the general level of fitness. We've played twenty games; if the players are not fit now they never will be. It's the old Liverpool philosophy – you play twice a week and in between you rest and recover.

President Núñez uses his traditional Christmas lunch with the press to back his coach again. 'We must let Bobby Robson finish the job he came here to do. It would be improper if we were to discuss sacking a man with his track record already. Some people say we've got a great team yet criticise Robson; but without him we wouldn't have built this team in the first place. He's the one who made the decisions about who to buy and attracted great players here. The days of hasty decisions at this club are over. We won't think about making judgements until the end of the season.'

Sport's deputy editor Miguel Rico is unconvinced by the club's public stance. 'Robson blames the press for the negative atmosphere at Barcelona, but if he's searching for the root of the problem he's looking in the wrong direction. Even as Núñez spoke, other board members were hinting that their biggest mistake was contracting Robson in the first place. The club just gets the press to do their dirty work, it's always been like that. In public, it's "Oh look, aren't we being fair", while behind the scenes they're stoking the fires of dissent. And if Robson wants to get tough with someone he should do it with his players. The problem is he got the job precisely because he's not a tough guy. After eight years of Cruyff the board had had enough toughness for a lifetime. Robson must be the only person in town who doesn't realise he's lost control of the dressing room. Barcelona are special in many ways but they do resemble other clubs in one sense; if they're going to win things they need the players to believe in the coach and his system. That's patently not the case at the moment.'

In his efforts to spread goodwill, Núñez also takes time out to back his beseiged youth team co-ordinator, who recently suggested that home-grown players deserve less money. Not surprisingly, the locals didn't agree. 'We all run the same, whether we're Chinese or from the Ivory Coast,' says Guardiola. 'As Catalans, we may love the club more, but when the time comes to negotiate, you do it as a professional.'

Robson's arrival and the president's decision to give him the money to buy a championship-winning side has seen *la cantera* (the home-grown talent) take a back seat. At a club where the presence of Catalan players has a political as well as sporting significance, the press have used the marginal status of De la Peña, Roger, Celades, Oscar *et al* as a convenient stick to beat Robson with. But whatever the rights and wrongs of the us-and-them debate, comparisons with the immediate past are misleading. 'No club has done more for home-grown players,' insists Núñez, 'but the Bosman judgement has seen all teams sign more foreigners, not just Barcelona. At least the players we've signed this season are in the team. That's not happened for at least three years.'

Self-serving or not, Núñez isn't exaggerating. The youngsters' impact last season was an accident born of Johan Cruyff's misguided shopping. If Hagi and Prosinecki hadn't failed miserably, Roger and Celades would never have been thrown in the deep end; if Kodro hadn't left his shooting boots at Real Sociedad, Oscar would never have been top scorer (with ten goals; what does that tell you about last year's team?) And the less said about Jordi Cruyff and his goalkeeping brother-in-law the better. By contrast, when Cruyff's Barça were accumulating the silverware, the home-grown contingent was reduced to Ferrer, Amor and Guardiola.

Pressure Barcelona-style is best illustrated by a comparison. Back in England, it's nothing but praise for Arsene Wenger who's led Arsenal to top spot in the Premiership: current record, 35 points from seventeen games. And Robson's appalling record? Thirty-four points (and twelve more goals) from a game less!

TUESDAY, 17 DECEMBER
Dawn raids have been rife for several weeks as Barcelona's art lovers scale lamp-posts and dangle off ledges to acquire one of the sought-after posters for the Andy Warhol exhibition at the Fundació Miró. Early risers today catch some Pop Art Barça-style. Graffiti on the walls at Camp Nou suggest that Núñez's defence of Robson and his comments about greedy locals misjudged the mood of the fans (or at least the spray-paint-wielding variety). 'Send Núñez to the firing squad.' 'More Catalans and less mercenary scum.' 'Gaspart = Judas.' And then Bobby's stuff. 'Send Robson to the old people's home.' 'Snowflake Robson Out.' And just in case he didn't get the message, 'F***ing Bastard Robson' in impeccable English.

Not to be put off, Robson has strong words of advice for the disgruntled Ferrer. 'My advice is that he does his talking on the pitch and in training. At Manchester United, Alex Ferguson has stopped David Beckham from talking, the same as he did with Ryan Giggs in the past. I can't stop the players from talking to the press here, but they have to be responsible and not answer every single question, especially if it's going to be controversial. What would people think if I suddenly started saying I had an offer from Blackburn or Bayern Munich?'

Robson's new club captain was also eager to censure Ferrer. 'The players should shut up and concentrate on playing football,' says Popescu. 'If he's got an offer from Madrid, he should be more discreet about it. And if he's got a problem he should talk to the directors, not to the press. If a player lets his bank balance rule his heart, he'll negotiate in a very different way to someone who values staying at the club most of all.'

Of course, Popescu doesn't play for money, does he? He's followed his heart from Universidad Craiova through Steau Bucharest to PSV and Tottenham and now Barcelona. And despite the fact that his agent recently flirted with Madrid, he's been a *culé* since he was a kid. Of course he has.

The perceived division between flunkies (Robson, Mourinho, Popescu) and the rest is not the only source of speculation at Camp Nou. If you believe the gossip in the press, the Brazilian clan, the Portuguese clan, the Spanish clan and 'Little Buddah's' home-grown clan form several mutually antagonistic groups in the dressing room. And then there is the maverick Bulgarian. 'Some players are so convinced that Stoichkov is the board's stool-pigeon they've dubbed him "the Squatter"'. Bobby Robson laughs at rumours that his dressing room houses a series of clans. 'There's a big difference between what is being written in the press and the reality,' he argues. 'There might be individuals who would like to be playing more – and with so many quality players you can't keep everyone contented all the time – but the image of disharmony is totally false.'

On a hot wire from Río, Giovanni sends the boss a peculiarly Brazilian vote of confidence. 'We take risks because we only play with two men in midfield,' says the midfielder, who when he's back in Barcelona won't say boo to a goose. 'We've got the best players in the world, but as a unit, we need to improve our tactical preparation. I respect Robson's philosophy but we need to bolster the midfield.'

Closer to home, Vítor Baía begs to differ. 'We should do our talking privately, not through the press. Robson's system will work because we're going to make it work together. How can you question a coach who is so committed and professional? Even when we were winning people were criticising him; they just want to cause problems for the club. We really have to stop shooting ourselves in the foot with stupid arguments.' Not a fortunate choice of words on a day when Spain loses its first two policewomen in the line of duty, gunned down by machinegun-toting bank robbers in Córdoba.

THURSDAY, 19 DECEMBER
Robson locks his men in the dressing room in a further attempt to lay down the law on the media crossfire. The players agree to keep any disagreements to themselves, but urge their coach and the board to practise what they preach. Out in the real world the divisions continue. The morning's training session is marred by a fight between security guards and a dissenting fan with a 'Come Back Soon Johan' banner. Later on, Robson laments the focus on what he sees as isolated protesters. 'It's only two or three people so why give them so much attention? And maybe those two or three people are really stupid? And why are they doing it? And why don't the press ask who is paying them?' No names mentioned, but rumours that a potential presidential candidate (whose employees include the daughter of a former manager) is waging a dirty-tricks campaign are commonplace.

The board issue a battery of statistics to refute claims that Robson is cold-shouldering the home-grown players. Just in case you wondered, Barça's Babes have enjoyed 4,256 minutes of first-team action! 'Ten of the twenty-four players used this season have come through the Barça ranks, compared with seven in Cruyff's first season,' states an accompanying press release. Ferrer, one of the lads born around the corner, is obviously convinced. 'To end all this fuss about Real Madrid, I've spoken to the manager and told him my intention is to stay here and fight for my place in the team.'

Alex Ferguson's policy on keeping his youngsters quiet clearly doesn't extend to Jordi Cruyff. Well aware of the situation at Barcelona, Jordi is busy canvassing for Dad. 'It's impossible for my father to return while the current board remain in charge,' he tells Ràdio Barcelona. 'But if the fans made it known they wanted him back in the future, he'd accept the offer with his eyes closed. The graffiti show that things are going badly, but blaming Robson is the easy way out. He just does what he's told, nothing else.'

FRIDAY, 20 DECEMBER
Ronaldo, *World Soccer*'s brand-new Footballer of the Year, returns to Barcelona in defiant mood. 'Robson needs to change his tactics,

not just for my benefit but for the whole team. His system might have worked at first, but as soon as we've faced stronger sides we've had difficulties. I prefer Zagalo's formation [*Ronaldo scored the only goal as Brazil beat Bosnia on Wednesday, in what was obviously a cracker*]: the team is more compact and I receive the ball more often.' John Toshack, for one, suggests that Ronaldo is a bit wet behind the ears to question his coach. 'When I was an eighteen-year-old at Cardiff, Bobby Robson tried to sign me for Fulham; that gives you some idea of his staying power. He might have a different approach to other managers here, but that doesn't mean he won't be successful. And though his system is diametrically opposed to Cruyff's, Barcelona are now scoring more goals. Just because they've lost two games you can't start doubting Bobby's methods, or talk of crisis.'

SATURDAY, 21 DECEMBER

At his weekly press conference, Robson offers his refusal to answer questions on side issues as a general recipe. 'People at this club should spend more time doing what I am doing today,' he suggests, following this with a long pause and a finger placed firmly over his lips.

Back in his room at the team's hotel, a more relaxed Robson admits that it's been a difficult couple of weeks. 'Whatever happens to me now, I'm fireproof; I've had my career so what can happen to me? In the current situation, a younger, more inexperienced coach would be going bonkers, but I can dismiss the pressure to a large degree . . . [*smiling*] well, at least enough so that I can sleep at night.'

He admits to being perplexed by the local habit of sending barbed messages through the press. 'I can't believe it sometimes. Everybody's at it: the board, the players. It's like the papers today with Ronaldo criticising my tactics again; he's twenty years old for Chrissakes . . . it's diabolical. Your only enemies in football are the people you play against. I've told the players they've got to keep their thoughts to the dressing room and put their own house in order before criticising me. Ronaldo says the system doesn't work, but he doesn't work . . . or he hasn't worked in the last few games. He wasn't complaining when we were winning eight-nil and six-one.'

Even a wily old campaigner like Robson admits he has to employ all his tricks to wind down. 'I always pick the team a day early so I can sleep well. I don't like doubts in my mind the night before a match. Otherwise, I don't find it easy to switch off. You're always thinking about your best team and asking yourself "Am I doing the right thing? How do we play against these guys? Do you play three in midfield or just two?" Your mind's not in turmoil, but you're constantly thinking about the next game. Or if things are going badly, you ask yourself what you're doing wrong. You're constantly trying to anticipate problems before they actually happen. It's a never-ending process.

'My wife often says to me on holiday, "Why don't you forget about it?" And she doesn't even have to say the word football [*laughing again*] ... I'll be sat on a lovely beach and she'll say, "Bobby, why don't you forget about it? We're here together on holiday in Bermuda, it's the beginning of June, and you're distant." The problem is that, as a football manager, what you do in the summer is as important, if not more so, than what you do in the nine months of the season. When I was at Ipswich, I tried to complete all my transfer business before I went on holiday. A lot of managers do it the other way round, but my way at least you've got some chance of switching off and enjoying the summer.'

When he was at PSV and Porto, Robson revelled in the free time the role of coach as opposed to manager gave him. As he has discovered, Barcelona is a different story. 'At Ipswich I was running things from top to bottom, but just coaching at a club like Barcelona is equally time-consuming, because the club is gigantic and the media pressure around you is greater. There is so much you have to do to keep the media industry happy. At a club like Barcelona you can't get away from it. My work-load would be just as heavy as, say, Alex Ferguson's. In England they seem to think that the Continental coach is finished by midday. Well, at a normal club you might get home at four, but not at Barcelona.

'I'm convinced now it's more difficult to coach Barça to the championship than lead a club like Ipswich to the UEFA Cup; because of the pressure and because every game is a big game, wherever you go they are waiting to take your scalp. For most Spanish clubs meeting Real Madrid or Barcelona is like a cup final.' And, of course, your opponents are not the only ones after your scalp. 'The weekend we drew three-all against Atlético Madrid and Real Madrid drew at home to Logroñes, I was a genius and Capello was an idiot; three or four games later, it's the other way round, so how can you take any of it seriously? That's the way football is here.

And the way things change is so arbitrary. A result turns on maybe one decision, and your life changes because of that one result. With so many daily papers they have to write something. Look what's happened to me. We lose to Real Madrid, and the next day seventeen players disappear, so I'm left with five or six players and sitting on a bad result for two weeks. Thirty guys are coming to the ground every day, there are no stories, no players to interview, so what happens? They go searching for stuff to write about. I'm the only one around so I get hung, drawn and quartered. With my experience and my record of success, I still get slaughtered. And even in the middle of the storm I was doing exclusive interviews for these people. I didn't particularly want to do them, but I thought, if that's the advice of the club, I'll do them.'

Robson may be baffled by much of the press criticism, but he's too honest to claim infallibility. 'Maybe I could have handled the captaincy thing better,' he admits. 'In England the manager always chooses his captain. When Bakero left the players perhaps thought we'd revert back to their way, that they'd go back to having a choice. But as I come from a northern football culture I wasn't aware of that. They maybe wanted a home-grown player because of the whole Catalan thing, which is fair enough. And off the record, I made a mistake getting involved in the bonus thing. In England or Holland, the club decides the bonuses, it's "There's your contract on the table and that's the club bonus that goes with it"; there's no negotiating. So when I said, "Take the club's offer and get on and play football," the players were very angry at me. They thought I was taking sides against them, but I didn't realise they had the right to negotiate. I was misquoted anyway. All I said was I hoped the players would accept the club's offer and get on and win the championship, nothing more. But it came out as "Oh, the players are bitching on about the payments all the time." Mind you, it's true.' He laughs. 'This was November and we'd still not sorted out the bonuses. The Spanish need a committee to decide whether to form a committee!'

A meeting with Popescu, Guardiola and Amor, followed by a private chat with Ronaldo to censure his rebellious attitude, means that Robson misses the second half of Real Madrid's televised draw at Valladolid. But what was he doing in a hotel on a Saturday night when he and all his players live within 20 minutes of Camp Nou? 'It's tradition, they've done it for years and they won't change it. I tried to change it in Portugal and drew a blank. The club didn't like

110

it; they said, "Don't take a chance, some of the players are young, they could go out at night, they could eat the wrong food, they might not get to bed by twelve. Here in the hotel you can control them, so do it." In England, we prefer to stay at home with our families on a Friday night. Different culture, different mentality; you couldn't change it even if you wanted to.'

SUNDAY, 22 DECEMBER
Barcelona 1, Celta 0 (Nadal 43)
Camp Nou, 90,000

Nadal (that's Christmas in Catalan) is a name that bespeaks good tidings. Sadly for Robson, the defender's first goal of the season delivers three points and inspires plenty of '*Bon Nadal*' headlines, but it fails to usher in the season of goodwill. In a week that saw Barcelona play host to Naomi, Claudia and Elle as the city joins the Fashion Café empire, whistling was always likely to be on the agenda. Unfortunately, the Camp Nou rendering had more to do with the wolf at the (manager's) door than the catwalk variety.

Ninety thousand fans at Camp Nou greeted their team with muted cheers. Sixty minutes into a lacklustre performance, the cheers had turned to jeers. The second half was an unbroken chorus, albeit selectively directed. Sergi and Luis Enrique have accumulated so much credit the fans will forgive them anything, while Amunike was given the benefit of the doubt on a nondescript debut. Giovanni, Figo and Ronaldo (aka the under-performing superstars) were less fortunate. Four weeks ago, the notion that Ronaldo could be barracked at Camp Nou would have seen you committed. Four goalless games, ten days' holiday, lots of in-your-face courting, and plenty of mo' money hustling later, his every failed dribble was met by a barrage of whistling. As the team trooped off, the fans said it with hankies again (depending on what else they do when they wave them, you get the picture).

If it's any consolation to the beleaguered superstars, it's always been that way at Barcelona. A couple of decent performances and Ronaldo and Co. will be back on their pedestals. As Robson admits, 'In England, it's inconceivable that a side that is beating awkward opposition and about to move within two points of the leaders would suffer the ires of their own public.' This, as he is now well aware, is not England. Barcelona fans are purists. If the football is mundane they'll respond with jeers, whatever the result. At least the fans are still coming. In Terry Venables's final season, things got so bad they simply stayed at home. 'A near-empty hundred-and-twenty-thousand-capacity stadium is one of the most depressing sights you can imagine,' said Gary Lineker shortly after arriving at Camp Nou. 'Sometimes it's so quiet it seems more like a theatre than a football ground. Mind you, if they played the game we do here in England nobody would go.'

Spanish football in the eighties was indeed dull, but what excuse did the current dissenters have? 'I can understand the supporters being disappointed,' says Robson. 'Everybody wants to win three- or four-nil. But after an infernal week, the team showed great spirit under pressure. I'm not trying to separate the players from the fans, but all the tension does make them nervous. Footballers thrive on confidence like everybody else; they need the crowd to get behind them. The phenomenal pressure at this club is something I was aware of, and as I'm the coach I'm always going to be caught in the middle, but in forty-five years in football I've honestly never experienced anything so intense. It's what Johan Cruyff called the *entorno* [*untranslatable, that's why Robson doesn't try; roughly, the negative atmosphere*]. The other day, somebody showed me a football magazine published just after Barça won their fourth consecutive league. The cover said, "Cruyff: Genius or Con-man?" Staggering!'

Robson may be privately critical of Ronaldo, but talking to journalists after today's game, he's nothing but supportive. 'I don't think the fans whistled Ronaldo out of disapproval, it was more a case of frustration. But you have to give him credit for trying the clever stuff on his bad days; the dribbles, the spectacular goals that made people go "Wow!" before. Despite the fact he's hit a dry patch and is not getting the run of the ball, he keeps going for it. And he was tired at the end after coming back from Brazil. He's not been in the same form since his injury, but if he keeps getting into good positions his luck will change, and being so young it was impossible to expect him to maintain that September and October form. I'm not worried about him not scoring – even the best strikers like Gary Lineker go four, five or six games without scoring; the key is to not put too much pressure on them.'

Unhindered by diplomacy, Celta boss Fernando Vázquez hinted that the Barcelona fans were indeed a burden. 'When you're not playing well you need to feel the warmth of the fans.' He also put his finger on the root of Barcelona's continuing defensive problems. 'When Popescu or Guardiola lose the ball they struggle to get back into position. As for Figo . . .' His outraised arms said it all.

Naomi ends her Barcelona night in a hotel suite with Spanish flamenco dancer Joaquin Cortés. As Naomi isn't noted for her linguistic talents and Pal Joey doesn't speak a word of English, whatever did they get up to? (Here's a hint: the inevitably bare-chested dancer claims his ambition is to have 'twenty children by twenty different mothers in twenty different cities'.)

MONDAY, 23 DECEMBER
Arriving in Brazil (again) for Christmas, Ronaldo is scathing about the Camp Nou hecklers. 'I've gone four games without scoring and have been unlucky in front of goal, but I'll soon be back to normal. I won't forget the fans that barracked me, though. They're just a group of frustrated individuals who go to football to let off steam and forget their problems at home.' Within hours, Barcelona's Penyes (the club's official supporters' clubs) issue a hearty protest. 'Ronaldo should do us all a favour and stay in Brazil. He got off lightly for being such a bloody clown, running around with girlfriends instead of concentrating on his game. We pay him a fortune to score goals, so he should shut up and start hitting the net again.'

TUESDAY, 24 DECEMBER
Bryan Robson claims that Middlesbrough have yet to give up on Nadal. 'We've been in touch with Barcelona and put an awful lot of money on their table,' claims the ace negotiator. 'The ball's in their court now.' Their court doesn't appear to be Bobby Robson's. As Manchester United flirted with Nadal, Robson the elder always insisted it was his decision. Now he lets slip that the defender's future is out of his hands. 'Middlesbrough have offered a lot of money for Nadal; I don't know what the club will do.'

The spirit of Christmas hasn't imbued Barcelona's oldest enemies. Josep Lluís Núñez reacts to Johan Cruyff's recent libel claims with a lawsuit of his own. According to Núñez, it's his former coach's declarations which are worthy of the thirteenth-century 'law of perpetual silence' (if you lose, you can never utter your adversary's name in public again). In an interview with Dutch television, Cruyff accused Núñez of being 'a soulless tyrant who deserves to live among wild animals. You never get run over by a gold car, always by a shit wagon [*maybe it loses something in translation*]. He's always been a despot and a dictator and has never been up to the job of Barcelona president. He's an embarrassment.' Say what you mean, Johan.

WEDNESDAY, 25 DECEMBER

In Barcelona, it's a typically sunny *Feliz Navidad*. And what do Barça fans get in their Christmas stockings? The sports papers knocking Bobby Robson, of course (you didn't seriously think these guys took the day off, did you?). *El Mundo Deportivo*, The World of Sport, do justice to their name by dispatching a team to England in hot pursuit of the bobbing and weaving coach. The unfailingly courteous Robson doesn't slam the door in their face, but the staple photos with *el bobby* prove more entertaining than a couple of spartan quotes. Otherwise, Camp Nou incumbents past and present enjoy a sprightly but sedate Christmas in England. After a lightning trip to pay his respects at Portman, Robson settles down in London for Christmas with the family. For Johan Cruyff, it's a seasonal trip to Manchester to spend the holidays with Jordi.

FRIDAY, 27 DECEMBER

Fabio Capello calls time out on his own knockers to express his solidarity with Bobby Robson. 'Maybe Barcelona aren't playing as well as at the beginning of the season. I'm a firm believer in results; how can you criticise a team that is so close to the top, regardless of whether the coach's system is convincing? If I was being selfish, I'd admit that the pressure on Barcelona helps us, but it's still not fair. Their fans should be more patient.' For Capello, it's a case of 'There, but for the grace of God, go I'. 'We've both arrived at new clubs and we're trying to impose our own systems, yet we're at the top of the league. What more can you say? Next year, we'll both have far less problems. We'll speak better Spanish, everybody will understand our systems and everything will be smoother.'

When Ron Atkinson was asked if he was having language problems during his time at Atlético Madrid, he quipped, 'I don't have problems; they're learning English very well.' Bobby Robson, who doesn't have Big Ron's line in one-liners (luckily, perhaps – Atkinson was sacked after two months), admits it's a headache. 'The language barrier definitely makes it more difficult to build relationships; it's not so natural to go up to Spanish players, say, and put your arm round them and talk. It wasn't so much of a problem in Holland because everyone spoke English very well, but it's more difficult here, especially gauging how to treat players as individuals. I still have one-to-ones with the help of José [*Mourinho*] – the other day I had a little chat with Iván and Roger about their disappointment at not playing more. But it's not easy. Still, it's important that players know your motives for doing things so you can't be afraid to try.

'Terry [*Venables*] would've had similar problems here. One of his strengths as a manager is that he gets on so well with his players, but apparently he didn't have the same relationship with his players at Barcelona. I'm sure that was because of the language, not his coaching style. It is difficult, though. If you're talking to an English player you can be more subtle; if you want to criticise him, for example, you can pitch it in a way that comes positively. That's very difficult in another language or through an interpreter. It's probably the single most difficult part of the job when you're managing abroad.'

SATURDAY, 28 DECEMBER

Ronaldo, Giovanni and Amunike return late from international duty and miss the first post-festivities training session. Robson responds by booking the transgressors into a hastily arranged New Year's Eve detention. Despite the fact he'll have to do time himself, the trio's spot of bad timekeeping is a blessing in disguise for Robson.

Ronaldo will now be forced to jettison plans to fly home (for the third time in a month) and spend the New Year in Río, a posture he'd refused to abandon despite energetic pleading. The club had claimed it couldn't stop him spending his time off wherever he chose, which raises one pertinent question – if you're paying a guy a fortune to kick a ball around, why exactly can't you demand they do so without the effects of jet lag? The incident also gifts Robson with an opportunity to demonstrate there's not one rule for the stars and another for the plebs (several of Ronaldo's cheesed-off teammates had remonstrated with journalists for hanging around the carpark awaiting the latecomers instead of concentrating on their training session).

'When the other players have their day off, these three will come in to train,' says Robson. 'I've told Ronaldo that it was a bad idea to fly to Río again, anyway. You can't do that kind of return journey in two days and expect to be in conditions to play. I've said, "Look, I've got England just an hour and a half away but I'm spending New Year's Eve in Barcelona." My place is here, it's my club and my work.' Ronaldo admits he is 'very sad' but chooses not to rock the boat further. 'I would have preferred to spend the New Year with my family, but I have to accept the coach's decision.'

In reality, it's a miracle he arrived at Camp Nou in one piece at all. To start with, the jet-lagged youngster couldn't remember where he'd parked his BMW. Then, after a ten-minute jog around the airport carpark, and in a scene reminiscent of O. J. Simpson's freeway carousel, Ronaldo's sprint to Camp Nou saw him shed all but the suicidal in the pursuing press caravan (either he's colour blind or red lights mean something different in Río). The thirteen kilometres between Barcelona airport and Camp Nou would normally take 20 minutes; Ronaldo did it in nine.

On *el Día de los Inocentes*, Spain's equivalent of April Fool's Day, it's widely reported that Barcelona have contracted Javier Clemente as Robson's successor. They will supposedly meet twice a week to discuss Barça's rivals and tactics, all with an eye to Clemente taking over the reins in the not too distant future. Believable? Unfortunately for Robson, all too believable. Elsewhere, a spokesman for Barcelona Dragons announces that Ronaldo's girlie will be joining them as a cheerleader. Believable? Well, if they'll employ Johan Cruyff's son-in-law as kicker ... Meanwhile, in enemy territory, the loquacious Susana makes the front cover of Madrid's *AS*, sporting a ball and little else. 'I'm a Real Madrid fan,' she says. 'Ronaldo made a big mistake signing for Barça, a mistake he's already regretting.' Believable? Fantasy football time.

MONDAY, 30 DECEMBER

For the second time in a couple of days, what is widely interpreted as bad news for Barcelona is, in reality, a blessing in disguise for Bobby Robson. Giovanni pulls up in training with a strained biceps and is ruled out of Saturday's game at Deportivo. 'I'm still not used to this cold,' he argues (of a sunny winter's day to kill for). Robson, who's privately admitted being tempted to drop his expensive midfielder, is thus presented with a headline-free opportunity to look at the alternatives. 'He's a bit timid sometimes,' he complains. 'There are whole matches when he doesn't get involved at all. And he's been moaning about the system when what he needs to do is look at himself in the mirror.' He denies, however, that a $7million price tag guarantees Giovanni a place in the team, especially when the alternatives, Oscar or De la Peña, are home-grown players. 'It's simply not a consideration. If he's not doing it he'll be out, and he's been close to being out for a while.'

Barcelona's final training session of 1996 ends with Robson's squad huddled in a scrum singing 'Auld Lang Syne' in what one of the players describes as 'macaronic English'. Singing along to songs you don't understand is no big deal Barcelona way. Pop into any club in the city and you'll find punters singing the latest by the Spice Girls or the Fugees (or perennial favourite Joe Cooker). Eavesdrop a little more closely and you'll discover a penchant for gargling what can only be described as indiscriminate noises; the Spanish have even got a word for it – *chapurrear*. Not surprisingly, then, the country's football terraces have never been a source of great songs; 'la, la, la' *ad infinitum* to the tune of 'Yellow Submarine' is about as good as it gets. Even those 'lyrics' aren't original; 'La, la, la' was Spain's only Eurovision Song Contest winner back in 1968. Legend has it that the anodyne ditty by Massiel (a kind of Iberian Sandie Shaw, though she graduated to taking all her clothes off) only outscored Cliff Richard because Franco laced the palms of the German delegation (something to do with Volkswagen plants and tax havens). Still, Spanish football fans may live in a musical time warp (na, na, na; 'Crocodile Rock' is another terrace stalwart) but at least we're spared the droning 'We Are The Champions' of lemmings everywhere else.

President Núñez is singing, too. Robson's praises. 'Even the best coaches need time to make a success of things, that's why I maintain my confidence in Bobby Robson and ask everybody to get behind him. It was the same when Cruyff first came here. In his second year, practically everybody was begging me to sack him [*strangely for Núñez, a fact*] but I stuck by him and we went on to win four leagues in a row.'

TUESDAY, 31 DECEMBER

Men in kit at the year's final training session (Robson, Mourinho, Ronaldo and Amunike) are outnumbered by journalists by ten to one. Six weeks shy of his 64th birthday, Robson participates with the energy of a man half his age. By pairing up with Ronaldo for sprint relays he draws sly smiles from press bystanders (who get out of breath going to the bar), but his zest deserves nothing but admiration. 'I still get a kick out of putting my kit on every day and training with the players,' he says, 'and I still feel young.' Nonetheless, he does make a slight concession to Father Time. 'I love to get involved with the players but I don't play too often because it makes the teams unequal! If there are seventeen players and we need eighteen I might get a game, though.' If Robson's enthusiasm is contagious, Barça are halfway to the title already. 'I have dreams like everybody else. I tell the players that I've still got a burning desire to win things. I tell them, "I want to win the league. Do you?" I've heard the fans go mad if Barcelona win the league. I want to go crazy down the Ramblas with them!'

Salvador Dalí, Joan Miró and Antoni Tàpies are Catalonia's most-fêted artists. Each boasts his own splendid gallery. Nonetheless, Barcelona's second most popular museum in 1996 was ... FC Barcelona's. Only the city's Picasso Museum could boast more visitors than the 729,221 who filed through Camp Nou's doors to contemplate Koeman's boots *et al*. It's been said that football holds an alarmingly central place in the cultural experience of working-class people in Britain. Ditto and then some.

WEDNESDAY, 1 JANUARY 1997

The New Year brings especially good tidings for Vítor Baía in the shape of a baby daughter. The occasional addition to the family aside, footballers in Spain rarely make anything but the sports pages. 'There are no twelve-pints-a-night men here,' says Robson, who, unlike his counterparts back home, doesn't lose sleep over the extracurricular activities of his charges. 'The lifestyle thing is totally different. Popescu couldn't believe it when he went to Tottenham and the players were all out on the razzle every Saturday night. It doesn't happen in other countries; players might have one glass of wine with a meal, but that's as far as it goes. When I was in England and we played away, the players would be boozing on the plane; the Spanish guys will drink bottles of mineral water. It's not imposed, it's just accepted behaviour.'

Robson's main worry today is whether any of his players choked to death last night. He admits to being 'dumbfounded' when at ten to twelve his New Year's Eve host plonked twelve grapes in front of him and barked, 'Swallow!' Spanish tradition dictates not hugging and kissing as the clock strikes twelve, but the gobbling down of a dozen grapes to the midnight chimes. 'I must admit I only got as far as nine,' he giggles. 'It was only afterwards I was told you can peel them and take the pips out first. You could make a fortune in Spain by selling seedless grapes!'

Overall, the Spanish smoke and drink more than anybody in the EU (the Guardia Civil have seized 200,000 unlicensed FC Barcelona products in the last four years; 147,000 were lighters). So why are their footballers so different? 'Well, they're very dedicated professionals and that breeds a positive attitude in terms of lifestyle,' says Robson. 'They realise the importance of fitness, they're educated at their clubs by coaches and directors, and they never get on that wagon.'

'Male socialising as a group doesn't happen,' says Kevin Moran, the former Manchester United defender who spent a season at Sporting Gijón. 'They might have little cliques of players who'll have dinner with their wives or something, but the players never go out as a group.' Robson agrees. 'In England, it's a man's world, you'll go with your mates and sit in the pub for two or three hours; that doesn't happen here. They've more respect for their wives and girlfriends so they'll do it that way. It was the same in Portugal; you never saw the players going out together in the evening. That's not to say that the British player is not more professional in other ways.' No boozy camaraderie in the pub means less bonding, full stop. 'He perhaps thinks about the team more, he's not so hung up on his own thing. He realises it's not about him as an individual, it's about the team.'

Premiership leaders Liverpool lose 1-0 at Chelsea today in their fourth game in ten days. Barcelona's game at Deportivo on Saturday will be their first in a fortnight, a mystifying comparison given that Robson's men play four more league games. The heavy fixture programme over Christmas and New Year in England is supposedly about customer demand. Of course, the fans are not the only ones it keeps out of the pub.

SATURDAY, 4 JANUARY
Deportivo La Coruña 0, Barcelona 1 (Pizzi 89)
Riazor, 35,000

A chilly night in La Coruña sees Robson renew acquaintances with an old rival. For a brief period in the late seventies/early eighties, John Toshack's Swansea threatened to emulate Robson's small-town

Ipswich. The parallels don't end there, either. Both men have managed Sporting Lisbon and both have tasted championship triumph abroad, Toshack's at Real Madrid in 1990. Before the game, the pair chatted amiably as their players warmed up. Robson admits to missing the relationship he had with other managers in England. 'I've got no problems getting on with Portuguese or Spanish coaches, football people are on the same wavelength the world over, but there was more camaraderie in England. Maybe two or three times a week you'd go to a match and you'd spend time after the game with Shankly or Cloughie. I do miss talking to other English managers about football, especially on those scouting missions. If you went to Leicester, say, there was bound to be at least five other First Division managers there and you'd all be put in the directors' box together, that's when you really got to know other managers. On match days, you'd get half an hour to say hello and have a drink, but then you'd have to get back to Ipswich on the coach from Liverpool or wherever. And after a match you didn't want to speak to your rivals anyway, 'cos at least one of you would be cheesed off!'

Tonight it was Toshack's turn to look glum. The game looked destined for a draw until a going-nowhere header from substitute Pizzi took a deflection and sealed the game. 'It's disappointing,' admits the Depor boss. 'Ronaldo had us reeling in the second half, but losing in the last minute to a fluke, especially when you're down to ten men, that really hurts.' Robson can only smile. 'That's football. Pizzi has played five minutes, touched the ball once and scored; Ronaldo's created all sorts of danger for ninety minutes and hasn't had any luck. Mind you, if he plays like that for the next twenty-five games I'll be very happy.'

The Brazilian's steadfast refusal to take a dive produced the game's most amusing sketch. One second-half dribble ended with Ronaldo hacked down in the box. Instead of angling for a penalty, he stumbled on and managed a scuffed shot. Robson's reaction to his youngster's tightrope act was to wave a castigating finger and do a touchline impersonation of Esther Williams. Later on, with the win safely under his belt, Robson admits he didn't want Ronaldo going the way of the rest of Spain. 'It's the same here as in Portugal; all the rolling over after you get fouled, all the diving. You don't get those theatrics in northern European leagues. Spanish players get bumped and immediately go down; an English player gets bumped and he stays on his feet. They're too willing to dive here; if you're really hurt you don't roll over four or five times; refs should know that to start with. One of the things I like about Ronaldo is that he never looks for the foul. Cheating players get the crowd going, too. That puts referees under pressure, so that makes their job difficult.' That doesn't excuse everything, though.

The Spanish Second Division's top scorer, Moisés, reveals he's off to Yorkshire for a trial with Sheffield Wednesday. 'I'm leaving because I can't see any chance in Spain for home-grown strikers,' says the Leganés player. 'Did you see the game at Riazor today? Practically all the players were foreigners [*fifteen of the starting 22*]. What chance have we got in that situation?' As Barça's De la Peña, Oscar and Roger would agree, the situation is especially difficult for creative players. Of the eight forwards/attacking midfielders who started the Depor v. Barça game, only Luis Enrique was Spanish, and he only abandoned his full-back slot to replace the injured Giovanni. Clearly, Moisés (that's Spanish for Moses) had it easier parting the Red Sea than his namesake has getting a game up front for one of the big guys. All that leaves is the wilderness they call the Spanish Second Division.

Moisés's farewell goal at Real Madrid B was witnessed by just 800 spectators; the weekend's top crowd outside the top flight was 7,000. Last season the average attendance was less than 5,000. On one occasion, a journalist at Marbella had the bright idea of counting the crowd; he fingered 78 people! As the former Palace and Spurs midfielder Andy Gray put it before escaping the Costa del Sol for Falkirk (think about it), 'If we were doing badly not even the ref would bother to come!' The door may be ajar post-Bosman, but a woeful standard of football, presidents who offer you time-share apartments in lieu of wages (Marbella again) and empty grounds (using the word grounds loosely), make Spain's nearly-league an unattractive proposition.

'It's not all good out here,' agrees ex-Norwich player Robert Ullathorne (or Ooh! La Thorne as the Spanish insist on calling him), now at Osasuna alongside former Bolton striker Fabian De Freitas. 'We're supposed to be the biggest club in the division and our best crowd so far was thirteen thousand. We've played at some places, Ecija, for example . . . oh my God, it's like playing at a local park. It's like playing at Goole Town again! For a country that's supposed to be so passionate about football the attendances are really low. Even in the top flight, you've got maybe ten or a dozen clubs that get massive crowds and the rest get nothing. There'll be big attendances when Real Madrid or Barcelona are in town but that's about it.'

The weekend's attendances bear out Ullathorne's view. Admittedly, Barcelona were playing away, and snow in the capital produced a season's-low 40,000 crowd at the Bernabéu (an experience so alien to Madrid supporters that Athletic Bilbao's wide players spent much of the game dodging snowballs), but today's nine-game average of 19,567 is an accurate reflection of the pulling power of Spain's middle classes. In the 1995/96 Premier League only five clubs (Bolton, Coventry, QPR, Southampton and Wimbledon) averaged less than 20,000. On current projections, fourteen or fifteen Spanish clubs will fail to do so in 1996/97.

SUNDAY, 5 JANUARY

'The real winner in La Coruña was sat on the bench,' writes Enric Bañeres in *La Vanguardia*. 'Bobby Robson was audacious when it came to making his changes and deployed his players masterfully. While Capello amassed defenders to safeguard a 1-0 lead at home to Bilbao, Robson refused to accept the draw at Riazor.' Elsewhere, headlines such as 'Robson's Courage' and 'Brilliant Barça' are the order of the day. Thirteen days after the 'Celta débâcle', it's Fabio Capello's turn to play the fall guy after another 1-0 win *à la Italiana*.

Robson may be delighted to be the flavour of the new year, but the sea change owes more to the whims of Spain's sports writers than a transformation in his own so-derided approach. Robson sent Stoichkov on for the tiring Amunike with a quarter of an hour to go and kept Pizzi on the bench until the 85th minute. That's surely a case of an obvious change (one left-sided attacker for another) and an arguably tardy one (Depor were down to ten men for the last fifteen minutes). The fact that Pizzi scored the winner was hardly born of the best-laid plans. As the player himself admits, 'When you come on as substitute you struggle to get into the rhythm of things; if you go on three runs you end up gasping for breath. In Riazor fortune smiled on me, but everybody knows you can't prove your worth in so few minutes.'

Pizzi's goal throws up two questions. Why is a player who scored 31 league goals last season and has scored five in just 403 minutes this term being used so sparingly, and why does Robson insist on making his substitutions so late in the day?

Meanwhile, Ronaldo, who has now gone 458 minutes without a

goal, is trying to bury his differences with the gaffer. 'I felt good on Saturday. We were much more compact and that was really positive for me. I was unlucky not to score, but it's just a question of spells. If the team had gone five games without winning then I'd be worried.'

MONDAY, 6 JANUARY

If Robson thought his standing had improved after Saturday's acclaimed performance, he's soon reminded of the precarious nature of his position. John Toshack's announcement that he is leaving Deportivo at the end of the season immediately fuels 'Toshack for Barça' stories (despite a rousing chorus of 'Good Riddance!' as a parting reference). Meanwhile, a cover story in *AS* claims that Barcelona have asked Louis Van Gaal, Raddy Antic and Jupp Heynckes to make no decision about their respective futures before talking to Barcelona. Nothing like hedging your bets, is there?

Atlético Madrid President Jesús Gil reacts furiously to stories linking Antic to Barça. 'Whenever things are going badly at Barcelona, they try and stir things up at other clubs. Who are they to tell my coach what to do? They're a bunch of village idiots; Gaspart is an imbecile and Núñez thinks he is God. I'm warning them, stay away from Antic. If the Ramblas dwarf [*a reference to Núñez's lack of stature*] wants war, he'll have it.'

Despite Bobby Robson's logical lack of complicity, Gil's also got time for an attack on the coach. 'Robson won't make it till the end of the season. Not that any coach worth his salt would join Barcelona in the first place. It's a nest of vipers and Núñez is the one who picks the team.'

Cent x Cent Fútbol is one of three weekly chat shows that dedicate 75 per cent of their screen time to FC Barcelona. On tonight's edition, presenter Pere Escobar cites a continuing source of discontent at Camp Nou – José Mourinho's inability to accept his place in the pecking order. In Portugal, Mourinho had the reputation of playing the bad guy to Robson's good cop. Being surly with the Spanish was obviously not such a good idea. After the victory at Deportivo, Robson's assistant suggested that his critics had better 'shut up'. 'It's an attitude that'll rebound on him the next time the team have a bad day,' says Escobar. 'The problem is that as Robson still has difficulties with the language, the press always go looking for a quote from Mourinho. Unfortunately, he's incapable of saying no.'

WEDNESDAY, 8 JANUARY

Rain stops play so it's in the gym for training. The singularity of the occasion reminds Robson of how lucky he is. 'The top Spanish and Portuguese players have a better touch than their equivalents in England; and that's largely down to the climate what you can do in training. The winter conditions at home mean quite simply, you can't stand around and do the more measured stuff. It's one degree in England at the moment and snowing in most of the country; when it's like that you're forced do a lot of hard running just to keep warm! There's more standing around involved when you're developing technique, so working on ball skills, controlling and passing, small-sided games – all those things go out of the window for three or four months. The kind of surface football is played on has a big effect, too. You could count the number of grass pitches in Barcelona on one hand. And when you're playing on dirt tracks and gravel pitches, you've got to develop a truer touch. If you're brought up on a bad pitch, then the football basics come easy when it comes to grass.'

The skill gap isn't just about favourable weather conditions, though. 'Spanish players spend more time on their technique, be it staying behind to practise free kicks or whatever; they're just that little bit more dedicated. And that's reflected in their performances. Tottenham fans loved Gica Popescu because he was seen as being far classier than your average defender in the Premier League. Over here, they're more used to seeing special players so the perception is different. Here he's run-of-the-mill, in England he stands out.' It's been suggested in some quarters that Gerry Francis let Popescu go because he couldn't handle the rigours of English football. More likely it's because he made the lads look bad. Several times this season, the Romanian has been spotted jogging around the pitch at Camp Nou on his day off.

One man doing less training today is Ronaldo. One of professional football's more curious rituals is how the world's famous find out if they're in the team and when, just as any football-crazy schoolboy would. At half past ten this morning, the missing-in-action Brazilian receives a phone call from his anxious employers. 'If the club hadn't called me this morning, I'd still be sleeping now,' admits Ronaldo later in the day. 'I forgot to look at the blackboard on the way out yesterday and Stoichkov told me training was at half past three. I didn't realise he was joking!' Luckily for Ronaldo (and Stoichkov),

Robson wasn't taking the misdemeanour too seriously. 'It was just a joke,' he tells journalists, gathered for news of reprimands. 'Let's not get dramatic about it.' Now go and write 'Never believe a Bulgarian' 100 times.

Kevin Keegan resigns as Newcastle manager. 'At this stage in my life, I simply don't need the pressures of football management,' he says. 'I've known about it for a couple of days,' admits Bobby Robson. 'I've said to friends in England, "These guys wouldn't last three weeks at Barcelona."'

THURSDAY, 9 JANUARY

Did those friends include Sir John Hall? Less than 24 hours after Keegan's departure, Robson receives Newcastle's headhunting entourage of Freddie Shepherd, Douglas Hall and Freddie Fletcher. Football's most fêted Geordie has often said he'd love to round off his career with one glorious championship-winning campaign at home. How could he possibly say no to that last crack at St James' Park of all places? Especially when Sir John is offering him silly money to join his crusade (£5 million over three years would make Robson the best-paid manager in England). What's more, it's no secret that his wife is homesick. How could the County Durham-born Robson, a Newcastle supporter as a boy for Chrissakes, turn all that down to stay at a club where his everyday existence is a lottery?

The Spanish read Robson's dilemma somewhat differently. *Sport* sum up the Barcelona consensus. 'The football world must have gone crazy if Newcastle seriously think they can lure a coach away from FC Barcelona. Newcastle may be a big club in English terms, but you can't possibly compare their international prestige or potential to Barcelona's.' Robson's employers don't seem to be losing sleep over Geordie sirens, either. 'Bobby's nothing if not a gentleman,' says Joan Gaspart. 'He rang me yesterday and told me that the Newcastle people wanted to come and talk to him. He didn't know whether it was to offer him a job or simply to seek his advice, he just wanted to receive them out of courtesy. We know he intends to stay here for two years and win things with Barcelona.'

Robson himself flatly refuses to get involved in the speculation. 'I'm obviously flattered that Newcastle are interested in me, but if you believe the stories doing the rounds they've offered the job to all kinds of people: Johan Cruyff, Kenny Dalglish, Bobby Robson, John

Toshack, even Jeff King if you like! I'm proud to be managing Barcelona, and that's where my heart is at the moment.' So he wasn't interested in the Newcastle job, then? His response is a less-than-emphatic 'No, I'm not saying that'.

FRIDAY, 10 JANUARY

'The only future I'm interested in is a successful one for FC Barcelona,' Robson tells a press conference that is even more packed than usual. 'Newcastle insisted on coming here to talk to me, even though I'd already given them a negative answer. It's flattering that they wanted me as their manager, and financially their offer is a once-in-a-lifetime opportunity, but I've got a contract with Barcelona, I'm very happy here and I'm still convinced we can win the league.'

Not even the threat of an ignominious *adiós* and a palpable lack of popular support (in one especially pernicious poll, 80 per cent of interviewees say Núñez should persuade Robson to go while 87 per cent insist he can't bury the memory of Johan Cruyff) have tipped the balance in Newcastle's favour. 'Right offer, wrong time,' he insists. 'People shouldn't forget that I had to turn the Barcelona job down on two occasions, as well – I've been dreaming about this job for eighteen years. I know I'm taking a risk and that three bad results could mean the sack, but that's football. I've got no idea what will happen in the future, I had to make a decision based on the situation now. All I'm asking for is a bit of patience. I had a long time to build my reputation at home; six months here is nothing at all compared with twenty years with Ipswich and England.'

Robson had called his players together before training to ensure them he was staying, too. Reactions suggest that his stock is highest among his foreign legion. 'We support him the same as we'd support any coach,' says Guardiola matter-of-factly. Luis Enrique's blessing is equally unadorned. 'It'd be a bad job if you weren't motivated by working at a club like Barcelona.' Amunike is more enthusiastic. 'I'm glad he's staying, a change now wouldn't be good for anybody. Robson's determined to triumph at Barcelona and demonstrate what he's made of.' Fernando Couto is equally supportive. 'He's started to build a new Barça and should finish what he's started. He's doing a grand job.'

Perversely, Robson's decision to stay also attracts praise from his erstwhile press critics. 'Everybody knows we're not big fans of Bobby

Robson,' says *Sport*'s Miguel Rico, 'but turning down the Newcastle offer says a lot in his favour. In the circumstances, his easiest option would have been to walk away, everybody here would have understood that. And maybe he's right, maybe six months isn't enough time to win over the sceptics.'

SATURDAY, 11 JANUARY
Barcelona ranks 56th in a list of Europe's 62 biggest cities for young people's job opportunities and economic aspirations. Try telling that to Ronaldo Luis Nazario de Lima. FC Barcelona issue a statement affirming that Ronaldo's contract won't be revised until the end of the season. It's safe to assume, however, that the youngster won't be going cap in hand to beg the rent. What Jordan is to basketball and Sampras to tennis, Nike want Ronaldo to become to football. A brand-new deal with the sportswear giants guarantees the youngster £1 million per annum for the next decade. And that's before we start talking the imminent launch of a Ronaldo leisurewear line. 'The contract with Nike isn't going to change my life,' he insists. 'Money doesn't make you happy. I know because I was poor and happy before.'

SUNDAY, 12 JANUARY
Real Madrid's goalless draw at Extremadura means Barcelona could recover the leadership tomorrow. 'It's always a bonus when your direct rivals drop points,' says José Mourinho. 'Madrid have been struggling recently and if we beat Hércules it'll tilt the psychological balance.' Given that tomorrow's second-to-bottom visitors are on a par with Extremadura for incompetence, he might have added, 'And the psychological effects of losing would be unthinkable'.

MONDAY, 13 JANUARY
Barcelona 2, Hércules 3 (Luis Enrique 8, Ronaldo 15)
Camp Nou, 75,000

It has been said before, but football's capacity to surprise is one of the reasons it holds such a tenacious grasp on the world's sporting affections. Hércules (a footballing misnomer if ever there was one) arrived at Camp Nou on the back of nine defeats in nine away games and a history that records not a single victory at Camp Nou in eighteen attempts. Early goals from Luis Enrique and Ronaldo amidst some genuinely flowing football soon had the crowd

127

celebrating with chants of '*Campeones! Campeones! Olé! Olé! Olé!*'
Down on the bench, Bobby Robson looked suitably contented. Hall's
gold? Who needs it?

Even when Hércules brought the scores level before the break, no
one could have envisaged anything but a swift return to the natural
order of things. At half-time, José Mourinho accused the team of
'defending like babies'. For once, it was understatement on the part
of Robson's brash assistant. Vítor Baía, or 'Barça's best-paid player'
as he's increasingly and mockingly referred to, was directly to blame
for the first goal and might have done better for the next two;
Laurent Blanc is an elegant footballer but as slow on the turn as an
oil tanker; and Albert Ferrer is a shadow of the tenacious defender
he was before suffering a succession of injuries. Unfortunately, the
defence's childish behaviour proved contagious. Ronaldo broke his
scoring duck and promptly disappeared as if his night's work was
done. De la Peña, making a rare start for the suspended Popescu, was
as anonymous in the last hour as he was inspirational in the first 30
minutes, and new boy Amunike looked like an actor who had
wandered on to the wrong set.

Robson's sedentary attempts to stall Barça's free fall into
impotency ('he's frightened to get off the bench because he knows the
crowd will barrack him,' quipped one journalist) proved fruitless.
With his Brylcreem sheen and gravelled forehead, Hristo Stoichkov
resembles a footballer from bygone ages; the ones who looked
middle-aged in their teens. Unfortunately, he's starting to play like
one. 'He only comes on to take the free kicks and corners,' sneered
another wag as Robson pitched the Bulgarian into the action. 'We
can't play like we did in the second half,' moaned the hardly guiltless
Ronaldo. 'I didn't see the ball, at all, we were just pumping it
forward in the air all the time.'

During the game the crowd were stunned into silence by the
bizarre nature of proceedings, but for the second successive home
game Camp Nou bade their team goodnight with ear-splitting
whistles and a choreographed hankie wave. As he trudged to the
dressing room, Robson must have reflected on the wisdom of turning
down an Indian summer in more familiar surroundings. Thirty
minutes after the final whistle, he appears before the press sporting
a disconcerting smile. The Wizard of Oz had grounds for sneering at
doom and chuckling at catastrophe; what's Bobby's excuse? Scared
shitless, perhaps? His first words are for the dissenting masses,

several hundred of whom are by now laying siege to the presidential suite chanting '*Núñez No, Cruyff Sí*'. 'I think the crowd were fantastic. I can understand their attitude in the last five minutes, they've every right to be disappointed, but that doesn't hurt me personally. I'm just sad that we've lost a great opportunity to go top.

'The game changed as a result of poor defending,' he continues, before pointing an accusing finger at journalists. 'Tonight demonstrated how important Popescu is to us; a player you have spent all season criticising.'

Earlier in the day, Espanyol's Pepé Carcelen had become Barcelona's first managerial casualty of the season. Robson will hope the neighbourly line in crisis management isn't catching. Or will he? Even before tonight's setback, Robson was clearly still torn between the Med and the Tyne. 'I must admit I've had sleepless nights over this, it's an unbelievably difficult situation. I've waited all these years to get here, yet Newcastle is tailor-made for me. They're in a wonderful position both on and off the field; with a little touch here and there, they still might win something. But look what I've got here, I'm at one of the world's greatest clubs and I've got the best squad in Spain. It would be difficult to give that up, too. Plus, I'm under contract. I've spent millions backing my judgement, so my president isn't happy about my talks with Newcastle.'

Newspaper reports in Spain suggest that, in fact, it's Robson who's unhappy with his president. Núñez has yet to pronounce the words 'Don't go' since the Newcastle story broke and Robson is allegedly demanding a public guarantee that he'll see out his two-year contract. Pure fiction according to Robson. 'Núñez has been brilliant and stayed out of the way. I'm not sure it would have happened anywhere else; other guys would have demanded to know what's happening.'

Robson was not the only person whose dreams were shattered by Hércules. One of the side effects of a Monday night fixture is that potential pools winners have to endure an agonising 24-hour wait for the fifteenth and final result. Why the pools company can't simply add another Second Division game from Sunday is anybody's guess. There must have been plenty of punters with the champagne on ice tonight as they waited for Barça to register the inevitable home win. In the end, a 76-year-old widow from Cádiz raked in £1.5 million thanks to the upstarts from Alicante. 'I haven't got a clue about football,' she admits, 'I just do the same combination every week.'

Confirming that strike-it-rich Brits don't enjoy a monopoly on eccentricity, she plans to splash out on a new allotment on which to rear her hens.

TUESDAY, 14 JANUARY

Bobby Robson takes just one day off a week. It's a day he uses to recharge batteries and to contemplate life beyond 22 men kicking a bag of wind around. The front pages of today's sports press are hardly conducive to a pleasant day off: 'Disaster', 'Debacle', 'Embarrassing', 'Humiliation'. Four headlines and a funeral, perchance? Admittedly, it's not 'In the Name of Allah Go', but there's no mistaking the sentiments. 'Real Madrid made fools of themselves at Extremadura,' argues *Sport*'s José María Casanovas, 'but Barcelona were a disaster against Hércules. However you look at it, the team is shipwrecked: Baía is not living up to his advance publicity, the defence is as vulnerable as ever, and the team falls apart in midfield. Some players are automatic choices however badly they play, yet Robson won't give a chance to at least half a dozen others. Even Ronaldo is beginning to look overrated.'

If Robson needed cheering up after browsing the papers, he'd have done well to avoid the midday news. A 'Barcelona in Crisis' report on Canal Plus wraps up with a spiteful conclusion: 'The only thing that can save this squad is if Robson joins Newcastle.' On the line from Manchester, Jordi Cruyff admits being 'dismayed' at Barça's latest setback, though he can't resist a dig. 'At least if Robson joins Newcastle it means we'll win the Premiership.'

A six o'clock press conference at St James' Park dashes Jordi's hopes. The new man in charge at Newcastle is Man United's nemesis, Kenny Dalglish. As the news breaks, Robson, holding court at a sports bar in Sitges, reacts with a resounding I-told-you-so. 'I've always insisted that my commitment is to Barcelona. If the club change their mind about me they change their mind – I'm not going to speculate about what might happen in the months ahead, but my ambition is to stay here until 1998 and win things. Half the stuff in the press is absolute nonsense; I'm sick of so many lies. I've seen reports saying I sent Núñez a fax demanding a vote of confidence. I haven't asked for guarantees, I've felt Núñez was a hundred per cent behind me from the day I arrived. Another paper said he met with John Hall and said I could go in return for four million pounds compensation; utter nonsense! Newcastle would have been prepared to pay compensation but it's absolute rubbish to suggest they discussed that with Barcelona.

'Maybe I'm crazy, or maybe I'm just an old-school manager, but whatever happens from now on – even if Barcelona sack me tomorrow – I'll always be proud that I didn't walk out on a contract. Maybe there's no place for loyalty in football nowadays, but it still means a lot to me. That's what my father taught me, and I've got his blood in my veins.' Not that Dad would be doing handstands. 'He would turn in his grave if he found out I'd turned down an offer from Newcastle,' admits Robson. 'I'll tell you one thing, Kenny Dalglish is a very lucky boy, but at least I can sleep soundly now.

'Monday was just one of those shock results, there's no reason to panic. Every great side has its upsets during a long season – look at Ajax, Manchester United and Juventus recently. I've always been the type of person who believes you can learn from defeats. I'm a fighter and I feel more motivated than ever. I've laid my prestige on the line by staying here, but I came to Barcelona with the aim of ending my career on a high note and that's still my heartfelt desire, that's why I've refused to move.'

Honourable sentiments, but those in the know question the wisdom of Robson's decision. Nobody at Barcelona is closer to the coach than José Miguel Terés. The club's press officer has all but abandoned his day job to mind Robson, both as translator and confidant. 'I really think *el mister* should have gone to Newcastle,' says Terés, his voice betraying a genuine affection for Robson. 'He'd have been at home there and they were offering him the kind of stability he'll never get at Barcelona. After yesterday's result his future here is hanging on a thread; the press are not going to forgive him another couple of results like that. But you have to admire his bravery, Bobby really is an honourable man.'

Emilio Pérez de Rozas, sports editor of the Barcelona tabloid *El Periódico*, could never be described as Robson's friend, yet he shares Terés's misgivings. 'If I was Robson, I'd be really worried by Núñez's indifference. Look at the fuss he made when clubs came calling for Nadal, Ferrer, Popescu and Celades. Yet when Newcastle come after Robson he responds with absolute silence. It's that silence that led Robson to demand a meeting and a show of support after the Hércules game. He might have got a yes, but it was so half-hearted he must suspect Núñez is losing faith in him. And you've got to understand the president's position. He's seen more white hankies in the last month than in eight years with Johan Cruyff. When Cruyff was in charge, Núñez was out of the firing line; given that Robson is such a yes man, he's got no one to hide behind now. From now on, if it rains the only one who gets wet is Núñez. He's spent a fortune trying to wipe out the memory of Cruyff, but nobody is convinced by the team. He is obsessed with presiding over the club's centenary in 1999. Failure on the pitch could mean failure in the elections. He simply can't allow Robson to continue if he doesn't get things right immediately.'

WEDNESDAY, 15 JANUARY

Never accuse Spanish journalists of underactive imaginations. It's been suggested in several quarters that the players threw Monday's game in an attempt to jettison their coach. Admittedly, the theory would explain an otherwise inexplicable capitulation, but footballers are no more prone to cutting off a nose to spite a face than the next man – remember, Barça would have gone top if they'd won. After an extensive clear-the-air session with Robson, the players are in magnanimous mood. 'We were to blame, not Bobby Robson,' insists Pep Guardiola, a player who generally has his finger on the dressing-room pulse. 'We're the ones who lost our concentration after we went two goals ahead. Everybody is looking for guilty parties here, but it's the players who have to make the difference when things go wrong during a game.' Or as Nadal put it, 'These things can happen to a defence full of internationals or to a bunch of friends in a village team – it was just one of those days.'

Not all the rumours flying around town are disguised as kamikaze footballers. It's also been suggested that Núñez has sought the counsel of several senior players, effectively asking them to sentence Robson. Apparently, their response was a resounding 'We play football, it's your job to hire and fire'. But what if they'd said 'Way to go, Joe'? Less than a week before sacking Terry Venables, Núñez claimed, 'If Terry goes it's over my dead body.' He justified his subsequent change of heart by claiming, 'The players begged me to sack him.'

Sixty-seven per cent of interviewees in another poll say yes, Bobby Robson is incapable of leading Barcelona to the championship, while 53 per cent predict he'll be sacked before the end of the season. Fifty-four per cent answer *Sí, señor* to the most pertinent question of all, 'Do you think Núñez's support for Robson will harm him at the presidential elections?' This on a day when Johan Cruyff's *consigliari*, Jaime Roures, attends a meeting of a new Núñez opposition group.

'It's at times like this that I look back at my Ipswich days and remember how contented I was,' admits Robson. 'I had a nice lifestyle in a laid-back part of the world at a club run by very blue-blood people. It was the perfect grounding for a young coach. But make no mistake, when you're at a club like Ipswich, your · dreams are about managing your country or coaching the Barcelonas.' Not that he saw the Ipswich job as a mere stepping stone. 'The club got bigger and better every year so I was very satisfied. I was never looking for another job, only towards the end, perhaps. I did have offers – I could have gone to Everton or Arsenal, and Don Revie rang me himself asking me to take over at Leeds when he took the England job in 1974. I turned that down and, of course, Brian Clough went there. I'm sure Cloughie's never forgiven me!'

THURSDAY, 16 JANUARY
Gica Popescu throws a lifeline to his under-pressure boss. 'A lot of people have criticised Bobby Robson, but he had the courage to stay, that means he's confident we can win the league. He's obviously not happy about all the criticism, but the players have told him we're on his side. And he seems very calm, I haven't noticed any change in him.' If the press have their way, he soon will have. 'Lots of talk about courage and honouring contracts,' claims the editorial in Marca, 'and it turns out Robson only stayed because Barcelona wouldn't let him out of his contract. He's told English journalists that if Núñez hadn't stopped him, he would have paid for his own ticket back to England.'

FRIDAY, 17 JANUARY
Robson tells journalists at his weekly press conference to ignore the 'I'd buy my own ticket' quote in *The Times*. 'They made up their own story using some loose quotes of mine and then put my name to it,' he contends. 'I don't understand why you guys want to harp on about it. I'm not interested in pursuing the Newcastle thing, they've got a manager now and I've pledged my future to Barcelona.' He also shakes his head at the suggestion that Cruyff's former assistant, Carles Rexach, is standing by to step into his shoes. 'I'm

not under the impression that my job is in danger. I rejected a five-year contract to stay here, after all. A week ago people were saying it was Barcelona's best start in thirty-three years. The season isn't over because of one result.'

With notable pathos in his voice, Robson draws proceedings to a close with a question of his own. 'Why is everybody against me?' After an uneasy silence, one journalist throws the question back at him. 'If everything's as positive as you say it is, why do you think everybody is against you?' Robson responds with a wry smile. 'I've often asked myself that question, but you're the only people that can answer that. All I know is that it's been like that from my very first day here. I accepted the challenge of coaching Barcelona knowing full well the pressure that surrounds the club, but I don't know what I've done to deserve such harsh criticism. But anybody who thinks I'm going to throw in the towel doesn't know me. I've never been one to surrender and I'm not about to start now. You people do your job, and you do it very well, but I won't let anybody put a blemish on my career. My job is to run the club and get results, that's what I'm going to do.'

SATURDAY, 18 JANUARY

It may be awards galore for Ronaldo beyond Spain's frontiers – on Monday he'll pick up FIFA's 1996 World Player award – but there's a growing domestic lobby who insist he's not even top dog on his own patch. Real Madrid's win at Atlético Madrid tonight can be summed up in two words, Raúl González. Madrid may have invested thousands of millions of pesetas in the likes of Suker, Mijatovic and Seedorf, but it's the nineteen-year-old local boy who steals all the plaudits. 'He's a fabulous player, as important to Madrid as Ronaldo is to us,' says Bobby Robson after watching Raúl's one-man show tonight. Real President Lorenzo Sanz may be biased, but he champions an increasingly popular cause. 'If he was called Raulinho instead of Raúl he'd be rated the best player in the world.' Even the prone-to-understatement Fabio Capello admits Raúl is 'one of the best two or three players in Europe'.

Raúl provides Madrid with an ingredient many reckon Robson's side is lacking. True grit. 'The problem with Barcelona's gifted players – Baía, Blanc, Guardiola, Figo and even Ronaldo – is that they only live up to their reputations when things are going well,' says *La Vanguardia*'s Enric Bañeres. 'Barça are a side with talent to spare, but there's a definite lack of character.' Character is what Raúl boasts in abundance. 'Fear is not part of his vocabulary,' says Juan Pedro Martínez, editor of the weekly magazine *Don Balón*. 'Julen Guerrero [*Athletic Bilbao's boy wonder*] has been part of the Spanish squad since 1993, yet he still blushes when Javier Clemente talks to him. Raúl, on the other hand, needed just one call-up to make his mark. You should have seen him in the team's hotel; it was "Raúl's here, I'm in charge now". He's only played three times, but a Spanish team without him is already unthinkable.'

SUNDAY, 19 JANUARY
Betis 2, Barcelona 4 (Luis Enrique 48, 61, 78, Ronaldo 73)
Benito Villamarín, 45,000

There's never a dull moment when what Bobby Robson describes as Dr Jekyll and Mr Barcelona are in town. Six days after surrendering a two-goal cushion against a team of no-hopers, Barça give highly fancied Betis a two-goal start before deciding 'Señor Heidi' deserves an airing.

According to an old baseball proverb, 'Some days, you win. Some days, you lose. And some days it rains'. When a Betis team schooled in year-long heatwaves defied torrential rain to score twice on the half-hour, Robson must have feared a defeat and a soaking (not to mention the sack). On a pitch so heavy it made running alone a monumental effort, and against a side whose motto for the night was clearly 'If it's wet and it moves, kick it', a comeback seemed out of the question. Luckily, Luis Enrique took it upon himself to conduct a one-man siege of the Betis goal. His appetite for the battle (he was on the end of half the fouls committed by Betis) was rewarded three minutes into overtime. With 21 saner participants contemplating warm dressing rooms and dry towels, he headed home the goal that changed the match.

After the break, Luis Enrique completed his hat trick and shamed the previously dormant Ronaldo into action. When the Brazilian gathered a loose ball 30 yards from goal, the Betis defence backed off, inviting him to have a go with one of those trademark dribbles. He glanced up, took in the retreating troops and unleashed a thunderbolt instead. Prats in the Betis goal belied his name and took evasive action. Despite that breathtaking strike, Bobby Robson reserved his respects for a more deserving cause. 'Louise Enrique's [*he gets about so much he not only multiplies, but has time for a sex change, as well*] first goal was the key, he's set a wonderful example for the rest of the team.'

Michael Robinson was in Seville commentating on the game for Canal Plus. 'By battling back from two-nil down against a side as tough as Betis, especially on a swamp of a pitch, Barcelona have shown what a great team they can be when they put their mind to it. Robson's side have answered some questions tonight. Have they got guts? Yes. Do their heads drop when the going gets tough? No. Do they know how to play football? Yes. Can they score goals? Yes.' That still leaves one unanswered question. Which Barça will we see next week?

MONDAY, 20 JANUARY
In Lisbon to collect his FIFA World Player award, Ronaldo strikes a modest pose. 'I still don't consider myself the world's best player; to be the world's best you should be a complete footballer and I've still got an awful lot to learn.' Alan Shearer, in third place behind Ronaldo and George Weah, sees little room for improvement. 'Ronaldo can do it all: he shoots with both feet, he's good in the air, and he knows how to play for the team [*why did we know he'd say that?*]. Only God knows what he can achieve in the next four or five years.'

As Ronaldo basked in the international limelight, the Spanish AFE (PFA) was meeting to debate their league's massive influx of foreigners. 'Clubs have blindly used their TV money to sign any player with a Brazilian or Yugoslav surname while Spanish players are going to waste,' complains Sergi. 'It's not about the Raúls and Luis Enriques, it's about the players who work their butts off in training for nothing. It's about youngsters like Celades, Roger, Oscar and De la Peña. Look at Abelardo, he's a fixture for Spain but doesn't get a look in at Barcelona.'

'It makes you wonder why we still talk about the Spanish League,' says Luis Enrique. 'In most teams there are only three or four Spaniards.' So why, pray, didn't they go abroad? 'It's mainly because our own league is such a good place to be. Just about every Spanish player, and not just the guys at the top, have had offers to go abroad. I've had the chance to go, but why should I when I'm so happy here?' Bobby Robson agrees, at least as far as going to England is concerned.

'They might be afraid of our climate and language, but basically the Spanish love Spain and its lifestyle so they don't want to leave. It's also because the British don't know much about Spanish footballers; they're more familiar with, say, Dutch, Italian or German football. Fernando Hierro is one of the top two or three defenders in Europe, but I'm sure nobody's heard of him back home. The Spanish domestic market is expensive, too. So I think it's a lack of knowledge and economics. That's why English players don't come to Spain, because they price themselves out of the market here. If a club in either country has to invest really big money, it's a case of better the devil you know.'

The AFE agrees to approach the government and sports authorities with two bottom-line proposals: a reduction in the number of non-EU players and an extension to the period South Americans need to work in Spain before becoming eligible for dual nationality (currently two years). Big names like Pizzi, Mauro Silva and Fernando Redondo have already slipped through that loophole and no longer occupy foreigners' spots; 86 of the 200 South Americans playing in Spain could follow their example next season.

The December/January transfer window has seen Spanish clubs invest another £32 million in reinforcements, all but the small change on foreigners. Tales of ordinary madness were rife. Seven months after packing his bags for East London, Florin Raducioiu returns to the sunnier climes of Barcelona and RCD Espanyol. The Romanian's back-and-forth saga begs at least two questions. Why did West Ham invest £2.5 million in such a dunce in the first place, and why on earth did Espanyol want him back? Gerardo González Movilla, president of the players' union, is dismayed by the ill-informed extravagance of Spanish clubs. 'I still think the Bosman ruling was a good thing, but our clubs have responded recklessly, not like Italian clubs who have applied the ruling with common sense. Look at Milan, they've studied the market and signed the best out-of-contract players like Reiziger and Davids for nothing. Our clubs should take note instead of throwing money away on senseless signings.'

TUESDAY, 21 JANUARY

Barcelona draw 2-2 with Standard Liege in another 'put pesetas into an agent's pocket' televised friendly. Fittingly it took place in Almería, Spanish spaghetti western territory and the location for *A Fistful of Dollars*, etc. If nothing else, the game gives Robson a chance to look at his underemployed youngsters. 'De la Peña has a great future in the game, he's shown tonight there's a place for him at Barcelona,' says the coach. The youngster himself isn't convinced. 'How can he say he rates me if he's only seem me in kickabouts or for the odd twenty-five minutes? And when I do get a chance I struggle because of a lack of match practice.'

Despite the impressive win at Betis, Barcelona's Fourth Estate (make that fifth column) continue to hound Robson with religious zeal. The editorial in today's *Sport* is a par-for-the-course tirade. 'Robson asks why everybody's against him? How about the following for starters: a) He does a good impersonation of a flunky who's more interested in defending Núñez and the board than his own players; b) He's signed too many foreigners and marginalised the young players; c) When Barça went 2-0 behind at Betis, he didn't once get off the bench to reorganise, yet he was quick enough to jump up and celebrate when Ronaldo scored the fourth goal. He's a friendly guy, but he lacks charisma and is incapable of motivating his players. He does everything he can to please but can't quite pull it off; when the team loses it's because of his system and when they win it's because of the individuals. People will soon be blaming him because it hasn't stopped raining since he arrived.'

THURSDAY, 23 JANUARY
Like most domestic cup competitions outside of England, the Spanish Cup lacks any real tradition. In fact, the big clubs take it about as seriously as Manchester United take the League Cup. In normal circumstances, Barça's opening tie would give Robson a chance to air De la Peña and Co. So much for that plan. The first two names out of the bag today are Barcelona and . . . Real Madrid. 'We could have done without the game at this stage,' moans Fabio Capello, 'this should be the Cup Final.' If the big guys didn't get a bye to the LAST SIXTEEN it wouldn't happen, Fabio.

FRIDAY, 24 JANUARY
Hristo Stoichkov's triumphant return home is proving anything but. A plague of minor injuries has limited his contribution to seven games so far and, now that he's fit again, Robson drops him from the squad to face Rayo Vallecano on Sunday. José Mourinho insists Stoichkov is out for 'tactical reasons', though word has it that it's a disciplinary measure (according to newspaper reports, Stoichkov

reacted to the news that he would be on the bench against Betis by faking an injury to avoid the long trip to Seville).

SATURDAY, 25 JANUARY

Bobby Robson denies that Stoichkov has been a naughty boy. 'There's no problem with Stoichkov. It's the same old story, the players that aren't in the team always make the news. I've got twenty-four players, so for every eleven that play thirteen are out and there's a story waiting to be written.' He also denies a vendetta against the 'Little Buddah Brigade'. 'People say I don't like De la Peña, Celades, Oscar and Roger – that's rubbish, I just can't find the moment to give them a game. I'd love to give them more of a chance, but I can only play eleven. They've got to be brave and accept that the guys who are playing are doing well. We've been lucky with injuries this season, and that's been bad luck for the kids.'

Robson's decision to drop Giovanni and Stoichkov undermines at least one persistent accusation. 'It's about time somebody started to stick up for Robson,' says Lluís Canut, presenter of the weekly football show *L'Ultima Jugada*. 'If he was really the president's flunky he wouldn't have dropped Giovanni and Stoichkov, Núñez's two personal signings. And Robson's attitude to Nadal shows his undogmatic nature; when Couto arrived everybody said Nadal wouldn't get a game, but he's been in splendid form and Robson has made him an ever-present at the expense of his own signing.'

SUNDAY, 26 JANUARY

Barcelona 6, Rayo Vallecano 0 (Luis Enrique 13, Sergi 19, Contreras o.g. 21, Ronaldo 34, 46 pen, Pizzi 75)
Camp Nou, 85,000

Four days before taking on the Real thing, Robson's men entertain Madrid's poor relations. Vallecas is a battered neighbourhood in the south of the capital with a team and stadium to match (if the Spanish FA were as demanding about its club's facilities as the Football League, Rayo would have been relegated to local league status years ago). Rayo's capitulation to Barcelona on a weekend that sees Premiership sides embarrassed by Wrexham, Bradford, Woking and Hednesford is a reminder that English football still boasts unprecedented strength in depth.

Struggling Premiership teams boast players – Ravanelli, Juninho, Le Tissier, McAllister, etc. – who would grace far better sides. In comparison, there's not a single player at mid-table Rayo who would get near the Barça bench, let alone make the team. Rayo's lack of talent is summed up by their bungling centre-forward, Klimowicz, an Argentinian who sounds like a Pole and looks like a giraffe. Rayo's last six visits to Camp Nou have produced six defeats and a goal difference of 25-2, so today's win by a tennis score is simply no big deal. Both Bobby Robson and Terry Venables before him have struggled to come to terms with demands at a club where trouncing the little guys is the very least the fans expect. In the same way that the nineties-model Rangers are expected to dismiss the likes of Motherwell and Raith without breaking sweat, Barça are in the same league as Rayo and Logroñes in name alone. The fans might accept once-a-century flukes *à la* Hércules, but they will never embrace a side that consistently performs in less than the manor born, irrespective of standing in the league table.

Before the game, the Barça players posed for photos with Miguel Indurain, the five-times winner of the Tour de France; Camp Nou's ovation for the retiring legend surpassed the response to Ronaldo's parading of his FIFA World Player trophy. The Brazilian responded with a brace of goals and post-match musings on his demanding audience (whistles at 6-0, would you believe?). 'I really don't know what the fans want here. If you ask me they've been spoilt. With six goals on the scoreboard they should be celebrating, not moaning.'

Barcelona may have scored 60 goals at lightning speed, but Bobby Robson still can't make it through a press conference without questions about *el sistema*. 'Things couldn't be better,' he insists. 'We're halfway through the season, we've got twenty goals and seven points more than this time last year, yet people are still complaining about the system. It's about time everybody forgot about Johan Cruyff [*the uncited ghost in the house*].' Rayo trainer Paquito, for one, would happily settle for Robson's kind of problems. 'Can you play badly and win six-nil?' he paraphrases headline-seeking journalists. 'Where do I sign?'

MONDAY, 27 JANUARY

There's only one topic on the Camp Nou agenda today. Why are the fans so bloody disgruntled? 'Where's the logic in barracking players for making one bad pass, especially when the team is winning five-nil?' asks Albert Ferrer. 'We might not be playing the best football ever seen at Camp Nou but we're playing reasonably well and scoring lots of goals. The crowd's attitude is really strange.'

Gica Popescu is equally baffled by the crowd's demeanour. 'I've talked about it with the rest of the players and we really don't understand what's going on. We'd love to feel that the crowd is on our side. If scoring five goals by half-time is not entertaining then I don't know what is. The fans are too on edge, they should try and relax more. Personally, I suspect the bad feeling is not aimed at the players. I don't know who they're getting at, but I don't think it's the team.'

A poll carried out before yesterday's game suggests Popescu may be right. While 87 per cent of *socis* still reckon Barça will win the league, 52 per cent say the club should call early presidential elections and 73 per cent insist the club should have let Robson go to Newcastle. (Ronaldo may be *O Rei* in the wider world, but the locals rate him a distant second as Barça's best player so far, the winner, Luis Enrique, polling a massive 68 per cent to his 17 per cent.)

'The fans expect far more given the players Robson has at his disposal,' says Santi Nolla, editor of *El Mundo Deportivo*. 'It's not that six-nil is to be sniffed at, the problem is expectations were too high; the fans expect goals, entertainment and convincing performances.' Effectively, Robson is suffering from the great expectations syndrome. If Big Brother in the press, aided and abetted by Capello, Toshack, Clemente *et al*, have delivered an unwavering message – Barça have the best squad in Spain, perhaps Europe – it's not surprising the punters are proving so demanding. In private, Robson admits his squad is, in fact, overvalued. 'Some of the players, maybe even a lot of them, are overrated. Of course, we have a good squad but we're not perfectly balanced, we're missing a natural wide player for a start. Figo tries and can succeed sometimes, but he's not a guy whose distribution you'd want to rely on. Cuéllar is a bit of a dribbler, too, though he's lost pace because of injury so he struggles to get away from people.'

Also in *El Mundo Deportivo*, it's claimed that Núñez had the veteran Croatian coach, Tomislav Ivic, locked up in a Barcelona hotel room watching Barça videos during Newcastle's flirtation with Robson, just in case. 'I took over from Ivic at Porto and I know what I did and what he left me,' says Robson, whose competitive edge is never more apparent than when comparing his own merits with those of other coaches. 'I won the Portuguese League, he didn't. I won the Cup, he didn't. I changed the character of the team, he didn't. My side played attacking football, his didn't.'

TUESDAY, 28 JANUARY

It's Robson's turn to take the Barça supporters to task, albeit diplomatically. 'The fans have every right to express themselves and if that means whistling, so be it. But if you'd asked them before Sunday's game to settle for five-nil at half-time they'd have agreed with their eyes shut. With a game against Real Madrid around the corner it was logical that the players eased off in the second half. People say we won six-nil against Rayo but there was no football. I wish somebody could explain to me how you can win six-nil without playing any football. It's an insult to the players, too. Are you telling me Ronaldo didn't play any football? Or Sergi? Or Luis Enrique? The problem is that if the media keep repeating "no football, no football, no system" a thousand times, people will end up believing it.'

THURSDAY, 30 JANUARY

Barcelona 3, Real Madrid 2 (Ronaldo 13, Nadal 70, Giovanni 78)
Spanish Cup fourth round, first leg. Camp Nou, 95,000

The last time Barcelona beat Real Madrid 3-2, Bobby Robson was on hand to monitor the boy Lineker's form. 'I was at Camp Nou in 1987 when Gary scored a hat trick,' he recalls. 'At one stage the giant scoreboards read BARÇA 3 (LINEKER 3) REAL MADRID 0. I'll never forget that.' As England manager, Robson was delighted with that *Gary Gol* hat trick almost ten years ago to the day, but as he admits, sitting in the dugout tonight as his side ended Madrid's nine-month unbeaten run was 'a higher plane altogether'. 'Tonight we've sent a message to the rest of Spain,' he purrs. 'Real Madrid can be beaten.'

Predictably, Barcelona's warring factions set aside their differences to focus on the common enemy. In a gesture full of symbolism, an army of volunteers placed paper hankies on all 110,000 of Camp Nou's seats – not white, but a mosaic-to-make in the colours of Barça and Catalonia. If that seems like unusual behaviour, even more bizarre is the visitors' annual ritual of responding to a cacophony of abuse (once likened to the noise a jumbo jet makes as it revs up before taking off) with a friendly wave from the centre circle: '*Hijos de puta! Hijos de puta!*' – sons of a whore; Spain may be lapsed Catholic, but it's still the ultimate insult here. Smile and wave. Smile and wave. Definitely a case of white rag to a Catalan bull. Barça's entrance was met by palpably democratic cheers as the man on the PA ran through the line-up. Doubtless, the first and last time this season the names of, say, Popescu and Amunike will be greeted with the enthusiasm normally reserved for Ronaldo and Luis Enrique.

For once, Spain's big game lived up to its billing. Especially when brute force in the shape of Roberto Carlos took centre stage. The Brazilian with football's most strapping thighs is no slave to reality. From 35 yards, 30 yards, 25 yards; a succession of impossible dead-ball attempts saw him getting closer and closer and Vítor Baía looking more and more nervous. Baía breathed a sigh of relief when Fernando Hierro whispered, 'My turn, Roberto' and stepped up to take a second-half effort from just outside the box. Fabio Capello is a man who rations his smiles with the caution of an undertaker; the semblance of a grin as Hierro set his sights urged caution. Even Ronald Koeman, for so long the dead-ball scourge of visiting 'keepers, never hit a ball as hard.

'Barcelona were dead after that goal,' claimed Capello. Dead maybe, but not buried. Within three minutes, Nadal had equalised from another free kick (ironically, it was Hierro's deflection that sent a tame effort in one direction as Illgner went flapping in the other). The last 20 minutes were a red-and-blue whirlwind, and not just the hankies. For once it wasn't Pizzi but Giovanni, another latecomer, who sealed victory.

The wonderful football was complemented by some exemplary behaviour. Ronaldo joking with Roberto Carlos in any given lull and then exchanging shirts at the final whistle (sacrilege), or Hierro giving Ferrer a bear hug as they trooped off at half-time, were examples of what sporting rivalry should be about. And when an avalanche of objects from the stands prevented Roberto Carlos from taking a second-half corner, Guardiola's response was to dash over, take the Brazilian by the hand and usher him to the corner flag himself. It was an admirable display of solidarity in a fixture not noted for such sentiments.

Bobby Robson could have done with a helping hand himself as he dodged the post-match snipers. He may have seen off the enemy, but his press conference degenerates into a barely disguised slanging match as he responds to hostile volleys with his own questions about the dubious press agenda. 'Last night I switched on the television on the eve of our most important game of the season, and I've watched a whole programme talking about Stoichkov and Couto. Not about the guys who would be playing but the absentees. I've only been in the game forty-five years, so I don't understand these things.'

Then it gets really personal. Questions about his system and the team's potential/performances are met with barely disguised contempt. 'Are you a football critic or a football lover?' Robson berates one journalist. 'Did you pay to get in?' he asks another. 'You've just seen a fantastic game and you're splitting hairs. Anybody who can sit here and criticise after seeing such a high-quality game doesn't respect football. If you don't like what you've seen you should go shopping instead!'

Things degenerate still further when the formal press conference ends. Half a dozen journalists approach the stage in placatory mood only to be greeted by an angry monologue. 'What do you people know? You know nothing, absolutely nothing. I've been in the game forty-five years; who are you, what do you know about football?' Robson's admonishments come with a gradual increase in volume. When he starts banging his fists on the table, as well, a worried-looking press officer grabs his arm and leads him backstage.

Robson's fiery attitude with the press is in stark contrast to his undemonstrative behaviour during the game. It took Capello barely three minutes to jump to his feet and berate his players from the touchline. Typically, there he stayed for the rest of the game. In contrast, Robson's touchline excursions could be measured in seconds.

In his defence, the language is still proving an obstacle. It's a dilemma familiar to most expats; you become so obsessed with the new lingo you start sounding like an Indian in your own native tongue – 'How you mean, no football?' And with the slightest mistranslation, the most innocuous question can become seriously barbed. On the subject of tonight's coloured handkerchiefs, Robson's translator omits the word coloured. The coach thus responds tetchily to what he thinks is another question about hankie-waving protesters. Then the question 'Given what you're teaching the players can Barça get even better?' is translated as 'Given what you're teaching the players should the team be playing better?' From such subtle differences are rants produced. Tomorrow, the big Barça chief will breakfast over 'Robson confronts journalists' headlines.

Robson could take lessons from Capello in dealing with the press. The language helps (Spanish is relatively easy for an Italian), but it's also about avoiding booby traps. The Italian's cagey manoeuvring at his press conference is in stark contrast to Robson's laboured attempts to make himself understood. Of course, having such a disagreeable aide doesn't help. 'I wanted to win to shut up you vultures' was Mourinho's post-match attempt to win friends (in the press) and influence people (who write editorials).

Robson may feel like it's me against the world at the moment, but there's help on the horizon. The self-styled 'Group for Respect, Justice and Support for Bobby Robson' announce the launch of a campaign in support of the under-pressure coach. And in the corridors of power, Josep Lluís Núñez has met with Catalan President Jordi Pujol to express his dismay at the way Televisió de Catalunya are treating FC Barcelona. An insider at Camp Nou admits that Núñez is unhappy at the local station's 'aggressive campaign to ridicule him for electoral purposes'. And guess who's stuck in the middle? 'The powerful anti-Núñez lobby at Televisió de Catalunya [*where key personnel are close confidants of Johan Cruyff*] are carrying out systematic attacks on Robson in an attempt to get at Núñez.'

Not surprisingly, Robson is chuffed about the launch of his support group. 'I'm happy that there are people in this city with a sense of fair play. Many of the press critics are dishonest, and I'm not talking about a one-off response to one game, I'm talking about the attitude of the last six months. There are some things I simply don't understand. If we were seven points behind the leaders maybe I could, but that's not the case.'

Tickets for Camp Nou may have been like gold dust, but elsewhere the Cup of cheers attracts anything but. Games at Atlético Madrid, Racing Santander, Lleida and Rayo Vallecano – all against top-flight opposition – attract crowds of, respectively, 15,000, 13,000, 3,500 and 1,000.

SUNDAY, 2 FEBRUARY
Barcelona 2, Oviedo 2 (Pizzi 60, Ronaldo 67)
Camp Nou, 70,000

After Barça's exhibition against Real Madrid, Bobby Robson advised the non-believers to go shopping rather than darken his door in critical mood again. As Camp Nou waved a collective goodbye to two more points against modest opposition, it seems many *culés* had taken at least half his advice. Unfortunately, white hankies are still the first item on Barcelona's shopping lists.

The Spanish say only a fool trips over the same stone twice. Three weeks after surrendering a two-goal lead against Hércules, Robson's men were doing their best impersonation of Pedro Picapiedra (Fred Flintstone) again. It took just 25 minutes for the fans to shed the goodwill generated by the Madrid victory and break into whistles. A Pizzi-inspired outbreak of football produced a two-goal lead after the break but that still wasn't enough to secure the points. When Ronaldo made it 2-0 in the 67th minute, Robson's gesture towards the fans was to take off Giovanni and Figo (woeful the both) to give De la Peña and Oscar rare outings. 'Little Buddah's' churlish response was to miss a pair of sitters that would have made the game collapse-proof even for Barça.

'I'm very angry,' moans a weary-looking Robson afterwards. 'We're two goals up and cruising and then we grant Oli the freedom of their penalty area.' Oli, Oviedo's centre-forward, did the rest; a case of another fine mess Robson's defence has got him into.

While the coach is bickering with the press over yesterday's 'dishonest' accusations, José Mourinho is doing his level best to improve things. Asked why the team had played so badly, the Portuguese charmer spits, 'You'd better ask the players that question.' Pizzi is first to take the test. 'I know everybody's saying it, but we're far too inconsistent and not performing as a team; that's the reality.'

Why Robson refuses to give the Hispano-Argentinian a decent run in the side is threatening to become a question of state. Pizzi – lest we forget, Europe's top scorer in 1995/96 and a stalwart in Spain's attack – has started just two league games this season. His seven goals in nineteen appearances have come at an enviable rate of one every 71 minutes. Today's cameo was typical of his speed out of the blocks. Entering the fray in the 57th minute, he hit the post with his first touch before opening the scoring three minutes later. Seven minutes after that, his defence-splitting pass sent Ronaldo clear for 2-0.

Robson argues that a side that has scored 62 goals in 22 league games has few problems up front. His critics claim that a team that's conceded 28 goals at the other end needs all the help it can get. 'I don't know what Pizzi has to do to get a run of games,' says *Sport*'s Miguel Rico. 'No player at the club works harder in training, he never complains about his situation, and when he comes on as sub he invariably scores. He works hard defensively and creates room for

Ronaldo. His teammates love him and rivals are frightened of him. At the end of the day, we're talking about a partnership between Europe's top scorer and the best player in the world.'

For the first time this season, a boardroom heavyweight goes on the record to express his dissent. 'What's happened today is unforgivable,' says Vice-President Nicolau Casaus, theoretically one of the pro-Robson faction and a man whose diplomacy is legendary (Franco had him banged up on Death Row, so he's hardly prone to exaggerate the importance of a football match). 'The side has committed monumental errors again; we are defrauding the fans.'

On a day characterised by overtime drama, things could have been worse. Sevilla manage to lose at home to Real Sociedad despite boasting a 2-0 lead with six minutes to go, a defeat that sees José Antonio Camacho become the eighth top-flight manager to lose his job in half a season, a reflection of outrageous levels of expectation in the so-called 'League of the Stars' (50,000 fans attended Sevilla's presentation day). Clubs like Zaragoza, Valencia and Sevilla reacted to the influx of television money and the Bosman ruling by investing massively in foreigners with little or no consultation with their coaches. With the long-running battle for TV rights finally settled, clubs are panic-stricken at the thought of losing their place on the gravy train. When the players don't perform nobody cares that the coach had little or nothing to do with putting the squad together in the first place (in Sevilla's case, at a cost of £20 million). At least Bobby Robson has still got a job.

MONDAY, 3 FEBRUARY

Robson's support group pick a rotten day to launch their 'Back a Bobby' campaign, and not just because Barcelona's newshounds are more interested in events at a local film festival (the premiere of an X-rated home movie, allegedly starring a teenage Norma Jean). Amidst speculation about a) the true identity of the blushing starlet, b) the reasons behind another Barça collapse, and c) Robson's future or lack of one, the manifesto in today's papers would have been relegated to no-man's-land even without its moralising tone. 'Long before the season began, a coach of recognised international prestige was condemned by the very same sports writers who remained silent during two years of arrogant failures. There isn't a coach in the world who can triumph if he isn't allowed to get on with his job. Morally, as Catalans and *culés*, we cannot tolerate this cowardly aggression against an exquisitely mannered and experienced professional.'

Cynics might suggest that the group's self-appointed spokesman, a local doctor called Jordi Gil, suffers not only from a bad case of get-a-life, but from serious problems with his timing. Two weeks after three Spanish medical volunteers were murdered in Rwanda, one of them a Catalan nurse, crusades in favour of downtrodden football managers are, at the very least, in bad taste (especially when donations are solicited). Unfortunately, dedication to less news-worthy causes doesn't convert perfect nobodies into prime-time telly fodder before you can say Isabel Gemio (Spain's Oprah wannabe).

Despite the protestations of Dr Gil and his Good Samaritans, it's not just the Catalan media who have their sights set on Robson. This is Brazil coach Mario Zagalo. 'Barcelona have a squad of extraordinary players, but the whole is disappointingly less than the sum of the parts. Robson's team lack tactical organisation and rely on individual inspiration. The midfield is uncompetitive and there's far too much space between lines; any decent counter-attacking side would have a field day against Barça.'

Today's training session kicked off late after another group therapy session. 'Sunday's slip-up was the players' fault,' says Guardiola, 'there's no point hiding behind the coach. I can understand the fans being uneasy – I haven't seen a *pañolada* [hankie protest] in eight years, now there's been three in the last four league games – but the only way to regain their confidence is to start winning games.'

As befits a man whose name translates as William Love, Guillermo Amor suggests less in-fighting would be a good idea. 'One day the press are putting us on a pedestal, the next you'd think we were neighbourhood buffoons, and Nicolau Casaus's declarations only help to create divisions.' However, Barça's longest-serving player reserves his real ire for José Mourinho, a man who counts his friends in the dressing room on one finger. After the win at Deportivo, Robson's assistant boasted, 'We gave our best performance of the season.' His 'Didn't we do well?' attitude on that occasion was in stark contrast to his 'You'd better ask the players what went wrong' response after the Oviedo game. 'We were the ones who let victory slip through our hands,' admits Amor, 'but does that mean people would have said we'd done it on our own if we'd won? I don't think so. When we win everybody wants to climb on board; and I include

Mourinho among the guilty parties. The difficult thing is to get behind the players when things are going wrong.'

For his part, Nicolau Casaus is not for turning. 'I was angry on Sunday, but I haven't changed my point of view. It's chaos on the pitch at times; there's a lack of chemistry between the star players and a lack of character. In all my years at the club, I've never felt so helpless. I know what I'd do if I could speak English, I'd go and talk to Robson. His track record speaks for itself and he seems like a sensible guy, but the language barrier is obviously a big problem. It makes it very difficult for him to communicate with the players.' Ominously for Robson, Josep Lluís Núñez (who doesn't speak a word of English, so imagine how he communicates with Bobby) comes out of hibernation to censor Casaus for his 'untimely outburst' but does nothing to appease his coach. 'Doesn't everybody say we've got the best squad around? Well, it's time they proved it.'

TUESDAY, 4 FEBRUARY

In a notable break from pre-match routine, Núñez invites Robson and his players for lunch. With more than a nod towards the club's fratricidal wars, he tells the gathering, 'If you beat Real Madrid it will be your triumph, but if you lose it will be my failure.' It's not the first time Núñez has tried to distract the press with gallant gestures on the eve of a big game. Famously, he broke down and cried during a television interview three days before the 1992 European Cup Final (on that occasion Barça won and he conveniently forgot that his tearful confession had included plans to resign, come what may).

Fresh from the hastily arranged lunch, José Miguel Terés suggests the pressure on Robson is beginning to take its toll. 'Bobby really feels he's getting an unfair ride,' says Barcelona's PR guru, 'but he shouldn't get drawn into a game of give-and-take with the press. If he rises to the bait there's only going to be one winner. These guys have got twenty-five pages a day to fill, after all. Not that it's easy for him. Some of the papers – *La Vanguardia* and *El Mundo Deportivo* – are fairly measured in their criticism, but the Madrid papers obviously take delight in slagging off Barça. And *Sport*, the paper that most influences public opinion in Barcelona, has gone way over the top. I've told Bobby to ignore the snipers but he's understandably worried; he's particularly afraid all this will filter back and damage his reputation in England. Like he says, after all the hard work he's put into his career he doesn't need negative press at this stage. The other day he showed me a *Daily Telegraph* article quoting a report in *Marca* that described him and Toshack as backward coaches. Now you've got a story in today's *El Periódico* suggesting Barça have reached an agreement with Louis Van Gaal for next year. Joan Gaspart denied it at lunch, but then again what's he going to say? Still, if Barça lose the next couple of games it may not get that far.'

Given the avalanche of negative press, it's not surprising Robson's sense of humour has taken a vacation. Celebrating the beginning of Spain's carnival fortnight, *La Vanguardia*'s colour supplement takes a dozen celebrities and dresses them up for the party. Pride of place on the cover goes to Robson as Lady Di (or Lady Dee, as the Spanish would have it) in ballgown and face-pack. Robson is furious. 'Nobody likes to see themselves dressed up like that, it's offensive and disagreeable, especially with all that's going on. I feel like I'm facing a firing squad every time I walk into a press conference. Sometimes I think the only thing that's missing is one of those "Wanted" posters.' And that other most-wanted? 'I know Van Gaal from my days in Holland and he's a grand person. But when I was coach of PSV and he was in charge of Ajax, I was the one who won the league.'

THURSDAY, 6 FEBRUARY
Real Madrid 1, Barcelona 1 (Roberto Carlos o.g. 68)
Spanish Cup fourth round, second leg. Santiago Bernabéu, 100,000

If taking on an adrenalin-charged Madrid after a week dominated by family tantrums was not bad enough, tonight Barça had to contend with another of their *bêtes noires*. Fittingly, dressed in black. History demonstrates that Spanish referees don't get to be internationals by being discreet. Manuel Díaz Vega is the role model for aspiring Spanish referees; he is haughty, controversial and FAMOUS. Unfortunately, he also has a major downer on FC Barcelona. This is the man who once said 'Johan Cruyff is only fit to coach kids', the bank manager by day who accused Barça's most celebrated coach of 'pissing in his pants every time he visits the Bernabéu'. Twice, Cruyff visited Madrid with Díaz Vega on hand as maître d'; twice Barça lost by the odd goal courtesy of a dubious penalty. Away from the big game itself, the man known as Darth Vader got his kicks by flashing red cards at Cruyff like they were going out of fashion. Shortly after the Dutchman was sacked, the clearly distraught referee was reduced to picking on the hapless Jordi instead (Cruyff Jr's sole sending off as a professional). Real Madrid's high-diving tandem, Mijatovic and Suker, have spent the last few days insisting that 'Díaz Vega is a great ref'. Well, they would, wouldn't they?

The first 30 minutes resembled a game of pass-the-parcel. Your ball. No, really, you take it. After that initial madness, Barcelona fended off Madrid's sterile territorial superiority with surprising ease. The inclusion of Pizzi (yes!) was another pleasant surprise. For once he didn't score, but his hustling presence allowed Ronaldo to produce his dribbling party tricks, if not his best finishing. In the second half, the youngster twice hit the post when it was easier to score. 'Even Núñez would have put those chances away,' he joked later. Plagued by his Bernabéu scoring jinx, the youngster turned to Roberto Carlos for help. Ronaldo's low cross posed no threat until his buddy collapsed in the box as if hit by a sniper – in went the ball off his thigh and Barça were ahead.

Desperate times call for desperate measures. With ten minutes left on the clock and Madrid going nowhere, Díaz Vega emerged from his shell to prove that Cruyff isn't the only Barça coach he's got it in for. Suker threw himself at Blanc with a theatrical dive. Guess what? Penalty. Fortunately for Robson, even a twelve-man Madrid proved incapable of producing a winner. Clearly his side are only for collapsing against the little guys. 'Every time we've suffered a setback we've bounced back with a good result,' says the delighted coach. 'I've been involved in lots of big games in my career, but this was one of the really big ones for me. If we'd lost tonight there was no second chance, and a defeat against Madrid has special repercussions.'

Despite Real's below-par performance, 100,000 acolytes rallied behind their team for the full 90 minutes (among them Julio Iglesias, who before crooning his way to exile in Florida was an apprentice goalkeeper at the club). Comparisons are inevitable. 'How do you think Camp Nou would have reacted if we'd played like Madrid did in the second half?' asks Guardiola. 'They only had one shot at goal and that was a non-existent penalty. I'd like to think our supporters will get behind us now.' He isn't taking bets, though. 'I'm not sure they will; it's not happened after other important victories.'

A report on Dutch television insists that Louis Van Gaal has agreed to join Barcelona in June. 'I've signed for one of Europe's biggest clubs,' admits the coach, who is busy learning Spanish, 'but I'm saying nothing until they announce it officially. However, I'm proud my name's being linked with a team like Barcelona.' What is the Dutch word for hint?

FRIDAY, 7 FEBRUARY
'Bravo, Barça.' 'El Madrid KO.' For once the headlines are good, though the quarterfinal draw allows Robson little time to savour them. There were plenty of plum fixtures as Javier Clemente put his hand in the bag: a winter break in Las Palmas, the chance to renew acquaintances with Rayo Vallecano, ties against lowly Racing Santander or Celta. So what does Bobby get? Last year's Cup Final hangmen, Atlético Madrid, that's what. 'It's the worst possible draw,' he winces. 'We're entering a two-game-a-week period again and I would have preferred weaker opposition so I could rest some of my key players. Ronaldo and Giovanni won't be available for the first game, either; Brazil are playing on the same day.'

SUNDAY, 9 FEBRUARY
Espanyol 2, Barcelona 0
Sarrià, 30,000

If local derbies provide the ideal occasion for the little guy to raise his game, Espanyol and FC Barcelona have clearly not been reading their scripts. The Budgies' previous victory against their bullying neighbours was back in 1987. Maybe they had been waiting for a suitable occasion. After 74 years at Sarrià, Espanyol's financial plight means they are being forced to sell their site in prime-time Barcelona and become tenants at the Olympic Stadium (their new ground, perchance?). A Barça win on their last visit to Sarrià would have been rubbing salt into the wounds.

Robson's men carried into the game the confidence that comes from beating Real Madrid; what they carried out was their collective tail, positioned squarely between their legs. As Robson admits, eight points behind the still-unbeaten leaders is 'a very big difference' in the context of the Spanish League.

A carnival weekend had begun with a university-style boat race. For Robson, the early morning exchange in the port evoked fond memories of his days by the Thames at Craven Cottage; a mere 20

Pep Guardiola – the piggy-bank.

Gica Popescu – '*El Mister* doesn't need any advice from anybody.'

Luis 'No Fear' Enrique.

Vitor Baia – the man who has everything.

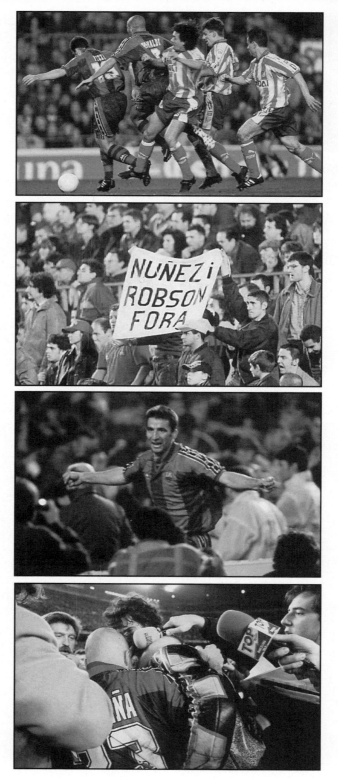

Barça 5 Athlético 4 – 'from disaster to triumph in ninety minutes.'

Robson shakes hands with Barça president, Josep Lluis Núñez. 'He doesn't speak a single word of English and that suits him.'

Robson with vice-president, Joan 'Pinocchio' Gaspart.

On yer bike! Robson in Holland.

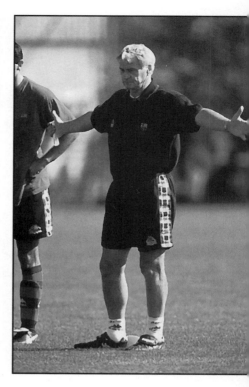

Bobby measures another whopper from th
press.

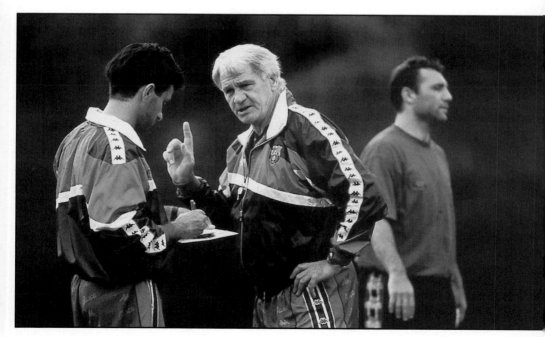

With friends like these … Robson with number two, José Mourinho, and Hristo Stoichkov.

Real Madrid *v* Barcelona – the mother of all footballing rumbles.

Ronaldo.

The world's best footballer and
'Little Buddha'.

Bobby Robson. On the sidelines but in the the firing-line.

Cup Winners Cup triumph. Gica lifts the cup while Bobby contemplates yet another medal.

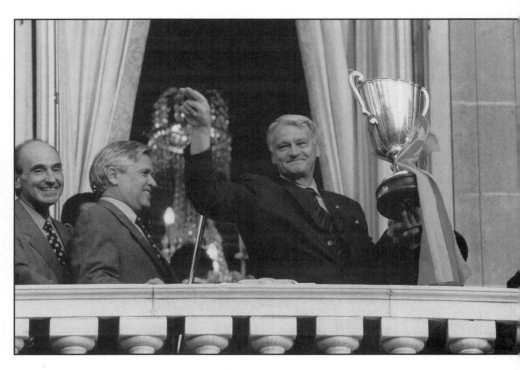

'This one's for you. Sou collonuts!'

minutes into the day's more serious proceedings and he must have felt like abandoning ship. By that time, the league's youngest referee, Megía Dávila, had gifted Espanyol the lead with a questionable (being generous) penalty and sent Figo back to the dressing room.

Former Barcelona coach Helenio Herrera once said that ten men were more effective than eleven. Barça don't seem to have read that script, either. Espanyol soaked up their timid attempts at a comeback and settled things when West Ham reject Raducioiu converted his second penalty of the night. Not until the 74th minute did Ronaldo manage Barça's first shot on target (a back pass dressed up as a goal attempt at that).

'I really didn't expect to lose this game,' admitted a shell-shocked Robson, 'but after the penalty and Figo's sending off we were always going to struggle. I try to avoid criticising referees, but that first penalty was as dubious as Madrid's on Thursday. This time it changed the course of the game.' If he was aware that Señor Dávila hails from Madrid, Robson preferred to keep it to himself (the Catalan press would compensate and then some).

As the match drew to a close, and with Robson burying his hands in his face on the bench, solace arrived from an unexpected source. 'We love you Bobby, we do! Please stay Bobby, please do!' chanted the fans. Unfortunately, it was Espanyol's *ultras* taking his name in vain. Meanwhile the 200 or so Barça fans cordoned off by as many policemen must have wished they'd left their carnival gear at home.

'The players gave blood in Madrid,' says Robson, 'and after just twenty-four hours to recover they've had to face almost a whole game with ten men. Anybody who's played football at this level will tell you that kind of physical handicap is decisive.'

Predictably, Luis Enrique was the last man to give up. Unfortunately, he took his fighting spirit off the field, too. Asked to apologise for decking a jeering Espanyol fan on his way out of the ground, he later described his victim as 'retarded'. Also in character, Ronaldo didn't hang around to muse on his personal disappearing act at Sarrià. Barcelona's carnival is too tame for him; he's off to Río de Janeiro and the real thing.

And then there was one. John Toshack calls time on a disappointing eighteen months in La Coruña with his much-touted side fifteen points adrift of Madrid. He's the ninth managerial casualty of the season. 'Any club in the English Fourth Division gives you more backing than Deportivo. When we were in the middle of a long unbeaten run nobody came to see me to say well done, it was, "Oh, what a great squad we've got". Yet now things have gone wrong it's all down to Toshack.'

One Anfield old boy whose job isn't on the line is Michael Robinson. He feels Bobby Robson's problems are common ones. 'Barcelona aren't the only side who get by on individual inspiration. There are lots of star players in Spain – I doubt if there's a league in the world that boasts more talent – but no super-teams. When Bobby first arrived, my first thought was, "I hope he knows what he's getting in to"; no experience prepares you for working here; it's not just what the coach does, it's what the press think of you, and of course, what Real Madrid are doing. Last week Bobby said there wasn't a single Premiership manager who could tame this bull – I think he now realises just how difficult it is managing Barcelona. I do feel he's been mistreated as a person, though. You might not like his style of football, but that's no excuse for personal attacks.

'There's been lots of talk about his English-style football not working, but I've never seen an English Ronaldo or Giovanni! Barça have signed lots of centre-halves – and our football is renowned for corpulent defenders – but otherwise, their style of play isn't particularly English. It might not be Cruyff, but it's not Fabio Capello either. If Capello had come here after Cruyff, the Barça fans would have said his team was too conservative and dull and we're not going to swallow it.'

Javier Clemente also has a message of support to Robson. 'If I was Bobby I'd keep on fighting. He's got the best squad around and it's way too early to write off their title chances.' Clemente's solidarity with Robson is in sharp contrast to his belittling of Raddy Antic. 'He's obsessed with being the centre of attention,' he says in response to Antic's suggestion that last week's cup draw was fixed. 'For the last fifteen days the papers have been talking about nothing but Real Madrid v. Barcelona and they've not given Antic a second thought; he's not even been in his own local paper, and he can't stand that. I'm sure he's spent his whole life cheating so he thinks everybody else does. He should concentrate on looking after his health, he's looking really bloated lately. I don't know if it's too much beer or too much work, but whatever it is he should look after himself.'

MONDAY, 10 FEBRUARY
'Espanyol OK, Barça KO', and Robson hanging on for dear life. The beleaguered coach had intended to fly back to London today for the

England v. Italy game and a temporary respite from his Spanish burdens. After being summoned to crisis talks this afternoon, it seems he is facing a more definitive trip home. Five hours locked behind closed doors with Núñez and Gaspart confirm Robson's worst fears. Word is he's been informed that a) his services will not be required for next season, and b) Ivic or Rexach will take over as caretaker if things don't improve in the next couple of games. In others words, it's definitely *adiós*; it's just a question of when. Robson's only observation as he rushes out of the meeting to catch a later-than-scheduled plane to England is, 'I realise that people are looking for a guilty party in these situations, and I'm not afraid to stand up and be counted.'

Barça Vice-President Joan Gaspart admits contingency plans are in place. 'We've told Robson how worried we are by the current situation and that we've approached coaches both for next season and as possible short-term replacements. We've talked about our coaching structure and about Ivic, as well. It's not about making overtures to coaches for the sake of it; football is a risky game and a club like Barcelona has to cover all the angles. Robson understands the situation perfectly, he's been in the game long enough to realise that a coach's fate always depends on results. And he's been in situations himself where he's taken over from guys halfway through a season. But one thing is what we intend to do if we have no choice, another what will actually happen. We still hope it's not necessary to take dramatic measures. Bobby Robson is an honest man and he's told us that nothing in his career had prepared him for such an extraordinary level of pressure. But he's still convinced he can win over the *socis* and deliver a winning season.' As for the Englishman's two-year contract: 'That's what's in the contract, another thing is what we've discussed with him.'

In Spain, the definition of a good loser is someone who doesn't lose too often. It's at least one thing the Catalans have in common with the rest of the country. Two decades on from Franco's demise, conspiracy theories are still the knee-jerk reaction in Barcelona whenever things take a turn for the worse. 'Referees are grinding us into the ground,' moans Gaspart, when he's finished backing Robson. 'As soon as that changes, our position in the table will improve. And why do the decisions always favour the same side? It's too much of a coincidence for my liking, yet nobody says anything because Real Madrid control the media.' Coming from one of *Sport*'s founding fathers and a man who feels giddy outside of smoke-filled rooms, this is a bit rich. Ask anyone to describe Gaspart and chances are the first sentence will include the word 'gangster' (off the record, naturally). The economic journal *Señas* recently described dealing with *la familia* Gaspart as a 'painful experience': 'Given the way they break contracts and stab their own shareholders in the back you'd have to be a peculiar kind of Good Samaritan to go into business with them.'

TUESDAY, 11 FEBRUARY
The day's sporting headlines offer scant variation on a theme: 'Robson's Days Are Numbered'. In terms of FC Barcelona, that seems a foregone conclusion, but as news of his stay of execution filters back to England, it's clear Robson's Spanish travails have not dented his prestige at home. His sudden availability has alerted several clubs, not least Blackburn Rovers. With Sven Goran Eriksson looking increasingly likely to snub Jack Walker in favour of Lazio, Robson offers a ready-made alternative. Many Spanish commentators believe Robson will only fly back to Barcelona to say *adiós*. 'It wouldn't surprise me if he hands in his resignation,' says *Sport*'s Josep María Casanovas. 'He must realise it's impossible to continue with the Sword of Damocles dangling over his head. Pride might tempt him to struggle on against the odds, but common sense should tell him he's lost the battle. He would be better off stepping down to avoid further suffering.'

On a day when the Ajax president tells Dutch reporters that Van Gaal is definitely on his way to Camp Nou, only Robson's players refuse to kick him when he's down. 'There's no reason why Robson should be made the scapegoat,' says defender Abelardo, from Alicante with the Spanish squad. 'He's perfectly capable of getting the team out of this situation.'

WEDNESDAY, 12 FEBRUARY
Crisis? What crisis? Every last Spanish paper leads today with Ronaldo's holiday snaps from Río. Discreetly clad in a gold lamé jumpsuit, glittering green shoulder pads, a star-spangled headband and enough blue feathers to fill a duvet, the youngster's idea of a quite break is to front the whole damn carnival procession. Bob Hope would be proud.

Not surprisingly, Ronaldo's carnival festivities go down like the hair of the dog back in Spain. 'The photos are an insult to everyone connected to FC Barcelona [*the shattered-looking youngster was also snapped at six o'clock in the morning crashed out on the back seat of a limo with the lovely Susana*],' grumbles an incensed Miguel Rico in *Sport*. 'The club's in the middle of a raging crisis and its biggest star is given special leave of absence to parade around at a carnival. It's beyond belief that Robson gave him permission to go to Brazil when he's got to go back there again next week for an international. What happened to discipline and the club's image? What must the fans think about his all-night partying when they haven't got over the Espanyol game? Not to mention the other players. Ronaldo is Brazilian, he's twenty, his girlfriend lives in Río, he's got two days off and plenty of money in his pocket – he's not to blame. If he thinks he can get permission of course he's going to take advantage of it.'

Ronaldo's teammates seem to agree. 'It's not about the dancing in Río,' says Guillermo Amor. 'It's about who gave him permission in the first place with all that's going on here.' Even fellow Brazilian Giovanni is mystified by Ronaldo's antics. 'I love the carnival too, but as a professional my duty is to be here. A return journey to Brazil for the sake of two days is really heavy going; even if I'd had the time off I would have stayed here.'

Ronaldo isn't the only guy who's under pressure for playing hookey. 'It's intolerable that Bobby Robson has taken two days off to commentate on the England game in the current circumstances,' says Josep María Casanovas. 'And the kowtowing to Ronaldo really is the last straw. One of the reasons Van Gaal is such a popular choice to take over is because he's big on discipline, something that's strikingly absent at the moment.'

THURSDAY, 13 FEBRUARY

Arriving back from London at midday, Robson's first stop is a newspaper kiosk at Barcelona's El Prat airport. Unremittingly hostile headlines would have convinced him his own shelf-life is severely limited. Van Gaal's smiling face (now there's a rarity) taunts him from the cover of *El Mundo Deportivo* while *Sport* leads with the soul-destroying result of yet another exit poll (Robson's?).

Hemmed in by journalists, Robson seems perplexed by the fuss over Ronaldo's ravings. 'I made the decision to let him go back to Brazil before the Real Madrid game. He played ninety minutes in both games last week and asked if he could miss Monday's session, which was just twenty minutes' recovery work. From now on we'll be playing twice a week, so it's the last chance he'll get to rest. When I stopped him going back for the New Year, I'd told him there might be another chance. He's young and he needs to see his family and friends.'

Later in the day, and strictly off the record, Robson is less understanding. 'I can't control players twenty-four hours a day. When they have time off I expect them to behave like professionals. Ronaldo was irresponsible and unintelligent. But he's only twenty, so you've got to look at the people who are advising him. He's always got his managers with him saying, "Sign this contract, more money, do this, do that," yet when these guys go to Río with him they don't say, "Hey, Ronaldo . . . duck!" I'd spoken to him and said, "Look, go back to Brazil, see your family and friends, but keep a low profile." Then I come back from England and he's splashed over the front pages like Joseph in his Technicolor dreamcoat.'

As for his own immediate future, Robson is reading a less colourful script than the rest of Spain. 'I'm not used to losing battles, I've never been one to panic and I'm not about to start now. The thought of quitting hasn't entered my mind, I don't care how much pressure there is.' Even the Van Gaal phenomenon (the papers are full of 'This Is Your Life, Louis' features) doesn't seem to faze him. 'As far as I'm concerned, I've got two years left on my contract and I fully expect to stay and win things.'

Half an hour after his coach's arrival, it was Ronaldo's turn to run the airport gauntlet. Unlike Robson, he spotted the bother a mile off. And unlike the veteran Englishman, diplomacy is NOT one of his virtues. After accusing journalists of being 'a pain in the neck', he then insisted he'd done nothing wrong. 'I'm not surprised by the fuss, nothing surprises me here any more. I've played lots of games lately so it's perfectly normal that I get a chance to spend some time at home. When I was at PSV, people didn't cause a row over this kind of thing, but the press here are different, they've provoked all the controversy. I suppose you [*journalists*] would have stayed at home if you'd had the chance to go to the carnival. Don't you guys ever get dressed up?' That's as wolves in sheep's clothing, Ron. As for the headaches his behaviour would cause the man who let him go, 'That's Robson's problem, not mine. I'm just a worker like anybody else, it's his job to run the club.' The words ungrateful and bugger spring to mind.

Josep Lluís Núñez's once unconditional support for his coach has shifted through lukewarm to downright nippy. After this afternoon's training session, Robson is summoned to yet another counselling session with Núñez and Gaspart. Ramón Besa, a columnist on Spain's bestselling broadsheet *El País*, sums up Robson's unenviable situation. 'Núñez was furious about the Ronaldo thing. He doesn't understand why several players have had three or four days off, nor what Robson was doing in England when half the squad is back in Barcelona training. Every single analysis of Barça's situation leads to the same conclusion; Robson's face doesn't fit at Camp Nou, Rexach is the most suitable caretaker and Van Gaal is the ideal long-term replacement. Whatever his past achievements, Robson has failed to live up to the legend of Johan Cruyff. The fans pine for the days of creative football, of a big role for the youngsters, and for a coach with the character to restore discipline and keep Núñez out of the dressing room. Van Gaal represents a return to the Ajax school without being Cruyff, that's why he's the perfect candidate.'

For the first time this season, the criticism is starting to get personal, too. In today's left-leaning *El País* it's suggested that only English bores vote for the Conservative Party: 'Robson is a renowned Tory; looking at his team, that makes sense.' Strangely for a man of mining stock, Robson is indeed a Conservative and proud of it. 'My dad was very strong Labour but as I moved on I've become a Conservative.' It must have been all those soirées in the company of the grandees at Portman Road. Sinking to uncharted depths, *Sport* columnist Antonio Hernáez accuses Robson of 'coming to Spain on a subsidised holiday for pensioners'. Some would say a contemporary of Robson's who is married to a teenage *cubana* has no right giving lectures on the etiquette of veterans.

FRIDAY, 14 FEBRUARY

Robson gathers his players to read the Riot Act. 'I'm still your coach' is his message. 'Ignore all the rumours, be professional and concentrate on winning football matches.' Robson's old-school faith in the goodwill of the average footballer is almost touching. Even in unguarded moments, he refuses to criticise his players. 'I still get the feeling that the players are with me; if I didn't think that I'd walk away immediately. As a manager you can sense different levels of commitment. It's not just games, you see it every day in training. I'm exceptionally happy with their attitude. The team has made mistakes on the pitch, but that happens, football is not a science.'

On a day when he doesn't make the eighteen-man cut to face Racing Santander, Abelardo could have been forgiven a moan. 'We don't have to come to training in carnival gear to prove how cheerful we are,' he jokes. 'Believe me, there's great camaraderie in this squad. I personally hope Robson stays for years, that'll mean we've been successful.' Guillermo Amor, another Spanish international struggling to get a game, is equally resolute. 'We're not even contemplating the possibility of Robson being sacked. He might know he's going to be dismissed, or maybe he's going to walk himself, but the players can't waste time second-guessing his intentions. It can't be easy being in his skin at the moment, but I'd say people have been writing him off prematurely. We're still with him, come what may.'

As usual, there's a discordant voice. Predictably, it hides a personal agenda. Iván De la Peña breaks a long silence to bemoan his marginal status, hinting that he will ask for a transfer if 'the current situation' (reading not very far between the lines, THE COACH) stays the same. Naturally, the youngster's assessors are aware that Robson is teetering on the brink of dismissal, so the timing of his outburst is anything but coincidental. You might think Robson would take it personally, if only he gave you the chance. 'A football manager can't let his heart rule his head, if you do that you're in trouble. Amor [*the player directly behind Iván in the midfield queue*] is a lovely lad and so reliable. He's a hundred per cent correct in everything he says and does and I'd love to give him a game every week. But you have to do what's right for the team, regardless of how well you get on with the players you leave out.'

SATURDAY, 15 FEBRUARY

That the Spanish sports press is at turns economical with the truth and downright mendacious is indisputable. In private, Robson admits he's hanging on to his job by a thread, but how thin? Today's sporting dailies offer four different versions; elementary mathematics suggest that at least three are 'mistaken'.

El Mundo Deportivo: 'Núñez has looked at the opinion polls, weighed up the advice of his board, and talked to the most influential players. For the moment, he's decided that it's not quite the time to dismiss Robson, so he will gauge the fans' response tomorrow and if there's no clear mandate he'll let things run their natural course. The club's options on Van Gaal and Antic are valid until 31 May, that's when the club has to either formalise an agreement or pay compensation.'

Sport: 'On Monday Robson managed to convince Núñez to give him another chance, but he was given an ultimatum; if Barça don't beat Racing, he will be sacked immediately. Even if he wins, there's a distinct possibility that he will resign.'

Marca: 'If the current situation continues nothing drastic will happen, but if Robson's side fall ten points behind Real Madrid, he will be sacked immediately and replaced by Rexach.'

AS: 'Núñez actually sacked Robson on Monday, but the Englishman begged for a one-game stay of execution before tendering his resignation. Rexach has been told he will be taking over on Monday, as have the senior players. Whatever the result against Racing, Robson will offer a staged resignation on Monday.'

You pays your 125 pesetas and takes your choice.

Maybe he didn't read the papers this morning, but Robson's mood as he surveys his Camp Nou domain belies his situation. On a splendidly sunny day, the only time he gets remotely flustered is when he thinks he's mislaid his sunglasses. A two-minute backtrack to the Hotel Princesa Sofia (once owned by the family Gaspart and still a Barça HQ by proxy) and a smiling Gica Popescu takes time out from an interview to wave the missing shades in the air. His Romanian skipper is as warm with Robson as three generations of *señoras* who approach the coach and insist they'd never use a handkerchief for anything amiss.

Back at Camp Nou, Robson chats warmly with a bunch of kids who grab an unexpected midday photo opportunity. 'Despite the best efforts of the press, the attitude of the fans hasn't changed at all,' says Robson. 'I feel a great deal of warmth and appreciation, that hasn't changed. The response on the street here is very high, it's hard to go anywhere without being recognised, but I find people extraordinarily nice; they've always got a smile for you, it's never "Go home you son of a bitch". It's always 'Oh, Mr Robson, good luck and *Visca Barça* (Long Live Barça)". I find them very supportive.'

Sat in his car in a secluded corner of Camp Nou, one of the few places in Barcelona where he can both see the sun and finish a sentence without interruption, Robson refuses to wallow in the irksome nature of his situation. 'I still thank my lucky stars that I came into football, even at times like this. I appreciate what a healthy and lucrative life the game's given me. If I didn't enjoy what I was doing it would be purgatory, but I'm still having fun, otherwise I wouldn't be here. The game – and right now that means FC Barcelona – still gives me everything I want: adrenalin, excitement and pleasure.'

Despite his refusal to over-dramatise the manager's lot, he shrugs off the notion that managers are a pampered breed, unworthy of our sympathies. 'Football fans look at all the money we earn and the supposedly glamorous side of things and say, "Blimey, I could do with that kind of pressure." But they'd soon change their tune if they tried, I'll tell you. I can understand why they say it, but you never know what it's like to be a bullfighter until you're in the ring, do you? Mind you, it's better being at a Barcelona or a Manchester United than a club with no money, struggling against relegation. I'm working at the sharp end and that's the best place to be.

'You can enjoy the lifestyle if you divorce yourself from the pressure. I'm quite good at that, that's why I've stayed in the game such a long time. I try to keep one day absolutely free – no interviews, nothing to do with work – and after games I always go straight home to my wife and have a quiet night in, we never even go to a restaurant.' As Robson admits, it's often his family which suffers the most. 'My wife doesn't like what people do to me,' he sighs. 'She thought that thing in *La Vanguardia* was degrading. I know there were other caricatures inside, but I was on the front page. After forty-two years of being married to me and football she'd prefer me to walk away from it, she really doesn't think it's worth it any more. Elsie likes Sitges, but we've met very few English people out here [*he pauses for several seconds, as if trying to convince himself*]; she's all right, she just wishes I had more time to enjoy the nice things with her. So do I. She needs to see a bit more of me, but unfortunately I can't give myself to her at the moment. And it's going to be a hectic two-games-a-week schedule until the end of the season.'

Yes, Robson is still talking about the end of the season. 'The club haven't told me any of that stuff about Van Gaal having signed a contract, or Rexach being lined up to take over. That's just what the papers say, it's simply not true. They've insisted they don't know what's happening at the end of the season. They're saying to me, "Look, you're the coach, we employed you and we're sticking by you." That's what I wanted them to say to me, all the other reports are rubbish. I'm on no time limit. I realise that if results don't go for us in the next two or three weeks, something will happen to me, but I've been in football long enough to know it's like that anyway. If we consistently lose, the people who run this club are put in a delicate position themselves. And if they're unhappy my attitude is "Well, sack me. You've got the contract, you can put an end to it". I'm not going to do their job for them.'

Nearly 30 years in management mean that Robson would be surprised if the board weren't covering all the angles. He also has first-hand experience of how the club handles these situations. 'Barcelona rang me up to see what my position was before Johan Cruyff was dismissed. They were quite correct about it, they didn't say, "Look, we're sacking Cruyff," all they said was, "If we decide to change coach next season, what's your position regarding your contract and is this job something that appeals to you?" It was near the end of his reign, so they must have been seriously contemplating it, or they wouldn't have called me, but they never said, "He's definitely going, we need you urgently." They were preparing the ground just in case.'

Despite all the talk of crises and managerial changes, Robson has yet to waver in public. Was he genuinely convinced he could turn things around, or was it merely a case of rallying the troops? 'Well, football managers are a bit like politicians, your job's all about keeping the eternal flame going. But I still think we can win the league and both cup competitions. I'm not saying we will, but we've got a fighting chance. If I was in England at the moment and second in the league and in the quarterfinals of the FA Cup and a European competition, I'd be labelled a bloody hero. Do you think back home they'd be thinking of sacking anybody in my situation, even at one of the top clubs? Not a snowflake's chance in hell! Spanish clubs are less patient, that's obvious from the number of managers sacked already, and quite honestly, I wasn't aware of how singular the Real Madrid v. Barça rivalry is. If we were in second place, Real Madrid were fourth or fifth, say, and Betis were top, there would be much less pressure. It's because Real Madrid are top, that's what creates the pressure. You're not measured by what the other twenty teams are doing, are you?

'When I went back for the Italy game on Wednesday, I recalled what it was like managing England. After being at Barcelona several months, I can assure you, the pressure here is much worse. That one week of an international game is very intense, but here you've got the forty, fifty guys hassling you every single day of every single week. As England manager you're in the papers every day for a week, here I'm in the papers every day of every week. So the pressure is more intense, you've even got journalists parked on your doorstep at Christmas when you've got no game for two weeks. Do you think anybody cares what Alex Ferguson does on Christmas Day?'

Whatever his problems with Barcelona's Fourth Estate, Robson insists he would never go down the John 'No Comment' Toshack road. 'I try to answer things constructively but it does depend on the questions. It isn't easy when you get asked so much rubbish. After the Espanyol game one guy tried to get at me because Ronaldo was caught defending. We were one-nil down and all the big guys had gone up for a corner. On the break, Ronaldo was the quickest back 'cos our defenders were in the opposing box; that's not being negative, we were trying to make it one-all. So the guy who asked that question doesn't understand football. It's either that or they're trying to catch you out; you'll use a word you didn't mean, and it'll be used out of context or get exaggerated. I try to be honest but occasionally you've just got to say, "Sorry, I can't tell you that." It's like the Stoichkov thing. His legs have gone and he isn't training very well, that's the truth. But at the press conference I'll say he's one of twenty-four players and I can only pick eleven. If I tell the truth, it's headlines and I've killed Stoichkov. I'd prefer not to do the press conferences – I hate doing them – but it's a condition of the club. I've cut down on the personal interviews, though, I pick and choose who I talk to now, you've got to control it or you'll be consumed by them. The press are after news, and nothing's better for them than talking to the coach every day and trying to catch you out. And if you don't talk to them they just make it up. It's like the stories saying I met with Emerson's agent in Lisbon; that's rubbish. I had to ring Bryan Robson to deny all the stories claiming we were tapping his player; our approach came later when Boro said they wanted Nadal. I'm still bemused by the media circus.' He sighs. 'I've never had so many people hate me. But they'll have to swallow their words if I win the league – I'd love to make them eat shit!'

Robson may field the odd enquiry about players from his former Captain Marvel, but the tenuous nature of football's friendships is demonstrated by his lack of contact with people back home. 'I keep in touch with Charlie Woods who was at Ipswich with me, and I occasionally speak to David Pleat, Alex Ferguson, Don Howe and Howard Wilkinson. I get family and friends over, but nobody from the game really. I've had some Dutch coaches here and a lad from Sheffield Wednesday came over to look at our youth system and watch the first team training. I think it's out of sight, out of mind, though. I used to be great mates with Jimmy Greaves, but I haven't spoken to him for years now, I don't even know what he's doing. If people do ring it's not to chat, it's because they want something: information on a player, a team I might be familiar with, whatever. With Don Howe or Dave Sexton it would be different, they might call just to talk. But if it was guys like David Pleat, it would be business.'

Robson is the former England manager, a famously accessible guy working at the biggest football club in the world, and nobody calls to say, 'Hey, can we come over and watch you work?' Didn't he find that staggering? 'Yes, I'm surprised people don't take advantage of that possibility. I've had the odd coach that has written to me, but not from professional or Premier League clubs. A lot of the younger managers – Robson, Wilkins, Hoddle – played for me when I was England manager, but they never get in touch for advice. That's the way football is in general, people don't ask for help. There's very little passing down of knowledge from generation to generation. It doesn't apply to everybody, and from time to time people do call you, especially if they're under severe pressure, but generally guys will think, "I'm on my own and I'm going to handle this." When I was a young manager I rarely turned to people for advice, either. It's a make-your-own-bed-and-lie-in-it world. As England manager I spoke to Ron Greenwood a few times. And when we qualified for Mexico I invited him to London to talk about his experiences and ask his advice. Glenn Hoddle might do the same, or maybe he'll talk to Terry Venables about his experience at the European Championships. I certainly found it useful talking to Ron. Mostly about the pitfalls, the things to avoid.'

Talk of managerial contacts inevitably leads to the Clemente/Antic war of words. 'Javier's problem is that he says the first thing that comes into his head. I heard about the argument over the cup draw, but I wasn't about to get involved. We've got a different mentality in England, haven't we? There's definitely more solidarity between managers at home, it's very rare to see managers criticising each other in the papers, that's why the Keegan/Ferguson thing last year was so striking.'

Not that the powers that be set an example for the guys in tracksuits. Wasn't it strange hearing other Spanish presidents describe Núñez as 'a dwarf'? Robson shakes his head, a bemused expression on his face. 'In all my years in football I've never come across anything like that, it's a totally different culture. One of the problems here is that presidents are always asked their opinions. In England, chairmen are rarely asked to comment and when they are, they'll either say "No thank you" or stick to being educated and showing respect for other people. Again, I suppose it's a case of so much newspaper space to fill over here. If you asked your average football fan in England to name a bunch of chairmen they'd probably manage their own and maybe John Hall and Jack Walker. If you asked a Leeds fan who the chairmen of Notts Forest or Liverpool were he couldn't tell you.'

Conversation turns to Robson's future. 'I came to Barcelona thinking it would be my last job as manager and I still think that, even if it went wrong over the next couple of weeks and I was sacked. That's the way I feel at the moment. Do I really need the hassle of another high-profile job? It depends who comes in; if the worst comes to the worst I'll take a month off – maybe stay in Sitges – and think about my future for a while. I came here on a two-year contract hoping to do marvellously well [*speaking now in a tone laced with melancholy*]. I thought, "What a finish for my CV, ending my career at Barcelona winning things." You really can't go out bigger or better than that, that would be the tops for me, but it hasn't quite worked out the way I'd hoped. But that's life in football, you never know. If we win our next couple of games and Real Madrid drop some points the situation could change. My biggest enemy at the moment is that Madrid are so solid-looking, they don't look like losing two or three games in a row.

'They've been very lucky, too. They've got nothing like the depth we have. If they lost, say, Raúl or Seedorf, they'd be up the creek without a paddle. But we've got no one player who is irreplaceable; even if Ronaldo gets injured Pizzi could come in and do a good job. Madrid have also won a lot of games by the odd goal. You feel that every club will have a dip at some point of the season; they've not had their bad run yet. We've had ours – let's hope we don't get another – and we're only six points behind them. We do need Madrid to start dropping some points, though. If they don't, and if we get two or three bad results, I think the board will do something about it. I understand that, the pressure on them is enormous, too. There are elections due, maybe as early as October, so Núñez's hand will be forced. He can't afford to not finish second, at the very least.'

Robson's more immediate future is Saturday's happy hour with the press. He does his best to preach tranquillity, even if his inquisitors haven't heard the one about kicking a man when he's down. Predictably, opening shots tackle the board's plans for his future. 'I don't accept ultimatums from anyone,' argues Robson, 'decisions yes, ultimatums no.' Not surprisingly, he pays the *AS* 'out on Monday' rumour equally short shrift. 'That's absolute nonsense,' he says in a tone pitched somewhere between incredulity and incomprehension. 'How does it go? I was fired last Monday but I'm still here. After forty-five years in the game, do you seriously think I'd stick around if I'd been sacked? The Madrid papers are capable of making anything up to damage Barcelona; there's no foundation to the story, it's totally false.' He also denies a suggestion that his future depends on the next result. 'If, if, if . . . it's always if. This girl asks such beautiful questions [*like most managers of his generation, Robson seems bemused by the notion of women sports writers, in this case a regular sparring partner from* La Vanguardia]. If you walk out the door and a car hits you, you're dead! But yes, if after all this time coaching at the highest level my future depends on one result, then I admit, that's a first.'

The next thorny issue concerns long- and short-term absences. 'Stoichkov isn't in the squad because I can only play eleven,' insists Robson. 'I told all the players at the beginning of the season, "If you aren't picked, respect the guys who are in the team."' As for Ronaldo's samba sojourn: 'I've told him he's got to be magic against Racing. He's always in the fans' hearts, tomorrow he'll be in their heads, as well. But show a bit of understanding. He's only twenty. I'd like to know what some of you were like when you were twenty.' 'Poorer!' ventures one journalist. Robson smiles. 'Not so rich maybe, but not as talented, either . . . seriously, I've had a word with Ronaldo and he knows he's got to prove that going to Brazil was good for him. I might not agree with how he spent his time there, but in principle, it was good for him to go back and see his family and friends. He knows he's caused a bad impression, but he's come back happy and in good form. Don't you think it's better that he's motivated for the future than concentrating on the past?'

Robson's good humour in fending off awkward questions prompts one journalist to joke, '*Mister*, you look more relaxed, are you hiding something from us?' Robson ignores the malicious intent (perhaps it's good news, as in 'I'm out of here on Monday'). 'Yes, off the record [*pauses for effect*], next year I'm going to the carnival with Ronaldo.'

SUNDAY, 16 FEBRUARY
Barcelona 1, Racing Santander 0 (Luis Enrique 42)
Camp Nou, 90,000

Even before Bobby Robson's men had saved his first managerial match point with this laboured win, the coach was fending off volleys from within his own ranks. José Mourinho's monologues for Catalunya Ràdio are part and parcel of Camp Nou's pre-match rituals. Five minutes before kick-off, the press box was replete with journalists fiddling with their trannies in the hope that Mourinho would put his foot in it again. Today, the man Robson calls Josie surpasses himself. Initially refusing to comment on his mentor's prospects if Barça fail to beat Racing, he messes up his sudden outbreak of diplomacy by scribbling two aeroplanes on a piece of paper and dubbing them 'Destination London and Lisbon'.

If boasting friends like that wasn't bad enough, Easy Jet go and choose today to unveil their latest cut-price flights at Camp Nou: 'Fly to London for less than ten thousand pesetas . . . One Way'. At least Easy Jet's hoardings went the distance. Several banners expressing support for Robson were confiscated under the pretence that they were obstructing the view. No wonder the coach suspects the world is against him. 'I almost feel like Gary Cooper in *High Noon*,' he jokes, kind of, at his post-match press conference.

Cometh the hour, Robson had abandoned his usual shades of grey for a beige blazer that was as bright as the weather. Like his decision to give Albert Celades a second game of the season, Robson's change of gear was interpreted as a desperate search for lucky charms on a day when only victory would do; in his eleven-game league career Celades has yet to play on the losing side. In reality, the change was forced on Robson by Ferrer's injury (more imaginative hacks would attribute it to Núñez's promptings).

'The Barça players are seized by fear when they take the field at Camp Nou,' said Valencia boss Jorge Valdano recently. 'Knowing that your first mistake will be met by a chorus of boos intimidates

168

even the best players.' The crowd's attitude to Celades confirms what a difference a positive vibe makes. The youngster made a pair of early blunders that almost cost Barça dear; the fans reacted by cheering his every touch. Giovanni, meanwhile, was the subject of derisory jeers for 72 minutes before Robson put him out of his misery with a mercy substitution. His replacement, Pizzi, was equally unfortunate, though his torture was self-inflicted. Two minutes after entering the fray, he was back on his way to the dressing room after a kung fu kick masquerading as a tackle.

Ignoring his coach's bidding, Ronaldo was anything but magic. When he was substituted in the last minute it was unclear whether the raucous protests were aimed at the Brazilian for leaving the samba spring in his step in Río, or at Robson for replacing his star man with an unwelcome guest, Amunike. On the final whistle, the protests were noisy and widespread. The list of guilty parties (the team for a dour performance, the referee for sending off Pizzi, Núñez and/or Robson as the usual suspects) converted the latest round of hankie-waving into a mystery as impenetrable as 'Who is Keyser Söze?'

Racing are managed by Marcos Alonso, a man whose playing days at Camp Nou are remembered for a spectacular cup-winning goal against Real Madrid and an equally spectacular falling out with Terry Venables (legend has it the result of a dalliance with one of El Tel's daughters). With the fans delivering a split verdict today, journalists did their best to get Don Juan to dictate sentence. Luckily, Bobby Robson has only got sons and thus avoided censorship. No wonder he is reduced to soliciting a kind word, albeit with a sore throat. 'You ask me if I can get on with my job with the crowd against me? Well, you can do something to control that, give me a better opportunity.'

His life would certainly be a lot easier if Ronaldo started hitting the net again. Typically, Robson defends the youngster. 'He's here for ten years, not ten minutes. Let's just be satisfied with him and concentrate on the good things that have happened today.'

MONDAY, 17 FEBRUARY

When the press have got a downer on you, best pretend you can't read. Robson's fan club could have adopted many a stance on Barça's victory yesterday, starting with 'Serious championship sides have got to win on their off days'. Instead, they choose to crucify the coach for taking off Ronaldo. The front cover of *AS* is typical: 'Scandal provoked by substitution – Robson intoxicates the mood of 90,000 fans.' Not surprisingly, the man himself is bewildered. 'People who criticise that decision don't understand anything about football at all. We're one-nil up, we're down to ten men and Ronaldo is shattered. So I buy some time and slow the game down. If we'd been two or three goals up I could perhaps understand the flak, but it's one-nil and we're on a knife's edge. Any coach worth his salt would have done the same; have these guys never seen an Italian game? How many times has Capello taken Suker off this season [*that's twelve times in 24 games*] and nobody [*except Suker*] knocks him.'

Otherwise, it's page after page of rumours about a 'dismayed' Núñez 'charging down to the dressing room for more crisis talks'. 'He popped his head round the door to congratulate the players,' groans Robson. Even Joan Gaspart is forced to defend his coach. 'Bobby Robson is not stupid,' he says. 'He knew he'd be criticised for taking off Ronaldo. But instead of worrying about his own reputation – especially after the week he's had – he made the decision he thought was best for the team. Instead of praising him for his honesty, the press prefer to criticise him.'

A brief encounter at Camp Nou this afternoon says everything about Bobby Robson the man. *Sport*, or *el comic* as its detractors call it, has been among the coach's harshest critics, and he knows it. Yet when their features editor approaches him with a request to say cheese with a birthday cake, Robson agrees without the slightest edge. 'I get on OK with him, so whenever they want something from me they use him,' he explains later. 'The guys who are slagging me off every day never show their faces. It's the good cop, bad cop trick. But I feel really sorry for him, it puts him in a really awkward position.' He feels sorry for him?

Diplomatic duty done, Robson continues to lament his situation. 'It's bloody horrible. In England I'd be a hero, here I'm living from game to game; it's an inhuman situation and the worse thing is I can't do anything about it – I'm just a political pawn. Nobody will say it out loud, but everybody's lining up their forces for the presidential elections. If it's not people trying to get at Núñez by criticising me, it's the Cruyff faction pitching for a candidate who will bring him back. It's got nothing to do with football.'

As he admits, Mourinho's willingness to fly the white flag doesn't help. 'That was really stupid,' admits Robson, though he takes the fifth amendment when asked just why everybody has got it in for his assistant. 'I trusted José, he knows my work and he interprets for me. He uses his ears for me, so I appreciate what he has done.' Clearly, it's not his style to criticise collaborators. It's not his style to rant and rave on the touchline, either. 'A lot of English coaches prefer to sit in the stand where they can see how the game pans out, especially in the first half. And if you do start screaming and shouting the referee will come and tell you to sit down; if you don't you're likely to be sent off. Here, the touchline theatrics are accepted practice. Those guys on the touchline are just working off their own adrenalin, though. At big, packed grounds like Camp Nou, the players can't hear you anyway. I tried to speak to Popescu three times yesterday but it was a complete waste of time. All I did was lose my voice; he couldn't hear a word.'

Spanish referees might turn a blind eye to amateur dramatics on the touchline, but as Robson admits, that's as far as leniency goes. 'They're better than Portuguese referees [*the mind boggles*] but way too officious, there's no dialogue with the players. They could save themselves lots of problems if they warned people early on instead of flashing the yellow card for the first foul. In England, it's "Hey, be careful, son, another foul like that and you'll be off". I don't think they're dishonest, but they could use a little common sense – Pizzi's sending off yesterday was correct, rules in hand, but it was an obvious case for leniency. He's just come on, he's cold and he's mistimed his challenge – a yellow card would have been more appropriate, instead he's in the *Guinness Book of Records*. It was the same with Figo last week. I spoke to him after the game and said, "Look, don't lie to me, what happened after the penalty?" He said, "*Mister*, all I said was, 'Why?' I didn't swear or anything." Five minutes later, Figo has a little push on one of their players, the referee's a bit petty and we're down to ten men. All the media focus on referees doesn't help, either. In England, a ref thinks he's had a good game if nobody's noticed him, here it's the other way around. They think by producing yellow cards and being officious they're controlling the match. Often they're doing anything but.'

Rexach may be touted as Robson's short-term successor but when they cross paths in the corridors at Camp Nou (Robson's here to pick up his monthly cheque; all those millions and they can't arrange a bank transfer?), Cruyff's former assistant does a convincing impersonation of a reluctant substitute. 'Don't let 'em get you down, *mister*,' he says with a big pat on Robson's back. 'And don't believe what you read in the press, I'm with you one hundred per cent.' Later, he sympathises with Robson. 'I feel terrible that my name is linked to the rumours of his sacking. I admire the way he's handling a difficult situation; lots of guys would have thrown the towel in by now. It must be his English phlegm! There really has been an indecent rush to make judgements. I agree with Bobby when he says that nobody in Europe has to work under such pressure. Cruyff's successor was bound to have a bad time, but not everything about Cruyff was good and not everything Robson does is bad. He's new to the club, so are lots of the players, and he's not having the slightest bit of luck.'

There has long existed an unwritten pact among the Catalan media – let's call it the dictatorship of the *culés*. 'Once again, the fans gave a lesson by getting behind the team,' reads the editorial in today's *Sport*. 'The demands of the fans are part of FC Barcelona's greatness.' Come again? Popescu whistled twice in the first ten minutes? Robson, Giovanni, Iván, Ronaldo and Amunike at turns? The whole team as they left the field? Barça may attract the world's highest average crowd, but biggest and best are not necessarily the same thing.

The Catalans' most celebrated virtue is *seny* – difficult to translate, but roughly a mixture of common sense and stoicism. Why then does Catalonia boast such a tumultuous history? This is how the Catalan writer Victor Alba squares the circle. 'The opposite of *seny* is *arrauxment* – an ecstasy of violence. But *arrauxment* is seen as an ultimate consequence of *seny*. The Catalans are convinced that when they act impetuously they are being sensible. When things are not the way they ought to be, when a situation is not sensible, the commonsense thing to do is oppose it abruptly, violently.' Anybody that has witnessed a slumbering Camp Nou respond suddenly and ferociously to a perceived injustice would have to admit that this paradox is reflected in Catalonia's sporting arenas. Unless Real Madrid are in town, Barça's own players are up there with MIB as prime targets when common sense goes out of the window; given the choice they'd probably opt for the more general tonic of lukewarm indifference.

In public, Robson has to play the game, but off the record he admits there's a problem. 'English crowds are definitely more loyal;

the Barça fans are much too quick to turn against you. English fans don't turn on their own team, even when they're losing. I think it's a Barcelona rather than a Spanish thing, though. Elsewhere crowds are considerably more volatile than back home; that makes it difficult for us away from home, too. English football fans are partisan but generally they're more sporting. Here they're very hostile to the opposition; all that *hijos de puta* business everywhere, and it's not just some eighteen-year-old hooligan. In England, you get the odd lager lout who'll do it, here it's everybody; the fans behind the dugout always shout and abuse you, and it's considered normal. In England they'd get turfed out by the police. And I've never seen objects raining down on English players as they're trying to take a corner, never.

'It doesn't help anybody when you've got the press harping on about how I'm going to be sacked next week; that gets through to the players, it's a handicap for the team. I have to accept the white handkerchiefs but I don't like them. I know it's the fans' way of expressing displeasure, but it's unnecessary and is soul-destroying for the team. The supporters pay their money and have the right to do whatever they please. But it's degrading for the players when the crowd is against them. You'd never see that in England, it's unthinkable, unthinkable.'

TUESDAY, 18 FEBRUARY
No, whatever the spin-doctors from *AS* may claim, we're not talking an optical illusion. That really is Bobby Robson slap bang in the middle of Camp Nou as his players sing 'Happy Birthday, Dear *Mister*'. 'In English,' says a smiling Ronaldo later, 'it's easy and it really cheered him up.' Twenty-four hours after what *AS* had billed as Robson's last day at Barcelona, the now 64-year-old coach is charging around at training with as much enthusiasm as ever. With Figo, Popescu and Baía away on international duty, he even gets a game.

Naturally, *AS* leads with an apology. Hah! These guys live in their own virtual-reality world. 'A sudden attack of pride on Robson's part broke his pact with Núñez. When he came back from England on Thursday, Robson told Núñez that it was the club's job to sack him if they considered him surplus to requirements. He refused to present his resignation yesterday so Rexach could take over; his attitude was, "After all I've suffered, I'm not going to give in now

and make it look like I'm the one who can't stand the pressure".'
Well, that's cleared that up, then. You guys make up a story, and
when it turns out to be bogus, you make up another one blaming the
guy you lied about in the first place!

One banner at the training ground today – 'Bobby Robson
Forever/Happy Birthday/We Support You' – suggests that not
everybody is baying for Robson's blood, and *Tot L'Esport,* the daily
sports round-up on Televisió de Catalunya, do their part by
dedicating a lovingly compiled video to the birthday boy. Whether
the Beatles singing 'Will you still need me when I'm 64?' was the
most appropriate choice of music is a moot point.

WEDNESDAY, 19 FEBRUARY

Could Robson's luck be about to change? Real Madrid's unexpected
defeat at Rayo Vallecano means Barça can close the gap to three
points if they beat Real Sociedad tomorrow. That Madrid should
lose 1-0 to their low-life neighbours is encouraging, that Fabio
Capello admits his side were outplayed even more so. The
honourable Capello aside, Madrid immediately set about unearthing
scapegoats. Mijatovic blamed the 'down and outs' who have
launched a campaign against his high-diving antics. 'The referee
ignored two clear penalties on me. Either he didn't want to give them
or he was scared to.' Scared to? Did somebody make him an offer he
couldn't refuse? If so, Lorenzo Sanz knows who's to blame. 'What
do our players have to do to get a penalty – get shot? We haven't
had a penalty since October; maybe we should retire now and let
Barça play on their own. Gaspart has got what he was after, though
now I suppose he'll say we're making excuses.' Surely not, Lorenzo.
'If I had the clout with the media and referees that Sanz says I do,'
responds Gaspart, 'Real Madrid would be in the Second Division.'

Before leaving for San Sebastián, Bobby Robson insists he's not
losing sleep over his future. 'I'm just concentrating on my job.' Albeit
in difficult circumstances. 'I don't know a single coach in Europe
who's holding on until his next defeat before getting the sack, that's
no way to run a football club.' However, he denies suggestions that
he's been banging at Núñez's door demanding a vote of confidence.
'Public backing would be positive, but I don't think there's a
president in the whole world who gives his coach a pat on the back
every week.'

THURSDAY, 20 FEBRUARY
Real Sociedad 2, Barcelona 0
Anoeta, 22,000

Robson's day starts with that pat on the back. Better late than never or an example of Núñez's fabled opportunism? (This is the man who lords it over a construction empire inherited by his wife.) It was certainly easier backing Robson this morning than it would have been, say, ten days ago, after the Espanyol defeat. 'There's been no ultimatum and my desire is that Robson finishes this season,' says Núñez in a rare television interview (albeit one-to-one and with a previously agreed agenda). 'Real Madrid lost yesterday and I haven't read any criticism of Capello, it's been accepted as a one-off defeat, it's not been converted into a drama. Yet when we lost to Hércules or drew against Oviedo the reaction was over-the-top criticism of Robson. That's the big difference between Barcelona and Real Madrid; the pressure on our respective coaches. If Robson is left to get on with his job then the team can still win the championship.'

A day of presidential decrees continues with the rather less camera-shy Jesús Gil crucifying Mijatovic 'in the name of the down and outs'. According to Atlético Madrid's owner, the Yugoslav is a 'gum-chewing pretty-boy, an Armani-clad mercenary, a coward and a cheat who only came to Spain for money. Brats whose speciality is diving belong in swimming pools, not in football stadiums.' Say what you mean! Of course, it doesn't help that Mijatovic plays for Real Madrid. 'I'm a hundred per cent anti-*Madridista*,' admits Gil. 'Nothing gives me more pleasure than seeing them lose; I had a sporting orgasm when they lost to Rayo.' Lorenzo Sanz responds to a previous attack on his striker by saying, 'If Gil is looking for epileptics and simpletons he should look at his own club.' This time he pledges to put the club's legal resources at Mijatovic's disposal, though this unusually formal response is undermined when a fellow director calls Gil 'a blubbering elephant'.

Against a background of crocodile tears from Madrid on the issue of referees, the last thing Bobby Robson needed tonight was another capital bureaucrat on his case, especially one whose role model took delight in closing the file on Brits. On the day a story breaks in Belgium claiming that Anderlecht bribed the Spanish referee Emilio Guruceta before their 1984 UEFA Cup semifinal victory against Notts Forest, Barça are well and truly grounded by José Núñez Manrique, an air force officer-cum-referee from Madrid whose self-confessed idol is . . . Guruceta.

When Guruceta wasn't Clough-bashing, he was damning Barcelona. In half a century of 'persecution at the hands of fascist referees in cohorts with Real Madrid', one incident looms larger than most in the Catalan consciousness. In the 1970 Spanish Cup semifinal between Barcelona and Madrid at Camp Nou, Guruceta awarded the visitors a decisive penalty for a foul committed a hop-skip-and-jump outside the area. After the infamous 'Cushions Riot' (to this day, *culés* can still hire plastic cushions to plonk on their seats, despite their misuse on that occasion), Guruceta, who died in a car crash in 1987, was suspended for six months and blacklisted from Barça games for fourteen years. As is inevitably the case in Spain, notoriety was a referee's best route to international recognition; hence his resurrection at Forest's expense.

It seems Núñez Manrique's route to fame is at another Englishman's expense. A first-half collision between Craioveana and Abelardo was an accident in any language. Make that a penalty and 1-0 in Manrique-speak. And when Real defender Fuentes stifled a Ronaldo dribble by grabbing the ball with his hand, Captain Biggles from Madrid waved play on. And they let this guy fly a plane? Barça then fluffed a succession of clear chances before Real settled things with a goal that summed up the visitors' night; De Pedro's grass-cutting corner was going nowhere until Guardiola and Sergi contrived to deceive Baía with extravagant dummies.

Twenty minutes after the final whistle, Bobby Robson is still incensed. 'I don't like to blame referees, but the first penalty was ridiculous and then there's a clear handball in their area and he ignores it. If the guy had made the correct decisions we're looking at a totally different game.' Despite his frustration, Robson admits that his team's failure to convert their chances was equally damaging. 'It doesn't help when vital decisions go against you, but if you don't score you're not going to win games. In the first six minutes, we've missed two open goals [*the hapless Giovanni, twice*]. If we'd scored then I'm sure we'd have gone on to win. It's just a strange result, and Real's second was the most absurd goal I've seen in my whole life.'

Asked whether the referee had been conditioned by Madrid's campaign, Robson opted for discretion. 'I don't think so, at least I hope not. What people have said or done previously should make no difference.' As usual, José Mourinho is less diplomatic. 'I thought this kind of thing only happened in South America,' he spits. To their credit, the players follow Robson's example. 'Looking at it coldly, the referee has influenced the result,' says Guardiola, 'but we were the ones who weren't up to scratch. If we'd taken our chances and won three or four-nil, nobody would be talking about the referee or his penalty decisions.' Ronaldo agrees. 'The referee's not the one who missed all the chances.' He then has a word for the real villains of the piece. 'I don't understand the attitude of Spanish directors. I'm here to play football. I wish everybody else would stick to their job instead of talking so much.' Guardiola is even more scathing. 'It's about time the guys in suits shut up and stuck to the business of running the clubs; that's why they're called directors.'

FRIDAY, 21 FEBRUARY

Say what you like about Bobby Robson, but like every last football manager in the world, there's little he can do about faculty-challenged referees and players who couldn't recognise a barn door from five yards, let alone hit one. 'It's not the coach's fault if the players can't put the ball in the net,' insists Guardiola, back in Barcelona. However, public opinion is unlikely to be so magnanimous while the media are so set in their anti-Robson ways. 'The defeat at Real Sociedad was manifestly unfair,' begins today's editorial in *Sport*, 'but given their performance, Barcelona didn't deserve to win.' So which was it, unfair or deserved? That's a case of have your cake and eat it, even by Spanish standards. Then again, how can you blame Bobby Robson for his team's defeat – as the editorial goes on to do – if it was all a question of bad luck?

Elsewhere, the defenders of the Barcelona faith rage against the men in black. The Catalans as a whole, and Barça fans in particular, need little excuse to dust off their 'No one likes us' theories (a survey in today's *La Vanguardia* leaves the Catalans holding up the rest of Spain in a nationwide popularity contest), but on this one they definitely have a case. Four penalties in three away games, only one of them remotely like a penalty in the real world, and three of them courtesy of referees from Madrid, are more than reasonable grounds for suspicion.

Presidential missives are still in fashion. Josep Lluís Núñez deposits an open letter with the press, denouncing a campaign to 'subvert FC Barcelona' and rallying his troops around common goals. Robson would have been delighted by one particular paragraph. 'We've got a new coach this season who given time will get the very best out of our squad. We ask everyone to unite behind him in this decisive stretch of the season. This is not the time to make judgements, it's the time to unite.' If it weren't for the capricious nature of the Camp Nou pitch, he might have added 'We shall fight them on the beaches, too'.

SATURDAY, 22 FEBRUARY

Johan Cruyff's habit of criticising his players in public inspired the raised eyebrows of even his allies in the Catalan media. Hristo Stoichkov once complained, 'When we win it's down to Cruyff, when we lose it's always the players' fault.' Strange, then, that Bobby Robson's refusal to lay any blame for disappointing results at his players' door, even off the record, has failed to attract him the slightest praise.

'It's not my job to score,' he tells his Saturday afternoon press audience, perhaps encouraged by his players' willingness to assume responsibility for their profligacy against Real Sociedad. 'I can't possibly get on the end of things sat on the bench. It's disappointing when we miss so many clear chances, but I'm not unhappy with the players. Their attitude is fine; taking chances is just a question of confidence.' Continuing his attempts to build bridges, he denies those alleged grievances with Núñez. 'I've never complained about a lack of support, though the timing of the president's letter is perfect because it transmits confidence to me and the players.' It was a calming voice he hopes will be contagious. 'It would be nice if the fans didn't lose their patience so easily. If they get behind the team when it's losing its way that really makes a difference. Camp Nou should be a fortress; our opponents should be the ones who are frightened of playing here, not us.'

Football reporting in Spain can be many things: over the top, gratuitous, fawning and occasionally readable; it is NEVER objective. In a country where vested interests are the name of the game, few men get more chance to air their views on Barça goings-on than Josep María Minguella. By day, he's one of Spain's most powerful football agents; by night he's a media gun for hire. Rarely, on his Sunday dates on the chat show *L'Última Jugada*, or in his weekly column for *Sport*, has he found anything good to say about Bobby Robson. Affable and eloquent, he argues a seductive case for the prosecution. Hardly surprising, really. The Englishman's arrival at Camp Nou has seen a diminishing of Minguella's influence; by sticking around, he's costing 'that impresario', as he refers to him, considerable income. Robson admits he is wary of agents and is particularly distrustful of Minguella. Moreover, his preference for familiar faces has seen Portugal's José Veiga assume Minguella's coveted role as the agent most likely to be seen in collusion with Gaspart & Co.

A feature in today's *Sport* reveals that the Barcelona-based Minguella has been touting César Luis Menotti as a short-term replacement for Robson (and as he's on their payroll, they should know). Now Señor Minguella is clearly entitled to land a client a job, but doesn't the fact that he stands to profit financially from Robson's demise compromise his journalistic opinions somewhat? Sadly, Barcelona way, nobody seems to think so. And naturally, it's mere coincidence that the players who have caused problems this season are either Minguella clients (Nadal, Guardiola, Oscar, Roger) or in his orbit (De la Peña, Ferrer).

The sad lack of objectivity in the sports media reflects a much wider reality. Barely a decade ago, Spain's only TV station, Televisión Española, was government-run; there are now several competing channels but the notion of impartiality remains a fragile one. Editorial lines that are not coloured by political sympathies are tainted by economic or personal interests.

Football's TV wars ended with the so-called Christmas Eve pact. In the short term, the creation of a joint company guarantees the formula of three live games a week – Saturdays through the grouping of regional channels which includes Televisió de Catalunya, Sundays on Sky lookalike, Canal Plus, and Mondays on Antena 3 TV. Pay-per-view from Canal Satélite Digital is just around the corner. With the erstwhile broadcasting enemies now bosom pals, the next battle on the agenda is a political one. In a display of populism Eva Perón would have been proud of, Spain's conservative government plans to introduce the so-called 'football law' ensuring that games of general interest – for example, Madrid v. Barça – are broadcast to the general public on free television. Altruism? If only. Sadly, the government's association with a competing digital platform is their motivating factor.

The pre-Christmas scramble for football rights saw democratic instincts routed as editorial offices echoed the party line of whichever media baron they belong to (Antena 3 TV is part of a conglomerate that also owns *Sport* and *El Periódico*, while Canal Plus and Canal Satélite Digital belong to the group that controls *El País* and *AS*).

Now there's a common bogeyman in town it's stories all round about how the government has threatened to jail the Antena 3 president for breaking an earlier pact with their digital buddies.

Given that each Spanish football club has signed an individual rights deal with one or other of the competing TV channels, don't go looking for a flat playing field in Spain's commentary boxes, either. Why, for example, should a television company tied to Real Madrid want to praise Robson and by extension Barcelona (i.e. their competitors)? Especially when their two leading executives are, respectively, FC Barcelona's former administrative director, a man who disparages Núñez at every turn, and the guy Barça's president rejected as his successor, despite vociferous lobbying. And then there's the influential Catalan commentator who lost the race to become Núñez's PR guru earlier this season. Guess what he thinks of the Bobby–Joe tandem. Is this beginning to read like the script to a bad soap opera? It gets worse. Johan Cruyff and Jorge Valdano have both worked for another media posse that has savaged Barcelona's football this season. All these guys are sworn enemies of Javier Clemente, who is, in turn, a disciple of . . . Bobby Robson. Guess what they think of the Englishman? As usual, economics plays a role, too. The tenuous grasp of Televisión Española (the Spanish Beeb) on a football audience is limited to Clemente's Spain. The guys who have the rights to everything else spend their lives rubbishing a Spanish side that hasn't lost since the 1994 World Cup. Surprisingly. And on and on it goes. The next time Bobby Robson hears somebody crucifying him for no good reason, the first question he should ask himself is not 'Who does this guy think he is and what does he know about football?' but 'Who does he work for, who does he drink with and which club do they finance?'

SUNDAY, 23 FEBRUARY
Barcelona 4, Zaragoza 1 (Abelardo 10, Ronaldo 40 pen, 46, 73)
Camp Nou, 85,000

In Spain they say, 'If you don't cry, you don't suckle.' After a week of blubbering about nasty referees, the cry-babies from Real Madrid had to wait three whole minutes before they were gifted a penalty against Oviedo, who were simultaneously reduced to ten men. Poor, persecuted Barcelona had to wait an interminable 38 minutes before Zaragoza 'keeper Otto Konrad received his marching orders and

Ronaldo a penalty. After the break, Xavier Aguado, he of the case of mistaken identity in the game at Zaragoza, joined Otto for an early bath. Try telling Zaragoza that referees have got it in for Barcelona.

In reality, there is only one winner when it comes to the crying game. Every single Spanish president will tell you his club are persecuted by referees; only a select few – Núñez, Gaspart, Sanz, Gil – make the front page for doing so. Zaragoza did get a penalty of their own when Gustavo Poyet took Baía's pre-match counsel to heart – 'Throw yourself to the ground and you're bound to get a penalty' – but by then it was 4-0 and all over. Not that Barça's victory was undeserved. Chants of *Olé! Olé! Olé!* after the break may have prompted Robson to ask if he was hearing right, but better that than incipient whistles in the first half as Barcelona struggled to break down an eleven-man Zaragoza. After a 'four-game goal drought' (that's Spain-speak) Ronaldo's hat trick was welcome, though the biggest cheer of the afternoon was reserved for Stoichkov. On as a late sub for his first game in a month, the Bulgarian's gallop down the flank for Barça's fourth goal was reminiscent of the good old days. Only Real Madrid failed to enter into the spirit of things. Like Ronaldo, Suker used his penalty as the launching pad for a hat trick as the leaders dispatched Oviedo 6-1.

Though Robson opens his press conference with a sop for the fans – 'There was a really nice atmosphere today and the players responded accordingly' – his response to a question about Stoichkov reflects his unease at the partisan nature of the Camp Nou congregation. 'Hristo came on at the right time and was involved in three really good moves, but the crowd got behind him immediately, that really makes a difference.' It says everything about the oppressive hegemony of Barcelona's fans that Robson feels obliged to thank them for such fickle support. Giovanni, consistently, and Guardiola, sporadically, were both whistled. As was the case with Ray Wilkins in his day, the midfielder attracts the ires of a minority for a tendency to play sideways. Hecklers aside, he would no doubt appreciate it if his coach stopped calling him Gladioli!

Zaragoza coach Luis Costa (thirteen sendings-off this season compared to Barça's four) and Oviedo's Juan Manuel Lillo (eight to Madrid's four) both lamented their treatment at the hands of referees, but hey, who's listening? Today's eleven top-flight games produced nine penalties, eight sendings-off and 52 yellow cards. Oh, how Spanish refs shun the limelight! Díaz Vega, widely perceived as Spain's most officious referee, averages an incredible 4.9 bookings per game. Incredible, because that makes him Spain's most card-shy referee.

Response to Barcelona's victory is generally positive. However, Robson's *amigos* at *El Periódico* are not for turning. Apparently, Barça's victory was deceptive because three of the four goals came from dead-ball situations. Don't they count any more, then? Does that mean Barcelona didn't really win the 1992 European Cup Final because Koeman scored the only goal from a free kick?

MONDAY, 24 FEBRUARY

Robson will be delighted that Popescu is fit again for Wednesday's cup tie at Atlético Madrid. Unfortunately, Ronaldo, Giovanni and Blanc will all be missing on international duty. 'We've lost three key players,' admits the fit-again Romanian, 'but we keep insisting we've got the best squad in the world, so now's the time to show it.' Against an in-form Atlético Madrid, no less. In a transparent bid to fire up his troops, Radomir Antic has revived controversies around the pre-season Super Copa, a trophy Barça won with the help of two very contentious off-side decisions. 'We've got unfinished business with Barcelona,' warns Antic. 'They robbed us of a trophy we deserved to win, now it's time for revenge.'

The International Association of Professional Footballers meets in Barcelona today to promote a Jean Marc Bosman benefit at the Olympic stadium in April. Fears that the AIFP will be a short-lived whim of the mollycoddled and the retired are not allayed by seating arrangements. At the top of the conference table are self-proclaimed president Diego Maradona, Alfredo Di Stéfano and Johan Cruyff. A dictatorship of the proletariat, we don't think. Nobody would deny we're talking three all-time greats, but gee, none of the three were models of solidarity in their playing days (though to be fair, Diego was good at getting his round in).

Hristo Stoichkov (a name-dropper if ever there was one) and Vítor Baía (never one to miss a photo opportunity) were in attendance, but the local guys and the rank-and-file stayed at home. 'I'm surprised at their attitude,' grumbles Maradona. 'The Bosman ruling was not our doing, but it's here to stay, and a good Spanish player could perform anywhere in the world. You don't seriously think a Brazilian or Argentinian is going to come here and take Raúl or Guardiola's place?'

One of Maradona's buddies who wasn't in town was his former Sevilla teammate Davor Suker. The Real Madrid striker takes advantage of a three-day pass to hit London with TV presenter Ana Obregón, once a friend of Diego's herself and a one-woman employment agency for the Spanish paparazzi. The press put two and three together and link Suker's dirty weekend to a bid from Arsenal. Ronaldo goes back to Brazil for three days and I get crucified, moans Bobby Robson. Suker is off in London shagging a bimbo from the telly and the press just talk about Arsenal. Well, all right, he might have done if he wasn't so gallant.

TUESDAY, 25 FEBRUARY

Bobby Robson can't work out what line to take over his missing Brazilians. 'The reason we've got such a big squad is so that we can cover the absence of the Ronaldos and Giovannis; I've got every confidence in the players who will come in,' he tells journalists, before changing tack. 'Of course we're going to miss them; it's not a question of feeling sorry for ourselves, but if you took Kiko and Esnaider out of Atlético's side they'd be in exactly the same boat.' He seems less confused by Antic's attempts to rewrite history. 'He should come and work here [*not the wisest of suggestions in the present circumstances*] if he thinks referees are against him; and he should forget about the Super Copa; Atlético only beat us in Madrid because we had six first-choice players missing. With our strongest side in the first leg, we beat them five-two.'

Robson is a self-confessed fan of Popescu. 'I really like Gica,' he says. 'It doesn't matter where you play him or what you ask him to do, he always does a job for you. He's a great professional.' Nonetheless, the Romanian is in his bad books today. An appearance last night on *Cent x Cent Fútbol* is to blame. 'Journalists ask me if it's a risk bringing him back for such an important game after injury, yet they're the ones who've got him in a TV studio until two o'clock in the morning! You'd expect me to get annoyed if he was spotted in a disco, well, it's practically the same thing. He's not in bed, is he? Gica says he'd agreed to do the show ages ago, but I'd expect him to be more responsible.'

'It's not my intention to stop the players doing radio or television,' he continues when informed that Johan Cruyff contained media overkill by personally controlling appearances, 'but please, not in the middle of the night.'

WEDNESDAY, 26 FEBRUARY
Atlético Madrid 2, Barcelona 2 (Pizzi 43 pen, 66)
Spanish Cup quarterfinal, first leg. Vicente Calderón, 45,000

Before the game, Barça centre-half Abelardo had said, 'If we sit back and defend we're bound to lose.' He might have added, 'And if we trade punches with Atlético, we're bound to get knocked out'. If Atlético Madrid were a boxer they'd be a Smokin' Joe Frazier. Antic's men are what the Spanish call *un equipo barriobajero*, a team from the wrong side of the tracks, and the neighbourhood daddy is a testosterone-charged Argentinian called Diego 'Half-Breed' Simeone.

Much to everyone's surprise, Barça take Atlético on at their own game. For the first time this season, Robson pitched all the big fellas into the same battle; Nadal, Abelardo, Popescu and Couto soon proved they can mix it with the best of 'em. An incredible 58 first-half stoppages were barely troubled by the intervention of the ball. Not surprisingly, the cuts men had a busy night, though a lengthy stoppage as Atlético's physio struggled to stem a blood-red geezer in Simeone's nether regions was something of a role reversal. Ten minutes after the Argentinian had put Atlético ahead, Fernando Couto mugged him with a more-than-passable impersonation of Jackie Chan; amazingly, the referee only produced a yellow card (he obviously didn't believe what he was seeing, either). Couto's 'come and have a go' response to Diego's goalscoring effrontery proved contagious. Pizzi's two-goal retort to Ronaldo's absence – the second with his first touch after a time-out with a bloody nose – looked to have secured Barça a deserved victory. As Bobby Robson put it: 'Kiko's equaliser was simply the kind of genius you can't legislate against.'

No sooner had the game started than Spain's radio commentators were lamenting Robson's 'conservative' tactics. Trying to find a football-free wavelength on big game night is nigh on impossible; finding a guy in the press box who's not tuned in to one or other of the sporting frequencies is impossible. Can't these guys think for themselves? Ninety minutes after his collective lecturing, Robson's decision to man-mark Caminero, Kiko and Esnaider was looking more than justified. 'We had to ensure Atlético never built up a head of steam; that meant shadowing them man to man and breaking up their fluency.'

Delighted as he is with the whole team, Robson reserves special praise for Pep Guardiola. 'He's been in exceptional form recently, and tonight he was outstanding.' Guardiola first emerged as a ball-playing pivot alongside Ronald Koeman. After a couple of seasons going backwards, he's been playing the best football of his career under Robson. While critics bemoan his deep-lying function, the 26-year-old has concentrated on proving he's the heart and soul of the side; his absolute refusal to waste a pass is worthy of a man whose surname means 'piggy bank' in Catalan. The dapper stylist who disappeared on his team's bad days is now one of Europe's most dogged footballers. Italy is watching closely.

On the other side of the globe, Brazil beat Poland 4-2 in the debut of the so-called 'Ro-Ro tandem' – that's Ronaldo and Romario as a strike force to die for. Giovanni, who kept Juninho out of the team, gatecrashed the party with two goals of his own. Once again, Ronaldo's presence back home brings bad tidings for Barça. His agents claim to be 'emotionally hurt' at Barcelona's failure to rubber-stamp December's contract upgrade. 'We've given the board plenty of time to finance the new deal; we can't wait much longer,' says Reinaldo Pitta. Alexandre Martins goes even further. 'The train was at Barcelona's station and they let it pass by. From now on, we're not going to say anything about Ronaldo's offers, we'll just let him get on with playing while we study his future. We only have to pay his buy-out clause and he can walk.'

THURSDAY, 27 FEBRUARY

A breaking story indicates that Fabio Capello will soon be heading back to Italy. Barely on speaking terms with Lorenzo Sanz, Capello is dismayed by Madrid's organisational chaos and their unwillingness to strengthen a squad he believes would be embarrassed in the Champions League. Like Bobby Robson at Barcelona, he is also furious at the way the club's internal business filters through to the press (including tonight's meeting when Capello tells Sanz he wants out). On the day that Bill Clinton's future is compromised by accusations that he rented out the Lincoln Room in return for donations to his presidential campaign, troubles at Spain's own White House, *la Casa Blanca*, can only be good news for Barcelona. 'Any situation like this carries over into the dressing room,' says Bobby Robson. 'It's a shame it didn't happen earlier.'

FRIDAY, 28 FEBRUARY

Either the boy isn't on speaking terms with his agents or he likes to spin a yarn. 'I'm very happy at Barcelona,' claims Ronaldo on arriving back from Brazil. 'The only thought in my head is to stay here and win things; there'll be plenty of time to sort out my contract at the end of the season. I know there are clubs prepared to pay my buy-out clause, but if Barça want me to stay I'll do everything possible to make sure they get their wish.'

So it's get on board the Ronaldo train, after all? Well, not exactly. He might put his own slant on things, but the player isn't denying his agents' version of the facts. 'The problem is that we signed a draft agreement and Barça haven't stuck to the 20 January deadline. They did ask for another week to sort things out, but that's long gone as well. I don't understand it, I actually had a ten-year contract in my hand to sign. We only left it because of a few minor details.' We may be talking a transparent attempt to force Barcelona's hand, but the club's leisurely attitude does seems strange. Don't they realise that £17 million (barely enough to buy you a couple of Hartson–Kitson combinations) for Ronaldo is beginning to look like a giveaway?

Lorenzo Serra Ferrer, Spain's longest-standing coach, celebrates THREE WHOLE YEARS at Betis today. Way to go, Lorenzo.

SATURDAY, 1 MARCH
Tenerife 4, Barcelona 0
Heliodoro Rodríguez, 23,000

In the build-up to tonight's game, Tenerife President Javier Pérez accused Spanish referees of being 'shit-eaters' for bowing to pressure from Barcelona and Real Madrid. With their boys on the wrong end of two more penalties and a double sending-off, we suggest the Catalan lobby revises its menu.

'Both red cards looked justified to me,' concedes a forlorn-looking Robson. 'We played reasonably well in the first half, even after Nadal was sent off, but the game finished as a contest when Abelardo went, as well.' The last time Barcelona lost 4-0, against Cádiz in 1991, they had just been proclaimed champions. If Real Madrid beat Espanyol on Monday, Barça's on-the-road blues (that's a three-game run of no points at 0-8) will leave them staring a runners-up spot in the face. 'That was a very sorry performance,' admits Popescu. 'Four-nil is four-nil, it doesn't matter whether it's against eleven, ten or nine players. We seem incapable of putting a run of three or four wins together. I really can't tell you why, it's not as if there isn't quality to spare in the squad.'

Ah yes, the squad, the latest buzz-word to haunt Robson. Ronaldo and Giovanni arrived in Tenerife last night after a second transatlantic flight in five days, yet despite the bags under their eyes both made today's starting line-up, as did Guardiola, despite a dead-of-the-night arrival after the eleventh-hour lifting of his suspension. Consequently, post-match debate was dominated by Robson's decision to sacrifice Amor and, above all, Pizzi, the two-goal hero against Atlético and understandably keen to play against his old team. Giovanni, who looks jet-lagged on his good days, wandered around in a trance for 45 minutes; Ronaldo was reduced to diving around looking for penalties. 'Ronaldo looked knackered,' said Tenerife midfielder Alexis. 'Maybe he has to play to justify his salary, I can't see any other reason.' Perhaps the youngster needed to take his mind off a more sordid reality. Just minutes before the game, he was told his dad had been arrested in Copacabana for cocaine possession.

'If I'd changed the team and we'd won, would anybody have asked me why I'd made the changes?' Robson asks journalists after the game. Probably not, but as *La Vanguardia*'s Enric Bañeres puts it, 'There's a growing feeling in the dressing room that several players have overstayed their welcome in the team, while others deserve more of a chance. After the praise for the way the team played at Atlético, it was a kick in the collective teeth to see the Brazilians start this game. And Robson can't be happy with certain regulars who aren't doing anything to save his head.' Even some of the peasants are revolting. 'It seems Robson counts on just twelve players,' says the Spanish international Ángel Cuéllar, 'however badly they play.'

Excessively loose talk about the world's best squad may be beyond Robson's control, but his own oft-repeated arguments regarding the need for a big squad threaten to rebound on him if he doesn't cast his net a bit wider. Nobody questions the untouchable status of, say, Ronaldo, Luis Enrique and Sergi, but the coach's tendency to field weary leading men is a slight on some more than capable understudies. Giovanni's performances in nineteen starts compare very unfavourably to Pizzi's in just three, and the ever-present Luis Figo has flattered to deceive while De la Peña has started just four games, and Celades, Roger and Oscar boast seven starts between them.

SUNDAY, 2 MARCH

Robson's stock response to poor reviews earlier in the season was to blind-side critics with favourable statistics. It's a tactic that threatens to backfire on him. Thirty-seven league goals conceded so far is Barcelona's worst defensive start in more than 30 years, and his side have now lost as many games as Johan Cruyff's in a farewell campaign described by Núñez as a 'disaster'. Addressing a supporters' club get-together, Barcelona's president adopts what have become familiar tactics when things are not going entirely as planned. 'In the last eighteen years, no other club has won as many European titles as FC Barcelona: in football, basketball, hockey and handball,' says Núñez, ignoring the fact that FC stands for Fútbol Club and that 95 per cent of Barça members frankly don't give a damn about the rest. Plan B is equally familiar. 'Real Madrid are more than fifty million pounds in debt while we're showing a thirty-million-pound profit over the last five years. If we compare our respective situations we're clearly the privileged ones.'

Núñez's notoriously creative book-keeping aside, the only deficit Barça fans are interested in is the one at the top of the table. 'I've always insisted that the time to make assessments is at the end of the season,' says the president. 'Let's not forget, this is a year of transition.' Unfortunately for one man, transition years at Barcelona tend to be between one coach and another.

MONDAY, 3 MARCH

Two goals by Raúl dash the hopes of both Barcelona's footballing *familias*. Real Madrid's 2-0 victory at Sarrià leaves Espanyol facing a relegation battle and Barça trailing the leaders by a season-high nine-point margin. Once a year, Catalonia's *Madridistas* sneak out of the woodwork and transform Sarrià into the so-called 'Little Bernabéu'. After tonight's recital, the 20,000 Madrid contingent had every reason to smile as they tucked their scarves back into plastic bags and headed back to their *culé*-occupied neighbourhoods. Even the chronically prudent Fabio Capello was contented. 'It's difficult to see anybody beating us the way we played in the second half.' More worrying for Barça fans were Lorenzo Sanz's matter-of-fact observations. 'Barcelona aren't even guaranteed second place now. Depor, Betis and Atlético are all breathing down their neck and in much better form.'

Earlier in the day, Núñez had broached the same delicate subject. 'If we finish second and don't make the Champions League, we'll compete in the UEFA instead. *No pasa nada.*' Núñez's blasé frame of mind extended to Ronaldo's future. 'I've no intention of renegotiating contracts until the end of the season, not even Ronaldo's. We never said that we definitely had sponsors to pay his salary increase, only that there were several interested companies.' Bobby Robson's future was next on his agenda. 'I can't guarantee that he'll continue until the end of the season, you can never say never. But it's the board's intention that he stays. All things being equal, Robson will be here until the end of the season.' Never say never? All things being equal? The Englishman would have been even less enamoured of the musings of club spokesman Josep María Antrás. 'Every board member is a frustrated coach, that's why we try and enrich Robson with our opinions. We'll offer our advice so that he can help the team become more consistent.'

Robson himself spent a tense 45 minutes before training giving his players some valuable advice. 'I've told the players a thousand times, "You can lose a game in a couple of seconds, you must maintain your concentration from the first moment to the very last, whoever the opponents." We need to talk more in training and on the pitch, that's the way to maintain our concentration.' Ronaldo half agrees. 'It's good to talk in the dressing room, but we should do our talking on the pitch. Three away games without a goal is worrying, but a team that wants to win the league really shouldn't concede so many goals.'

Josep Lluís Núñez had time today for an unsolicited attack on his previous coach, summed up by the laughable phrase 'It's thanks to me that Johan Cruyff was so successful at Barcelona'. Like most people, Michael Robinson believes it was the other way round. 'When Cruyff was at Barça, he not only built a great team, he also polished Núñez's public image because he didn't have to speak in public. Now Cruyff's not here to cover him, Núñez is walking on a tightrope without a safety net.'

	P	W	D	L	F	A	PTS
Real Madrid	27	18	8	1	59	22	62
Barcelona	27	16	5	6	67	37	53
Deportivo	27	13	11	3	40	20	50
Betis	26	14	8	4	53	28	50
Atlético Madrid	26	14	7	5	51	31	49

TUESDAY, 4 MARCH

Robson reacts to suggestions that the board will tender their counsel with resignation. 'Nobody has said anything to me. No director has to give me ideas about football.' And if they tried? He covers his ears deliberately and smiles. 'I don't accept advice. There are three million coaches in Barcelona and every one has got their own opinion. But I'm not going to listen to other people's, I'm only interested in my own.' '*El mister* doesn't need advice from anybody,' agrees Gica Popescu, among others.

The Ronaldo negotiations are threatening to get out of hand. The player's response to Núñez's latest snub is as clear as it's disconcerting. 'If the president said they didn't agree terms with us, then there's really nothing more to be said.' His men in Ipanema are even more forthright. 'The only way Ronaldo will stay at FC Barcelona after 30 June is if we don't receive a single offer from another club,' says Alexandre Martins. Patently not the case. 'These Brazilians change their tune every five minutes,' responds Núñez. 'One day they're saying they'll take Ronaldo somewhere else, the next they say he'll stay here for eight years. Which story are we supposed to believe?' Perhaps the president should take Bobby Robson's advice. 'The more that's said in public about Ronaldo's contract, the more difficult it'll be to handle the situation properly. I've told the lad to forget about it for now and I suggest everybody else does the same.'

WEDNESDAY, 5 MARCH

Barcelona's débâcle at Tenerife is not looking any better with age. A goal by a 25-year-old part-timer called, appropriately, Sand earns Brondby a 1-0 UEFA Cup win on the isle. Not surprisingly, then, Bobby Robson won't be taking his own Scandinavian opponents lightly. 'If that's not a warning I don't know what is. I've told my players that AIK Stockholm will treat tomorrow as the game of their lives. We have to be at least as committed, only then can we make our quality pay.' All Bobby really wants is a nice quiet night. 'There's too much drama in our games, we have to avoid making silly mistakes that create dramatic situations.'

If six million Catalans with an attitude weren't bad enough, some guy called Pelé is on Robson's case. 'Just because a team has the best players doesn't mean it's going to win the league,' says Brazil's sports minister, once a decent footballer himself. 'Despite all the money they've spent, and despite having a stronger squad than Real Madrid, Barcelona are not top, are they? Bobby Robson is an experienced coach, but I think he's lost control of things.'

THURSDAY, 6 MARCH
***Barcelona 3, AIK Stockholm 1** (Popescu 2, Ronaldo 55, Pizzi 80)*
European Cup Winners' Cup quarterfinal, first leg. Camp Nou, 55,000

Come on, *chicos*, what did the boss say about less drama? Less than a minute into the game and Carlos Busquets goes walkabout and gifts AIK's Pascal Simpson the easiest goal of his life. As number thirteen Busquets stared at the ground for an escape route, Robson contemplated the heavens with an expression that read 'Why me?' Luckily for Barça's reserve 'keeper, the nice Swedes immediately invited Popescu to equalise.

Before the game, Guardiola had also warned of the dangers of complacency. 'AIK are in the last eight of the Cup Winners' Cup,' he said. 'They can't be cripples, can they?' Perhaps not, but if UEFA president and former AIK player, Lennart Johansson had dusted off his boots and vacated the presidential box, he wouldn't have looked out of place in the worst side to grace Camp Nou in years. That Barça scored just three times was a mixture of bad luck, worse finishing and David Elleray's inability to pronounce penalty in Spanish. Obviously a case of 'when in Barcelona'. Maybe Robson should simply accept the inevitable and train for a ten-man game. Only late subs Pizzi, who naturally scored after ten minutes, and De la Peña could take any pride in their performances. 'I love playing with Iván because he's always looking to play that killer ball,' said Ronaldo in a broad hint to the boss.

As the news filtered through that Betis were thrashing Sporting Gijón to draw level with Barça, the crowd's humour shifted from bad to worse. Robson had reacted to Busquets' blunder by geeing up his 'keeper from the touchline. A shame the fans who barracked him for the rest of the game didn't adopt his line in solidarity. For his part, Bobby Robson refused to comment on the whistles that reverberated his way every time he left the bench. 'During the game I'm only thinking about making the right decisions. I thought we reacted well after that disaster in the first minute; we could have easily scored eight goals.'

FRIDAY, 7 MARCH
Once again, Robson reaps the dubious rewards of a gripe sown by a hostile press. 'I feel humiliated,' said Julen Lopetegui, the latest player to catch the 'give us a game' disease from the suddenly

democratically inclined media. 'I'm not attacking anybody, but Robson told me he picked Busquets because of his international experience. Who's he trying to convince? I'm the one who's played for Spain. If he doesn't rate me, I should have been told at the beginning of the season.' Meanwhile, Gica Popescu, one of the guys the press would like to see less of, reacts tetchily to Ronaldo's wowing of De la Peña and match reports suggesting that 'Little Buddah' did more in 20 minutes than he did in 70. 'Iván is a quality player and yesterday he made three good passes, but that was in favourable circumstances in one specific game. It's not always like that. Other times, things haven't worked out for him.' In other words, I'm the midfield pivot in this side and don't you forget it.

SATURDAY, 8 MARCH

Robson responds to the debilitating Morse coding in the press. 'I can't control what journalists say but I've told the players to be more responsible and to show more respect to their teammates. I've told them, "You get paid to play football, not to talk, so shut up and play." Picking the team is none of their business. They're employed by the club to play ninety minutes or one minute; to be on the bench or waiting in the wings. I'm trying to create a good atmosphere here but there's always someone to light the spark. What does Lopetegui mean when he says he feels humiliated? I can understand him being disappointed, I would be, too, but humiliated?' Robson also had harsh words for Giovanni, who claims he needs more time to adapt to Spanish football. 'It's a good job he hasn't got my job. All he has to do is put his shirt on and play, and the truth is we've given him lots of opportunities.'

SUNDAY, 9 MARCH

Barcelona 3, Compostela 0 (Blanc 5, Stoichkov 24, Ronaldo 63)
Camp Nou, 90,000

A combination of injuries, suspensions and Atlético Madrid waiting around the corner sees an unrecognisable Barça sweep aside a rival so feeble that even another Madrid-born referee can't save them. For the first time this season, Robson's side dance to a Catalan tune: Busquets, Ferrer, Sergi, Amor, Roger and De la Peña making it an unprecedented six home-grown players in the starting line-up. Fittingly, it was Guillermo Amor's 500th game in the famous

192

scarlet-and-blue stripes; Guardiola may get the popular vote, but Amor is the guy his young teammates adore.

Bobby Robson normally spends his post-match parleys stoking the fires of everybody else's debatable enthusiasm; today he struggles to dowse a sudden outbreak of the stuff. For the first time since opening day, 'Little Buddah' and Stoichkov, increasingly the totems of popular discontent, make the same team. If journalists were to be believed, they were the men behind 'Barça's best performance of the season'. Naturally the zealots have a hidden agenda. Robson knows that if he concurs, the press will crucify him if his line-up reverts to type. 'It was a good result in a comfortable game, but it wasn't spectacular and Compostela are not Betis or Atlético, are they? They played with one forward and never put us under pressure in defence. After our second goal it was a very straightforward game.'

Crippling nepotism/blatant marketing push sport off the front pages of the specialist press, again. The Barça v. Compostela game marks the debut of pay-per-view television in Spain (attracting 1,625 viewers at £5 a time). Today's *AS* reads like a cover ad for the revolution; that's absolutely nothing about how the best games will no longer be free, but plenty of 'Oh, aren't those nice people at Canal Satélite Digital doing football fans a favour'. A reminder: *AS* and Canal Satélite are part of the same media conglomerate.

Otto Konrad is not having much luck in his debut season in Spain. In a sinister turn on the craze for using 'keepers for target practice, the Austrian suffers first-degree burns to his eyelid after a firework fells him at San Mamés. 'It's bad enough someone throwing a bottle on the pitch in a moment of frustration,' he moans, 'but a firework involves premeditation.' Vítor Baía, forgetting perhaps that the guys behind his own goals are among the worst culprits, sympathises. 'At the Bernabéu, my box ended up littered with coins, lighters, batteries and a full two-litre bottle of Coca-Cola.' No wonder 'keepers in Spain are so fond of punching; it's not easy playing football with one eye on the ball and the other on rogue missiles.

'Vítor punches the ball all the time because he comes from a different culture,' says Bobby Robson. 'That's the Continental way of goalkeeping, it's always been like that, it was like that forty years ago when I was playing. In England we train 'keepers to secure the ball; we think it's better to catch the ball and hold on to it than do a diving punch for the photo and get the Oohs! and Aahs! of the crowd. Every day in training I shout at Busi and Lopetegui and Vítor,

"Secura el balón, secura el balón!" but they still go punch, punch, punch.' As the word *secura* doesn't exist in Spanish, not altogether surprising. 'The other day the ball went to Vítor in the first minute and all he had to do was say "Thank you" and catch it, but he's gone [*leaps out of his seat to demonstrate*] Ping! and punched it straight in the air with both fists. His wife could have caught it. But it's ingrained in them, perhaps it's because they've never played cricket!'

MONDAY, 10 MARCH
Real Madrid beat Racing Santander 2-1 to restore their nine-point lead. Two weeks after Robson was censured for taking Ronaldo off in the last minute against the same opposition, Fabio Capello reacts to Madrid's second goal by replacing Suker with a defender with more than 20 minutes to go. 'And not a whistle in the house,' says Robson. 'I'd love to know how our press would have reacted if we'd played as badly as Madrid did against Racing and been so lucky.'

TUESDAY, 11 MARCH
Atlético Madrid centre-forward Juan Esnaider, the scourge of Arsenal and Chelsea when at Zaragoza, was sent off on Sunday for feigning a head-butt, an incident that led teammates Simeone and Geli to compliment the referee on his eyesight. Barça should do the same, without a trace of irony. The Atlético trio are suspended this morning by the Spanish FA, and as there's no hanging around when it comes to suspensions, Antic's side will face Barça in the second leg of their cup quarterfinal with three key absentees, a decision that sends Jesús Gil into one of his famous strops. At 4.30 this afternoon, he sends word to Madrid airport, ordering his players back home. 'I have to consult with my lawyers, but if it's up to me, we won't play. This is the biggest outrage in the history of Spanish football. If justice isn't done, I'd prefer to pay the price [*elimination, bans, compensation*] than go down on my knees to a bunch of nobodies.'

Like most people, Bobby Robson is convinced Gil is bluffing. 'If we get through to the semifinals without playing, I'll say *muchas gracias*, Atlético, but I don't seriously think it'll happen. My job is to make sure the players don't get confused or distracted by the situation.' Neither does he rule out a measure of cod psychology on Gil's part. 'He could be trying to influence tomorrow's referee. Do you seriously think Atlético would be threatening a boycott if the result had been different in the first leg?'

At this morning's disciplinary meeting, it's also decided to close San Mamés for two games and fine Athletic Bilbao £5,000 for their firework display. That's to say, a bad impersonation of a Glaswegian kiss and a few harsh words are considered as serious as sight-threatening artefacts. Amazingly, Bilbao announce they will appeal because the sentence is 'excessive'. 'Konrad only suffered slight injuries, after all,' argues skipper Julen Guerrero. No wonder Robson says, 'Let's just say the decisions made by the Spanish disciplinary committee are very different to those in other countries.'

WEDNESDAY, 12 MARCH
Barcelona 5, Atlético Madrid 4 *(Ronaldo 47, 50, 72, Figo 67, Pizzi 82)*
Spanish Cup quarterfinal, second leg. Camp Nou, 80,000
Barça: Baía, Abelardo, Blanc (Pizzi 40), Couto, Sergi, Guardiola, Popescu (Stoichkov 40), Luis Enrique, De la Peña, Figo (Nadal 88), Ronaldo.
Atlético: Molina, López, Prodan, Santi, Toni (Solozábal 55), Aguilera (Vizcaino 70), Bejbl, Pantic, Paunovic (Roberto 75), Caminero, Kiko

The game that nearly wasn't turned out to be one Robson admits he'll 'never forget'. Barely a week after he'd asked his players for 'less drama, please', a 0-3 deficit at half-time left Barça looking dead and *el mister* buried. Five goals later, and we were talking one of the 'all-time great comebacks' instead.

Like most of life's great nights, it kind of sneaked up on you. The Spanish FA ratified the triple suspension at midday; Jesús Gil ummed and ahhed until teatime before succumbing to reality. Consequently, Atlético's squad arrived at Barcelona airport less than two hours before kick-off; as some seriously vexed expressions revealed, hardly ideal preparation for a vital football match. A combination of subway strikes and a walkout at Televisió de Catalunya added to the suspicion that this was the game somebody didn't want us to see. The lack of public transport kept the crowd down to 80,000. After an eleventh-hour compromise, housebound *culés* did get to see the game, but with no sound (some would say a strike was never better timed; how could words have done justice to such a memorable game?).

Watching their first-half no-show, you'd have thought Barça's players were the ones who'd spent two days hanging around at airports. By half-time, Bobby Robson was hanging on to his job by the slightest of threads as choruses of 'Núñez Out! Robson Out!'

195

resounded around the ground and fights broke out between stewards and fans who tried to unveil an anti-Núñez banner. Desperate times call for desperate measures. A double substitution before the break (Stoichkov and Pizzi for Popescu and Blanc) demonstrated that, at the very least, Robson was determined to go out with a bang. It was Atlético, however, who were blown to pieces in the second half as Ronaldo's treble, a remarkable volley by Figo and a last-gasp winner from Pizzi provoked collective frenzy.

Spare a thought for Atlético's Milinko Pantic. The first ever visitor to score four goals at Camp Nou and he trudges off a loser. Vítor Baía, whose lamentable performance gifted 'Panty' at least two of his goals, was equally inconsolable. As the 'keeper was led off weeping, De la Peña raised his arm like a victorious boxer, a gesture that provoked a thunderous ovation from a suddenly contrite Camp Nou (they'd barracked Baía all night). Up in the stand, the invariably lachrymose Josep Lluís Núñez was also blubbing away while Joan Gaspart, in what has become a ritual in nail-biting situations, had to be rescued from a toilet after locking himself in after the fourth goal.

'We've gone from disaster to triumph in ninety minutes,' croaks Bobby Robson in what is left of his voice. Asked what the hell had gone on out there, he admits it was a game that defied analysis. 'God knows. You'll have to give me time to sit back and take it all in. I've been in football a hell of a long time and I don't remember anything remotely like that second half. We've just seen something special, so let's take some time to enjoy it. At half-time, I told the players to take a look at the shirt they were wearing, think about what those colours meant, and go out and win 4-0 in the second half. Scoring two goals straight away was the key; that inspired the players to fight back while they still had gas in the tank.'

The second half saw Barça's full attacking arsenal – Ronaldo, Pizzi, Stoichkov, Figo, De la Peña and Guardiola – on show together for the first time this season. It prompted the inevitable question. Why didn't Robson play them together more often? 'You can't play like that in every game. If it was possible, why don't you think anybody has ever done it? Like I said, tonight was a very special game. We've got great players but every game is different. Football's not like bullfighting, where you know that the bull always has to die at the end.'

Louis Van Gaal, on hand to spy on Atlético, was one very confused observer. The Ajax coach started the game by taking copious notes; come the second half he threw away his exercise book to stand up and cheer with the best of 'em. 'It was a marvellous match between two great sides. I can't remember the last time I enjoyed a game so much.' A week before Ajax's Champions League visit to Vicente Calderón, Van Gaal would have been tickled to bits by Atlético's collapse. As favourite to take over from Robson, he would have been delighted by Barça's comeback. Whichever hat he's wearing, he'd do well to ignore that first half.

THURSDAY, 13 MARCH
The soul-destroying reality of Robson's lot at Barcelona was never more evident. What should have been a day for savouring an epic comeback sees the Englishman on the rack. 'Robson lost the first half 3-0, the players won the second half 5-1,' writes Emilio Pérez de Rozas in *El Periódico*. 'The comeback took place because the players finally broke out of the coach's strait-jacket.' The editorial in *AS* is even more implacable. 'Poor Robson. All the time you were sitting on this awesome attacking machine and you didn't know it. Instead you wait until you've got a rope around your neck before abandoning your own futile tactics. You're in debt, Señor Robson, not just to Barça supporters, but to football fans everywhere.'

'I've defended Robson against the witch-hunt until now,' writes *El Mundo Deportivo* columnist José María Ducamp, 'but after the Atlético game it's clear he's reached his sell-by date. The players have never believed in him; now they ignore him. Before the game, the board ordered him to play De la Peña, and before the second half the players could be seen in a huddle working out their own tactics.' *La Vanguardia*'s Dagoberto Escorcia, another of the erstwhile Robson-ites, backs the claims of anarchy. 'Robson didn't dare open his mouth in the dressing room at half-time, it was Stoichkov who had to break the silence and gee up his teammates. Then Guardiola insisted all was not lost so the players started to organise things among themselves.'

Whatever his role in the dressing-room revival, everyone from Van Gaal to Antic agrees it was Stoichkov's sheer willpower that changed the course of the game. 'He was their most important player,' says Antic. 'Psychologically he made all the difference, he lifted them up when they were finished.' Unfortunately for Robson, Stoichkov takes advantage of his acclaimed performance to throw a match on the bonfire. Incensed at starting the game on the bench, the Bulgarian was overheard cursing the 'damn Portuguese' (Baía, Mourinho, Robson, the whole clan?) as he stomped off at half-time. Today, he remains in belligerent mood. 'Van Gaal, Antic and the Barça fans understand football, not like others who still haven't got the picture. I've done enough to deserve a place in the team, but it's down to Robson and he doesn't seem to be willing. Knowing him, he won't change, either. I'm sure we'll go back to the same old tactics at Logroñes. As for that stuff about looking at the shirt, that's rubbish. If you've got no heart you shouldn't be playing football in the first place.' Asked if he would be playing on Sunday, he spits, 'Ask the president.'

FRIDAY, 14 MARCH
A slightly better day for Bobby Robson. A semifinal draw against Second Division strugglers Las Palmas is handsome reward for eliminating Madrid's heavyweight duo in the Cup. The players are doing their bit to cheer him up, too. Amor, Luis Enrique and De la Peña censor Stoichkov for his untimely declarations, while Guardiola pooh-poohs the notion that Robson doesn't pull the strings. 'People can't blame Robson when we lose and then say it's got nothing to do with him when we win. He made the changes in the same way he always does; he was the one who told the players what to do and where to play. We're happy to assume our responsibilities on the pitch, but it's Robson's job to decide the tactics; it's simply not true that we rode roughshod over his instructions. Robson is in charge, we limit ourselves to playing football.'

SATURDAY, 15 MARCH
An incensed Robson refutes the puppet-on-a-string accusations. 'Nobody interferes with the team,' he tells journalists gathered at Camp Nou after training, 'and nobody tells me who to play or what system to play. The first time somebody does, I'll say, "Here you are, you train the team then." And can you please explain something to me? I brought Stoichkov and Pizzi on ten minutes before half-time, so who made that decision? [*He gestures as if talking on the phone.*] Núñez, Van Gaal, Antic, the club doctor, you lot?

'You'd think it was the first time this season we've played attacking football or come from behind to win. Do you really think we'd have scored so many goals if we played conservative football? It doesn't make sense when people say we haven't got a system; scoring goals is the most difficult thing in football, if not games would finish 11-10 all the time. How can you score goals if you haven't got a system? That's the stupidest thing I've heard in my life. And you can't possibly say the team has lacked guts, or that I have when it comes to picking the team. I'm the same coach I've always been.'

Robson is one who goes easy on his players in public, however unruly. 'I've spoken to Hristo face to face and he assures me he wasn't talking about me [*this despite the fact that Stoichkov's unambiguous comments were made on television*]. But I've still had strong words with him. I asked him if he'd played in a World Cup and he answered yes. I told him, "Me too, so we're on the same level."' Whatever Robson said behind closed doors, Stoichkov seems to have got the message. 'Bobby Robson is Barcelona's coach and his is the only opinion that counts. He has to decide whether I'm in the team or not.' The boss himself is keeping tomorrow's side to himself. 'The fans can dream about the line-up that beat Atlético, but there's a romantic and a realistic side to football.'

SUNDAY, 16 MARCH
Logroñes 0, Barcelona 1 (Amunike 82)
Las Gaunas, 18,000

'No two games in the history of football are ever alike,' said Robson before the game. You can say that again, Bobby. Ignoring his own better instincts, the coach paid homage to Wednesday's exploits by starting with his second-half heroes. Forty-five minutes of dour fare later Pizzi manages Barça's first shot on target against relegation-bound Logroñes. If the locals had gone on to take their chances in the second half, it could have been even worse. Luckily, substitute Amunike began to pay back Robson's blind faith with his first goal for Barça. 'Robson has got twenty lives,' joked *Sport*'s Antoni Closa as the unlikely saviour was mobbed by his teammates at the final whistle.

MONDAY, 17 MARCH
AS cite a spokesman at Nike who claims the company can't justify their investment in Ronaldo if he stays at Camp Nou. 'We can't possibly wait three years until Barcelona's deal with Kappa ends, that's three years of Ronaldo photos in another kit.' The inside source also suggests that Real Madrid are in a position to link up with Nike and place themselves at the head of the Ronaldo queue.

Meanwhile, a story from Italy claims that Juventus are prepared to pay Ronaldo's buy-out clause and offer him $25 million for eight seasons.

The front cover of Friday's *AS* boasted a photo of Barça's eleven second-half heroes and the legend 'The New Dream Team'. The message? Drop them if you dare! Two days later, *AS* claims 'Robson got it wrong by playing the same team'. No reasons given.

TUESDAY, 18 MARCH

Nike issue a statement denying any involvement in decisions about Ronaldo's future. 'Our job is to manufacture sportswear for the world's best athletes, we are not involved in deciding which clubs our stars play for. Speculation about Nike's involvement in Ronaldo's negotiations with Barcelona or any other club is simply absurd.' Madrid President Lorenzo Sanz concurs. 'We've had absolutely no contact with Nike or Ronaldo.' Almost simultaneously, Juventus factotum Luciano Moggi calls a press conference to insist that his club 'cannot afford to sign Ronaldo'.

So that's another *AS* story and anonymous source rubbished. But why the inventions? Apart from the obvious – a 'Ronaldo for Madrid' cover sells papers – there are interested parties at work. According to a report in today's *AS*, Ronaldo's agents have cancelled a Río press conference and the announcement that their charge would leave Barcelona at the end of the season. Why? How about because Núñez panicked at the Madrid/Juve stories and called to say, 'Cancel the conference, we'll sit down and talk on your terms.' As Jorge Valdano, the former Real coach and a man with an exquisite sense of history, puts it: 'If Ronaldo joins Real Madrid it'll be history's second Di Stéfano case.' The mere thought was enough to set the alarm bells ringing at Camp Nou. For Ronaldo's entourage and their allies in the press, a case of mission accomplished.

Bobby Robson steers clear of the 'Ronaldo for Madrid' speculation, preferring to concentrate on the player's more immediate future. 'I spoke to him about his fitness on Monday. I want him to eat properly, to sleep well and get plenty of rest. He plays an awful lot of games, in most cases for ninety minutes, and then there's all his journeys to Brazil. When he gets back he hardly has time to recover; that's hard for a twenty-year-old kid.' So why not give him a rest? 'He's our player, we paid a lot of money for him and we want to use him. If Brazil haven't considered giving him a rest, why should we?'

200

Robson then turns to those rumours about Wednesday's train of events. 'I'm angry, very angry. Today there's a newspaper [*El Periódico*] that's printed a pack of lies. They say the players were the ones who decided on the changes we made against Atlético. Absolute rubbish! I make the tactical decisions, me and me alone. I understand people criticising me when we lose to Hércules, say, but when we beat Rayo six-nil and the press still say we played badly I'm the one who should be complaining. Whoever started these stories, or the ones about the president calling to say I had to play De la Peña, is simply a liar. And I'm furious with the rest of the press for going along with it.'

'It's a mystery how the rumours started,' admits Amor, who was alongside Robson on the bench against Atlético. 'There's no truth to them, whatsoever.' Even Stoichkov is backing the boss. 'I'm not going to get into a war with the people who wrote this because it'll only give them more publicity, but these things hurt everybody at the club. And it's not the first time the press have tried to use me by writing this kind of rubbish.'

Away from the glare of the cameras, Robson continues to reflect on a momentous night. 'I've never been as involved in anything as big as the Atlético comeback; three goals down and scoring five in forty-five minutes to turn it around, and we missed two sitters, as well! Those are games for the fans and for the press – they're good stories – but for the coach [*he shakes his head then breaks into nervous laughter*], believe me, as a coach you get more pleasure from going to Deportivo and winning one-nil. We conceded awful goals – Vítor Baía made the kind of mistakes you wouldn't expect from a park 'keeper – but because you're in charge, you have to take responsibility. After their first goal we crumbled; so from a coach's point of view there were some awful things that happened out there. We then pulled back to three-two and Baía makes another error with a kick 'cos [*whispering*] his head's gone.

'I'm furious with the way the press are claiming the players made the changes. I could stick knives into people who say things like that. They should grab hold of the video and take a look at the bench; the players have all got their heads in their hands like this [*cradles his head*] going, "Oh my God, we're 3-0 down." Only me and José kept our heads. The doctor's like this [*grabs his head again*]: "Oh, *mister*, ooohh, *mister*." And the stuff about me saying nothing in the dressing room at half-time is bloody ridiculous. Things like that get

201

me so angry at people. I don't know where those stories come from; nobody in the game seriously believes that stuff. They wouldn't believe that in England or Portugal.

'Chances are I'd have been out of a job if we hadn't turned things around, but that wasn't going through my mind on the bench. All I was asking myself was, "How can I recover this situation?" At three-nil we were on to a hiding; we could have chased the game and ended up losing five-nil – I've taken two defensive players off and we've got De la Peña in midfield; he's not going to defend, is he? When we were three-nil down I knew I'd be in a difficult position if we lost, even though our mistakes had nothing to do with me, but during games you divorce your mind from what might happen in the future. Anybody who says the players made the changes either doesn't understand football or has ulterior motives. They're vicious, bad people writing bad stuff.'

And what about the people in his own camp? Robson's gut reaction is to deny the undeniable. 'Was Stoichkov referring to me?' Once convinced, he's pitiless. 'That's a hot-headed statement. How does he know what goes on in Van Gaal's or Antic's head? I can lose Antic, I've lost him all season [*he counts off the results one by one*]. Stoichkov's frustrated because he wasn't in the team. He's gone, finished in many ways. He can't run so how can he play? He's all right for half an hour, but long term he's finished. We put him on because he can play for an hour and we needed someone who can score goals. We used what he still has – his character – and to be fair to him, he did it for us. But because he's had a frustrating season, he now wants to be the big boss, again. He knows he's contributed so he makes these "I'm bigger than anybody" statements. Hey [*leans over and adopts a conspiratorial tone*], in England they'd cut his fucking head off. He's not a bad bloke, he's just a big kid who says the first thing that comes into his head.'

The Spanish may be unpunctual, but they occasionally get their act together if there's money to be made. Today's *El Mundo Deportivo* comes with the video of 'Barça v. Atlético: The Great Comeback', complete with shots of a smiling Dutchman in the stand. 'I don't understand why Van Gaal is on the video,' complains Robson. 'I'm the coach so why are they promoting him?'

WEDNESDAY, 19 MARCH

A story in *El Mundo Deportivo* claims that Fabio Capello has offered his services to Núñez. 'It seems like all the world wants to come to

Barcelona, the only one who doesn't want to come is Mickey Mouse,' says Robson, adding without a smile, 'but I suppose even Mickey's better at making the substitutions than me. I'm beginning to understand Cruyff's complaints about the atmosphere here. Not that I'm going to try and change it, that's a job for a martyr. I've just got to ignore what's going on around me and concentrate on the football.'

Atlético Madrid lose 3-2 at home to Ajax in the Champions League. Ronald Koeman, back in Spain to commentate on the game for Spanish television, is one of the toughest characters around, but even he admits relief at escaping the everyday madness that is FC Barcelona. 'They were six years of intense pressure, in the end I was overwhelmed by it, I needed to leave Barcelona to recover. Now I only bump into three journalists a week, I can watch my three children grow up and my wife says she's got me back. I'm a different person.'

THURSDAY, 20 MARCH
AIK Stockholm 1, Barcelona 1 (Ronaldo 12)
Rasunda stadium, 37,000

Any doubt about the outcome lasted the dozen minutes it took Ronaldo to put Barça into the lead. Even a team as unpredictable as Robson's were never going to concede four goals against such limited opposition. *La Vanguardia*'s Enric Bañeres described the final result as 'a stupid draw'. In fact, the team's softly-softly approach to a foregone conclusion was wise given the perils of a rock-hard pitch and blustering opponents. The same cannot be said of Guardiola and De la Peña's ability to pick up yellow cards for, respectively, a handball on the halfway line and encroaching at a free kick. 'I'm disappointed with the bookings,' admits Robson. 'If ever there was a game for avoiding yellow cards it was this one.' Both players will miss the first leg of the semifinal against Fiorentina.

SUNDAY, 23 MARCH
Barcelona 4, Sevilla 0 (Oscar 57, Ronaldo 67, Pizzi 74, Luis Enrique 79)
Camp Nou, 85,000

And the winner is ... The day before Hollywood bows to *The English Patient*, there was only one man to steal the show at Camp Nou, and it wasn't Barcelona's own *paciente inglés*. Oscar (who else?) has barely managed an hour of first-team action under Bobby

Robson. Last season's top scorer finally gets the role he's coveted and fittingly scores the goal that breaks Sevilla's already fragile morale. It proves to be a great afternoon for the García i Junyents. Ten minutes later, Oscar's little brother Roger dissects the Sevilla defence with a precise through ball and Ronaldo makes it two. Pizzi scores with, you guessed it, his first touch, and Luis Enrique makes it nine goals in two blinding second halves.

In reality, the Andalusians offered scant resistance. Even in a goalless first half it was clear Barça would win simply because Sevilla gave them no choice. In Spain, there's a kind of football team they call *inocente* (it translates roughly as naïve). On the evidence of this afternoon's showing, Sevilla would bend over in front of the Artful Dodger. The only discordant note of a placid afternoon was a scolding for Robson when he replaced Guardiola with Popescu. Not surprisingly, he was dismayed by the crowd's reaction. 'I took Guardiola off as a precaution, we've got a Cup semifinal on Wednesday and two games a week for the immediate future; against Las Palmas, Popescu and the Portuguese players will be missing on international duty, so a fresh Guardiola is crucial. I wish the fans would appreciate the changes, and respect my reasons for doing it. The barracking shows a lack of respect for the player coming on, too.' What it won't do is condition Robson's decisions. 'I'll continue to do what I think is right for the team. I have to use my experience and look at the big picture, not just think about today's game.'

At least the masses are finally getting De la Peña and the run his talent deserves. Predictably, 'Little Buddah's' media lobby still find a way to knock Robson. 'Any coach who takes twenty-five games to find a place for Iván doesn't deserve to be at Camp Nou,' suggests a news report on Canal Plus. 'Robson then proved he's as clumsy as ever by taking off Guardiola, just in case the fans started enjoying themselves, we suppose.' *Sport* are equally ungracious. 'Even Robson has realised what a difference Iván makes, but the team has still to perform over 90 minutes, we still get two different sides every game.' Ronaldo's goal against Sevilla was Barça's 100th of the season. It's a good job for the opposition that they only perform in fits and starts.

Unfortunately for Robson, his rivals are proving as stubborn as his critics. Real Madrid and Betis are both on impressive winning streaks while Deportivo's victory against Oviedo means they become the season's first team to win six consecutive games; that's the half a dozen games since Carlos Alberto Silva took over from John Toshack. Robson should thank his lucky stars the Welshman didn't walk earlier.

	P	W	D	L	F	A	PTS
Real Madrid	30	21	8	1	65	24	71
Barcelona	30	19	5	6	75	37	62
Betis	30	18	8	4	68	32	62
Deportivo	30	16	11	3	46	21	59

MONDAY, 24 MARCH

Enough already! *La Vanguardia* leads today with a bombshell. 'If any club is willing to pay Ronaldo's 4,000 million peseta buy-out clause, they will be welcomed with open arms. He may be the world's best footballer but Barcelona have decided he's more trouble than he's worth.' Coming as this does from one of Spain's sporting tabloids, you might have fobbed the story off as gossip; coming from Catalonia's earnest broadsheet, and a paper with reliable sources (one of their chief football writers was Barça's press officer until last season), it bears the aura of fact.

Apparently, two factors have turned the tide. One scenario is that the 'bye-bye to the itinerant Ronaldo' auction is his agents' responsibility. His latest musings put paid to the notion he is an innocent bystander. 'I speak to my managers every day, I know all about the offers and who they're talking to. I'm happy enough at Barcelona but circumstances could dictate that I'm gone on 30 June. We had an agreement with the board but they've not kept to it.' Then there's the AWOL factor. Brazil's FA have persuaded FIFA (presided over by homeboy João Havelange, of course) to confer bona fide status on a number of quasi-official tournaments. Now it's one thing losing your star player for the last three league games of the season because of the Copa América, it's another altogether losing him for marketing exercises in Miami or Christmas kickabouts in the United Arab Emirates.

Brazilian coach Mario Zagalo had originally said Ronaldo would be rested for next week's friendly against Chile. One hastily arranged meeting by Nike (sponsor of both Brazil and Ronaldo) later and he'd changed his tune. 'A coach depends on victories and it's my obligation to pick the best players.' In other words, Nike expect Ronaldo to play in all 21 of Brazil's 1997 fixtures.

TUESDAY, 25 MARCH

Lazio President Sergio Cragnotti announces that his club are prepared to pay Ronaldo's buy-out clause and offer him $4.1 million a year for eight seasons. 'We're working on the loose ends with financial backers, but Ronaldo has agreed to join us.' Once again, the movers and shakers are the money men. Cragnotti is patron of the Cirio food group, a company with major interests in Brazil (shares up 8 per cent in the wake of Ronaldo interest) and Lazio intend to float on London's stock market on the strength of their new acquisition. On Monday, Lazio met with Ronaldo's agents at Nike HQ in Los Angeles; according to a report in today's *Corriere dello Sport*, Nike have 'given Ronaldo permission to join Lazio'. As *Sport*'s Miguel Rico observes, 'Ronaldo is a Barça player, but he also plays for his sponsors, notably Nike and Brahma [*a Brazilian brewery*]. And there's one important difference; he gets more money for his commercial work than he does from FC Barcelona.'

WEDNESDAY, 26 MARCH

Las Palmas 0, Barcelona 4 (Ronaldo 43 pen, 76, Pizzi 57, De la Peña 75)
Spanish Cup semifinal, first leg. Estadio Insular, 23,000

Twenty seasons after Ipswich knocked Las Palmas out of the UEFA Cup, Barcelona guarantee Robson a date at the Spanish Cup Final with a stroll on Gran Canaria. For most of the first half, the Second Division strugglers had Barça on the ropes, but if you don't take your chances against the big guys, everybody knows what happens, especially when you're saddled with a star-struck referee and a goalkeeper who handles the ball as if catching sand.

Until his legs went in the second half, Vinnie Samways gave as good as he got. Booked after a par-for-the-course eleven minutes (he was sent off after twelve minutes of his debut, suspended for four games, and then sent off in his first game back), Samways has been a revelation since arriving from Goodison in December. Could this really be the same Vinnie Samways who used to ponce about White Hart Lane to such questionable effect?

SUNDAY, 30 MARCH

Valencia 1, Barcelona 1 (Ronaldo 69)
Mestalla, 48,000

A 5-2 win at Valencia was Barça's most memorable performance in Terry Venables's championship-winning season. As a well-informed

Bobby Robson admits, trips down the Mediterranean coast are rarely so agreeable: 'It's normally a real war when Barcelona go to Valencia.' Especially with the *Chés* still fretting over Ronaldo's hat trick at Camp Nou. 'A kick hurts him the same as anyone else,' growls defender Fernando Cáceres in lieu of a welcome.

'Considering the game in isolation it was a good result,' argues Robson after a bloodless draw. One game less to play and an 'as you were' situation at the top and it doesn't pass muster. 'We've played well at a ground where Barcelona lost four-one last year, and we've come back from a goal behind. But because we're still nine points behind Madrid people will say it's a disappointing result.' Including the more realistic players. 'A draw is no good to us at all,' admits Nadal after the game.

Ronaldo flies to Brazil leaving behind a clear message about his priorities. 'My future doesn't depend on whether we win the league; it's a purely economic question.' At a club where ingratiating players have long fed supporters the 'I love Catalonia, truly, deeply' line, at least he can't be accused of hypocrisy.

TUESDAY, 1 APRIL

Joan Gaspart is the vice-president with the clout, but FC Barcelona boast an interminable number of vices of more dubious influence. Jaume Sobrequés is VP of communications and the guy shuffled out to relay the party line on the television. On Sunday, he described Ronaldo as a 'troublemaker' and his agents as 'birds of prey'. Bet he's one hell of a poker player. 'I'm furious,' says Ronaldo from Brazil. 'Pitta and Martins are like parents to me and Barça should show them more respect. They've been looking after me since I was fourteen, and my life has changed for the better thanks to them.' One of his surrogate daddies is even more pitiless. 'The more fuss Barcelona kick up the worse for them,' says Reinaldo Pitta. 'They're the vultures; they promised to improve Ronaldo's contract and haven't kept their word.'

WEDNESDAY, 2 APRIL

Robson's press conference ahead of tomorrow's formalities against Las Palmas is a monologue that speaks volumes about who makes the decisions at FC Barcelona. 'I'm the coach, it's not my decision to take sides in this argument. But if the club's decision is to sell Ronaldo I can understand it. I've got my own opinion, but Núñez still hasn't asked me. I was the one who said "Buy, Buy, Buy" in the summer, even when they warned me the price was going up. But however much I insisted it's the board who pay, they have to make the final decisions about what's right for the club. It's not my job to decide what the club's economic criteria should be, no matter how exceptional the player.

'Ronaldo is probably the best footballer in the world but a club can't depend on one player. I suppose Núñez doesn't want the other players feeling aggrieved. It's a problem that's difficult to solve and if Ronaldo does go, you're transferring the problems to another club. It's also a race with no end in sight. In the summer we thought he was worth the twelve million pounds we paid for him, now it's twenty-five million, but where does it end?' Given the logic of his following observations, never. 'This situation is caused by his agents. Ronaldo is their principal source of income so they're constantly testing the market and the possibilities of making a fresh profit. But if I was Ronaldo I'd look closely at what I'm getting into; he might earn more money elsewhere, but he'll pay more tax and more commission to his agents. And where's he going to find a better club and city than Barcelona? It makes me laugh when his guys say one of the reasons Ronaldo wants to go is because he doesn't like playing in my system. Can anybody tell me what club Martins played for? Who has he coached? Did I miss the World Cup he took part in? The day I take any notice of what an impresario says about football is the day I'll be ready to retire. Meanwhile, I'll treat their declarations with the contempt they deserve.'

The total cost of acquiring the Ronaldo package has been estimated by Núñez at £80 million. The youngster's stock may have risen further today as he shares four goals with Romario in Brazil's 4-0 win against Chile, but that's still one heck of an investment. 'Personally, I doubt if there's a club in the world capable of taking that kind of cost on board,' says Robson. 'I've spoken to Joan Gaspart and I've said, "Look, he's on an eight-year contract, he was delighted to sign that a few months ago, and the difference between what he gets and what the other players do is already like this [*arms wide*]."' He ends an unusually light-hearted press conference in joking mood. 'I was the one who insisted we buy him, so if Barça do sell Ronaldo I'll be in Núñez's office asking for my commission.'

THURSDAY, 3 APRIL
Barcelona 3, Las Palmas 0 (Oscar 15, Luis Enrique 28, Couto 65)
Spanish Cup semifinal, second leg. Camp Nou, 25,000

Barring unforeseen developments, Bobby Robson's last game as Barcelona coach will be the Spanish Cup Final against Betis on 28 June. In his own words, the return leg against Las Palmas was a 'friendly kick-around'. The fact that only 25,000 fans bothered to show up and that a Spanish referee managed 90 cardless minutes says everything about the cordial nature of the game.

SUNDAY, 6 APRIL
Barcelona 4, Sporting Gijón 0 (Giovanni 13, De la Peña 45, Ronaldo 61, Pizzi 90)
Camp Nou, 75,000

A victory in third gear (well, OK, fourth) against Sporting says lots about the mediocrity of Spain's middle classes and plenty more about Barcelona's priorities as the season hits the final stretch. Robson's side have no choice but to keep winning in the league and pray that Madrid slip up. If they can do so while cruising, and with an eye on Thursday's game against Fiorentina in a competition they can realistically win, all the better.

Cruising or not, Robson's team (you know, the one pre-season critics claimed would be more defensive than a George Graham fantasy) have now scored 80 goals in the league, and at 2.5 goals per game are on course to beat Cruyff's season-high return of 91 in 1993/94. It wasn't all good news, though; Luis Enrique limped off with an ankle injury and is out for Thursday. 'This gets worse and worse,' groans Robson. 'Sergi and Celades are already out so I'm practically left without full-backs.' At least Ronaldo will be around to show the Italians what he's worth, though his move to the *calcio* seems to be on ice again. After a parley with Núñez, Ronaldo tells journalists, 'There's more possibility of me staying now. Núñez has told me he wants me to stay, and he knows that I love it here.'

MONDAY, 7 APRIL
At a press conference originally scheduled to announce the Ronaldo coup, Lazio's Sergio Cragnotti admits that not only is the ball firmly in Barça's court again, but they are serving, as well. 'I've told Ronaldo's managers that we accept their economic conditions, now

it's just a question of waiting. I'd love to bring him to Rome, but as he's already in Barcelona it's easier for them to reach an agreement. We don't want this thing to turn into a soap opera, so our offer only stands until the end of the month.'

A couple of weeks ago, Núñez insisted that if a club put the money on the table Ronaldo was history; now that Lazio have called his bluff he's changed his tune. After his chat with the youngster yesterday, he adopts the paternalistic mood he favours when buttering up the help. 'I'd advise Ronaldo to stay. Italian football is extremely complicated, that's why so many great players struggle there. Look at Laudrup; he was a great player but things didn't work out for him in Italy, yet he was happy here in Barcelona. Maradona was the best player in the world and things still didn't work out for him at Nápoles [*Erm, excuse me, don't the club's only two* scudetti *count?*]; Romario hit his peak and won a World Cup while at Barcelona, too. Ronaldo has just come back from Brazil so it was important to talk to him and clear up the confusion about what's been said. I've spoken to Guardiola, too, and I've told him that not only will we improve his salary but we'll extend his contract.'

That football is close to Catalan hearts, and that Guardiola embodies nationalist sentiments like no other player, is no secret. At twelve, he was already living at La Masia, the club's residence in the grounds of Camp Nou, and if the club had any intention of finally letting him leave home, a poll organised by Catalunya Ràdio suggests they think again. In a top of the pops of the century's most illustrious Catalans, young Josep comes seventh, behind the likes of Gaudí, Pau Casals and Salvador Dalí, but ahead of a who's who of cultural icons and civil war heroes. Stand on any street corner in Barcelona and shout the names Josep or Jordi and 90 per cent of male passers-by will stick their hands up, but there's only one Guardiola.

WEDNESDAY, 9 APRIL

Talking to the press ahead of tomorrow's game against Fiorentina, Robson suggests his team are hitting their peak at the perfect moment. 'The players are growing in confidence every day, their concentration is more intense and they've stopped making stupid mistakes. Ten games unbeaten proves how difficult we are to beat now.' As are any representatives of the *calcio*. 'Italian sides are always true to their philosophy; Fiorentina will come here to defend and destroy our momentum. Our forwards won't get many goalscoring opportunities; that means they'll have to be right on their game.'

It's a big game for Gica Popescu tomorrow. For the first time this season, the skipper finds himself out of favour with his principal advocate, as Robson opts for De la Peña as Guardiola's midfield partner. 'I know people will make comparisons, the same thing happened when I took over from Ronald Koeman, so I'm used to it. People say that now I'm not playing [*he's not started the last seven games*] the team is winning, but earlier in the season they said the opposite. I do feel rejected by the crowd, though. It's hard when the fans boo the first time you make a bad pass, and the reaction when I came on against Sevilla really hurt. Personally, I believe the press are to blame. I know what I do isn't as spectacular as others, but people forget I'm a defender who's being asked to play in midfield. But if that's what Robson wants there's nothing more to be said.'

Bobby Robson would never criticise his captain, but in private he admits his change of heart over De la Peña has indirectly affected Popescu. 'Until the night of the Atlético Madrid comeback, I didn't think Iván and Pep could play together, I thought we'd be too vulnerable defensively. But they played so well together in that second half they deserved another chance. De la Peña's beginning to take on board the things we've said to him, too. He's making better decisions about when to make the decisive pass and when to play it simple. He's not trying to be so sensational, he's a bit more professional.'

Giovanni's fall from grace has also helped the youngster. 'When you come into a new job and you've got players the club have paid a lot of money for, you feel obliged to have a look at them for a couple of months. You can't pay seven million dollars for Giovanni and leave him on the bench straight away. And we've bought eight new players, so there's more competition for places. You've got to remember the young lads had their chance with Johan Cruyff last season and didn't win anything. Cruyff didn't play Iván very much, either. I'll bet you De la Peña will end up playing more times this season; he'll certainly start more games. Roger, Celades and Oscar have had more chances recently, as well.' He denies that his new taste for rotation is a response to criticism. 'Earlier in the season, the team was playing very well, so I didn't want to change it. I felt I'd wait until my hand was forced by injuries and suspensions, or when players looked a bit tired. If I'd changed it too early we might have lost one or two more games. Can you imagine the stick I would have got then?'

THURSDAY, 10 APRIL
Barcelona 1, Fiorentina 1 (Nadal 42)
European Cup Winners' Cup semifinal, first leg. Camp Nou, 100,000

If Gabriel Batistuta, Argentina's all-time leading scorer, had buried his chances, Barça's bid for Euro-glory would have gone the same way as Liverpool's (dispatched 3-0 at Paris Saint-Germain). Happily for Robson, 'Batigol' rounded his night off with a ludicrous booking and gets no chance to make amends in the return. 'They won't be so dangerous without Batistuta,' argues Robson, 'and we'll have our missing players back. They'll play defensively, even at home that's the Italian way, but if we get one goal the situation gets very interesting.' As might have been expected, the absence of Guardiola and De la Peña reduced Barça's creative streams to a trickle; Nadal's header apart, the giant 'keeper Toldo had a placid night. Clearly Robson was not going to criticise Popescu and Amor, though he did concede, 'We lacked that intelligent final pass.'

Batistuta may have been profligate but his persistency paid off with a characteristically slamming equaliser after the break. Ronaldo, meanwhile, was anonymous to the point of invisibility. 'It was a difficult night for him, he always had two men tight on him,' argues the ever-tolerant Robson. Josep Lluís Núñez, meanwhile, leaps at the opportunity to hammer home his theories on the bottomless pit that is Italian rearguards. 'Fiorentina have given Ronaldo first-hand experience of what I told him about Italian football; he'd have far more problems in a league where the accent is on defence.'

As is customary on big European nights, Camp Nou was jam-packed and dressed to the nines. As the players took the field, the whole north end of the ground paraded one of those amazing made-in-Spain multicoloured mosaics, BASILEA 79 – BARCELONA 82 – BERNA 89, recalling the sites of Barça's three previous Cup Winners' Cup triumphs. However, a colourful stadium an intimidating arena does not make. 'We're not worried about Camp Nou being full,' said Batistuta before the game. 'The fans are a long way from the pitch, and forty thousand fans in Florence will make far more noise.' As did 4,000 *tifosi* in Barcelona. Batistuta had been well informed; Barça's support may be numerous, but it comes nowhere in the decibel league. Juventus patron Gianni Agnelli once said that 'forty years of dictatorship leave their mark, that's the only way you can explain how one hundred thousand people make so little racket'. That once-a-year noise binge against Real Madrid aside, things haven't changed.

Half an hour into tonight's game and Barça's *ultras* were moved to recriminate the silent majority with a familiar chant: '*Dónde está, no se ve, la afición de los culés*'. That's 'It's all gone quiet over HERE'. And it used to be worse. 'At least the ground is more or less full these days,' says Jordi Sant, spokesman for the *penya almogavers*, an independent and influential grouping of young Barça fans. 'When the side isn't doing so well you've got this cavernous stadium with wide open spaces but with no possibility of the general public gaining access to the vast majority of seats. In England, the atmosphere at grounds is created mainly by the "ends". For us it's very difficult to get together and impose our presence on the stadium. It's made worse by the fact that where we congregate [*behind the Gol Nord*] is a flat rather than stepped terrace, which makes us less visible.' So why did the *ultras* choose this area? The answer is simple: they have no choice. Looming above are four huge banks of seating where virtually all places are the permanent property of *socis* – fans who own seats in perpetuity after a one-off purchase. The young, the spontaneous and the poor can only aspire to one-off tickets in the blustery heights of the *general*. 'Given the passivity of most of the *socis*,' admits Sant, 'that translates into zero atmosphere.'

A recent survey in the journal *Europe's Environment* rated Barcelona the second-noisiest city in Europe (Sofia is the noisiest, which probably explains why Stoichkov feels so at home in Barcelona). Maybe your average punter goes to Camp Nou for a bit of peace and quiet?

FRIDAY, 11 APRIL

Josep Lluís Núñez's campaign to portray the *calcio* as the big bad wolf of European football gets a helping hand from an unexpected source. Ninety anonymous minutes against one of their own is enough to convince the Italians that the boy wonder is overrated. *La Gazzetta dello Sport* tots up his grades. 'Ronaldo's performance was very unimpressive: he demonstrated a woeful lack of initiative and the mobility of a 1950s centre-forward.' A Spanish sports media terrified at the prospect of losing their licence to print money reproduces every last detail of the character assassination.

'The comparisons don't bother me,' shrugs Ronaldo. 'Let's see who comes out on top before passing sentence.' Bobby Robson agrees. 'If I was Ronaldo, the criticism would only motivate me for the second game. Personally, I'd never judge a player on one game;

he wasn't at his best on Thursday, but that doesn't make him a bad player overnight.'

SATURDAY, 12 APRIL

This time last year, Johan Cruyff's side were alive and kicking in three competitions. A ten-day spell then saw them lose the Cup Final, knocked out of the UEFA Cup by Bayern Munich, and waving goodbye to the league after a home defeat against Atlético Madrid. Tomorrow's visit to Atlético is the first date in Bobby Robson's own season-defining ten days, and he knows it.

'Time is running out so we're facing the pressure of having to win every single game,' he admits. 'The day we lose and Real Madrid win we've had it. But I'm not afraid of history repeating itself; the important thing is to still be alive on three fronts at this late stage. It's always better not to concentrate on one competition. Look what happened to Atlético; they centred all their ambitions on the Champions League and then found themselves too far adrift in the league. A week after we beat them five-four in the Cup, their season was finished off by Ajax.' Radomir Antic has said his players are 'psychologically unprepared for a game against Barcelona' while Jesús Gil claims 'he couldn't care less about the result'. Robson is convinced they're bluffing. 'I'm sure they'll see the game as a chance to restore their reputation.'

SUNDAY, 13 APRIL

Atlético Madrid 2, Barcelona 5 (De la Peña 40, Ronaldo 42, 58, 75 pen, Figo 88)
Vicente Calderón, 52,000

Your typical Spanish football match finishes 1-1 (45 times and counting this season). It's a result that suggests order and restraint; if the truth be known, it's also the kind of result managers are quite fond of. Barcelona v. Atlético Madrid, on the other hand, is football's equivalent of chaos. Six confrontations this season have now thrown up 37 goals at more than six per game; that's the kind of sequence that sends managers to the emergency ward.

The final instalment was typically anarchic. Despite the result, Antic reckoned his side 'deserved to win', and he could make his case without a strait-jacket in sight. Five minutes before the break, Atlético were 1-0 up and a daydreaming Barça were grateful for the nil. Rub a lantern and enter the bald genie: Ronaldo forced a free kick just outside the box and De la Peña's swerving strike did the rest; 'Little Buddah' returned the favour with a deft assist and it was suddenly 2-1. Who said football was supposed to be fair? After the break, Simeone and Santi got themselves sent off, allowing Barça to put a generous gloss on the final score.

The subject of merciless barracking all night, Ronaldo celebrated his fourth hat trick of the season in out-of-character fashion. After scoring his second, a single finger to the lips sent an unmistakable message to his tormentors. He dedicated his third goal to Atlético's *ultras* with the 'Up Yours!' gesture Catalans call a sausage and which Ronaldo described as a 'banana'. 'It was just a spontaneous reaction,' he smiled. 'They spent the whole game insulting me and my girlfriend.'

Bobby Robson reckons he should take it as a compliment. 'Atlético have a great crowd and they always get behind their team, whatever the score [*unlike some, he must have been thinking*]. They were on Ronaldo's back because they realise he's a constant danger; it's a sign of respect.' Barça's number nine may be causing the club headaches off the field, but he's nigh-on kept his goal-a-game promise on it. His treble in the capital brings his tally to 40 in 41 games.

MONDAY, 14 APRIL

It appears the boys from Brazil have won their game of call my bluff with the Catalans. 'Barcelona have accepted our conditions and a contract that'll keep Ronaldo at the club until 2006 is waiting to be signed,' says Reinaldo Pitta. Mind you, they add insult to injury before cashing in their chips. 'As soon as we receive a bank guarantee confirming the money is available, we'll come straight to Barcelona to sign contracts. We don't want to come over in vain again.'

TUESDAY, 15 APRIL

Bobby Robson has never failed to stand up for himself, but it must be nice to do so from a position of relative strength. Looking bronzed, self-assured and slick in Barça's new spring gear, this is a man in control; and about to go on the attack. An article in *AS* dubbing him 'the worst coach in the world' has left Robson fuming. Before setting off for the game at Valladolid, he lambasts his capital critics. 'I've just read in *AS* that I'm the worst coach in the world; I find that disgraceful, it shows a complete lack of respect. If you said that in my country, where they also understand football [*pauses for effect*], you'd be considered a fool and an idiot. And if I'm the worst coach in the world I must be on one hell of a lucky streak. It's true we've played badly on occasions, but it's just as true that we're now on a roll; it would be impossible for a team playing badly to get our results. Popescu and Amunike [*also rubbished by* AS] deserve more respect, too. Gica has played seventy-five times for his country and been to World Cups and European Championships. Nigeria has an Olympic gold thanks to Emmanuel. How may Pulitzer Prizes has that guy on *AS* won?'

In reality, nothing the Spanish press throw at their victims is as vicious as the convulsions of their English counterparts; the problem is their persistence. Being called a plonker once every couple of months may be bloody annoying, but the far less insulting 'Robson is not up to the job' repeated *ad infinitum* is far more insidious.

WEDNESDAY, 16 APRIL
Valladolid 3, Barcelona 1 (Ronaldo 6)
Nuevo Zorrilla, 26,000

After a season characterised by trouble at sea (Bilbao, San Sebastián, Tenerife), Robson's championship dreams are dashed in Spain's most landlocked city; and in the cruellest of fashions. For 30 glorious minutes even the cautious veteran must have believed the title was at his fingertips. Ronaldo put Barça ahead before anybody broke sweat, while in the capital Real Madrid were two down against Sevilla before you could say *Sorpresa, sorpresa*. A four-point gap. If only. Things started to go wrong when Fernando equalised for Valladolid on the half-hour. Ten seconds after the break a second from Víctor, like Fernando once a Madrid apprentice, stunned Barça into instantaneous submission. Meanwhile, at the Bernabéu, Real took a cue from their old boys to storm back and win 4-2. A ten-point deficit with eight games to go provides reasonable grounds for surrender.

A disappointed Robson is unusually scathing about his team. 'The players have thrown away a winning position at one-nil; I think they thought it was easy. We tried to talk ourselves back into the right frame of mind at half-time but when Valladolid scored their second so quickly it killed us off. We went to pieces after that: we looked tired, our concentration went and we could have conceded even more goals.'

In the build-up to the game, a report on Televisió de Catalunya claimed that Louis Van Gaal's lawyers were in Spain finalising the details of his contract with Barcelona. Disgruntled he may have been, but Robson was unwilling to speculate. 'I'm not interested in hearing that from the press. It's a situation I'll discuss with the appropriate people at the club, no one else.'

PS. Why are so many Spanish footballers known by their first name only: Fernando, Víctor, Roger, Sergi, Oscar, Raúl, etc.? Can you imagine a number nine called simply Alan, or Ian, or Robbie?

THURSDAY, 17 APRIL

Guess who the press are blaming for Barcelona's title *adiós*? There was nothing baffling about yesterday's defeat; after twelve unbeaten games and the wear and tear of a three-pronged campaign, Robson's men simply didn't have the legs for a Valladolid side that are sprinting their way to a place in the UEFA Cup. In reality, Barça made their fatal errors long before they arrived in Castille. But that doesn't make for eye-catching headlines, does it? 'ROBSON Throws the League Away In Valladolid.' Now that's what you call a headline.

Sport open for the prosecution. 'Robson's ridiculously timid tactical approach was trashed by Cantatore [*the Valladolid coach*] on the blackboard and on the pitch.' Elsewhere, they inform us that when 'Robson berated Roger for his defending on Valladolid's second goal, the youngster told him to shut up [*highly unlikely*]. His teammates applauded him for doing so [*untrue*]. We do, too.' Ooh, aren't we the tough guys, now?

Michael Robinson's clout at Canal Plus doesn't extend to getting his buddies to go easy on fellow Brits. 'It's Robson's fault that Madrid are going to win the league. He's spent the season living off occasional outbursts of talent from one of the best squads in the world. When a game goes crazy – for example, Sunday's win at Atlético – Barça's stars get Robson out of jail, but when the game is about tactics – against Fiorentina or yesterday – a guiding hand is sadly missing. Cantatore gave the Englishman a lesson; Barça were a tactical disaster. The only consolation for Barcelona is that it looks like Ronaldo is staying. Having the best player in the world for just one season and he coincides with Bobby Robson is what you call a sad case of mistiming.'

Not surprisingly, Robson doesn't share the Canal Plus theory on the benefits of chaos. 'Frankly, they don't know what they're talking about. Sometimes things can work out for you in a crazy game, but it can also be very dangerous; it's precisely the coach who has to make sure he doesn't lose his head. They don't understand a thing about football, they're just making statements off the top of their head. I find that disgusting.'

Josep Lluís Núñez denies that Barcelona were wrapping up a deal with Van Gaal yesterday. 'I can personally guarantee that nobody has been in Holland or anywhere else negotiating with Van Gaal. Bobby Robson has been informed that FC Barcelona cannot be run by or through the media [*now, that is news*] and that he cannot doubt my support [*hold the front page!*].' Despite himself, Núñez can't resist an unwelcome rider. 'Robson's got a contract and his future is in his own hands. I'll continue to back him – if anybody has defended Robson it's been me, I've even sent letters to the *socis* asking them to be patient – but he has to accept whatever decision we make. The fans will make their feelings known at the end of the season, that's when I'll talk to him about his future.'

Robson spends his afternoon at Barcelona's Godó tennis tournament. In between watching Thomas Muster lose to Cédric Pioline, he gives his side of the story. 'Until the president and the board tell me any different I'll continue with the same motivation and try to ignore the rumours about Van Gaal. All the speculation hardly helps the team, though. We'll keep battling away in the league but it's going to be difficult to reduce the difference now.' That's not quite raising the white flag, but his priorities clearly reside elsewhere now. 'The second leg against Fiorentina is the most important game of the season. I'd just hope everyone can forget about all the rumours and concentrate on being right for Thursday.'

Also at the Godó, Hristo Stoichkov offers an unexpected source of support. 'It's not Robson's fault we lost at Valladolid, he doesn't play, does he? And it doesn't help anybody when two hours before a vital game the press are saying Barcelona are about to sign Van Gaal.' Surprisingly, the Bulgarian's legendary optimism has gone missing. 'The league's lost now; even if I said we were going to win it nobody would believe me. Thursday was embarrassing. I'm sure Real Madrid haven't stopped laughing at the way things swung round. If we lose against Fiorentina it's going to be hell until the end of the season, there'll be a thousand silly stories about who's coming, who's going, rumours about contracts, TV deals . . .'

218

FRIDAY, 18 APRIL

If Josep Lluís Núñez is to be believed, Robson could be staying, after all. 'We've lined up two new coaches as we restructure our technical staff, but both men have been told that Bobby Robson has another year on his contract, and there's nothing to suggest he won't fulfil it. One of the new coaches will be overall director of football and the other director of transfers, but I've always insisted, Robson has a contract until June 1998 and FC Barcelona won't break it.' Núñez also takes the unprecedented step of sending an open letter to 'My Dear Friend Robson' through the EFE agency, assuring the coach he enjoys his total support.

Robson's presence on the first-team bench for a further season is being interpreted in some quarters as an attempt to avoid the traumas of the past. The theory goes, Van Gaal's year in the wings will give him the chance to learn the language and familiarise himself with the idiosyncrasies of the club. Those familiar with Núñez's scheming nature say he is simply playing the good guy because he knows Robson won't accept the snub.

Núñez also takes time today to deny a list of Van Gaal discards (Baía, Busquets, Couto, Abelardo, Oscar, Amunike, Cuéllar, Ferrer, Popescu and Stoichkov) published in *El Mundo Deportivo*. 'The only person with the power to make any such list is Barcelona's coach and that's Bobby Robson.'

SATURDAY, 19 APRIL

Robson reacts to Núñez's open letter in grateful fashion. 'Before the Valladolid game I received a message from the president telling me to ignore the Van Gaal story; he's now published this open letter so that everybody knows exactly what the situation at the club is, for once and for all. And I've spoken to the players and told them to forget about possible comings and goings; the list of rejects is false.' Nonetheless, Robson does admit he needs to talk to Núñez about his own future. 'The president has convinced me he's behind me, but I don't know much about the signing of two more coaches for next season. I'm sure we'll talk about it in the near future.'

Vítor Baía is rich, famous and has a wife who is almost as pretty as he is. So what do you give the man who has everything? Well, not that old punch-line, to start with. Barça's 'keeper turns up for training this morning complaining of a sore ear, so the club doctor prescribes a swift penicillin jab. One allergic attack later and Baía is ruled out of tomorrow's game against Bilbao.

SUNDAY, 20 APRIL
Barcelona 2, Athletic Bilbao 0 (Abelardo 49, Ronaldo 64)
Camp Nou, 60,000

Barça's lowest crowd of the season is proof positive that the fans have bid *adiós* to the league. Fiorentina on Thursday is what really counts now. More evidence of the new realism? How about not a hankie in the house when Robson takes off Ronaldo, De la Peña and Giovanni in the second half? The belated dose of realism comes on the day when Josep Lluís Núñez finally pronounces the words Van and Gaal in the same sentence.

After the game, Núñez gathers journalists in his presidential pulpit to preach the latest gospel. 'There should never be a power vacuum at the club; so to ensure continuity we're going to appoint two more coaches, one of whom has already signed his contract.' His very next words are 'We'd like Van Gaal to form part of that structure'. Draw your own conclusions. It is enough to wipe the smile off Robson's face as Núñez's musings filter through to the press suite. He opens proceedings with a question – 'Are we going to talk about football here?' – to which he already knows the answer. 'In my opinion the club haven't decided on the exact structure. I'll come into that structure, but it's too early to be more explicit.' He then continues on autopilot. 'I'm working hard and concentrating on winning things this season. What's going to happen to me, Ronaldo, Guardiola and Figo; that's all part of the future.'

Despite looking out of sorts, Ronaldo equalled Romario's 30-goal first season at Camp Nou. 'If you give Ronaldo that much space he'll score even on an off day,' says Michael Robinson, in town with Canal Plus. And doesn't Núñez-for-president-again know it. 'We've found a sponsor who'll enable us to keep Ronaldo at Camp Nou. The money has been deposited in the bank and his new contract is just a question of paperwork.'

'I know the board have made a big effort,' says Ronaldo, 'and I'm extremely grateful. I spoke to Núñez last week and my mind's now at rest. Although I've received serious offers from Italy and England I'd always told my representatives that I wanted to play for Barcelona. I'm very happy to be staying.'

MONDAY, 21 APRIL

Real Madrid's draw at Valencia leaves Barça eight points adrift with seven games to go. 'It's nice to pull a couple of points back, though I'd have been happier if it was three,' admits Robson, conscious that time is running out on a comeback. Looking further ahead, he denies a story on Sky claiming that he met with Everton chairman Peter Johnson yesterday. One man who is definitely looking for a coach is Lorenzo Sanz. Real Madrid's chief reacts angrily to Núñez's suggestions that Capello is leaving because of 'family problems' (i.e. he won't give Sanz Jr a game). 'That's sinking really low, even for Núñez; he's obviously as lacking in morals as he is in stature. And knowing what an intelligent guy Van Gaal is, I wouldn't be surprised if he imposes three hundred and twenty-seven conditions before signing for Barcelona.' As opposed to 328 or 329.

TUESDAY, 22 APRIL

Bobby Robson arrives in Florence for the Cup Winners' Cup semifinal with a less immediate future still dominating the headlines. 'All this talk about Van Gaal infuriates me when I'm trying to prepare the most important game of the season,' he complains. 'When I get back to Barcelona I need to have a serious chat with the president.' Meanwhile, he prescribes a recipe for his players. 'My way of ignoring the fuss is to not read the press or listen to the radio. I'm concentrating on Fiorentina, that's what we should all do.'

Robson's cause is championed by an unexpected ally. Louis Van Gaal admits he's 'negotiating' with Barcelona, but bemoans the surrounding publicity. 'I'm really annoyed my name is being used to hurt people; it would have been better to have kept things quiet until the end of the season.' He also derides the notion of a blacklist. 'That's rubbish, the imagination of sick minds. I'm not so demanding . . . and I can't type!'

Another Dutchman is cleared of talking rubbish today. A long-running legal battle between Johan Cruyff and Josep Lluís Núñez ends with both men cleared of libel. If the judge is to be believed, Núñez's statements about Cruyff were 'hard-hitting but not defamatory', whilst tapes of Johan's televised diatribe on his former employer have been 'lost' by Dutch TV. Cruyff's attacks might qualify for the sticks-and-stones category, but Núñez accused his former coach of organising pre-season games for backhanders, signing players for 'personal reasons', forcing seriously injured players into action, and taking commission from political parties and presidential candidates. So what exactly is considered libellous in Spain?

WEDNESDAY, 23 APRIL
Barcelona celebrates St George's Day with four million roses, not as some strange homage to their under-siege English coach, but because Sant Jordi is also the patron saint of Catalonia. It's a day when tradition dictates a rose for the señoritas and a read for the boys; among the 400,000 books shifted today were copies of FOUR new biographies of the twenty-going-on-twenty-one Ronaldo.

Installed at the Villa Cura, a neo-classical mansion on the outskirts of Florence, Bobby Robson's own day begins with an unwanted bouquet. In a radio interview late last night, Núñez's response to the question 'Did you make a mistake signing Robson?' was, at best, equivocal. 'Don't forget that I suddenly found myself in June with no coach, with no planning and in a hurry,' he grumbled. 'All the other teams had signed reinforcements and all the best coaches were tied up.' It might not be the 'My Bobby Blunder' of this morning's headlines, but 'I didn't have much to choose from' has to go down as a lukewarm vote of confidence.

Núñez immediately dashed to Florence in an attempt to get his foot out of his mouth. 'I'm annoyed by what I've read' was Robson's curt description of a tense meeting. 'The president says he's been misinterpreted and that his words have been taken out of context, but in my opinion, he's said some unnecessary things.' The words are measured, but Robson's expression is a tale. He has had infinite opportunities to feel aggrieved since his arrival at Barcelona, but for the first time he makes no attempt to cloak his disgust in a smile. 'A club like Barcelona can't afford a situation like this forty-eight hours before a European semifinal,' he complains, 'and we had exactly the same problem before the Valladolid game. I've got to fight a battle practically every day; this would kill a younger, less experienced coach.' For once, he isn't about to shoot the messenger. 'This is a situation created by the club itself.' At least the players seem to be taking his side. 'This is really dangerous,' says Amor. 'It's not the players' job to take sides, but we've got a crucial game and Robson knows he can count on us.'

THURSDAY, 24 APRIL
Fiorentina 0, Barcelona 2 (Couto 30, Guardiola 35)
Cup Winners' Cup semifinal, second leg. Artemio Franchi, 47,000

Barça's two-in-one Italian job leaves their supporters with decidedly mixed feelings. Early into the club's fifth European basketball final it was clear that a fifth straight defeat was on the cards (remember, this is a club that loves a tale to end in tears; the footballers have lost three out of four European Cup finals, too). At least FC Barcelona's capitulation to Olympiakos in Rome (73-58, basketball's equivalent of a 6-0 spanking) solved one dilemma for *culés* back home: what to watch on the telly. Josep Lluís Núñez must have wished he'd stayed in Florence after his audience with Robson. For his part, the coach will be hoping his gaffer's presence at the final against Paris Saint-Germain proves less of a jinx. Legend has it that the basketball team want to save their diminutive president the ignominy of posing at their knees in a victory photo. Perhaps Robson should pick the little guys for the final, just in case?

Couto's thumping header and Guardiola's free kick quickly ended the game as a contest. Only Nadal's sending-off spoiled the show. Reaching a European final is another victory for Robson in his daily battle against the world, though in elegant fashion he refuses to talk of revenge. 'I don't take revenge on presidents, I just do my job and let people make their own conclusions. My statement to the president is that I've taken his team to a second final. Yesterday was difficult for me, but I wasn't going to let it affect my motivation. The team's always supported me, that's the thing that means most to me. It's all a coach can ask for.'

Never one to spurn the plaudits, Núñez was happy to bask in the reflection of Robson's glory. 'I'm the only one who's defended him,' he boasts, displaying a remarkably short memory. 'While ninety-nine per cent of the press were doing everything possible to get rid of him, I stood alone beside him, and *Mister* Robson knows that.'

Barça's victory provoked a predictable reaction from Fiorentina's infamously volatile crowd. Coins, lighters, bottles and seats rained on the pitch in the second half as the disgruntled *tifosi* played target practice with all things Spanish. Both Sergi and De la Peña were felled by UFOs, and on several occasions the referee was forced to halt proceedings and threaten to suspend the game. Each successive appeal for calm by loudspeaker was met with jeers and a fresh avalanche (UEFA would later force Fiorentina to play their next two

European games at least 500 miles away from Florence). Dante, the city's favourite son, would have been proud.

The Barcelona press corps' reaction to tonight's result was less violent, but more ominous for Bobby Robson. 'I've never seen as many sad faces in my life as on the journalists' bus back to Pisa airport,' admits *La Vanguardia*'s Enric Bañeres.

FRIDAY, 25 APRIL

Robson arrives home in the early hours of the morning, tired but optimistic. 'Now let's get after Madrid in the league!' he tells journalists at the airport (like stetsoned lookouts, these guys don't sleep either) before heading for a well-deserved break on the Costa Brava with his wife. José Mourinho stays behind to do what he does best. 'A lot of the players were disappointed to see their names on Schindler's List,' says Mourinho of Van Gaal's alleged discards, 'so victory in Florence was doubly satisfying. Bobby's got every reason to be proud of his achievements; as he said after the game, his record speaks for itself. He's too experienced and well mannered to blow up, but he won't forget. If people are embarrassed by the way they've treated us that makes me happy. If I'd had to put up with what Bobby has it would have killed me.'

It's only the second time Barcelona have reached the Spanish Cup Final and a European final in the same season. The last coach to do it was Terry Venables in 1986; Bobby Robson will hope he doesn't end up with two loser's medals, as well. History contrives against Robson in other ways. The final takes place at Rotterdam's De Kuip stadium, the scene of Barça's defeat in the 1991 final against Manchester United. And then there's the opposition. 'It's going to be very, very tough,' says Guardiola. 'Not only are Paris Saint-Germain one of the toughest and most consistent sides in Europe, they also make a habit of beating Spanish teams.' Real Madrid (twice), Deportivo and Barça themselves (in the 1994/95 Champions League) bear witness.

SATURDAY, 26 APRIL

Just when Barcelona thought the Ronaldo soap opera was over, his agents move the goalposts again. Not only do they want their boy to earn $5 million a year, apparently they want Barça to pay all his tax, as well. The teetotal player takes time off from shooting a commercial for a São Paulo brewery to change tack again. 'I still

224

haven't agreed anything with Barcelona, I've not even received a concrete proposal from the club,' he says. 'The board are saying they've reached an agreement with several sportswear manufacturers, but that's impossible. In the first place, I'm not going to get involved with more than one company, and in the second place I've got a contract with Nike.'

Javier Clemente, for one, is tired of football's growing tendency to play Monopoly for an audience. 'I don't blame Barcelona for wanting to renegotiate Ronaldo's contract, they're only reacting to market forces, but flaunting silly money around is not on. People struggling to make a living have every right to be furious at talk of hundred-million-dollar salaries.' Clemente's sense of solidarity extends to an old friend. 'It's April, Barça are alive in three competitions, yet people are still questioning Bobby Robson. It could only happen in Catalonia and at Barcelona; Barça are the club of great loves and great hates. It's a question of marketing, too. There's an orchestrated campaign by people who want Núñez's job; getting at Bobby is just a smokescreen. Johan Cruyff used to complain about all the politics, but things were nowhere near as bad for him, and in his first season he didn't come close to achieving what Bobby has. If anybody has reason to complain it's Bobby Robson. Capello said it's ten times more difficult for a coach here than in Italy, yet in comparison it's been a bed of roses for him at Madrid.'

Maybe somebody should have a word with Louis Van Gaal, as well. Even BEFORE he arrives at Barcelona, the press are on his case. 'You've got to seriously answer questions about a coach who doesn't rate Baía, Couto, Pizzi and Abelardo,' suggests an article in *La Vanguardia*. In other words, one paper (*El Mundo Deportivo*) invents a blacklist, then another from the same publishers criticises Van Gaal for its contents. Needless to say, Robson was crucified for buying Baía and Couto in the first place.

SUNDAY, 27 APRIL
Bobby Robson spends the day in Figueres, getting away from it all with a visit to the Salvador Dalí Museum. Back in Barcelona, his future takes an increasingly surreal turn. Five days after hinting that he signed Robson because there were no alternatives, Núñez, or 'Mister President' as his fawning interviewers address him, appears on the football chat show *La Portería* to renew his vows with Robson. 'Bobby Robson will be our first-team coach next season.

We're preparing a new technical hierarchy, but any restructuring is based on respecting his contract; there will be a clause in the new coaches' contracts which states clearly that Robson is in charge. Anybody who doesn't accept that doesn't come. We've not even considered Robson continuing as anything other than first-team coach.'

Interestingly, Núñez airs his now familiar 'I'm Robson's guardian angel' line, but also hints that senior players had helped save the coach's head. 'I spoke to players at critical moments and they told me the dressing room had never been so united; that there had never been such a good atmosphere. The big problem this season has been that a minority of fans have been swayed by a campaign of misinformation and incoherent criticism.' Núñez's own incoherence is reflected by his attitude to Barça's Most Wanted. After 20 minutes elaborating the financial minutiae that will keep Ronaldo and Guardiola at Barcelona, he answers a question about Luis Figo's future by saying, 'Who does he think he is? We can't be negotiating players' contracts during the season, he'll have to wait like everybody else.'

MONDAY, 28 APRIL

'There have been too many rumours flying around this club,' says Robson in response to Núñez's latest turn on the box, 'not just in the last couple of weeks but all season. I'm delighted that the president has cleared the situation up. Let's hope that's the end of the story.' He then succumbs to realism and admits he is completely in the dark on the nature of the proposed changes. 'I need to see Núñez in the near future to talk through the new structure; the responsibilities of the new coaches have to be clearly defined to avoid misunderstandings.'

Robson may be exasperated by off-the-field turmoil, but he refuses to use it as an excuse for on-the-park setbacks. 'It might have had some influence, but I think it's a small one. At the beginning of the season we produced some good results so people forgot we were basically a new team. You have to be patient with new players and a new coach; football's like anything else, you need time to shape things. We dropped silly points at home to Hércules and Oviedo and that's where all the doubts start, but those were mistakes made by the team. It had nothing to do with outside pressure.'

Mention of Hércules leads Robson to reflect on the day he closed the door on Newcastle. 'When John Hall originally got in touch, he wanted me to manage the club at first-team level. The initial offer was a two-year contract with a one-year option. He thought I might not want to be at the sharp end of it after two years. "Think about it as you go along," he said. But they wanted me to stay at the club in whatever capacity I chose, so I was offered a five-year contract. Two and one at the sharp end, plus another two. The idea was that I could eventually become technical director and oversee the club's footballing structure. And now there's the football academy which they're keen to set up; John Hall still says I'm the ideal person. He's told me "That job is there, and it's there whenever you want it." But I wouldn't take the academy job unless Kenny was happy and gave me his support. If he thought I was a threat, I'd say, "That's fine, I understand that, carry on, fella," but personally, I'd have no problem working with him.

'I went through all sorts of things that night against Hércules [*wincing*], it was easily my worst moment of the season. I'd spoken to Gaspart earlier in the day and asked for a meeting with him and Núñez after the game. I thought we'd be in a marvellous position; losing to Hércules was the worst thing that could have happened to me. Maybe that was the day I should have bloody gone, but I stuck to my guns. I said, "Look, I feel absolutely terrible, I've had a disastrous night and we've lost a game I could never have imagined losing, but it makes no difference to me – whether it makes any difference to you I don't know – my head and my heart are here at Barcelona. I wanted to be standing in front of you as league leader to say my mind was made up before the match, to tell you unequivocally [*raises his voice*] I AM STAYING." It's not true that I was unhappy with Núñez – I knew they didn't want me to go at that time – but my mind was in a turmoil after the game. For the first twenty minutes it looked like we'd score six or seven. I remember looking at their coach and thinking, "I feel sorry for this bloke, he's going to lose six-nil." And he finishes up winning! He wasn't sorry for me, I'll tell you. What a disaster, it was just awful.

'Newcastle had told me Kevin Keegan was resigning a couple of days before he actually went and they wanted me to take over straight away. By the time Kevin went on the Wednesday, I'd already turned down the offer on the phone but they came over to pressure me to take it. I'd told Joan Gaspart the day Keegan resigned or maybe the day before. I knew it might get out, so I went to see him and I told him, "Joan, I've been offered a job and I've turned it down." Then the guys from Newcastle came over and it all blew up. On the Friday, I called the press conference to say I wasn't interested, that I'd turned the job down. That was the end of the story as far as I was concerned, but the press would never let me go. There were all the rumours and reports that I'd met with Núñez and Hall, that we'd reached an agreement for me to go in June, and so on and so forth. But there was never a meeting and we never discussed the possibility of a later deal. The whole thing was the result of overactive imaginations in the press.

'I'd taken eighteen years to get to Barcelona, I was at the biggest club in the world and the team had everything to play for, even after the Hércules defeat. Newcastle was a tempting offer, both financially and from a football point of view; it's where I come from and the job was tailor-made for me. My wife and the rest of my family wanted me to go, too. Elsie was sick when I turned it down, but honestly, there was never a moment when I seriously thought I'd go. There were a couple of hours when I turned it over in my head, but I don't like walking out on contracts.'

So there was no truth in the *Times* version? 'I was surprised at that; you'd expect that from the *Sun*, but not from *The Times*. I said that [*talks slowly and surely*] on any other day, on any other occasion, I'd have bought my own ticket back home to take the Newcastle job. They changed it to "if Núñez had been prepared to let me go, I would have paid for my own ticket home". And the Peter Beardsley thing never came up in the talks, either. That was another press invention, it was never mentioned. We never got beyond the basic offer. After the Newcastle guys came to Barcelona, there was no more contact, they took my no as definitive and went ahead and got Kenny Dalglish. I found out he'd got the job the day of his press conference, the same as everybody else. All the stuff about John Hall calling me or coming to Barcelona to change my mind was fiction. And I never said come back and talk to me at the end of the season, either. Could you understand the logic of that one? Everybody knew they needed to hire a big-name manager because of the share flotation, and it had to be immediate and permanent.'

TUESDAY, 29 APRIL
Josep Lluís Núñez and Joan Gaspart have spent the last few days hinting that Fabio Capello is a closet *culé*. 'He's in love with FC

228

Barcelona,' claims a smug Núñez. 'He approached me earlier this season about joining us,' insists Gaspart. Fabio's idea of falling in love with Barcelona is to elope with their leading man. 'I've got it on good information that Ronaldo will be playing for an Italian club next year,' says Lorenzo Sanz, on the day his coach calls a press conference to confirm the worst-kept secret in Spain: come the end of the season he's going home to Milan.

'Four or five clubs are willing to pay Ronaldo's clause and Milan are top of the list,' admits Reinaldo Pitta from Miami, where his money-maker is in action for Brazil. 'He wasn't born in Barcelona, he was born in Brazil. It was a business decision to leave PSV and join Barcelona; he went there to make money. If he receives a better offer from elsewhere, he'll go. Business is business.'

WEDNESDAY, 30 APRIL
The plot to keep Spain's World Cup campaign off the front pages continues. Despite the efforts of six Barça players in tonight's draw in Yugoslavia, Spain's chances of grabbing tomorrow's headlines in Catalonia disappear with the announcement that the King's youngest is getting hooked. As *la infanta* Cristina has decided to marry FC Barcelona handball ace Iñaki Urdangarin, Clemente's team won't even make the sports covers.

THURSDAY, 1 MAY
An early morning flight to Barcelona means Bobby Robson, who was at Wembley last night to see England beat Georgia, doesn't get time to vote for the losing side. When he arrives back at Camp Nou, his squad is looking as decimated as the Conservative Party. Election day in England is the first of two days off in Spain – if one of their Bank holidays falls midweek, the Spanish don't move it to a Monday or Friday, they simply take *un puente*, a bridge, and make it a four-day weekend. Catching, then? Well, no, actually half of Robson's squad are still away on international duty.

In what is a season's first, it's all quiet on the Barcelona front while life at table-topping Real Madrid resembles a battlefield. 'I don't know if Capello approached Barça or if Gaspart approached Capello,' says Lorenzo Sanz. 'It's difficult to know who to believe with two liars. But every pig gets his San Martín in the end [*Spain's pig-slaughtering season begins on St Martin's Day*]. Whatever the truth, Capello has deceived us, he's stuck around to do half a job because of the money and now he's threatening to throw games if we don't let him go.' He adds with a smirk, 'Let's see if he gets paid come the end of the season.'

FRIDAY, 2 MAY

For once, Ronaldo arrives back from Brazil in time for training; Bobby Robson tells him to go home and get some rest anyway. Unlike Phileas Fogg, Ronaldo hasn't been around the world in just 80 days; four times around the globe in a season is nonetheless some serious flight time. The youngster's latest trip means he has clocked up 160,000 kilometres and ten countries since September. Where to next? 'I know which team Ronaldo is going to sign for and how the deal has been done,' says Lorenzo Sanz. 'We'll be laughing soon.' What does he mean? Here's a clue. Ronaldo's European agent, Giovanni Branchini, confirms today, 'Ronaldo has a new club and it's Italian.'

SUNDAY, 4 MAY

Fabio Capello's word may not be his bond (he tore up a contract with Parma to join Madrid, so why is Sanz getting on his high horse?) but few would deny the man's balls. Despite a barrage of niceties from admirers at the Bernabéu, he spends today's game against Sporting Gijón in his customary pitchside position and pose (that's very gesticulative). The players may not like Capello very much but his resolve is clearly infectious – for the eighth time this season Madrid come from behind to win. 'I'd like to dedicate the victory to the fans,' says the coach after the game. 'They're sensible and intelligent and I'm satisfied with the way they've treated me.' What is Italian for 'sarcastic bugger'?

'It's a shame we won't pick six points up against Extremadura next season,' said Bobby Robson earlier in the season. Cometh the hour, this term's second three are not a foregone conclusion either. Inspired by the mid-season arrival of Argentinians Montoya, Basualdo and Silvani, the men from Almendralejo have staged a remarkable comeback and have a fighting chance of staying up. Former Boca Juniors 'keeper Navarro 'Monkey' Montoya has proved a particularly inspired signing; Extremadura haven't conceded a goal at home for NINE matches now. Not surprisingly, the level of expectation in the small town is enormous. When Robson and his men land at nearby Badajoz airport, 3,000 fans are waiting to say *hola*. A wave or two instead of the routine blinkered stare suggests that Robson's players are not oblivious to what the occasion means to the wide-eyed locals. Even Ronaldo permits himself half a goofy smile.

'If we don't win tomorrow, beating Madrid will be no good to us because the league will be over,' Guillermo Amor tells local journalists. Privately, his boss admits the league is a pipe-dream, whatever his side achieves between now and the final day. 'In my heart of hearts, I knew after the Valladolid game that we were struggling,' concedes Robson. 'That was the night it could have gone for us. Real Madrid have lost one game in thirty-six, so realistically there's no chance they'll lose two or three in six. I don't think it's fair when people say we've thrown the league away; you have to give credit to a side that has only lost one game. Madrid have been very consistent, they haven't played exciting football, but they win on their off days; we haven't done that. I've seen them struggling to beat people at home, but they don't concede many goals so they get out of jail. They've had a bit of luck on their bad days, as well. We've had two very unfortunate games: two stupid penalties and the sendings-off doomed us at Tenerife, and we had rough justice at Espanyol with the penalties and Figo getting sent off early on. That's two games we were given no chance of winning.'

Those lost opportunities are not the only thing bugging Robson. 'Capello said he has a conversation with two people at the club and the next day it's in the press. It happens here, too. People can't keep their mouths shut. Everybody knows everything. It never happens in England; you'd never read what David Dein said to Arsene Wenger in private, never. Yet all this mouthing off in public, and when you really need to talk it doesn't happen. Núñez has been on the telly and radio talking about my future, and I've had to request a meeting with him, to talk to me about it. He's avoiding me because he doesn't know what's in his head.

'I need my position clarified so that we can talk about next season; the squad doesn't need a lot to win the league, but a club like Barcelona has to produce star signings. That's fine, but to buy two you need to let two go. One of my problems is that I've got too many good players already – it's impossible to keep them all happy. I've had to leave Nadal and Oscar out for tomorrow, Roger is suspended and Celades is injured and I'm thinking THANK GOD [*chuckles*], two less to choose from! Having too many good players causes a problem, because the press have always got frustrated guys to write about. Madrid have got fifteen or sixteen players and beyond that nothing; there's not going to be headlines about who Capello leaves out. Whichever sixteen I pick there are a minimum of five players who'd walk in the team anywhere else. If I get rid of a couple of players in the summer, the people we bring in are going to be even better, so it'll be even worse!'

Even the guys who see plenty of the bench agree it's a headache. 'It's difficult moulding so many stars into one team,' says Hristo Stoichkov. 'Not a day goes by that I don't think about what a hard job Robson has got on his hands.' His former teammate, Ronald Koeman, who to the relief of defensive walls everywhere is hanging up his shooting boots at the end of the season, insists that too many leading men in the same play poses particular problems at Barcelona. 'The sheer size and quality of the squad is a real headache for Robson. Choosing who exactly to leave out must be a nightmare, and trying to give everybody a game doesn't help him build a settled team. Worst of all, there's always the disgruntled stars – knowing how the Barcelona media works that's a big problem.'

Núñez may be vacillating, but there's no doubt where Bobby Robson wants to be this time next year. 'If it was my choice, I'd stay here to try and win the league and have a serious crack at the Champions League, that would be my dreamboat,' he says emphatically. 'I've spoken to Everton and Celtic and I know I'm top of their list, but my priority is here. I'm not really interested in the Celtic job, going to Scotland would be a step backwards, but I need to sort things out with Barcelona because Everton won't wait. If Núñez says to me, "Look, Bobby, you're sixty-four, we're bringing in Van Gaal as a long-term option, but he needs time to get used to the club and learn the language, so next year you're still in charge, you're the first-team coach," I could understand that. No problem, just tell me what's happening.'

A common request in the Robson household. 'I said to him in Florence, "If you don't want me as your coach just tell me now, I'll pack my bags before the game and go" . . . [*puts on a sobbing voice*] "No, no, it's not true," he said, "I've always supported you, blah, blah, blah." He knew he'd put his foot in it, that's why he rushed from Rome to talk to me. And all that stuff about it was June and he didn't have any choice; I could really make him look silly one day. I've got it all written down in my diary – they got in touch with me in March last year, it was all "Everybody's sick of Johan Cruyff, he's got to go, can you take over?" [*jumping up and down to make his point*] This was in MARCH, not June.

'It's going to be difficult finishing second 'cos Betis and Deportivo are pressing, but if we do, my view would be that qualifying for the Champions League and winning two cups is a better season than Madrid's. I don't know if Spanish fans would see it like that, though. We've played fourteen games more than Madrid – and we haven't lost one of them – on a financial level that's fourteen televised games, so it's good for the club as well. And my intention is to go one better and win the league next year, that's why I'm going to let the Everton job go.'

MONDAY, 5 MAY
Extremadura 1, Barcelona 3 (Ronaldo 10, Luis Enrique 33, 80)
Francisco de la Hera, 12,400

On a pitch so Subbuteo-like a disbelieving Robson had it measured during the warm-up, Ronaldo took ten minutes to break the hosts' 841-minute clean sheet. The locals swiftly drew level at 31 goals each (that's Extremadura 1996/97 v. Ronaldo), but 'Monkey' Montoya, clearly intent on doing his turn with banana skins, immediately gifted Luis Enrique Barça's second. Robson's jack of all trades settled things after the break with his fifteenth league goal of the season, one more than he managed in five campaigns at Real Madrid.

If Barcelona can beat Madrid on Saturday, they'll cut the gap to five points and give themselves a morale-boosting send-off for Rotterdam in the process. Ironically, many Barça fans have more chance of getting to the Cup Winners' Cup final than *el derby*. Only 11,000 tickets are available for the Camp Nou showdown; once 8,000 tickets are shared among official supporters' clubs that leaves a paltry 3,000 for the general public (and those are for the so-called *general*, a vertigo-inducing fifth tier from where the players look like ants). There are times when a 115,000-capacity stadium is just too damn small!

Two hours after going on sale this morning, the 3,000 *entradas* were gone. And who do you think all those shady-looking types buying up wads of tickets were? Ask a silly question. Outside of Real Madrid day it's never a problem getting in at Camp Nou. Even if tickets are at a premium at the box-office, there'll be *socis* hanging around to offer spare season tickets (their brother's, uncle's, etc.) at face value or near as damn it. However, when Madrid come to town even *socis* who use their membership as VIP cards for the rest of the season tend to show up, thus the spivs who spend the rest of the year hoodwinking tourists on the Ramblas turn their attentions to football. The *culé* desperate for a ticket for Saturday had better take out a second mortgage. Meanwhile, you can get to Rotterdam and back on a Barça-organised coach for 60 quid, ticket included.

	P	W	D	L	F	A	PTS
Real Madrid	36	24	11	1	76	29	83
Barcelona	36	23	6	7	91	44	75
Betis	36	20	12	4	74	36	72
Deportivo	36	20	12	4	55	25	72

TUESDAY, 6 MAY
Bobby Robson's intimate supper with the boss resolves absolutely *nada*. Robson remains tight-lipped as he exits to grab a cab (given his inveterate loquaciousness, a giveaway in itself) while Josep Lluís Núñez simply utters platitudes to waiting journalists. 'Robson hasn't got to worry about me, I'm an angel,' he declares. Deadpan. 'And he didn't ask for guarantees about his future.' That's two white lies, or pious lies as the Spanish call them, sandwiched between what most Catholics would consider sacrilege. Robson IS worried and DOES want guarantees, that's precisely why he requested the meeting.

WEDNESDAY, 7 MAY
Robson may be blind-siding the press about last night's talks, but in private he is seriously cheesed off with his procrastinating president. 'Frankly, I didn't get what I was looking for,' he says, unable or unwilling to mask his exasperation. 'Núñez keeps talking round and round in circles but he doesn't want to make a decision. All I want is a simple yes or no, but he won't give it to me. I'm going to have to think seriously about my future over the next couple of days. If I don't make a decision soon I'll end up back in England sweeping roads. My season here runs till the end of June; clubs back home can't possibly wait that long to see what I'm doing. But whatever happens, believe me, I'm not going to walk away from this as the guilty party. I'll humiliate Núñez if he messes me around.'

Despite the fact that Robson has drawn a veil over last night's talks, the media have concluded that an ostensibly cordial supper (ritual photos of the smiling participants were taken before *aperitivos*) means he is staying. As Núñez spends today telling anyone who'll listen that 'Bobby Robson has got a contract and wants to stay', for once the press can be excused their bad call.

THURSDAY, 8 MAY

Today's *Sport* boasts a cover photo of Robson and Capello musing over a chessboard at the paper's HQ in the heart of Barcelona. 'Bobby Robson was kind enough to accompany us to Madrid before the league game in December,' writes editor Josep María Casanovas. 'On that occasion, Fabio Capello promised he'd repay the compliment.' Shortly after that winter tête-à-tête, *Sport* accused Robson of 'lacking personality' for wasting time in Madrid instead of concentrating on his job. Quote: 'Can you imagine Fabio Capello flying to Barcelona for a photo opportunity with Robson in the build-up to Spain's most important game?' Well, *sí, señor*. And given that he'd already promised YOU GUYS to do just that, so could you. Needless to say, there are no editorials today bemoaning Capello's lack of personality. Elsewhere in today's edition of the fearless organ, we're informed that 70 per cent of readers think Robson should be sacked even if Barcelona win one of their cup finals. With the kind of insidious campaign the coach has suffered at the hands of the opinion-shakers, it's remarkable that 30 per cent of their readers defy the witch-hunt.

The build-up to a Barça v. Real Madrid is invariably marked by a slanging match between respective godfathers. Don Núñez sets the ball rolling today at a lunch to gee up the troops. 'Count yourselves lucky to be at Barcelona,' he tells his players. 'It's not just Capello who wants to come here; I've had calls from four Madrid players begging to join us next season. I've told them, "Stay calm, don't sign for anybody else, and we'll sit down and talk at the end of the season."' When he'll no doubt make them an offer they can't refuse.

Halfway through dessert, Núñez pulls Ronaldo aside to lecture him personally on why he should remain part of *la familia*. 'I told him that if he listens to my advice his problems are over,' says Barcelona's president. 'I still feel guilty for letting Maradona leave so young; if he'd stayed here he'd be much happier now. I don't want the same thing to happen to Ronaldo; I'll be like a second father to him.' The youngster's vexed expression suggested he could do without the patronising. Either that or he doesn't like having his *pudín* interrupted.

Luis Figo was the president's next dupe. A couple of days ago, Núñez boasted that Figo was 'going nowhere' despite a much-flaunted compromise with Milan. 'My spies in his hair salon tell me Luis wants to stay,' he claimed, without moving his tongue anywhere near his cheek. Now it seems he has something more concrete to go on than the confessions of a hairdresser. 'Figo's escape clause is 15.6 million pounds, not the six million everybody's been talking about,' he gloats. Asked to clear up the confusion, Figo just looks perplexed (admittedly his favourite expression). 'My clause must have gone up, I suppose.' We suggest he has a word with his agent.

Meanwhile, Milan Vice-President Adriano Galliani reveals there will be traffic in the other direction. 'We've agreed a 6.5-million-pound fee with Barcelona for Michael Reiziger and Christophe Dugarry, now it's up to the players to agree terms.' But with whom? 'I'll have to talk to Van Gaal to find out what his plans are for me,' says Dugarry. That's news to Bobby Robson. 'I don't know anything about their transfers,' he says. 'I haven't given them my OK so it's not definite they're coming. Don't believe everything vice-presidents tell you.' And he should know.

FRIDAY, 9 MAY

Capital Don, Lorenzo Sanz, reacts to his Barcelona rival in kind. 'That imbecile Núñez has got things ass backwards again. I'm the one who's been tapped: by Figo, Ferrer and a third big fish [*Ronaldo, we're invited to assume*].' Hristo Stoichkov, never one to pass on a Barça v. Madrid scrap, reacts by claiming, 'The only traitors are in Madrid's dressing room. Suker and Mijatovic [*who have both accused the Bulgarian of being a has-been*] are nobodies who have won nothing; until they do, I suggest they keep their feet on the ground or they'll fall over. Somebody should tell them that the Bernabéu [*Real's pre-season tournament*] is not the European Cup. And my Golden Boot and Golden Shoe aren't made of wood. Madrid have lost their bottle; I'm convinced they can't handle the pressure and will blow up altogether.'

Núñez continues his mendacious games concerning his coach's future. 'Robson has got a contract, he wants to continue and we're very happy with him.' Privately, Robson is chomping at the bit at Núñez's deceit, but he guards a prudent silence in public. Despite the

236

persistence of both the locals and reporters over from England (900 accredited journalists are expected tomorrow, twice the normal number), he refuses to discuss his future. 'I've got nothing to say about contracts or offers from other clubs. The only thing that's certain about the future is that I'll be four days older on Thursday.' And no better at maths.

SATURDAY, 10 MAY
Barcelona 1, Real Madrid 0 (Ronaldo 47)
Camp Nou, 110,000
Barça: Baía, Ferrer, Abelardo, Nadal (Stoichkov 23), Sergi, Guardiola, De la Peña, Figo (Pizzi 89), Luis Enrique, Giovanni (Popescu 15), Ronaldo
Madrid: Illgner, Panucci, Hierro, Alkorta, Roberto Carlos, Víctor (Amavisca 47), Seedorf, Redondo, Raúl, Mijatovic, Suker (Ze Roberto 70)

Crash! Bang! Wallop! It was a collision Bobby Robson had seen coming. 'Barcelona and Real Madrid is the only fixture in the world that draws more than a hundred thousand fans twice a year,' he'd said on the eve of the game. 'Throw into that equation all the history, the politicking and the media attention, and you're looking at a powder keg.' Especially when the opposing coach is on a one-man crusade to revive the bad old days of Italy's *catenaccio*. Fabio Capello had obviously told his men to test Barcelona's resolve early on. Would Robson's players be up for a scrap four days ahead of a European final? The answer was a resounding yes, but at a cost. Roberto Carlos took less than 20 minutes to dispatch Giovanni and Nadal to the dressing room on stretchers as Real embarked on a 90-minute attempt to foul their way to a stalemate. Unpunished.

Carmelo Rodríguez is the kind of referee that will continue to feed Catalan bleatings. The more incensed Camp Nou became, the more blatantly he leant, though he did bow to the inevitable and award Barça their match-winning penalty when Roberto Carlos upended Figo. To their credit, Robson's side competed without rising to the bait, with the exception of, no prizes for guessing, Stoichkov. Booked soon after replacing Nadal, he should then have been sent off for spitting at Panucci.

It was a scrappy game won by an even scrappier goal; after Illgner parried Ronaldo's featherweight penalty, the Brazilian had little choice but to nudge home Figo's point-blank assist from the rebound. It was also a defeat for Spanish football and its much-heralded *artistas*. The game was broadcast to a global audience of 200 million; that's some 45 countries where there are now serious doubts about those 'best league in the world' claims. If you wanted to acquire the 22 players in the starting line-ups, it would cost you more than £220 million in buy-out clauses alone. That's much ado about nothing on this evidence. Ronaldo, the hottest property of all, was infuriatingly apathetic. In the white corner, Raúl produced his fourth anonymous turn of the season in *el derby*, Mijatovic missed a trio of sitters, and Suker was a passenger until Capello hauled him off with the customary 20 minutes to go.

'I was surprised at how hard Madrid were,' admits Bobby Robson afterwards. 'They were definitely the most aggressive side we've seen here this season.' Logically, he lays the blame for a disappointing spectacle in his opponents' court. 'It was impossible to play better football because Madrid kept interrupting the flow of the game with fouls. Even when they went behind they knew that one-nil was a decent result for them, so they just fought to hold on to that.'

Effectively, even if Barça were to peg back the five-point gap, Madrid's 2-0 win at the Bernabéu would make them Champions by virtue of their superior goal difference in the head-to-heads. 'We knew a second and third goal were vital, but it's not like drinking a cup of tea, you know,' sighs Robson when asked why his team hadn't gone for the jugular. 'We did everything we could but Madrid are very resilient.' Asked if beating Real was a catch-all cure at Barcelona, Robson replies, 'Not for me,' though he knows what a personal hangover defeat would have provoked. 'Madrid haven't won here for fourteen years, so I knew I was facing a mountain if we lost.'

The less than salubrious nature of proceedings was not limited to the game itself. Whoever decided to defy etiquette and seat Spain's Minister of Industry between the rival presidents should be praised for their foresight. Josep Lluís Núñez spent the game in a barely controlled frenzy, bouncing around and contorting his face to extremes Matthew Simmons would be proud of. Thankfully, Lorenzo Sanz didn't react with a flying kick, though his face was more poetic than anything the bard Cantona has ever produced. 'The mores of the directors' box may be a pantomime, but everywhere else in Spain people manage to control themselves,' complains an indignant Sanz. 'Núñez spent the game screaming and shouting, and then Gaspart tries to pick a fight with me. Their behaviour was deplorable, they can keep their box, their stadium and their team, I won't be coming back here, and they're no longer welcome at the Bernabéu [*not that they go, anyway*].' He then wishes his *amigos* good luck for Wednesday. 'I've never seen a Spanish flag at Camp Nou so I'm glad when Barça lose in Europe [*the teams entered the fray today to a backdrop of a 20,000-card mosaic of the Catalan flag*].'

Never one to turn the other cheek, Núñez accuses Madrid's players of everything but rape and pillage, and 20 minutes after the final whistle, Gaspart is still prowling around the VIP suite in intimidatory mood. 'If Sanz has got something to say, let him say it to my face,' he boasts with quivering voice. 'And if he doesn't know how to lose he should stay at home and bite his nails.' Two households both alike in dignity?

SUNDAY, 11 MAY
SCANDAL is the buzz-word in today's match reports. Depending on which side of the Barça–Madrid divide they stand, the press are rocking their high horse to the tune of Madrid's rough-and-tumble or Núñez's antics in the box. Meanwhile, attacks on Real Madrid's bus (windows shattered on the way to Camp Nou) or the treatment dished out to Bodo Illgner (at least one bottle missed him by inches, and on several occasions he had to practically wrestle the ball back from ballboys) barely warrant a mention. Clearly acceptable behaviour on these occasions.

Worst of all, yesterday's real scandal passes by unnoticed. Roberto Carlos may be the villain of the piece in Catalonia, but even the Real-leaning media don't consider the treatment dished out to him worthy of comment. That a dark-skinned footballer has to suffer 'Ooh! Ooh! Oohs!' every time he touches the ball, or monkey impersonations and flying objects (sticks, fruit, a golliwog) every time he approaches the sidelines, is lamentable enough in itself. That absolutely nobody among the participants or in the media thinks that behaviour worth a SINGLE WORD of admonishment is something Spanish football should be thoroughly ashamed of. It shouldn't make a difference, but for the record, the racial abuse started before Giovanni or Nadal were carried off. And as the latter acknowledges, 'You can't expect Roberto Carlos to stand by and admire while I line up a shot.' A feature in today's *La Vanguardia* likens the 'Barça faithful' to a 'guard dog, always ready to go to the aid of their team'. If nothing else, that's an insult to Camp Nou's impeccably behaved Rottweilers.

Earlier this season, Roberto Carlos was rubbished in Catalonia when he suggested Barcelona fans were the most racist in Spain. Maybe, probably, they're not (Madrid's *Ultras Sur* take some beating in the xenophobic stakes) but finishing runners-up in a race between bigots is nothing to boast about. 'That was the worst experience I've ever had as a footballer,' says Roberto Carlos. 'The fans didn't stop insulting me for the whole ninety minutes, and Guardiola, Sergi and Luis Enrique seemed more interested in turning the crowd against me than playing football. I didn't mean to hurt Giovanni or Nadal, the surface was very quick [*very*] and they were fifty-fifty balls, I'm the one who's owed an apology.' Don't hold your breath, Roberto. There are already voices in Barcelona suggesting the Brazilian be deported before dawn. Even the city's equivalent of the Hampstead set are on his case. 'Compared to Roberto Carlos, Hugo Sánchez [*the Antichrist*] was like Mother Teresa,' says Josep Carreras, the Barça-crazy tenor. Hopefully, he'll be making more agreeable sounds at a Camp Nou concert in July with Plácido Domingo (Real Madrid) and Luciano Pavarotti (Bologna).

'When Barça play Madrid the atmosphere is far too charged,' admits Bobby Robson. 'You don't see that level of hostility in most other countries. I suppose it's the Latin temperament, but that's no excuse for the racist stuff, I hate that. All the monkey chants and the bottles being thrown, that's just about uneducated people. And the fact that the press prefer to ignore it offends my sense of decency. I couldn't believe it when Roberto Carlos couldn't take a corner because people were throwing rubbish at him again.' Not that Saturday's display was on an Italian scale for waste disposal. 'Fiorentina was the worst behaviour I've ever experienced,' continues a disgusted Robson, shaking his head. 'I've played in some very hostile, violent atmospheres – I remember something similar in Greece once – but I've never seen anything like that amount of stuff thrown on the pitch. That's a disgrace to football. I seriously thought the game was going to be stopped; we were winning two-nil when things got really bad, and I was thinking, "How does this effect the result?" The referee was young and inexperienced and you could see him thinking, "What do I do here?" One of those big bottles of water hit me on the face. Fortunately it just glanced my cheek; if it had hit me straight on it would have knocked me down, 'cos those bottles are bloody heavy. I was lucky. In England we've got cameras on every person in the ground so you can identify culprits, throw them out and never let them back in. That's how we dealt with the hooligans; here no one seems interested in tackling the problem.'

Least of all the otherwise occupied powers that be. 'I'd be embarrassed to be president of a team as violent as Real Madrid,' Josep Lluís Núñez tells a supporters' club gathering. 'In my nightmares last night I was being kicked all over the place; I could see Nadal with his leg in plaster, Ronaldo with a bandage on his head, and Giovanni and Figo with broken legs. I kept waking up in a cold sweat and running to the bathroom to check I didn't have blood on my face.'

Lorenzo Sanz may have slept soundly, but he didn't wake up in a more conciliatory mood. 'When Núñez spends his weekends visiting *penyes* and insulting Real Madrid, you know there's an election around the corner.' However, he reserves his real bile for the president's sidekick. 'They should put Joan Gaspart in a strait-jacket. He's got no place in a VIP box, he should spend his weekends at the psychiatrist's.'

Middlesbrough's relegation today has Bobby Robson musing on the comparative strengths of Europe's big leagues again. 'The sides that go down here certainly haven't got players like Ravanelli, Juninho or Emerson [*laughs*] – although the problem with Boro was the other seven. But those three alone would get you out of jail in Spain; the bottom sides here have got nothing like that kind of quality. The English League has got more potentially big clubs, too. Even in Spain and Italy you can only talk about two or three, but the Premiership has got Liverpool, Everton, Man Utd, Arsenal, Tottenham, Newcastle, Leeds, Villa, and even in the First Division you've got big clubs like Manchester City, Notts Forest, Sunderland and Wolves.

'Maybe the top Italian teams are better in the head-to-heads – look how Juve murdered Ajax, and they were too good for Man Utd – but there's definitely more strength in depth in England. The Spanish League is a very tough league, but the Premier League is stronger in the middle; an Everton or a Blackburn are stronger than, say, Sporting or Celta. The Italian League used to be one rung up the ladder, but I think that difference has gone now. It's gone from being the league that everybody admired to being in a debatable position

241

compared to England and Spain. That's shown by a lot of Italian players walking out of it and going to the Premiership.'

MONDAY, 12 MAY

FC Barcelona's flight to Rotterdam is delayed by four hours after warning calls claim there's a bomb on board their Iberia 747. It's a good job it turned out to be a hoax. Despite the fact the phone calls were logged in at 2.30, Barça's plane was still taxiing leisurely around the runway fifteen minutes later, and it wasn't until 3.35 that Bobby Robson and his men were advised to disembark. *Mañana,* always *mañana.*

Despite the disquieting rumble of fire-engines, Bobby Robson initially reacted in good spirits. 'It's a Real Madrid bomb!' he joked, preferring to ignore the presence of bomb-disposal experts dashing past him on the runway. As it became clear the delay would be an extended one, his good humour disappeared. 'Just when I thought nothing else could go wrong for me here, this happens. Talk about bad luck!'

At least the hanging around would have dampened the excessively high spirits Robson had bemoaned earlier in the day. 'There's a real feeling of euphoria, I can sense it everywhere; I'd prefer the players to be feeling nervous and on edge.' And so he should. History dictates that FC Barcelona are never more vulnerable than when cocksure of themselves. Terry Venables led his men to Seville in 1986 for what was prematurely billed as the club's maiden European Cup triumph. Defeat against a gatecrashing Steaua Bucharest was the beginning of the end for El Tel. Similarly, Johan Cruyff's supposedly invincible team were steamrollered by Milan in the 1994 final; the beginning of lean times for *el flaco*, 'the skinny one'. Pep Guardiola, a survivor of that 4-0 débâcle, winces at the memory. 'Three days before we played Milan we'd sealed our fourth consecutive championship, so we headed off for Athens like the Mambo Kings; the whole world was on a high. Now we're arriving off the back of a big win on Saturday, while PSG have had two weeks to prepare. It was the same before the Milan game; we were recovering from a last-gasp title win and they'd had a gentle build-up.'

In common with the rest of the players, Guardiola spends the four-hour delay ensconced behind the closed doors of El Prat's VIP suite. Ronaldo and his Brazilian clan – Mum, his 'secretary' Cesar, a bodyguard who'd pass for the Notorious B.I.G., his secretary, *et al* – recover from the shock in a secluded corner. When normal service is resumed, it takes all Ronaldo's powers of persuasion to get Moms back on board. Given the way Giovanni sprinted off the plane (if only he'd show half as much energy on the pitch), Brazilians clearly prefer to do their flying on the football field. Only Hristo Stoichkov abandons the protective cordon to mingle with fans in the airport café. He may be eternally at odds with his teammates, but Hristo's standing among ordinary *culés* is no quirk of fate.

TUESDAY, 13 MAY

Bobby Robson is accustomed to sticks and stones at his press conferences in Barcelona; a change of scenery produces the real thing. As he fiddles around with his microphone before taking questions at the De Kuip stadium, Robson's jaw drops when a fight breaks out among lensmen jostling for position. His initial astonishment soon turns to humour. As the main offender is dragged away, he jokes, 'Hey, can he play for us tomorrow?'

Not surprisingly, the Dutch are taking a keen interest in the final: Cruyff, Neeskens, Koeman, Romario, Ronaldo and now Van Gaal have long made Barça big news in Holland, and of course Robson is also a familiar figure. So did playing the final on Cruyff and Van Gaal's patch mean anything special? 'It would make absolutely no difference to me if we were playing in China,' Robson insists. 'I had two extraordinarily happy years here at PSV, so I've got a special relationship with Holland, but that's as far as it goes.'

Back on familiar territory and, when it comes to European finals, lucky territory (Ipswich sealed their 1981 UEFA Cup victory at nearby AZ 67 Alkmaar), Robson has the chance to write himself into FC Barcelona's history books. For the Cup Kings *par excellence*, tomorrow represents a record-breaking fourteenth European final, and if they win, Barça will equal Madrid's record of eight European trophies. Even so, we're not talking about mere par-for-the-course success. In manoeuvring his way through the minefields of a tortuous season, Bobby Robson is the first Barça coach since the 1950s to reach the last month of the season with the chance of doing a treble.

WEDNESDAY, 14 MAY

Barcelona 1, Paris Saint-Germain 0 (Ronaldo 37, pen)
Cup Winners' Cup Final. De Kuip stadium, Rotterdam, 45,000
Barça: Baía, Ferrer, Abelardo, Couto, Sergi, Guardiola, Popescu (Amor h-t), De la Peña (Stoichkov 84), Figo, Luis Enrique (Pizzi 88), Ronaldo

Paris Saint-Germain: Lama, Fournier (Algerino 58), N'Gotty, Le Guen, Didier Domi, Leroy, Raí, Guerín (Dely Valdés 69), Cauet, Loko (Pouget 77), Leonardo

The last time Barça visited the stadium locals call 'the Bathtub' they got a dousing at the hands of a Brit reject. Mark Hughes's goals in the 1991 Cup Winners' Cup Final were sweet revenge for a player who was derided in his brief spell at Barcelona. After Man United's victory six years ago, Hughes refused to dwell on his personal calvary at Camp Nou. Surplus to requirements after one season or not, Bobby Robson is equally quick to dismiss notions of getting even. 'The word revenge is not part of my vocabulary,' he tells a packed press conference after the game. 'As far as I'm concerned, tonight was simply a great opportunity that we've grabbed with both hands. It's not about me, it's a success everybody deserves for their efforts over a very complicated season.' But was it a victory that could keep him at the club? 'Well, a European title is not bad for starters,' he muses, 'but that's a question you'll have to ask the president.'

Robson's demeanour for most of the night was that of a man several steps removed from his surroundings. Admittedly, any chance that he'd get too excited during the game was destroyed by UEFA plc – a double file of advertising hoardings in front of the benches left Robson caged in and the sidelines of 'the Bathtub' resembling a moat. But even as Guardiola, Sergi and Ferrer unfurled Catalan flags and led the fans in celebratory chants of '*Madrid cabrón, salud al campeón!*' (roughly, 'Madrid you w**kers, bow down before the champs!'), Robson remained several paces off the fray (trying to find him in the victorious group photos is misspent time). His almost beatific smile suggested, 'There, I've done my job, but I'm no longer part of this'. It was Clarence the angel revisited at the end of *It's a Wonderful Life*.

Whether it's the beginning or the end of his reign, Robson's advocates insist he can be proud of himself. 'Barcelona have forged a link with their most brilliant past,' says *La Vanguardia*'s Enric Bañeres. 'It's a kick in the ass to the peddlers of gloom who have tried to poison the team's season. Outside of Spain, and away from self-serving critics, Robson's team inspires nothing but admiration. If he does go, he'll leave his successor a real "Dream team", one that has absolutely nothing to envy Johan Cruyff's.'

Strangely enough, Barça's victory in the land of total football was forged on their often maligned defence. The teams may have taken the field to the tune of *Star Wars*, but it was not a night for intergalactic leading men. Ronaldo shook off the attentions of N'Gotty once in 90 minutes, provoking the defender's one mistimed tackle before stroking his penalty past Lama (in the 'keeper's last game before a five-month ban for marijuana consumption). However, the real stars were Ferrer, Sergi, Abelardo and Couto at the back (the 'Robson has got too many centre-halves' school were predictably quiet tonight) and the colossal Luis Enrique everywhere else. Lama may leave the odd blade of grass unsmoked, but Luis Enrique covers every inch of the pitch and then some. Robson's appraisal of a dour encounter was somewhat baffling – 'It was a flowing game, a game of counter-attacking and a game with danger at both ends' – but hey, who cares? Sometimes it's not what you say, but how you say it. And the glow in his eyes suggested an inner contentment. As Guillermo Amor, a survivor of the 1991 final, put it: 'It doesn't matter how you play in a final, the only thing that matters is winning. I know, I lost a Cup Winners' Cup on this same pitch.'

Even the guys who have been periodically at odds with Robson are benevolent in victory. 'A coach who has won the Cup Winners' Cup, taken us to the Cup Final, and still has a fighting chance of leading us to the title has earned another chance next year,' says De la Peña, whose impermeable frown is replaced by a grin so wide it threatens to split his face. When the team arrive home in the early hours of the morning it is yawns all round, yet 'Little Buddah' is still smiling like a kid at Christmas. José María Bakero, whose everyday existence is now a relegation battle in Mexico, is equally generous. 'Barcelona have grabbed the chance to begin a glorious new epoch. It's just reward for Bobby Robson after several very difficult months.'

In fact, it was a night when almost everybody was on their best behaviour. Sorry, did anybody say Hristo Stoichkov? Hristo has been embroiled in a feud with *les français* ever since Bulgaria denied France a trip to the 1994 World Cup in a dramatic qualifying game in Paris. As the rest of his Barça teammates revelled in their victory with 12,000 travelling *culés*, Hristo sprinted towards the PSG fans and unfurled a Bulgarian flag – good job about the moat! It was a vindictive touch on an otherwise trouble-free occasion. The Dutch police reported only thirteen arrests; of the five Barça fans banged up before the game, four were nabbed for stealing a bag of cakes from a bakery. The only other *culé* to miss the victory countdown was Joan Gaspart, who in his umpteenth display of ordinary madness spent the second half pacing up and down outside the ground. After Barça's European Cup triumph at Wembley in 1992, Gaspart carried out a pre-match promise and took a midnight dip in the Thames.

THURSDAY, 15 MAY

Bobby Robson has often said he wanted to go crazy down the Ramblas with the fans. Today he gets his wish. If anybody doubts that Barça are indeed 'more than a club', they should be tied to a balcony in the city centre and made to witness the outpourings of *Catalanismo* that surround their title celebrations. If they can't make it in person, lock them in a room with the videos; that's four hours' live coverage on two different channels.

First stop on a well-established route is the city's Basilica and a symbolic offering to the church. Robson is suitably respectful as *la iglesia* bestows its blessings, but some of his younger charges can't resist the wedding giggles at the formality of it all. After the whole squad have kissed a statue of Barcelona's patroness, Our Lady Mercè, they move on to the city's political centre at Plaza Sant Jaume (one of the rare occasions when the socialists at City Hall and their conservative rivals across the square are not at daggers). As the players take their cue from politicians with lots of talk of Barça flying the flag for Catalonia, Robson again shuns the limelight, though he manages a brief message from the town hall balcony. 'This one's for you, long live Barça, long live Catalonia!' He signs off with the day's catchphrase in Catalan, '*Sou collonuts!*' – You're the dog's bollocks!

A Catalan's pride in his or her language is practically limitless; just about the biggest gaffe you can commit among Catalans is to refer to their language as a dialect; Catalan is in fact no more a dialect than Castilian Spanish; in many ways it is more similar to French. All three, like Italian, are dialects of Latin. This pride is understandable. Franco's victory in the Civil War unleashed a vicious campaign against the Catalan language. Meanwhile, Castilian, 'the language of the empire', was wielded as a cleansing and unifying power. It's a pride, however, that sometimes translates into a bewilderingly fawning attitude. Popescu's brief discourse in Catalan from the balcony attracts rapturous applause both *in situ* and from the press. Now no one's knocking Gica – he's been here less than two years and is already speaking more Catalan than some of his Spanish teammates who've been here years, and they didn't have to learn Castilian first (as the common language, inevitably the first linguistic port of call). But let's be frank here. These guys are earning silly money for representing Catalonia's most celebrated institution. And they don't work in the afternoons. Isn't it the very least they can do to learn a bit of the lingo?

Ronaldo, who is not exactly Mister Gift of the Gab in his mother tongue, had to be dragged to the microphone to say *gracias*. Another one who knows he's on his way? Or maybe he was smarting from the lack of acclaim. He may be the world's best footballer, but the masses make it clear he's got some way to go before competing with an evergreen idol. Despite his marginal status this season and a five-minute cameo last night, 'Hristo! Hristo!' was still the day's most boisterous chant. Only the cheers for a still-buzzing De la Peña and Luis Enrique (proving as popular with teenage girls as he is unpopular with opponents) came near to Stoichkov's on the decibel scale.

Some of the guys who have been on Robson's case all season have the grace to hold up their hands today. 'Bobby Robson has won his own particular war,' admits the editorial in *Sport* (though one insider suggests the change of heart is because Núñez has threatened to withdraw the licence for their lucrative sideline in Barça products). However, *El Periódico*'s Emilio Pérez de Rozas refuses to let up on his crusade, claiming that the team he has criticised Robson for sabotaging all season is not really the coach's, after all (i.e., in the aftermath of a European victory). More surprising is Johan Cruyff's attitude. Fears that the Dutchman would spend the year attacking his successor have proved unfounded. 'He's been very good,' Robson has admitted off the record, 'though to be honest I didn't expect anything less. People in the game are usually reluctant to criticise a fellow professional.' Cynics would claim he's let his cronies at Televisió de Catalunya do the dirty work. Today, Cruyff himself is doing his best to put the dampeners on festivities. 'The final wasn't a good game to watch, but what do people expect? It's been like that all year. The results might have been good but the football hasn't been entertaining. And remember, in the Cup Winners' Cup you're not competing against the best teams in Europe, they're only second best or worse.' Given that it was his team that finished third in the league and thus qualified as beaten cup finalists, hardly something he can blame Robson for.

'If you sign a coach whose sides always plays a particular way you'd be stupid to expect something different from him. Maybe a lot of people don't like Robson's methods, but he's worked like that for twenty or thirty years, so what did they expect?' At least Cruyff admits that Robson has carried the players with him. 'They've been very united, anybody who says different is mistaken.' As for Núñez's new coaching structure, 'It's garbage,' says Cruyff, 'too ridiculous to even comment on. Nobody at the club has the slightest power except Núñez. Anything else is a montage. I'm amazed people still can't see that.'

If Cruyff is right, Don Leviathan's failure to pronounce on Robson's future must be worrying the Englishman. Post-Rotterdam, Núñez continues his smug posturing without guaranteeing his coach's future. 'When everybody was begging me to sack Robson, I said wait until the end of the season; logically my position isn't going to change now.'

That lukewarm show of support is accompanied by the umpteenth paean to the Amsterdam school. 'We need to emulate the Ajax model, that means appointing a person responsible for monitoring the transfer market and not depending on what intermediaries offer us; a person with time and resources to convince players to join us. The first-team coach will give his opinion but he won't sign anybody directly.' But who will that coach be? Here's a clue. 'Van Gaal will bring two people with him, his assistant and a goalkeeping coach.' Question. If Van Gaal is going to be sat in an office, why would he bring his training-ground lieutenants with him? 'He wouldn't, would he,' admits Robson privately. 'I want to stay, but not as second-in-charge. I knew I was at the point of being sacked earlier in the season, but I said to the board, "Be loyal and patient, the season lasts nine months, not two or three." I think I've proved my point, but who knows what they think now?'

Whoever is in charge next year, his chances of counting on Ronaldo are reducing by the day. His agents fly out of town this morning without exchanging a single word with Núñez; neither did they speak to anybody from the club in Rotterdam. Núñez and Gaspart immediately drag Ronaldo to supper in an attempt to find out what's going on. The youngster's gruff 'I've got nothing to say' as he leaves is unencouraging, but not as ominous as his comments earlier in the day when asked to record a message for the club's forthcoming website: 'What if I don't stay, what good will I be on the Barça Internet then?'

MAY 1997

SATURDAY, 17 MAY

'Winning the UEFA Cup at a club like Ipswich was a minor miracle, but I'm aware I'm nearer the end of my career than the beginning now, so the Cup Winners' Cup victory is extra-pleasing,' says Bobby Robson, whose Vía Crucis (make that Vía Cruyffis) began exactly one year ago today when he agreed terms with Núñez at a clandestine rendezvous in Madrid. 'To do it for a club as big as Barcelona in my first year, despite all the hassle and criticism [*he pauses and sighs*] – you name it, I've had it thrown at me – to come through all that and win a European trophy is a nice piece of management. I enjoyed the celebrations, the hundreds of thousands of people on the streets. Admittedly, all the religious stuff was a bit strange, but that's been here for centuries, it's part of their culture. I tried to savour everything, after the game and at the town hall. I let everybody else jump around and go mad, that's not me anyway, I can't be like that. I've always said that if you can treat victory and defeat with an even temperament, you're a much better manager. I try not to get over-excited or over-depressed, whatever happens, but inside I was elated.'

SUNDAY, 18 MAY

Given Barça's treatment at the hands of referees who hail from the capital, Real Madrid must have shuddered when the name came out of the computer for yesterday's game against Valladolid: Catalonia's finest, Llonch Andreu. Predictably, 'Calamitous and biased' was today's post-match verdict. Less predictably, from Barcelona. Even Bobby Robson was moved to complain. 'Madrid's penalty was a very dubious decision and the referee had already disallowed a perfectly good goal at the other end, so they've won one-nil instead of lost by the same score. Referees' decisions in Spain are always about context; given the pressure he was under, the guy was lucky he gave the penalty. I hope he can sleep after seeing it on the telly, though being Catalan he deserves a couple of sleepless nights.'

A belligerent Robson also responds to attempts to belittle Barça's Cup Winners' Cup triumph. 'Any player would be proud to win a European title; Cruyff and the Madrid players [*that's Mijatovic and Suker again*] are just jealous. It's not the Mickey Mouse Cup we've won; there are only three European champions a year and we're one of them.' Try telling the president that. 'You'd think my relationship with Núñez would have improved, but life goes on the same. I still don't know how this saga will end, but I haven't got a positive sensation about next season. I haven't spoke to Núñez since Rotterdam, I'm still waiting for him to respond to a pre-season schedule I gave him weeks ago. I've talked to him about the players I'd like to stay and possible incorporations, but he still hasn't asked me for an exact list.'

One player going nowhere but home is Eric Cantona. 'I'm stunned by his retirement,' exclaims Robson. 'Somebody phoned to tell me and I thought they were winding me up. I can't work out why he's retiring.' Despite the Frenchman's scowling disposition. 'He always had that frown and that glum appearance, but I think that was a pose, he wanted to be seen as a son-of-a-bitch character on the pitch and nobody was going to change him. That's not to say he didn't get a thrill from the game.'

MONDAY, 19 MAY
Celta 1, Barcelona 3 (Oscar 29, 39, Ronaldo 64)
Balaídos, 24,080

Barcelona clearly take favourably to the air on Spain's Celtic fringe. A convincing win in Vigo makes for a Galician full house after earlier victories at Deportivo and Compostela. With Depor and Betis again dropping points at home, it's a win that all but guarantees second place and classification for the Champions League.

Once again, Barça demonstrated their strength in depth. Starting only his second league game of the season, Oscar's first goal was a long-distance beauty. His second, a volley from even further out, was an instant contender for goal of the season. 'Hitting the ball first time like that is football's most difficult art,' purrs an admiring Robson. 'You'll rarely see one player score two such spectacular goals in ninety minutes.' Another fringe striker was nowhere near as fortunate. Coming on in the 77th minute, Pizzi was booked in the 82nd and carried off clutching his knee in the 86th. That could spell bad news for Robson with Ronaldo set to join Brazil for Copa América preparations next Sunday. Asked if Saturday's game against Deportivo would be his last for Barça, Ronaldo answers, 'We'll see.' Very promising. At least he'll say goodbye as a record-breaker. Scoring tonight for the ninth consecutive league game, he overtakes Mariano Martín's 1942/43 total to become Barcelona's top marksman in a season with 33 goals.

250

Despite the fact that Celta's keeper was sent off for glancing at Amunike in no-man's-land, the campaign in the Catalan press to credit referees for Real Madrid's success is unlikely to wane. 'Madrid are the most consistent side in Spain,' goes the argument, 'every week they persuade the ref to do them a favour.' Today's Barcelona editions are full of accounts of alleged favours, flashy graphics *et al.* And don't expect the other side of the story. Even one of the more measured broadsheets described the referee's performance in the game against Madrid as 'genocidal'.

The Celta game was Josep Lluís Núñez's 700th as president. In his nineteen years at the helm, ten coaches have occupied the Camp Nou bench. If, as is presumably the case, Robson defies early season odds to make it to the end of the season, he'll move into fourth place behind Cruyff (306 games), Venables (116) and the German Udo Lattek (60). For the moment, his winning percentage (65 per cent) is the best ever.

	P	W	D	L	F	A	PTS
Real Madrid	38	25	11	2	77	30	86
Barcelona	38	25	6	7	95	45	81
Deportivo	38	20	14	4	56	26	74
Betis	38	20	13	5	78	41	73

TUESDAY, 20 MAY

Ronaldo for Inter. If you believe the Italian press it's all over bar the formalities. An eight-year contract at $4.5 million a year (plus more perks than a shady backbencher could ever dream about) has apparently done the trick. 'Everything's ready to take Ronaldo to Italy,' announce his men in Brazil. 'He loves Barcelona – the city, the club, the fans – but we've got to do what's best for him financially. FC Barcelona have contributed enormously to his popularity, but tax changes in Spain next season mean Barça can't possibly match financial offers from Italy. We can't let him renew and lose money.' Or us, they might have added. A 1992 deal signed by Ronaldo's father when the player was still a minor guarantees Martins and Pitta (through the Gorting Corporation in the tax paradise of the Virgin Islands) 10 per cent of any Ronaldo transaction until 2002. No wonder they want him to move. 'Money is their god,' says Bobby Robson, 'and Ronaldo is great business for them, but he should realise there isn't a better club or city in the world than Barcelona.

Once you've earned a certain amount, money shouldn't be the priority.'

Robson, who according to a Portuguese press agency will join Real Madrid next season (!), is hoping that Luis Fernández is a man of his word. 'I'm not an enemy of Barcelona,' says the Athletic Bilbao coach, whose side meet Bobby's future employers on Sunday. 'We need to beat Madrid to get in the UEFA Cup next year.' He also rubbishes notions that Barcelona are offering fiscal incentives. 'If anybody offers me money, I'll denounce them immediately. I'm one of those guys who likes to look in the mirror in the mornings. I don't understand all this talk about cash-filled briefcases and laundered money. Yet it seems it's standard practice in Spain.' It is indeed common knowledge that clubs are fond of investing money come the end of the season in order to stimulate the legs of teams facing their championship rivals, fellow relegation contenders, etc.

'If it's not illegal and it's not frowned upon then it will happen,' says Bobby Robson. 'I find it disgusting that clubs or players will accept money from third parties to try harder [*practically spitting by now*]. Clubs paying money like that in England would be banned; even if it was a Real Madrid they'd be put in the Second Division. They'd be fined and relegated for cheating. It's diabolical. Football's supposed to be a sport, you shouldn't be able to buy anybody. It's the federation who should take responsibility for it; they should find out exactly what's happening and convince players that it's wrong. It's amazing how all the coaches and players go on telly saying it's OK as long as it's for winning. If clubs break the regulations, they have to be fined and relegated. Swindon were hammered by the FA for something that was far less serious; it was silly, that's all. When I was at Porto I was told that it happened there, too. I don't have anything concrete here, but everybody talks about it so much you have to suspect it's happening. It just abuses the spirit of the game.'

FC Barcelona are Spain's basketball champions after beating Real Madrid in the decisive play-off game in the capital. The Barça players had to sprint for safety as objects rained down on them at the final buzzer, a fact considered unworthy of comment by at least one Madrid-based TV station. Step forward, Canal Plus, always willing to adopt the moral high ground because Bobby Robson's team doesn't play what they consider aesthetically pleasing football. They could take a lesson in priorities from their neighbours at *Marca*. Sergi Albert is a columnist for the Madrid daily and a weekly guest on

Cent x Cent Fútbol. On last week's show the former referee described Roberto Carlos as a 'monkey'. *Marca* immediately told him where to take his column. It's a shame Televisió de Catalunya didn't follow suit – the show's presenter shrugged off the incident by claiming, 'Anybody can make a mistake.'

Real Madrid are similarly undiscerning when it comes to their fellow travellers. It's no secret that both individual board members and players have long underwritten the *Ultras Sur*. Not everyone goes as far as the late Juanito or, more recently, Alfonso, self-confessed *ultras* on the pitch, but woe betide the player who refuses to dig deep for the mob's seasonal raffles. Top boy José Luis Ochaíta was arrested at a game against Atlético Madrid in February in possession of a catapult, ball-bearings and knuckle-dusters; behaviour not considered serious enough to lose him his parking space at the Bernabéu or some 500 free tickets per game (tickets he then sells to finance the *Ultras Sur* activities). And certainly not enough to keep him out of his ringside seat for the basketball. Luckily, the police dragged the foaming-at-the-mouth thug off the court before he could get to the Barça players.

WEDNESDAY, 21 MAY

As the season reaches boiling point, you wouldn't expect anything less than fighting talk from Luis Enrique (either he's sponsored by the 'No Fear' factory or he spends all his money on their gear). 'If there's a genuine chance to cut the difference it has to be this weekend. We let everybody down when we allowed Madrid to open the gap in the first place. Now it's getting tight, we can't give the league away, we have to make sure they lose it. A month ago nobody gave us a prayer, now people are beginning to have their doubts and Madrid are getting nervous.' And with good reason. The Basque Cathedral of San Mamés is as Madrid-hostile as Camp Nou, UEFA-chasing Bilbao are desperate for the three points, and both Suker and Mijatovic are suspended.

Monday has been confirmed as D-Day for Ronaldo. Meanwhile, Guardiola's agent confirms that the club has until Tuesday to respond to an offer from Parma. 'It would be a tragedy if Barça lost Ronaldo and Guardiola,' says Bobby Robson, who plays no part in the negotiations. 'The best club in the world should have the best players, so Barcelona should do everything in their power to keep them.'

Gary Lineker, in town to interview Stoichkov for the BBC, reckons they should make a similar effort to hold on to his former England boss. 'Bobby has suffered plenty of criticism in his career but he's always managed to overcome it. Being coach at Barcelona always means massive pressure, especially if you're behind Real Madrid, but he's used to this type of situation. He rode through similar crises as England manager, but in the end, he always ended up the hero. And if Barça do offer Van Gaal his job, Bobby will walk away with his head held high. He's not the kind of person to create problems.'

That depends. 'I'm confident that when the season is over I can cause Núñez a problem,' says Robson, though he swiftly lapses into realism. 'What will he decide? I've got a contract for another year, but what does a contract mean here?'

THURSDAY, 22 MAY

You would have thought a side that has lost just twice all season would feel reasonably comfortable about needing seven points or less in their last four matches. So why are Real Madrid giving off those Keeganesque run-in vibes. 'I look into my players' eyes and I see fear,' laments Fabio Capello. 'They seem petrified at the thought of losing the league in the last game of the season again.' Ah yes, the dreaded Tenerife syndrome. In both 1992 and 1993, Barça were proclaimed champs on the season's final afternoon as Madrid rounded off record-breaking collapses in the Canaries. 'With just four games to go it's vital we use our heads and not our hearts,' pleads Capello. 'We're not running out of gas, our problems are psychological. The players have been in a state of shock since the defeat at Camp Nou; they've gone completely.'

At least Ronaldo won't be around to haunt Madrid in the run-in. 'I know I'm leaving at a bad moment,' says the youngster. 'I'd love to play the last three games and the Cup Final, but I can't split myself in two.' But would Saturday signal the final curtain or just a temporary parting of the ways? 'I don't know, all I can say is that it'll hurt me to go,' says Ronaldo. 'I've got a great lifestyle here. This morning I was sunbathing by the pool in my garden and I said to a friend, "Gee, if we were in Holland now, we'd be locked inside watching telly." But I've got to think about my future well-being and my family, too. If I do go it'll be purely for money. Barcelona is the best football club in the world, but life doesn't begin with Barça, Manchester United or Milan. If I have to leave, *no pasa nada*. Life goes on.'

FRIDAY, 23 MAY

After stealing a kiss from Bobby Robson after today's training session, Carmen Sevilla, once a fifties movie idol and now the gaffe-prone presenter of Spain's lottery draw, describes the Englishman as 'a naughty boy and a flirt'. The Catalan poet Pere Gimferrer is more literary, but less complimentary. 'Bobby Robson is like an alien who's landed on another planet. He's so out of place you can't help but like him. It's as if Don Quixote had landed on the moon!'

SATURDAY, 24 MAY

Barcelona 1, Deportivo 0 (Ronaldo 89)
Camp Nou, 95,000

Ronaldo's last goal of the season in the last minute of possibly his last game in Barça colours leaves his team with both feet in the Champions League; and Real Madrid looking very nervously over their shoulder. 'Madrid will not like this result . . . one bit,' says Bobby Robson. 'We've put a lot of pressure on them for tomorrow, let's see how they handle it.'

It may seem churlish to criticise a 20-year-old who has scored 45 goals in 48 games in his debut season at the FC Barcelona pressure-cooker, but for the umpteenth time this term Ronaldo seemed determined to prove he's an extraordinary footballer despite himself. Like a raging tornado, the young Brazilian is an unstoppable force of nature; like a sea breeze on a siesta, he's also as indolent as he's unpredictable. Tonight's game was billed as the showdown between Brazil's finest. Rivaldo, of feline glide and seductive left foot, has been in such awesome form since Christmas that he leads Ronaldo in many of Spain's Footballer of the Year contests (annoyingly, there are scores, so you never get just the one MVP). With his teammates entrenched in their own half, he constantly dropped deep to try and make things happen.

In contrast Ronaldo looked disinterested and when the ball was forced upon him he seemed intent on playing on his own. His future in the balance, you'd have thought a heaving Camp Nou would have been at pains to make their boy wonder feel wanted. On the contrary, there was not a 'Please Don't Go!' banner in sight or a token chorus of 'We love you, Ronaldo, we do'. In fact, the 20-year-old superstar was whistled as early as the eleventh minute, and then successively, for his flagrant individualism. The lack of communion was summed up perfectly, if inadvertently, by the kit man's oversight; Ronaldo spent the first half in a shirt minus the Barça badge.

He was back in proper gear after the break, but despite the significance of his late winner, Ronaldo's behaviour at the final whistle was indicative of where his heart really lies. While his teammates headed for the centre circle to say goodbye for the season to the fans, Ronaldo preferred to exchange pleasantries with Depor's Brazilian clan on the touchline. When he eventually trooped off, he did so without so much as a token glance at the arena that has embraced him, let alone a wave. And yet, and yet. He doesn't do much, but what he does. Four and a half seconds of pure magic with 44 minutes and 46 seconds on the clock. Springing to his feet like a panther after being knocked to the floor, he rode lunges from Djukic and Flavio Conceiçao, flew past Mauro Silva, and thrust the ball past Songo'o to keep Barça in the title hunt. Blink and you'd miss it. Pure Ronaldo.

One hundred thousand *culés* exploded at the final whistle, but for 89 minutes of stalemate they'd suffered in bewildering silence. 'You'd never believe the title was on the line,' observed *Goal*'s Michael Hodges, halfway through the second half. When the fans did open their mouths it was for all the wrong reasons. So Roberto Carlos got the bird because he's stroppy and plays for Real Madrid, did he? Try telling that to Jacques Songo'o, Depor's laid-back 'keeper from the Cameroon.

Barça's fifth win in a row eliminates Depor from the race for second place. 'They were easily the best team we've seen at Camp Nou this season,' admits Robson. As for that best player, despite the persistent efforts of journalists, the coach refuses to badmouth Ronaldo. 'He may not be playing as well as he was at the beginning of the season, but he's still winning games for us. He's twenty, and he's still got a lot to learn about football, but you don't want to take away his ability to do things nobody else in the world can. He needs to learn when to pass and when to combine with others, but it's not easy for him; a split second after receiving the ball he's got an opponent clattering into him, so he doesn't get time to think. I just wish we weren't losing him for crucial games. We've paid all this money for him and he's leaving.'

Off the record, Robson admits that Ronaldo got himself out of jail with his goal. 'He didn't have a great game, but he gets off the ground and wins the game with a remarkable goal so everybody writes about him. But his performance in the game didn't merit more marks than some of the other players; Sergi, for example. He was up and down the left flank non-stop for ninety minutes; it was like watching a tennis ball going backwards and forwards. Ronaldo was very static and he's lost the ball a lot. Maybe it is a case of getting by on natural talent, but he'll improve and participate more. When he learns exactly when to be selfish, he'll be even more effective.'

Before the game, Barça's basketball team tempted fate by parading the spoils of Madrid around the pitch. Only once have FC Barcelona been proclaimed Spain's basketball and football champs in the same season, and that was as long ago as 1959. More recently the revolving-doors syndrome has been unnerving: the tall guys won the league in 1987, '88, '89 and '90; Cruyff's men did the honours in 1991, '92, '93 and '94, and the basketball team again in 1995, '96 and '97.

SUNDAY, 25 MAY

If Fabio Capello read fear in his players' eyes last week, then he'd better look the other way altogether this week. Madrid's spineless display in a 1-0 defeat at Athletic Bilbao leaves Barça just two points adrift and a growing sensation of déjà vu in the capital. Five games ago, defeat at Valladolid left Robson's side ten points adrift and seemingly beyond redemption. Madrid's subsequent impersonation of a journeyman team with no legs and even less bottle (Tenerife 1992 and '93) is reflected in just one goal (and that a non-existent penalty) in three games. You know something's amiss when naming names is the capital rage: Sanz is busy fingering Capello and referees, Capello the players and press, the players Capello and Stoichkov, the fans any of the above.

Of course, what's really got them worried in the capital is that Robson's team are on the kind of 'Ain't no stoppin' us now' roll Barça championships are invariably made of. Seven wins in 30 days have seen them secure a European trophy, shake off Depor and Betis, and equal the club's all-time goalscoring record of 96 in a season. All this despite those perilous cup-winning hangovers and injuries to Nadal, Blanc, Giovanni, Popescu and Pizzi.

No wonder Bobby Robson was looking chirpy today as he swapped stories with King Juan Carlos on a yacht at Barcelona's

Club Naútico. 'We chatted about the club and success, and he told me how happy he was for me. He said he hoped I liked it in Spain and would be here many years. That's still a thrill; football has got its downside, but it's got its privileges, too. Only this kind of job would give someone from my background that kind of opportunity. Not many people get the chance to become acquainted with the King, it's the kind of thing you still ring home to tell your family. I've had friends ring me and say [*laughs and puts on airs-and-graces voice*], "I see we're talking with the King now"!'

	P	W	D	L	F	A	PTS
Real Madrid	39	25	11	3	77	31	86
Barcelona	39	26	6	7	96	45	84
Deportivo	39	20	14	5	56	27	74
Betis	38	20	13	5	78	41	73

MONDAY, 26 MAY

A six-hour meeting between a bunch of characters who wouldn't look out of place in a Tarantino movie attracts such a crowd to the offices of Núñez y Navarro Construction that police are forced to set up barricades. Another controversy over Núñez's plans to knock down listed buildings and erect one of his 'street corner' monstrosities in their place? No, in fact the dudes in dark suits, darker shades and carrying suspicious-looking briefcases are here to decide the future of the 20-year-old merchandise they call Ronaldo. In the early hours of the morning, the rival clans – Josep Lluís Núñez, son Joe Jr and Joan Gaspart in the Catalan corner; Alexandre Martins, Reinaldo Pitta and Italian associate Giovanni Branchini in the Brazilian corner; an army of bodyguards (well, OK, financial consultants) on both sides – call it a night. 'We're agreed on ninety per cent,' says Núñez as he scampers out of a side door.

One man missing was Ronaldo himself. The player headed for Oslo this morning to join the Brazilian squad for a game against Norway. 'I'll be in touch by mobile,' he tells journalists at the airport, 'and contrary to what's being said, my managers work for me, not the other way around. They'll follow my instructions, and I want to stay.'

There's good news on the sporting front, too. Betis's draw at Valencia guarantees Barcelona's presence in next season's Champions League. If they get beyond the preliminaries, they could encounter a familiar face. Ronaldo may or may not be staying, but word has it that Guardiola has decided to join Parma. His agent has long described Barça's offer as 'derisory', but until now the player himself has opted for a discreet silence. His words today are a dead giveaway. 'I've made my decision,' he says after training, 'but I'd prefer to keep it to myself until the end of the season. I don't want to cause a fuss when the most important thing is focusing on winning the league.' Given that it would cause NO fuss WHATSOEVER if he decided to stay, it looks like destination Parma.

TUESDAY, 27 MAY

'RONALDO STAYS!' After a morning of intense negotiations, a four o'clock press conference delivers the news all Catalonia has been waiting for. Amidst *mucho* macho backslapping and kisses between the big fellas, it's confirmed that Ronaldo is, in the words of Josep Lluís Núñez, 'Barcelona's for life'. The player's existing contract will be extended until June 2006 with a rising wage scale that will net him an average £2.3 million a year. As Núñez has kindly agreed to meet Ronaldo's tax obligations, as well, it's a package that will cost FC Barcelona a cool £55 million. The club backed down on three other bones of contention: a) Ronaldo will be paid all his salary directly by the club, not by participating sponsors, b) he is not obliged to offer commercial services in return for the latters' contributions, and c) his new buy-out clause is fixed at £42.5 million, not the £64 million originally agreed in December.

'I've spoken to Núñez to thank him for the club's efforts,' says a delighted Ronaldo, whose immediate reaction to the news was to order a bottle of *cava Codorniu* (Catalan 'champagne') and spray it Formula One-style over Barcelona's press contingent in Oslo. 'If I'm World Player of the Year it's thanks to Barça; when I was at PSV I scored just as many goals but nobody noticed. My managers had told me not to build up my hopes, and I'd convinced myself that moving to Milan was not the end of the world; it's Italy's fashion capital and Inter are a big club, too. But I was so desperate to stay I couldn't take in what they were saying. So I insisted and insisted and now they've finally settled it. As I'm getting more money I'll have to score even more goals! This year I've scored thirty-five, but next year I want to do even better. My aim is to smash the Spanish record.'

Actually he scored 34, but unlike the rest of Spain, Ronaldo insists, 'I'm counting the Rayo one, as well.' Thirty-four league goals and he's claiming what was a clear own goal as well? It's an anecdote that says everything about the goalscorer's obsessive nature. 'I'll do anything for Barça now,' he continues. 'I'll even take dual nationality if it helps them. And if I've got a Spanish passport I won't have to queue so much at Barcelona airport [*laughs*]. With a Brazilian passport they always tell you to wait or get in the queue.' That's obviously Espanyol fans, then.

WEDNESDAY, 28 MAY

'RONALDO GOES!' At eight o'clock last night Barcelona's lawyers sat down with Ronaldo's men at Núñez's HQ to dot the i's on the contract. Five hours later, the Brazilian's team leave the building with long faces. Reinaldo Pitta tells journalists, 'As soon as we began to draw up the definitive contract the problems started all over again.' Two hours later they call Núñez to say the deal is off. A day of rumours follows until Barcelona's president emerges from the office of his financial assessors at seven o'clock and admits, 'It's all over, Ronaldo is going.' Two hours later, the player's agents release a statement confirming there will be no more negotiations. What Núñez described as a lifelong matrimony didn't last 24 hours.

Later in the evening, a disconsolate Ronaldo launches a bitter attack on the Barcelona board from his hotel in Oslo. 'It's all over. They've spent seven months deceiving me. I'm leaving and that's that. We'll never sit down to negotiate with Barcelona again; the only thing that matters now is our dignity, it's not an economic problem. Núñez can say whatever he likes but my managers were working for me and I know exactly what happened. He's a liar and he'll carry on lying. We've tried everything to reach a deal but we can't trust the board any more, they're not men of their word. If they treat me like this, given half a chance they'd kill the other players. They blame my representatives, but I trust them far more than Núñez.'

And that is all that counts. Ronaldo believes his managers. Not surprisingly, the united forces of *Barcelonismo* set their sights on the player's unholy trinity. Rumours and more rumours. They'd already accepted $5 million commission from Inter (Giovanni Branchini lives in Milan and is a close confidant of the Inter president). They only sat down with Barcelona to mollify Ronaldo. They wanted his salary for the ninth and tenth season paid across years one to eight.

'I'm sure they'd already made a deal with Inter,' claims Núñez. 'After we shook hands on terms, they spent the next hour on the phone to Italy. They admitted they didn't expect to reach an agreement, and they used any excuse to try and slow down negotiations. It was obvious they wanted talks to break down. I accepted things I never should have: they asked for five million pounds by ten this morning and we said yes; they asked for ten million more in seven days and we said yes; they refused to pay five per cent of Ronaldo's taxes as previously agreed and we said, "OK we'll pay them." We even agreed to pay everything in dollars. Then they refused to accept that Televisió de Catalunya could pay fifteen per cent of Ronaldo's contract or my word as guarantee. It's clear they only came here because Ronaldo forced them to. I feel sorry for him; when I spoke to him yesterday he was so happy.'

'We're not interested in a war of words,' responds Alexandre Martins. 'We're just sorry that once again it's been impossible to get down in writing what was agreed verbally. Barcelona knew Ronaldo's heartfelt desire was to stay and they thought they could take advantage of that. It takes a marathon of meetings to agree anything with them and we still have nothing on paper. We really can't trust them any more.' Reinaldo Pitta describes the rupture in more melodramatic terms. 'We're disappointed by all the cowardly lies and deception. They told us Televisió de Catalunya would pay fifteen per cent of Ronaldo's contract but when we asked for guarantees they couldn't give us anything, that's why we broke off negotiations. I don't understand how their attitude changed after lunch yesterday. It's like a husband who trusts his wife and gets home to find she's cheated him, or when Christ was betrayed by Judas. They tried to wear us down with sheer wear and tear – we may be Brazilians, and we may be from the Third World, but we're not idiots.'

The last thing Bobby Robson needs today is a another stroppy Brazilian. Here's Giovanni on his case from Oslo. 'If Robson stays I'm going. He doesn't like me and he makes me play in strange positions. He never speaks to me, even when I'm injured. He's a gutless coach who has never repeated a line-up this season because he's afraid of putting people's backs out, that's why he rotates so much. He's a coach with no personality or character; he's bad, very bad.'

After training, a furious Robson gathers journalists together to answer in kind. 'I wouldn't normally talk to the press about one of my players, but if that's the way Giovanni wants it, so be it. I spoke to him three times about his fitness before the Cup Final and it was obvious he wasn't ready. The fact that he then broke down in training and missed the next two games shows I made the right decision. His arguments are ridiculous; it's his own fault he's lost his place, he's had loads of opportunities and most of them in his natural position. He's had a poor season, particularly away from home; he should concentrate on his own performances instead of opening his big mouth.'

Borussia Dortmund beat Juventus in the Champions League final. As the Spanish and English leagues go overboard on the exotic, Bobby Robson points out that Borussia's winning team was 'very, very German'. 'Any intelligent club will always have a strong home-grown nucleus – the Germans have done that and they should be admired for it. They are a race that really believe in themselves, too, so I think they'll continue to have the major league with least foreigners. Of course, there are economic reasons, too. English clubs were like that once, but their philosophy has changed because the price of home-grown players has gone crazy. Teddy Sheringham has said he wants to leave Tottenham and at thirty-one years of age the club are talking about a six-million-pound fee. That's not a viable proposition, so what do you do? You look further afield. Sheringham is talking about going abroad, but that's rubbish. I can guarantee you no foreign club would pay half that for him.'

THURSDAY, 29 MAY

Ronaldo's departure could prove very good news for Pep Guardiola's bank account. As a letter to the editor in today's *El Mundo Deportivo* puts it, 'Ronaldo is gone, if Guardiola follows him, the next to go should be Núñez.' Just in case the president doesn't get the message, *Sport* launch a 'Don't go, Pep' campaign. Losing a 'money-grabbing' Brazilian is one thing, losing the home-grown symbol of *Catalanismo* is quite another. The fans may have made no discernible effort to persuade Ronaldo to stay, but Barça's training ground sports plenty of 'Pep for ever' banners today. Meanwhile, a group of dissenting *culés* are busy pinning up flyers outside Núñez's office. They read, 'If Robson, Núñez and Gaspart have a plane crash who is saved first? *La pedrera i el Barça* [home-grown players and Barça]'.

'If Ronaldo was as happy as he says he was and really wanted to stay, I don't understand how he can say no to nearly fifty thousand pounds a week,' says Núñez. 'It could be he was playing a three-way game all the time to push up offers from elsewhere.' Not surprisingly, Ronaldo begs to differ. 'They had seven months to sort things out with my managers and all they did was mess us around. I'll never let my people sit down with Barça again, there's not that much money in the world. All I'm interested in now is having a great season in Italy and preparing for the World Cup in France. I know Núñez is trying to justify himself by blaming us, that's natural. I just hope the fans understand me. While I was there I did everything to make Barça champions – my conscious is clear.'

Anybody who'd seen Ronaldo in Oslo on Tuesday, leaping over Giovanni and shouting, 'I'm staying, I'm staying,' and the Ronaldo of this morning – bags under his eyes after a night crying, goofy smile nowhere to be seen, asking to be excused breakfast with the rest of the Brazilian party so he could retire to his room – would have to agree; either he genuinely wanted to stay or he's a mighty fine actor.

SATURDAY, 31 MAY

The fact that Ronaldo is under contract until Inter pay his buy-out clause has led to suggestions that he could play in the Cup Final if Brazil don't make the final stages of the Copa América. Wishful thinking, it seems. 'I know I'm still a Barça player,' says Ronaldo, whose listless performance as Brazil lost 4-2 to Norway yesterday reflected his mood, 'but I've got no desire to wear the Barça shirt again – I don't want to go within a mile of Núñez or anybody else from the board.'

No one seems to have noticed, but there's a decisive game against Hércules tomorrow. 'I'm trying to run a football team here and we've spent all bloody week talking about Ronaldo,' complains Bobby Robson. 'Everybody's forgotten about the other players and how vital it is to win and keep the pressure on Madrid – that's what we should be talking about.' That's not to suggest Robson doesn't care what happens to Ronaldo. 'It's very sad what has happened this week; the best player in the world was ours and now it seems we've lost him. It's out of my hands, but all I'd say to the president is keep fighting until he's signed on the dotted line elsewhere. And I'd say one thing to Ronaldo: maybe clubs like Inter have got the money to take him away from Barça but that doesn't make them better clubs. Look at Ronaldo now and Ronaldo when we signed him; this club have given a lot to him.'

Unlike everybody else in Barcelona, Robson feels the player has still got the final word. 'It's logical that his managers fight to defend his economic interests but Ronaldo's the one who has to make the final decision. He has the key, he has to decide whether he wants to play in Spain or Italy.' And if he does go? 'It would be very sad news for everybody. There are other great players around, but there's only one Ronaldo.'

As for possible replacements, Robson admits, with his own job still on the line, he's in the dark. 'I've given Núñez a list of players but he's not saying anything to me. They must have made their minds up about next year but they still haven't told me anything.' His obvious frustration is mixed with an unusual sense of pessimism, at least off the record. 'We'd win the league if we had Ronaldo, Pizzi and Giovanni available. As it is, I've got no centre-forward. The Ronaldo thing is a mess.'

SUNDAY, 1 JUNE
Hércules 2, Barcelona 1 (Luis Enrique 4)
Rico Pérez, 30,000

A bad week in the office finishes with an even worse day on the pitch. Losing Ronaldo and the league in the space of a few days? The kind of accident you'd only just wish on your worst enemies. Some would say that Barça – who contrived to lose to already relegated Hércules for the second time this season, the only side to do so – are their own worst enemies. 'That was our worst performance for months,' admits Robson, 'perhaps our worst of the season.' With Madrid beating Extremadura 5-0 to go five points clear, Capello's team need just one point from two games to be proclaimed champions.

'Mathematically we've still got a chance,' says the smiling coach afterwards (he'd done all his fretting on the bench), 'but realistically it's very difficult now. The players have made a superhuman effort in the last couple of months; we've played so many big games and everybody has got a limit.'

This time last week, Madrid's defeat at Bilbao was looking good to kick-start a tumultuous week in the capital; instead attention has focused on the Ronaldo saga. Talk about giving your rivals a timely morale-booster. Typically, Robson will not accept excuses. 'Today's result had nothing to do with Ronaldo. The players knew how important the game was and they were determined to show they could win without Ronaldo. But sometimes you just can't dredge up any more reserves.'

Unlike his boss, José Mourinho is never one to look a gift excuse in the mouth. Word on the media grapevine has it that Hércules were on a third-party bonus of £30,000 a man to beat Barcelona. 'I've spoken to people in the Hércules camp and they've confirmed there were cash incentives,' says Mourinho. Gica Popescu agrees. 'They were already relegated yet they celebrated at the end as if they'd just won the Cup. I can't see any reason for so much joy that's not financial. What really gets my back up is that Hércules are on their way to the Second Division with the six points we've gifted them – that's six points that would leave us top of the table.'

Josep Lluís Núñez, who met yesterday with executives from Nike, claims the sports empire are desperate to see Ronaldo stay at Barcelona. 'They described Inter as a second-rate club,' he says. Nike's Spanish office confirms moves could be afoot. 'Nike would like the best player in the world to play for the world's biggest club; we'd be delighted to bring the two parties together.' Before Barça fans get too carried away, Giovanni Branchini continues to insist it's an Italian job. 'If it was just about money Ronaldo would go to Glasgow Rangers, theirs is the best offer he's received [£4.25 *million a season plus bonuses*]. But he wants to play in Italy.'

Predictably, the media are blaming Ronaldo's absence for today's defeat. 'Barcelona have proved they can't win without Ronaldo,' claim Michael Robinson's buddies at Canal Plus. 'He's missed three games and they haven't won one. When the outcome depends on Robson's tactics Barça always lose.' As Pizzi puts it off the record, 'Of course, they've forgotten Ronaldo's woeful performance against Hércules at Camp Nou.'

	P	W	D	L	F	A	PTS
Real Madrid	40	26	11	3	82	31	89
Barcelona	40	26	6	8	97	47	84

MONDAY, 2 JUNE

Laurent Blanc once described Ronaldo as being like a ping-pong ball. He obviously meant off the pitch, as well. 'Nike have called me and they're keen to help Barça resolve my renewal,' says Ronaldo from Brazil's training camp in Lyons. 'Going back to Barcelona is the best thing that could happen to me. I'm annoyed with the president, but I'd go back for the fans and because I feel at home there, that's what really counts. After the way the board have acted, I'd only ask for one thing, fair play. I haven't spoken directly to Núñez or Gaspart over the last couple of days – to tell you the truth, I think they're scared to talk to me after going back on our agreement – but if they want to do the right thing, they should call me. I've said it a hundred times and I'll say it again, I'd love to stay at Barcelona.'

TUESDAY, 3 JUNE

'Nothing has changed, I didn't open any doors. My decision is made and I'm not interested in talking to Barcelona again, no way.' Ronaldo, naturally. His latest change of heart coincides with the arrival of Alexandre Martins and Reinaldo Pitta in Lyons. 'We have to forget about Ronaldo,' admits Barça Vice-President Joan Gaspart. 'His representatives have got too much power over him.' *La Vanguardia*'s Enric Bañeres agrees. 'Ronaldo no more controls his career than Mike Tyson does. In the same way Don King controls who and when Tyson fights, Ronaldo's agents will decide who he plays for.'

Ronaldo's mobile hasn't stopped ringing in Lyons: fellow baldie De la Peña and the Portuguese-speakers – Couto, Figo and Baía – have all been on the blower urging him to think again. Back in Barcelona, Vítor Baía also offers his support for Bobby Robson. 'I know it's not supposed to be the players' business, but Robson has got a year left on his contract and he deserves to stay. The critics have gone way over the top, you can't attack a coach just because he steps off an aeroplane left foot forward, or because he's got white hair.'

WEDNESDAY, 4 JUNE

After breakfast with Ronaldo in the gardens of the Château du Pizay, Martins and Pitta jump in a cab and head for Orly airport. Destination Milan. *Modus operandi*, Massimo Moratti's private jet. Less than an hour in the early morning shade was enough to convince Ronaldo to ignore Vic, Nike, Uncle Tom Cobbley and all. And didn't he look happy about it (actually no, he looked devastated). Whatever his agents' hold over him, it's clearly vice-like.

Giovanni Branchini was waiting at the airport to whisk Martins and Pitta into the arms of a grateful Moratti. Back in Lyons, a glum-looking Ronaldo confirms the worst. 'My decision is final – I've just signed the documents confirming my *adiós* to Barcelona. Inter are offering the same money but there are more guarantees in the form of payment. It's the same decision we made several months ago (!?) and there's no reason to change it. Nike are my sponsor but this decision has got nothing to do with them. I was misinterpreted the other day, I can assure you my future is in Italy.' And maybe he's not the only one. 'If Barcelona treat Guardiola the same way they've treated me then he'll leave as well. That's for sure.'

THURSDAY, 5 JUNE

Let the legal battle commence. According to FC Barcelona, both domestic legislation and FIFA rules dictate that only Spanish clubs can sign players using the buy-out clauses. 'As the same norm doesn't apply in Italy, there's obviously some confusion,' says Josep Lluís Núñez. 'Ronaldo is not on the transfer list and Inter are breaking FIFA rules by negotiating with him behind our backs. He can only join an Italian club if they reach an agreement with FC Barcelona. He can go ahead and rescind his contract via the buy-out clause, but the right to grant his international transfer remains in the power of the Spanish authorities. If Ronaldo doesn't want to play for us he can't play for anybody.'

Ronaldo is not impressed. 'They should try reading my contract more carefully. It clearly states I can go to any club I choose on paying my buy-out clause. It was one of the details we took longest to negotiate when we drew up the contract last summer in Miami. We specifically asked that the clause be valid for Spanish or foreign clubs to avoid this kind of problem. At least this will show Barça fans why I'm leaving; the board don't even want to respect what's written in contracts.' According to his agents, this is just the latest stage in an underhand campaign. 'One of the biggest mistakes Barcelona have made is to act behind our back with their dirty tricks. Their second big mistake is that they tried to buy us off. They wanted to give us two million dollars more when negotiations broke down; we felt like telling them to stick the money up their ass.'

If Ronaldo's buy-out clause was only valid in Spain, there would, of course, be an easy solution; use another Spanish club as a stepping stone. And don't Real Madrid know it. 'Maybe we can get our own back on Barcelona for paying off Sampdoria to stop us signing Karembeu,' says Lorenzo Sanz. 'As president of Real Madrid it's my obligation to try and weaken Barcelona, and doing so seduces me. It's not our war, but if we can take advantage of it . . .'

Relaxed on a leather sofa in one of Camp Nou's inner sanctums –
an etching by Picasso peering over his shoulder – Bobby Robson is
struggling to come to terms with losing Ronaldo. 'I still can't believe
he's going,' he sighs. 'I always thought he'd stay when it really got
down to it. The problem was the board's inability to get along with
his managers; they've never managed to sit down with them and
clarify all the problems. It's a crime that boy's leaving here. And it's
crazy that the boy's been in Barcelona eight or nine months and the
decisive negotiations are going on while he's in Oslo. My impression
is that Ronaldo really wanted to stay, but his guys have influenced
him, I don't think there's any doubt about that, at all. But regardless
of what Inter Milan have offered him or his agents, the board
obviously waited for the wrong moment. It's a shame. He was a
popular, easy-going lad, and he got on well with the other players.

'Whatever combination we get up front, we can't possibly be a
better team without him. Where are we going to find a player to score
thirty-four goals for a start? A Barcelona with Ronaldo at twenty and
improving all the time are far better off than a Barcelona without
him. I'm very sad.' Even so, he does agree there was a lack of rapport
at Ronaldo's farewell game. 'I agree the crowd were a bit quiet
against Deportivo, I don't think they thought it was really going to be
his last game for Barcelona. If they had, the atmosphere might have
been different. But he doesn't need special attention, he knows he's a
hero here.' Though not on a par with Stoichkov. 'Hristo's been here
five, six years, Ronaldo has had eight months, that's the difference. If
Ronaldo had stayed a couple of years he would have achieved that
idol status, but I think it's a bit much to ask for it in eight months.

'Stoichkov is like a god to the Catalans; I've never seen anyone so
popular. That's why Amunike has had problems, because he's taking
over from a legend; it would be like me trying to stand on a stage
and sing after Sinatra.' Of course, Stoichkov has also gone out of his
way to woo the public and eulogise all things Catalan. Others could
take note. After training this morning on an adjoining pitch, Robson
strolled alone across Camp Nou to the cheers of scores of kids up in
the third tier. Naturally, he was all smiles as he waved his way to the
dressing room. Five minutes later, De la Peña and Popescu manage
to walk the same 50 yards without a hint of a wave. Now no one
expects footballers to be role models, but a minimum of civility and
education is surely not too much to ask?

'It's not difficult to look up and wave,' agrees Robson. 'You do wonder why they can't do it. A little wave is everything to the kids, it produces a nice feeling of attachment so it's the least players can do. When I'm on the team bus, I never stop waving, but I'm practically the only one. English footballers definitely have more rapport with the fans, they celebrate their goals with the crowd rather than among themselves. That's another reason Stoichkov is so popular, because he always goes to the fans.' Former Sevilla striker Toni Polster once said, 'You can't expect people to cheer you on match days and then ignore you if they see you in the street.' Words that should be pinned up in the Barça dressing room.

Today's papers are chock full of reports about Van Gaal's furniture-removing arrangements and Bobby Robson's isolation from Barça's decision-making hub. And if Robson isn't packing himself, why on earth is that Gica Popescu saying 'Hello' in dubious English on Barça's brand-new website (http://fcbarcelona.es). The coach makes no attempt to hide the fact that he remains in the dark about his own future.

'The problem is I don't know what is happening, I HAVEN'T GOT A CLUE. Aghh! It's crazy, I'm very angry. I shall be seeing Núñez next week to give him an ultimatum, but whatever they do to me at the end of the season, I'll still have a year left on my contract. I'm sure they can keep me at the club as something other than first-team coach, so I can't resign. If Van Gaal is bringing his own assistants he's obviously going to be on the bench. And I don't know who all these signings are, do you? I've seen talk about Dugarry and Reiziger, and now Rexach is in Brazil looking at someone called Dodo. Who the hell is Dodo? When I see all this stuff about the signings, of course I feel mad at the president. And the quicker English clubs know what's happening the better; there comes a time when they'll pass the point of no return and won't wait for me. I can't play that game of poker much longer, I've got to get a decision from Núñez. I keep asking him and he says, "We have to wait, we're doing very well, we're very happy, you have to win the Cup, blah, blah, blah, bow, wow, wow." And despite what you read in the papers, clubs at home are not hanging on the end of the telephone waiting for me to call. I turned down Everton four or five weeks ago, I told them I couldn't make a decision until the end of the season, and I haven't spoke to them for weeks. They haven't appointed anybody else so the press keep the story alive.'

Robson recently said that one year at Barcelona wears a coach down like five years anywhere else. So why, pray, did he want to stay? He laughs aloud. 'Well, maybe it's like three years . . . it's because you're working at the biggest club in the world, and if you get good results it's the best feeling in the world. I wouldn't want to work here for too long, but I've only been here one season. It's a great place to work and I'd love another crack at it. Despite everything that has happened with Núñez, if it's my choice I still want to stay. Yeesss! But basically I'm interested in coaching, I want to be out on the pitch with the first team.'

FRIDAY, 6 JUNE

As everyone gets in on the legal debate – FIFA, UEFA, the Spanish FA, authorities in international labour law – Ronaldo's Brazilian cabinet insist we're talking a smokescreen. 'If Barcelona are trying to get us to negotiate again they can forget it,' says Alexandre Martins. 'Ronaldo's clause is very clear, he can choose to go to the club he wants.'

'Ronaldo is mine,' boasts an equally unflustered Massimo Moratti. 'I've given myself a present.' If it's any consolation back in Catalonia, Moratti's gift-wrapped scoring machine is having none of that *culé* nightmare scenario. 'I'm not going to Real Madrid because it's unnecessary,' says Ronaldo. 'Once I pay my clause I can go wherever I want. Barça are powerless to stop me.'

SUNDAY, 8 JUNE

Spain beat the Czech Republic to effectively guarantee their place at the World Cup finals. Not that you'd notice amidst the latest headlines about Ronaldo ('Inter Go For Ronaldo/Romario Duo') and Italian sirens tracking Guardiola, De la Peña, Nadal, etc. 'To be honest we're all sick of being asked about Ronaldo every day,' says Abelardo, shortly before helping Spain beat the Czechs 1-0. 'Ronaldo's monopolising the headlines and nobody has talked about this game. And it's worse in Barcelona; you go out on the street and it's the only thing people are talking about. Last week everybody seemed to forget we were two points behind Madrid with the title on the line. It's about time we forgot about Ronaldo and concentrated on the league and the Cup Final.'

TUESDAY, 10 JUNE

They say you should measure your response by how it serves your goal, not how it serves your fury. Bobby Robson's capacity to ignore a slight is undeniable, though it's reaching the point where you have to ask what is his goal exactly? A gold medal in how to be humiliated and come out smiling? Another session at Núñez i Navarro with the press gang, and Robson is still no closer to a straight answer on his future. According to the local press, Núñez insisted on talking about the next three games, avoiding the subject of Robson's future altogether. 'Do you fancy our chances in the Cup Final, *Mister*?' 'Yes, but it won't be easy, Joe. Betis are a dead handy side.' Ten minutes maybe, but more than an hour? Pleaaase. 'We've got three important games left, that's all that matters,' shrugs Robson as he jumps into a cab, 'not my future.' In his tracks, José Mourinho. Unlike his boss, Mourinho has a face like an open book. If looks could kill.

Five minutes later, Joan Gaspart emerges telling porkies again. 'Robson knows as much as we do, whatever we do will be with his blessing. We've agreed not to talk about his future because there are more important things on the agenda. Robson understands that, he knows we have to avoid distractions.' Does the word Ronaldo not ring any bells? 'Bobby Robson has spent twelve months thinking Joan Gaspart's word was as good as the president's,' says *El Mundo Deportivo*'s Joan Poquí. 'Has he never read *Pinocchio*?'

WEDNESDAY, 11 JUNE

'If we pay one player a quarter of a million pounds more, another will ask for three hundred thousand, another three hundred and fifty thousand, and in the end, we'll have to sell Camp Nou. FC Barcelona haven't got a licence to print money.' That's Josep Lluís Núñez pleading poverty again. It makes you wonder what they do with their money. Even if they don't pick up an unsolicited cash bonus for Ronaldo, Núñez admits Barça will make an £8.5 million profit this season. 'We're the most economically sound club in Spanish football, the only one that could realistically float on London's stock market and compete with English clubs. We've no immediate plans to float but we've commissioned feasibility studies and our projected share value is 1.275 billion pounds [*nearly three times Manchester United's present quote*]. If we can devise ways to ensure shares are spread evenly among our fans and thus prevent control by a single group, flotation is a possibility.'

Joan Hortalà, president of the Barcelona exchange, admits

investors would queue around the block to buy shares in FC Barcelona Ltd, but as a fan he has his reservations. 'In theory, a flotation would see the club's *socis* become shareholders; in reality, the club would probably fall into the hands of a wealthy minority. That's the reason talk of turning Barça into a limited company is considered heresy by most Catalans. As a businessman I'd love to have shares in Barcelona, but for sentimental reasons I'd prefer to see the club stay as it is.'

In between scraping around for pesetas, Núñez tells a meeting of the Fundació del Barça (an independent, charitable trust that has contributed £2.8 million to the club's coffers this season) that he has tied up a £90 million/ten-year kit deal with Nike, despite the fact that the club's present contract with Kappa doesn't end until June 1999. Those nice men at Nike have even agreed a £9 million down payment. Meanwhile, FC Barcelona remain the world's only major football club who don't have a sponsor's name emblazoned across their shirts, despite the fact they've been offered as much as £4 million a season to do so (the board argue it would soil their image as Catalonia's ambassadors). And Ronaldo is walking over a few bob?

THURSDAY, 12 JUNE
Giovanni Branchini is photographed sneaking out of the Bernabéu after a rendezvous with Lorenzo Sanz. If that's not enough to strike fear into Barcelona hearts, the Madrid press hammer home the point with shock-horror montages of Ronaldo dressed in white. 'If the Inter transfer runs into problems we've agreed to sit down and negotiate,' says Sanz. 'We're interested in Ronaldo, and not just for a year.'

FRIDAY, 13 JUNE
Ronaldo's defection moves Barcelona to get out the cheque-book and safeguard their other divas. Today, Iván de la Peña, Luis Figo and Luis Enrique sign lucrative, long-term contract extensions designed to keep Italian suitors from their doors. 'Little Buddah', whose agent has spent the last week flirting with Roma, is now gold-plated; at 20 years old, an annual £1.4 million cash in hand is nice work if you can get it. In return, he now boasts a £42 million buy-out clause. The club's generosity sits somewhat uneasily with the president's latest musings on the Ronaldo saga. 'I felt as if God had

helped me when the talks finally broke down,' admits Núñez. 'As we said yes to all the Brazilians' pretensions, I had the feeling we were putting the club's future in danger, not just because of the overall investment, but because of its repercussions; nobody should forget the dressing room is a collective. I had serious doubts about committing so much money on a player who wasn't going to be available for crucial stretches of the season.'

Off the record, the sports editor of one of Spain's broadsheets, a man as close to Núñez's inner circle as any journalist, suggests the Barcelona president will in fact be delighted to see the back of Ronaldo. 'Núñez never really wanted to sign Ronaldo in the first place. After he was sacked, Cruyff said that Barça's money should be on the pitch and not in the bank, so Núñez was under lots of pressure to come up with a big name last summer. Even then, he went on record during Euro 96 saying the Czech Republic were the way forward – a genuine "team" with no big names. Then there was his famous "Even my concierge could sign players for ten million pounds" quote. On the day Ronaldo arrived, he spat at journalists, "You signed Ronaldo, not me." He's never been happy having a player whose cost represents such a high percentage of the club's budget, especially when Ronaldo was uncontrollable because of the whole Brazil/Nike thing.

'When Barcelona failed to meet the January deadline for revising Ronaldo's contract, Núñez didn't even bother to get in touch with his agents. In those kinds of cases, it's standard practice to make a down payment that's equivalent to their commission. If you keep the agents happy, you've generally got the player. Here in Catalonia, Ronaldo's entourage have been depicted as the villains of the piece; now I'm sure they're getting a nice commission from Inter, but basically their version is true. After the press conference to announce Ronaldo was staying, Núñez did try to change things again and couldn't provide guarantees of the monies to be paid by Televisió de Catalunya [*supporters of Espanyol might ask why the state-funded channel is using their taxes to lace the pockets of Barça players in the first place*]. It's all right him saying it was only a small percentage, six or seven per cent, but six or seven per cent of fifty million pounds is three and a half million! Ronaldo's guys wouldn't have been doing their job if they hadn't demanded guarantees.'

Which begs one question: why exactly did Núñez go through that charade of a press conference? 'Basically because he's very cunning;

he knew he could then say, "Look, I agreed to everything, you saw how happy I was that Ronaldo was staying, but the Brazilians then betrayed us." Never underestimate how devious Núñez is.' (The president's detractors would ask why big-name players – Maradona, Schuster, Laudrup, Romario and now Ronaldo – always leave Camp Nou in a huff. His acolytes would point out that Cruyff and Maradona, like Ronaldo the world's best in their Barça playing days, only won one championship between them in six seasons.)

'The club have acted intelligently in sealing their contracts,' says Bobby Robson, reacting to news of the guys who are staying. 'All three are great players who've still not reached their peak; in all the meetings I've had with the president this year, I've insisted on how important they were.' He cannot say the same of the incoming Dugarry and Reiziger. 'I've not seen enough of them to tell you if they will make the grade at Barça. I didn't recommend them, it's the club's decision.' As for his own future, Bobby Robson fobs off a query with a joke. 'Who knows? But if I do stay, there's probably not enough money left to give me a rise.' He also admits, rather less enthusiastically, that he is in the dark about Núñez's promise of a Sunday 'bombshell'. 'I've no idea what it is [*sighs*]. I suppose I'll read about it in the papers.'

Another thing he'll be reading about in the papers is a barney with Guardiola in training. Robson smiles. 'Pep is always mouthing off and arguing about decisions. I just ignore him. He's always going [*whines*], "Oh, *mister, mister*." I just say, "Ah, fuck off and get on with the game!" I could stop training, send him off and make a big "Oh look, I'm in charge" thing of it. The press would just love that, wouldn't they? That'd make a fantastic story, but I'm not going to cause a split in the dressing room just to keep journalists happy. You can't win, though. You still read the stuff about problems in the dressing room. WHAT A LOAD OF RUBBISH; there are NO problems in the dressing room.'

SATURDAY, 14 JUNE

Real Madrid beat neighbours and reigning champs Atlético 3-1 to avoid last-gasp agonies and keep the silverware that matters in the capital. Naturally, the real fall guys were some 621 kilometres away. As one of Madrid's vice-presidents put it at the final whistle, 'It's now three years since Barcelona won the league, that's 1,095 days, or 26,280 hours, or 1,576,800 minutes.' Counting, was he?

Fabio Capello's reward for a mere nine months' grind is the big one. And Bobby Robson? He can't even say 'Maybe next year'. With absolutely no exceptions, the Spanish media are pitching tomorrow's game against Betis as his Camp Nou swan-song. The Ronaldo saga may have relegated debate about Robson's future to secondary billing, but the shift from 'Will Robson go?' to 'When he goes' is nonetheless striking. Such unanimity can only mean one thing: the board have leaked their verdict to the press. It's the Brother Luis show next year, and whatever Núñez may have claimed in the past, the Dutchman clearly doesn't want elder relations looking over his shoulder.

'The season has been just that little bit too long for us,' says Robson, after watching Real Madrid beat Atlético 3-1. 'I'm not saying Madrid aren't worthy champions, but the race for the title has been so frenetic that when it got close to the wire all those extra games made a difference. We've played nearly sixty games, you know [*blows his cheeks*]: when we were two-one down at Hércules you could see the players didn't have the energy to fight back. Our fans would never have put up with the football Real Madrid have played – a lot of it has been very drab; a lot of one-nils. The means have served the end, I suppose, but their performances don't compare to ours at Camp Nou. Barça fans would never have accepted that kind of football, the supporters here are far more demanding.'

SUNDAY, 15 JUNE
Barcelona 3, Betis 0 (Oscar 43, Stoichkov 74, Luis Enrique 82)
Camp Nou, 55,000

Twenty years to the day since Spain celebrated its first democratic elections the fans vote with their feet as Barça beat Real Betis in a Cup Final dress rehearsal in front of the season's lowest crowd (a 'disappointing' FIFTY-FIVE THOUSAND). The game was widely billed as Bobby Robson's farewell, but one 'Bobby, Thanks And Forgive Us' banner aside, you'd never have noticed. The reality is that Robson's reign is coming to an end against a background of absolute indifference, though the uncompetitive nature of the fixture didn't help. No one was getting too carried away by the result, either; Real Betis will be an entirely different proposition come 28 June.

At the final whistle, the Barça players did take a token ramble to the centre circle to bid their fans farewell, but the formalities lasted all of ten seconds. After that it was a race to see who could get out of the place quickest (one of the marvels of even a packed Camp Nou is how quickly it empties). Luis Enrique's goal saw Barça reach 100 league goals in a season for the first time in their history, but even that wasn't enough to make the fans hang around to applaud. Real Madrid 27 (championships), Barça 14 are the weekend's only numbers that matter.

Celebrating a second league title two weeks shy of his 20th birthday, Raúl summed up the bottom line. 'Now I feel like I've really won the league; when we were champions two years ago our main rivals were Deportivo. This time we've beaten Barcelona, that's what really counts.' At last night's celebrations, the youngster stuck his nose into TV cameras and sang, 'Barça, Barça, aaagh, you're SHIIIT' to the tune of the FC Barcelona hymn. It's fair to say that at that widely televised moment, Barça fans didn't give a Raúl about the Cup Winners' Cup or those 100 goals.

Robson was on autocue at his final Camp Nou press conference. Whether paying his respects to the players for their 'motivation, spirit and character' for exactly the 41st time of the season, reminding us that Barça had made their 'best start in thirty-three years' and only gone off the rails with the fixture pile-up, or claiming that his season had been a 'fantastic experience', it all sounded terribly valedictory, though he refused to admit that the game was anything but his 'last of the season' at Camp Nou. Only when asked to commentate on a second-half streaker did he abandon a familiar script. 'I thought it was the president's bombshell,' he joked, in reference to the news Núñez had failed to deliver at a packed pre-match press conference (he simply confirmed the De la Peña, Figo and Luis Enrique deals).

Quite frankly, the 64-year-old Bobby Robson was looking weary. Would, say, a 44-year-old Robson have taken Núñez's continuing snubs without a fight. Not that everybody agrees it's about age. 'I've never met a good English coach,' says the legendary Helenio Herrera, a champion with both Barça and Inter Milan, and still sprightly at 81. 'Age has got nothing to do with it; the coach doesn't have to run, his job is to think. If Ronald Reagan can run America at eighty [*admittedly, not the best example*], then don't tell me a sixty-four-year-old can't run a football team.'

	P	W	D	L	F	A	PTS
Real Madrid	41	27	11	3	85	32	92
Barcelona	41	27	6	8	100	47	87

MONDAY, 16 JUNE

Josep Lluís Núñez's bid to preside over Barcelona's centenary begins here. Taking his opponents by surprise (that's the idea), Núñez announces presidential elections for 27 July. 'We can't possibly go through another season like this one,' he claims. 'In August we've got the preliminary round of the Champions League and if we win the Spanish Cup, the Super Copa, as well. With such a hectic month and a new first-team coach it would be the worst possible moment to launch an electoral campaign for a September or October poll.' A NEW FIRST-TEAM COACH. So Joe finally goes public. But what's happening to Bobby? Núñez limits himself to confirming, 'I'll present our new coaching structure on 1 July.'

The fact that the media are far more interested in reactions to Núñez's early elections (as most Catalans go on holiday the last weekend in July, opponents immediately dub him an anti-democratic fascist) confirms that Robson's dismissal was long since taken as read. Ninety-one thousand *socis* (if you're under age or joined less than a year ago, you don't get to vote) will make the call on Núñez. One man has marked Robson's card, and he still hasn't told him. Perhaps it just slipped his mind. Núñez had intended to announce the election date yesterday – his bombshell. Then he was reminded that the club's statutes demand he inform the rest of the board first.

TUESDAY, 17 JUNE

On page fourteen and fifteen of today's *El Mundo Deportivo*, several Barça players suggest concentrating on the Cup Final instead of politicking, comings and goings, etc. 'We fell into the trap of talking about Ronaldo more than Hércules and were made to pay for it,' says Stoichkov. 'I hope the same thing doesn't happen with the elections.' That's pages one to thirteen, Hristo.

Late last night, Josep Lluís Núñez claimed, 'If Bobby Robson had won the league, he'd still be Barça coach next year.' Robson spends the day fencing with journalists seeking an indignant response. 'I hope Louis Van Gaal has learnt the lesson, then. He's got a year to win the league; if he doesn't I take it he'll get the sack.' Irony aside, Robson continues to insist he's 'waiting to see what happens'. 'I prefer to keep my thoughts to myself for a more appropriate moment. The last thing we need is a war of words in the build-up to the Cup Final. Of course, I've read that Van Gaal is signing as first-team coach, but until the club tells me different I am coach until June 1998 and my intention is to continue. That's why I turned down the Everton and Celtic jobs.'

WEDNESDAY, 18 JUNE

An unblushing Núñez admits he's still not told Bobby Robson the club's plans for him. 'I haven't spoken to him personally, it's a matter that we'll resolve at the end of the season. We've touched on the subject, but not officially. We'll make the final decisions after the Cup Final, but Robson will be a strong presence in the new set-up. We've already agreed seventy times that we'll decide our coaching line-up at the end of the season, though clearly the situation is not the same now we've lost the league. The only thing we're interested in now is taking the pressure off the players and coach for the Cup Final.' That's to say a) Núñez hasn't told Robson personally what he has announced in public, and b) he thinks pissing people around is likely to cheer them up. Is that a peculiarly Catalan form of motivation? 'This club's a disaster, a disaster,' moans Robson before leaving his office for training. 'Can you believe they've still not told me anything? I'm on a big-money contract, so I'll just wait to see what they come up with; there's no need for me to panic.'

Barcelona justify their decision to oust Robson by leaking a club-commissioned poll that leaves the Englishman holding the smoking gun. Placing his decisions in somebody else's mouth is Núñez's favourite tactic, though in this case contradictory given that he hung on to Robson earlier in the season when polls were even more damning. Of course, with elections on the horizon, he needs a brand-new knight in shining armour to guarantee his re-election. 'The way he's been treated, Bobby Robson will end up leaving Barcelona like a martyr,' says *Sport*'s Miguel Rico. 'Between one thing and another, it's been torture for him here.'

Meanwhile, Van Gaal is busy pulling the strings from the sidelines. Gabriel Batistuta and Monaco's Sonny Anderson top his shopping list while Núñez has already been told who's surplus to requirements. Laurent Blanc signed for Olympique Marseilles today; Popescu, Cuéllar, Amunike and Lopetegi, among others, will almost certainly follow him out of the door. What was that about deciding the coaching hierarchy in July? Robson admits, 'I haven't been consulted on any of these decisions.' Even Joe isn't denying it. 'The only person who can decide on comings and goings is next year's coach, not the one who's here now.'

THURSDAY, 19 JUNE

After Saturday's game at Camp Nou, Betis coach Llorenç Serra Ferrer spent his press conference fending off rumours that he would be the second piece of Barcelona's new coaching jigsaw. Today the news is confirmed. The Cup Final will be Serra Ferrer's last game before joining Barça as director of youth development. Betis President Manuel Ruiz de Lopera, a shady character even by Iberian boardroom standards, had Serra Ferrer locked in a room for several hours today, insisting he either sign away his right to defect or be sacked before the Cup Final. Only the late-night intervention of his players avoided a ransom note.

Bobby Robson's days at Barcelona may be drawing to a close, but he's still one of the winners in the managerial rat race. Of the 22 top-flight coaches in place at the beginning of the season, only FIVE – Atlético's Raddy Antic, Bilbao's Luis Fernández, Valladolid's Vicente Cantatore, Compostela's Fernando Vázquez and Racing's Marcos Alonso – will make the cut for the 1997/98 season. Even allowing for the fact that Serra Ferrer, Fabio Capello and Jupp Heynckes are walking of their own accord, that's a stunningly high casualty rate. Taking into account the serial-killer nature of several top-flight presidents, a staggering FORTY different coaches have been on Spain's payrolls since September.

'Twenty-two teams and a turnover of twenty odd coaches, that's a disgraceful figure,' says Bobby Robson, shaking his head. 'Spanish clubs don't believe in continuity; two or three bad results and they panic. Often they make changes for no other reason than change for change's sake. The Mallorca coach was sacked with his team top of the Second Division with six games to go! Can you explain that to me? [*Víctor Muñoz was in fact the SECOND coach to be sacked with his side top of the Second Division; Merida's Sergio Kresic suffered the same fate in February*] Continuity is very important in England; stability is not even considered here, it's a purely results-based philosophy. My advice to Louis Van Gaal is to win, but even that won't free him from the pressure. If Barcelona sack their coach every time they don't win the league, there'll never be stability.'

Given the trigger-happy competition, Josep Lluís Núñez can still claim without gagging that 'Bobby Robson has triumphed'. Nevertheless, it's time for a change. 'The season has been a successful one, though I'd swap one of the cups for the league title; losing out by two points leaves a bitter taste in the mouth. On 30 June I'll weigh things up and do what's best for the club. I'll talk to Bobby clearly and sincerely.' That's as clearly and sincerely as a pathological liar who is about to plead guilty can. 'I made the mistake of not calling elections at the beginning of the season. If I had, Robson wouldn't have suffered everything he has and we'd probably have won the league. We've paid a high price for the campaign against our coaching duo.'

FRIDAY, 20 JUNE

Ronaldo is no longer a Barcelona player; his lawyers deposit a 4,000 million pesetas cheque (about $27 million given the free-falling peseta) at league headquarters in Madrid, leaving him free to join the Spanish club of his choice. Meanwhile in Bolivia, Inter Milan take the next steps as read and sign their man on a five-year contract worth $7 million gross a season plus a $10 million signing-on bonus. It's still a case of wait and see, though.

Barcelona have lodged a formal complaint with the Spanish League insisting that Inter Milan are in breach of FIFA regulations because Ronaldo is not for sale and his buy-out clause is only applicable in Spain. In response, the league announce they won't accept a unilateral rescission of Ronaldo's contract and will withhold his international transfer until the matter is resolved with their Italian counterparts. In other words, Ronaldo is in no-man's-land. The players' entourage insist they will take the case to FIFA's executive committee (president, João Havelange) if there is a problem. Not surprisingly, Bobby Robson is clear who will win the legal battle. 'The club should forget about Ronaldo and start looking for a substitute.'

Before squeezing into a car to seal the deal with Ronaldo and Inter technical director Luis Suárez, Alexandre Martins admits his boy took some convincing. 'Ronaldo was upset with us in France because he wanted to stay at Barcelona, but we convinced him that the best thing he could do was go to Inter. We told him again, "Keep your sentiments for Brazil, you play in Europe to earn money." He understands that now, he's calmed down and accepts we've all got our roles – his job is to play football, ours is to take care of business. Barça's season has been authentic chaos, a coach with no authority and an impostor for president. When Núñez discovered there was a genuine possibility of losing Ronaldo he panicked and tried to negotiate with him and his mum behind our backs, then he tried to bribe us with more commission. And when we sat down to draw up the contract he tried to change what were net amounts in the draft into gross amounts. You'd expect that kind of behaviour from a second-hand car salesman, not from the president of a club of Barcelona's prestige.'

The presence of Luis Suárez in Bolivia rubbed salt into old wounds. Suárez was also poached from Barcelona by Inter only months after being crowned European Footballer of the Year (he's still the only Spaniard to win the award). Five years before Alan Ball became England's first £100,000 footballer in 1966, Barcelona received a staggering £125,000 for the 24-year-old Suárez. Nonetheless, Núñez & Co. will be praying that an undeniable sense of déjà vu ends there. In ten glorious years in Italy, Suárez inspired Inter to three championships and two European Cup triumphs. Meanwhile, Barcelona, champs with Suárez in 1959 and 1960, would have to wait until 1974 for their next league title. 'I played against [*whispers the name in awe*] Luis Suárez for England at Wembley,' says Bobby Robson. 'I've never forgotten that name, he was a fabulous player.

'Ronaldo loves it here,' he continues. 'He's not going to Inter Milan because he likes spaghetti, he's going because his people have told him, "Go to Milan for the money." But I don't share the criticism of those who say "Oh, Ronaldo only went for the money" – what do they work for? Do the guys on the sports press work for nothing?'

SATURDAY, 21 JUNE

At his weekly press conference, Bobby Robson surprises everybody when he abandons his 'my place is on the bench' line to insist he is staying, come what may. 'My decision is to stay at Barcelona. After the Cup Final, we'll talk about my new role, but I know more or less what I'll do. It's my life and my decision. If I didn't want to stay here, I'd go.' Not that he pretends to understand his marginalisation. 'I can't give you a reason for the change. I suppose it's because the club's long-term planning is in the hands of Van Gaal. And I don't see any relationship between the elections and the criticism I've received. I don't know how much it affected me the president not calling elections at the beginning of the season. One day he'll sit down with me and explain why I've had to suffer this situation for a year.' So would he vote for Núñez? Robson smiles. 'Yes, *seguro*.'

SUNDAY, 22 JUNE
Rayo Vallecano 1, Barcelona 2 (Stoichkov 8, Roger 86)
Vallecas, 14,000

A Barça shadow side – no Baía, no Luis Enrique, no Guardiola and, naturally, no Ronaldo – send Rayo into the relegation play-offs. Real Madrid's line-up take their last-day obligations rather less seriously, losing 4-0 at Celta, who thus stay up. It has been widely reported that the Barça players were on cash bonuses from Celta. On the evidence of Madrid's no-show, suspicious minds would say it was the champs who got the bung. As Bobby Robson puts it after the game, 'I'm sure if Madrid had been playing for the league at Celta the result would have been very different.'

Johan Cruyff (five points behind Real Madrid in his first season, eleven points adrift in his second) abandons the golf course to evaluate Robson's year. 'You'd have to classify it as a good season,' he admits begrudgingly, 'though some fans say there's been a lack of entertaining football, despite the hundred and two goals. The difference between Madrid and Barcelona is that Capello made his team the priority, not the stars; it's been the opposite at Barcelona. It's not been easy for Robson, though. He's been under suspicion from the first day and the board have never stuck up for him.' As usual, the Dutchman reserves his real venom for the occupants of the boardroom. 'The club have caused a woeful impression – the Ronaldo saga, the way the Van Gaal thing has been handled, how they've treated Guardiola, and now all the rubbish with the buy-out clauses. On the one hand they're saying Ronaldo's clause is worthless, on the other they're throwing money at Iván and Figo in return for higher clauses. So which is it?'

Despite his disapproval of the current regime, Cruyff insists he won't get involved in the presidential campaign. 'People can forget about me during the elections; it's no secret I'm anti-Núñez – I constantly disagreed with him in my eight years at the club so I'm not going to change now – but I don't want to be linked to any candidate. All I'd say is that I hope the opposition can unite.'

	P	W	D	L	F	A	PTS
1. Real Madrid	42	27	11	4	85	36	92
2. Barcelona	42	28	6	8	102	48	90
3. Deportivo	42	21	14	7	57	30	77
4. Betis	42	21	14	7	81	46	77
5. Atlético Madrid	42	20	11	11	76	64	71
6. Athletic Bilbao	42	16	16	10	72	57	64
7. Valladolid	42	18	10	14	57	46	64
8. Real Sociedad	42	18	9	15	50	47	63
9. Tenerife	42	15	11	16	69	57	56
10. Valencia	42	15	11	16	63	59	56
11. Compostela	42	13	14	15	52	65	53
12. Espanyol	42	14	9	19	51	57	51
13. Racing Santander	42	11	17	14	52	54	50
14. Zaragoza	42	12	14	16	58	66	50
15. Sporting Gijón	42	13	11	18	45	63	50
16. Celta	42	12	13	17	51	54	49
17. Oviedo	42	12	12	18	49	65	48
18. Rayo Vallecano	42	13	6	23	43	62	45
19. Extremadura	42	11	11	20	35	64	44
20. Sevilla	42	12	7	23	50	69	43
21. Hércules	42	12	5	25	40	77	41
22. Logroñes	42	9	6	27	33	85	33

Real Madrid and Barcelona qualify for the Champions League, Betis for the Cup Winners' Cup, Deportivo, Atlético Madrid, Athletic Bilbao and Valladolid for the UEFA Cup. There is no getting away from the fact that Spanish football is woefully bottom heavy: Merida and Salamanca, both relegated last season, return to the top flight as champions and runners-up of Division Two; they will replace Logroñes, Hércules and Extremadura, who all go straight back down. Rayo Vallecano will play Mallorca in a promotion/relegation play-off decider for the second successive season. Only Sevilla's case of throwing money at bad is a relative surprise.

TUESDAY, 24 JUNE
'This week there should only be three words on people's lips at Barcelona,' pleads Guillermo Amor. 'They are cup, final, and win.'

Right. And how about Ronaldo, Ronaldo, Ronaldo? Or money, money, money?

'Ronaldo is still a Barcelona player,' insists Josep Lluís Núñez. 'We haven't cashed the cheque and the Spanish League won't grant Ronaldo his transfer until FIFA reach a decision – and they've confirmed that the buy-out clauses are only valid domestically. FIFA's general-secretary has said they won't approve the transfer until Barcelona and Inter Milan reach an agreement.' In other words, if the Italians are to get their man, they'll have to sit down at a table with Joe and talk more pasta.

'All we are asking is that our clubs compete on equal terms,' says Gerardo González, of the Spanish FA. 'If a Spanish team has to negotiate with Juventus for, say, Del Piero, surely it should work both ways. I'm sure this is a game that'll last all July in Zurich; there'll probably be extra time and penalties too!' Massimo Moratti doesn't seem too worried at the prospect. 'Ronaldo is going to be at Inter for ten years, so we can afford to lose a few months,' insists the Inter president, safe in the knowledge that the Italian FA are backing his club all the way. 'I'm not losing any sleep,' Ronaldo tells reporters in Bolivia. 'I'm now an Inter player. When FIFA read my contract they'll realise that once I'd paid Barça the buy-out clause I was free to join Inter.' And if Núñez was really convinced Ronaldo was staying would he be so busy looking for a replacement? (Today Fiorentina turn down $20 million for Gabriel Batistuta.)

WEDNESDAY, 25 JUNE
Jupp Heynckes is officially presented as the new coach of Real Madrid. Asked how he'd handle the pressure, he answers, 'I was Bayern Munich coach for four years, and in Bavaria they say if you can survive Bayern you can survive anything.' Didn't Bobby Robson say something similar about Barça and having managed England?

THURSDAY, 26 JUNE
Looking tanned and improbably healthy for a 64-year-old, Bobby Robson strolls into his private chambers alongside Camp Nou's dressing rooms. He has just conducted his final training session as Barcelona's first-team coach, but don't expect him to look back in anger. Tomorrow the team he is so proud of heads for Madrid and the Cup Final; Robson remains as chirpy as ever. 'It's my last game so you can imagine how much I want to win,' he begins. 'Not that

it will be easy. Betis don't get to many Cup Finals [*that's two, compared to Barça's 31*], so it's a special occasion for them and their fans. And you don't stay in the race for the Champions League till the death if you're not a good team. But none of that, or whether their fans outnumber us by two to one, should matter. When the game starts it's eleven against eleven, and I'm confident we have the best players.'

Unlike the green-and-white half of Seville, the city of Barcelona is not stricken by cup fever. 'At times like this the routine pressure at Barcelona actually works to your advantage,' argues Robson. 'I remember the build-up to the FA Cup Final at Ipswich; you knew something special was going on because of all the media attention and the atmosphere in the town. Here it's just another week at the office, with scores of journalists and hundreds of fans [*though summer holidays bring a more polyglot bunch to Camp Nou and the Barça museum today*]. I'm not changing our habits, either. We'll fly to Madrid tomorrow; after the amount of time the players have spent away from home this year, they'll be much fresher and rested if we stay here.'

His Portuguese clan – Figo, Baía, Couto and Mourinho, all looking like they've just stepped off a catwalk – wave 'Bye, *mister*' to Robson as they pass through on the way to a side door (thus avoiding the press). Núñez has admitted off the record that Carles Rexach, Cruyff's former number two, will also be part of Van Gaal's coaching staff. Didn't Robson now wish he'd appointed a local to steer him through the intricacies of life at Camp Nou? 'I was happy to bring José,' he insists, 'but maybe I should have had a Spanish assistant, as well. I've had Alexanco [*captain in Venables's championship-winning side and still on the staff as general dogsbody*] whose reports on our opponents helped me, especially in the first half of the season – but he's not been too involved. José and I were both inexperienced in terms of Barcelona and the club's dimension, so maybe it would have helped if we'd had someone to tell us who to watch out for, who to talk to . . .'

La Vanguardia's Enric Bañeres is a big fan of Robson, but insists his Portuguese assistant has proved a dead weight. 'Mourinho put people's backs out from the very first day – it's one thing being haughty and arrogant if you're Cruyff, quite another if you're a nobody. Robson would have been far better off if he'd had a number two who was familiar with the club and the players, somebody with a bit of a deft touch at handling people.'

As he continues to reflect on a tumultuous year, Robson is matter-of-fact rather than vindictive. 'It's disappointing to miss out on the league but it's not getting another crack at it next year that really hurts – and I would have loved to have had a go at the European Cup, I've never won that. If we win the Cup on Saturday, I'll have given this club more things than any other coach in Europe – no other club has won two major competitions and qualified for the Champions League. Now I'm familiar with the players and Spanish football, and know how this club works, I'm sure we'd have won the league next year.

'Looking back, you'd have to say I was unlucky. Everybody talks about those two Hércules games, but to be honest, they were games we lost because we played badly. If you look at the run of away defeats in February and March – Espanyol, Real Sociedad and Tenerife – they were games we had no chance of winning because of stupid goals and awful decisions by referees. That was the period when Real Madrid opened up a lead because of our misfortune.'

When Robson arrived at Barcelona, pundits predicted an *adiós* to the free-scoring days of old. They got that one wrong. Unfortunately, 100-plus goals for the first time in Barcelona's history and NO league title means something clearly went amiss at the other end. Ironic, given that Robson was simultaneously hailed as a manic defensive who would dismantle Cruyff's attacking legacy. 'We conceded too many goals because of a lack of concentration and individual mistakes, it had nothing to do with my tactical system. People said we conceded too many goals because the midfield was a sieve. In fact, my complaint would be that we made too many individual errors in and around the box. And with all the goals we scored there was obviously nothing wrong at the other end. Throw in a few bad decisions by referees and that's why we didn't win the league. We've finished just two points behind the champions and won twenty-eight games – one more than Madrid – that shows we always played to win.'

It's now several days since Robson acknowledged the Van Gaal handover, though he admits he'd known a while longer. 'I was told about two weeks ago, after the Hércules game, that was when the president said to me, "Yes, Van Gaal is definitely coming." They've told me there's still a job for me here. They've mentioned a couple of things, but not in detail, and I've promised them I'll say nothing until after the Cup Final. I even said, "Pay me the year left on my contract and I'll walk away without making any fuss," but they said, "No, you've got a year on your contract and we'd hate you to go." I'll meet Núñez and Gaspart on Sunday and we'll discuss exactly what the options are. I've said in principle I'll stay, but if I'm not happy and something comes my way that I really fancy, I'll go. Otherwise I'll stay here and take a sabbatical year. The press are saying I'm staying for the money, but I could blow the money. I could walk away from it all tomorrow and never work again. I could drink champagne every day for the rest of my life.

'If I've got a job here next year on good money why walk away until something I prefer comes along? I'm not going to leave Barcelona for Turkey or Scotland, forget about it! I'd rather stay here. It's the same with Everton, I'd be there from nine o'clock in the morning until seven o'clock at night, seven days a week, up the M1, down the M6 ... and it's a long-term job; I don't want a four- or five-year programme, the kind of job I'm interested in is at a club that needs just a little retuning – a Newcastle [*he grimaces and nods several times*] – there's the job I should have gone for. Fabulous club, fabulous opportunity. But my attitude was Barcelona is the biggest club in the world, why walk out on this? I also thought I'd have a chance to do something here that I couldn't do at Newcastle: win the league and have a go at the Champions League [*shrugs*] – now it turns out they'll be in exactly the same position next season. The academy job is still there, but I don't fancy that, at least not yet.

'There's not a lot of jobs that fit the bill – Liverpool maybe, if they don't live up to expectations in the first couple of months – so I'll sit here and when people know I'm available we'll see what happens. Better here than being in Istanbul – why go to Turkey with all that tension and pressure in a hostile atmosphere? Or Celtic on less money and a hiding to nothing? And I'll make the job here – technical director, technical adviser, looking at players – I've got some ideas of my own. I know what the club lacks – so do they – they know the club needs continuity. And if that works out, and I convince the president it's worthwhile, I might be here a few years yet. I'll go away in July, though. Van Gaal doesn't need me around stepping on his feet. I only know him slightly, but I do know he's been in charge of everything at Ajax. That won't be the case here.

'He doesn't know what he's let himself in for,' he continues, echoing Michael Robinson's words of a year ago. 'He comes from a similar background to mine at PSV; you only get two or three

journalists waiting for you after Ajax training sessions. The first time
he finds the training ground surrounded with cameras and journalists
he'll go mad. He's an intimidating character and he'll ban them all
from training, so his problems with the media will start from day
one. It's not just about fighting the ghost of Johan Cruyff, either. Any
coach needs character to face the pressure here – Van Gaal will soon
find that out.

'At my age I wasn't going to be a long-term bet, but I honestly
thought I was coming here for two seasons. In retrospect, you'd have
to say the club hired me as a one-year stop-gap; Van Gaal had
already gone on record saying this would be his last season at Ajax.
In my opinion, Barcelona got in touch with him and he told them to
wait a year. I think they've known all along that he was coming.'

Miraculously, Robson bears no grudges. 'The president of
Barcelona is like the prime minister in England, he goes to the polls
when he thinks he's got an advantage. Núñez has called the elections
now because it suits him; and he sees Louis Van Gaal as his friendly
budget, it's an asset he thinks will help him get elected. We are all
pawns, he uses people and situations within the club – he's solved
the De la Peña, Luis Enrique and Figo contracts, he thinks he can get
Guardiola to stay – but he'd be bloody stupid if he called the
elections at a bad moment. The other day I said I'd vote for Núñez.
I should have said I'm neutral, but honestly, is there anybody better
than Núñez in this city? I doubt it. Van Gaal is a good long-term bet,
too. I can't disagree with that, I'm just annoyed at the way they
handled it; all those bloody meetings and absolutely refusing to give
me a straight answer.'

So how come Robson hadn't exploded? 'They've lied in public and
messed me around, but I'll still stay here if it suits ME, that's why.
As a younger coach I might have been more impetuous, I would have
been like José [*Mourinho*], he's angry and twisted and keeps
growling, "They've treated us badly." He wants to go, OK, let him
go. I'm terribly annoyed, too. It's not the decision – that's their right
– it's leaving it so late. I think they could have been straight with me
a long time ago because they knew what was happening. I've spent
whole meetings with them trying to get them to say to my face what
everybody else was going on about for months. Their argument was
always, "We don't know what the situation will be until the end of
the season; let's see what we win and lose and then make a decision
about you and Van Gaal." What could I do? They run the club, not

me. I tried to get them to clarify our position but they always shunned us and said you've got to wait.' Having Gaspart as his main interlocutor and a mute president didn't help, either. 'Núñez doesn't speak English, not one word, and that suits him,' shrugs Robson.

On that note, he leaves for a photo opportunity; Núñez's, naturally. The outgoing president has taken little heed of his own advice – 'Forget about the elections until after the Cup Final' – and has embarked on a flurry of activity that is the FC Barcelona equivalent of kissing babies (Robson says cheese as Núñez hands him a Cartier watch, a perk for winning the Cup Winners' Cup) and promising more hospitals (next stop is the unveiling of the 'Family Barça' theme park, a £30 million project that includes a hotel, a shopping mall, and an artificial beach). Don't ask who's building it.

Just in case anybody missed that one, 'the club' have chosen this precise moment to send out a limited-edition *History of FC Barcelona* to its 103,038 *socis*. Silver wedding? Golden? No, a nineteen-year history, actually. That's nineteen years (and 40 photos) since Núñez was first elected. Not surprisingly, other presidential candidates are furious. 'It reminds me of the way the fascists used to rewrite history,' says Jaume Llauradó. 'When I was a kid, history books said everything that happened after the Civil War was good and everything before was bad. This history is the same, it's as if Barça didn't exist before Núñez. And worst of all, the *socis* are paying for it out of club money.' The glossy brochure includes tributes to Josep Lluís from Juan Antonio Samaranch, president of the IOC since 1980 and a former career fascist, and FIFA's João Havelange, another man who knows a thing or two about personal fiefdoms. At least nobody can accuse Núñez of hiding his intentions.

FRIDAY, 27 JUNE
Bobby Robson may have been anxious to keep well away from Madrid tonight, but Los Angeles? 'It's hell,' says Robson of the club's overnight HQ at an urbanisation in Los Ángeles de San Rafael, 70 kilometres from the capital. Collapsing beds, musty rooms and spiders figure among a litany of complaints. When asked at his press conference if it was a personal choice (London's hotels have a very bad reputation in Spain), Robson could not have been more explicit: 'Nooooooo!' So who did choose the digs? When Josep Lluís Núñez told Jesús Gil he was looking for a hotel, the Atlético Madrid president quickly recommended LA. Not altogether surprising, given

that he owns it. 'It can't be that bad,' says Núñez, who fails to explain why he's doing business with a man who even in a good mood refers to him as a dwarf. 'Atlético use it and they did the double last year. And Robson wanted somewhere quiet.'

Jesús Gil uses the team he owns to market the LA entertainment complex he built, and boy does it needs some promoting. Gil spent a year in jail in the early seventies when one of the buildings at San Rafael collapsed, killing 52 people. Only a year? Suffice to say that Franco granted him a pardon and Gil has been known to boast, 'I'm proud to be a fascist.'

Núñez, who in all honesty has never constructed a building that has collapsed, shares a candlelit supper with his coach. Afterwards, he spars with journalists who have belatedly seen the Robson light. 'Let's be serious,' he pleads, 'you can't spend the whole year attacking Robson and demanding his resignation in editorials, and now say you want to save him [*here comes the one about the pot and the black kettle*]. You've got short memories; go back and read what you've said all year, I'm the only one who has defended him.'

SATURDAY, 28 JUNE
Barcelona 3, Betis 2 a.e.t. (Figo 45, 114, Pizzi 85)
Spanish Cup Final. Santiago Bernabéu, 85,000
Barça: Baía, Ferrer (Oscar 84), Abelardo, Sergi, De la Peña (Popescu 100), Guardiola, Figo, Luis Enrique, Stoichkov (Amunike 66), Pizzi
Betis: Jaro, Jaime, Vidakovic, Ríos, Merino (Ureña 64), Alexis, Cañas (Pier 71), Nadj (Olías 86), Finidi, Alfonso, Jarni

Your star striker has done a runner. Your best defender is crocked. The crowd is on your back. Before you've had time to settle on the bench, the opposition fluke a goal. Your boys fight back to equalise, but fall behind with time running out. Dredging up reserves from God knows where, they draw level again. Then one hundred and fourteen minutes into the last game of the longest season, they score the winner. The Spanish Cup Final. Bobby Robson's season in a nutshell. Against the odds. Epic. Triumphant. The spectre of Ronaldo, Nadal's injury, a Betis majority at the Bernabéu, a fifth-minute goal that flew in off Alfonso's face, Finidi's strike with ten minutes to go, extra laps after a marathon: now bring on some real obstacles.

Barcelona's titanic encounters against Real and Atlético had breathed life into a competition normally reduced to an afterthought;

Betis and their impassioned support were the icing on the Cup cake. A staggering 85,000 Andalusians made the pilgrimage to Madrid for the final, the ticketless half delighted just to soak up the atmosphere. Never was the club's celebrated motto – 'Long Live Betis! Even if we lose!' – more appropriate. Inside the Barça half of the Bernabéu, 35,000 unusually boisterous *culés* bathed the Real temple in the colours of its adversary – the scarlet and blue of Barcelona and the yellow and red of 20,000 Catalan flags. And as Robson's men celebrated their triumph, the unthinkable – the FC Barcelona hymn blasting out of the speakers. '*Tot el camp, és un clam, som la gent blaugrana* [roughly, *we're the smiley, happy red-and-blue army!*] . . . BARÇA! BARÇA! BARÇA!'

'I don't know if we'll ever seen that again,' confessed Núñez as *über*-director Gaspart charged around the pitch brandishing a *Boixos Nois* (Crazy Boys *ultras*) scarf and the *culé* ranks threw a chorus or two back in Raúl's direction (Lorenzo Sanz was already complaining to the Spanish FA, so the answer is probably no). Sergi, one of Barça's home-grown players, was happy with just the once. 'To win at the Bernabéu and see the ground full of Catalan flags is as good as it gets . . . and then hearing the hymn FOUR times, it's fuckin' unbelievable!' As red and blue fireworks lit up the sky back in Catalonia, 'Little Buddah' led the fans at the Bernabéu in a chorus of '*Asi se quema, se quema Madrid*' (Madrid is burning, it's burning Madrid).

As his players milk every last drop of the adulation, Bobby Robson is facing the Spanish press for the last time. 'I'm happy and sad at the same time,' he admits, though his face suggests solely the former. 'If this is my last game it's a great way to finish. The Bernabéu is one of world football's great arenas, so it's a wonderful honour to win a Cup Final here. I've made history, too – I must be the first coach to win three out of four titles in his first season at a club and not get the chance to carry on. And I've now won five out of five Cup Finals in my career so I must be very lucky!'

Naturally, even after Robson's triumphant last stand there would be dissenting voices. Seconds before extra time kicked off, his players had huddled together in a scrum in the centre circle. The coach's detractors immediately jumped on a few fraternity house 'Ra! Ra! Ra!'s as another example of the players' so-called 'self-management'. Madrid's sporting mafia and their unwitting (?) allies in Barcelona would subsequently churn out a now familiar line: 'Núñez made a mistake signing Robson', 'Robson took an eternity to hit on the right formula', and, wait for it, 'it was Robson's fault Ronaldo left'. Happily not all the media are so obtuse.

Televisió de Catalunya have taken some convincing (friendlies included, that's FIFTY-FOUR live Barça games this season), but commentator Pere Escobar's first words at the final whistle were not for any of the on-field heroes (a special word for two-goal Luis Figo, who finished on the losing side to Robson's Porto in a Portuguese Cup Final, Pizzi, who must have been a cavalry officer in a previous life, and the dynamic duo, Sergi and Luis Enrique), the president or the fans, but for the much-maligned coach: '*Senyors i senyores*, Bobby Robson has just won his fifth Cup Final.'

Robson's knockers at *Sport* also hold their hands up. 'Barcelona have rounded off an absolutely brilliant post-Cruyff season,' says editor Josep María Casanovas. 'Robson has set a very high standard for Van Gaal – not just in terms of trophies, but by building a team with the caste of champions; a side that rebels against adversity and has demonstrated it can win things without Ronaldo. Bobby Robson can sleep soundly – it's a triumph for a man who never lost faith in himself.' *La Vanguardia*'s Albert Turró agrees. 'No Barcelona coach has ever been the victim of such fierce, unjustified and indiscriminate criticism as Bobby Robson. He deserves nothing but praise; one of the club's best ever seasons may not be enough to save his job, but his chivalry and professionalism have earned him a place in the hearts of the fans.'

José Mourinho is rarely a spring of wisdom, but in a season of contradictions, he best sums up a contradictory situation. 'Bobby and I have felt abandoned this season – the only thing that's kept us going has been the players' backing – but now that we've won the Cup I suppose all the hangers-on will be queuing up to get in the photo at the town hall. Núñez says the dressing room is more united than ever. So what's he going to do? Change the coach! People ask me if it's strange being kicked out after what we've achieved. It's not strange, it's ridiculous.'

SUNDAY, 29 JUNE

Louis Van Gaal spends his first afternoon in town sat in a room at the Hotel Princesa Sofia watching Barça's televised celebrations. He would have seen the streets full of fans singing 'Pep Don't Go' and barracking Ronaldo mercilessly. He would also have seen Bobby

Robson standing to one side of the town hall balcony, clutching the Cup as if his life depended on it. Typically, the coach let his players hog the limelight with their silly speeches and impromptu songs, but the gesture was a fitting one. If the trophy belonged to anyone, it was Robson.

Van Gaal would also have observed Josep Lluís Núñez embracing the coach whose death sentence he signed months ago. With barely an hour left on Robson's last day at the helm, newspapers and press agencies receive an official fax from FC Barcelona confirming that Louis Van Gaal is the club's new first-team coach and that Bobby Robson will continue as director of signings. As Núñez leaves the club's celebratory dinner, he confirms the news. 'Robson has been a great coach and I thank him. Justice has finally been done; he's reaped the rewards of a gruelling season. This has been a year of triumphs, one of FC Barcelona's best seasons ever, because of the support I gave Robson. Now it's time to organise for the future. I'll always be by Louis Van Gaal's side, the same as I was with Bobby Robson.'

The big Dutchman will sleep soundly tonight.

BOBBY ROBSON AT FC BARCELONA
SEASON STATISTICS

APPEARANCES

	League	Cup Winners' Cup	Spanish Cup	Total
Guardiola	38	6+1	5+1	49+2
Vítor Baía	37	8	5	50
Ronaldo	37	7	4	48
Luis Enrique	35	7	6+1	48+1
Figo	34+2	8	5	47+2
Sergi	34	7	6	47
Popescu	26+3	8	4+1	38+4
Blanc	25+3	5	4	34+3
Nadal	25+2	5	4+2	34+4
Giovanni	24+6	6+2	1+3	31+11
Couto	23+3	4	4	31+3
Abelardo	19+2	5+1	3	27+3
De la Peña	17+16	4+2	3	24+18
Ferrer	16+2	5	5	26+2
Stoichkov	13+9	5+2	3+1	21+12
Roger	12+4	1+3	1	14+7
Amunike	11+8	—	1+2	12+10
Amor	10+16	2+4	3	15+20
Oscar	6+8	—	1+3	7+11
Cuéllar	6+2	0+2	0+1	6+5
Pizzi	5+28	2+5	5+2	12+35
Busquets	4	1	2	6
Celades	3+1	1	1	5+1
Bakero	1+3	0+1	—	1+4
Arnau	1	—	—	1
Prosinecki	—	2+1	—	2+1

SEASON STATISTICS

GOALSCORERS

	League	Cup Winners' Cup	Spanish Cup	Total
Ronaldo	34	5	6	45
Luis Enrique	17	—	1	18
Pizzi	9	1	5	15
Giovanni	7	3	1	11
Figo	4	1	3	8
Stoichkov	7	—	—	7
Popescu	4	1	—	5
Oscar	4	—	1	5
Abelardo	3	—	—	3
De la Peña	2	—	1	3
Nadal	1	1	1	3
Roger	2	—	—	2
Couto	—	1	1	2
Amunike	1	—	—	1
Bakero	1	—	—	1
Blanc	1	—	—	1
Sergi	1	—	—	1
Guardiola	—	1	—	1

	P	W	D	L	F	A
LEAGUE	42	28	6	8	102	48
EUROPE	9	5	4	0	14	5
CUP	7	5	2	0	21	11
TOTAL	58	38	12	8	137	64